Encomiums

Thanks & awe for your Villadrome, which helped us to climb the heights of Sicilian poetry.

— Marcel Duchamp

From the very beginning, Villa was so advanced that, even today, his initial writings or graphemes appear ahead of the times and even the future, suspended between a polymorphous sixth sense and pure non-sense.

— Andrea Zanzotto

Emilio Villa was the greatest Italian poet of the forties, never mind Montale.

— Nanni Balestrini

I was awestruck by this blasphemous character who didn't care about the gods, let alone men.

— Patrizia Vicinelli

As the universe expands and its galaxies grow further apart with a speed proportionate to their respective distances, so does the linguistic universe of Emilio Villa.

— Adriano Spatola

I called him Zeus (to always associate him with greatness, as well as his translation of the *Odyssey*) and Rabelais (for the excesses, his physical and mental voracity for gigantic meals, dictionaries, and all languages).

— Giulia Niccolai

At different times there is Villa the archæologist, the translator, and even the scenographer skilled in historical reproduction (for John Huston's film *The Bible*), apart from Villa the poet & writer, the tireless experimentalist, the clandestine promoter of 'poetic events,' and the underground initiator of mysteries.

— Luciano Caruso & Stelio Maria Martini

The Selected Poetry

of

Emilio Villa

Other Works by Emilio Villa

forthcoming from Contra Mundum

Selected Writings

The Hebrew Bible, tr. by Emilio Villa

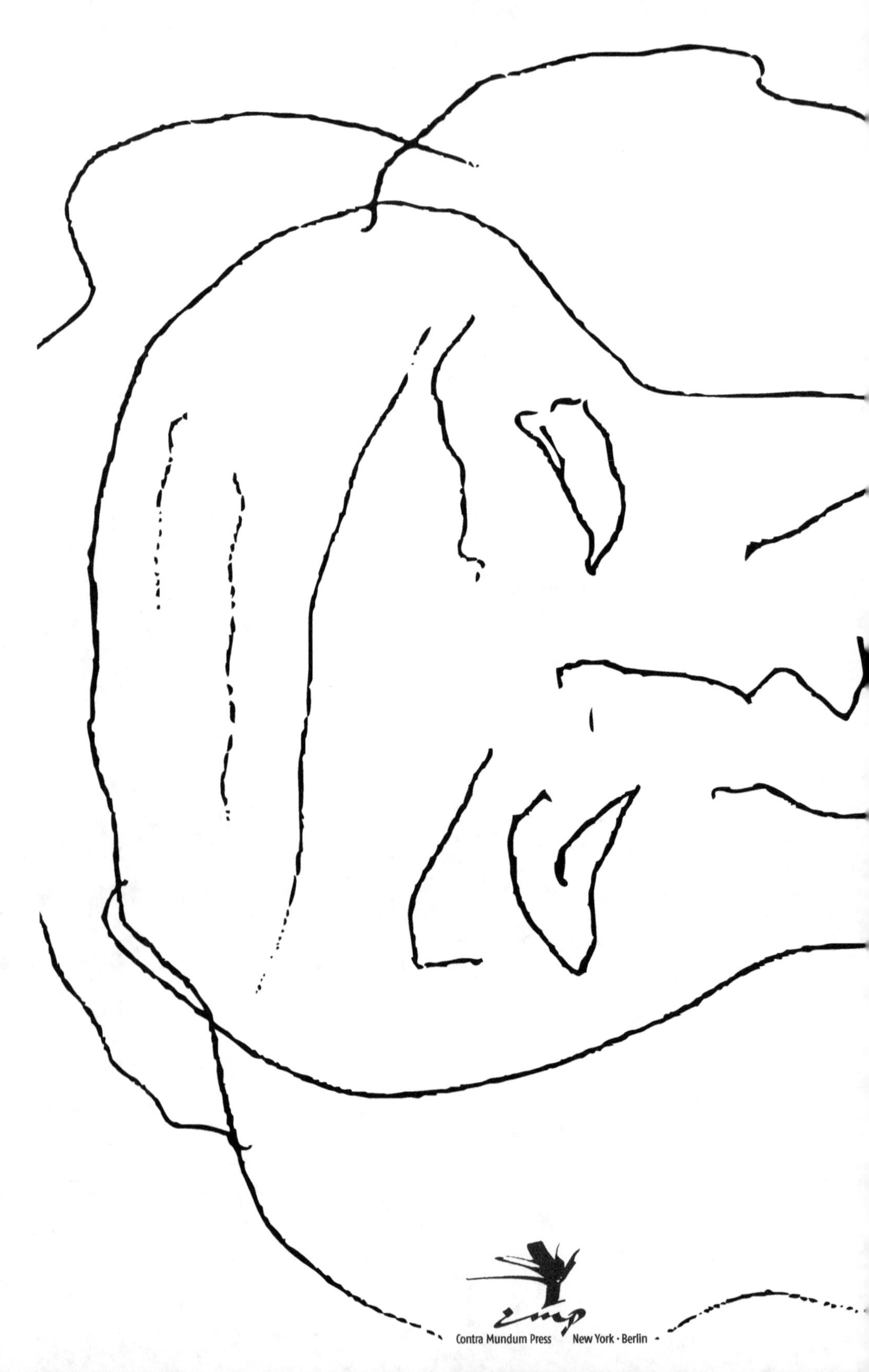
CMP
Contra Mundum Press
New York · Berlin

The Selected Poetry of Emilio Villa

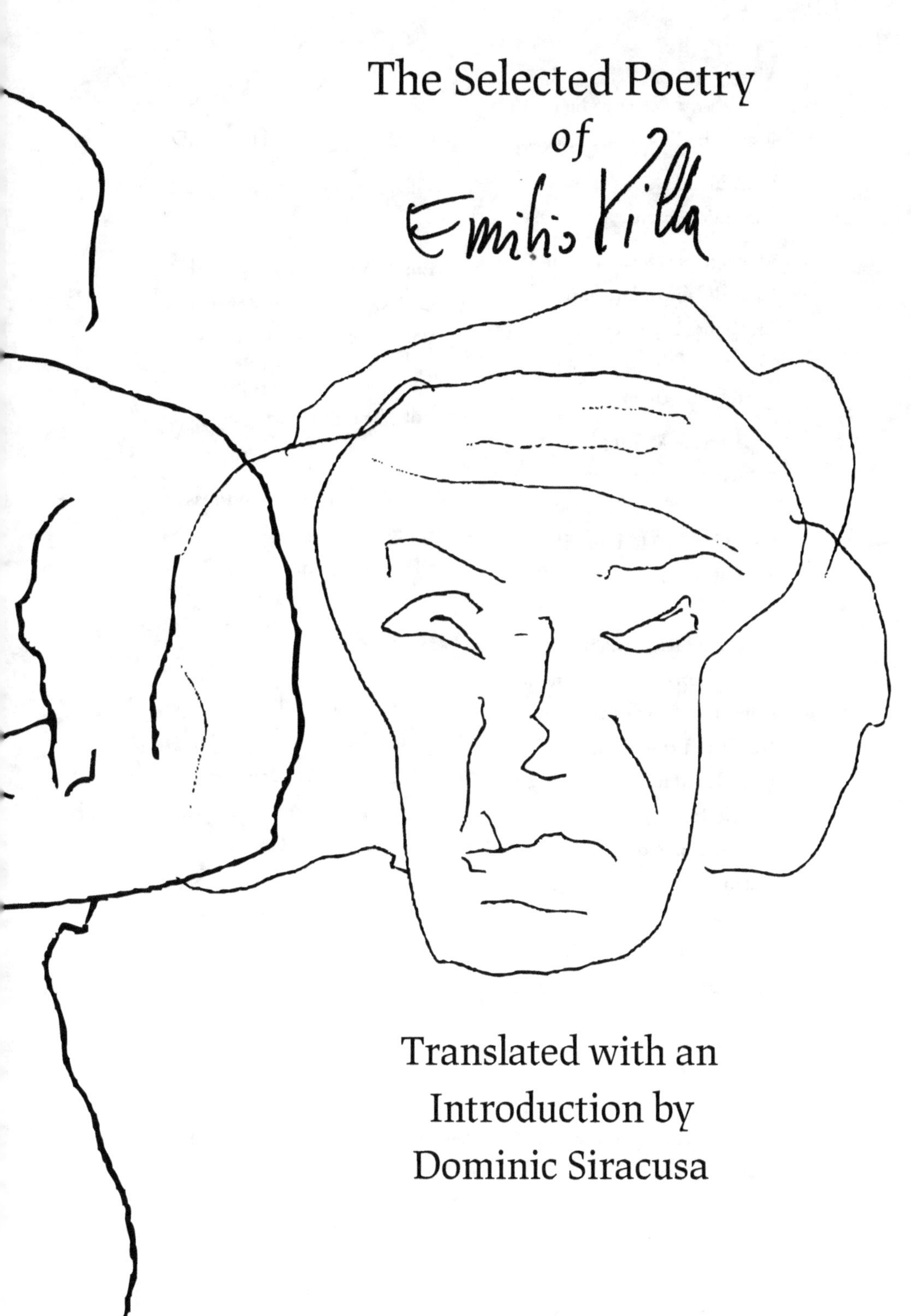

Translated with an
Introduction by
Dominic Siracusa

First Contra Mundum Press
edition 2014.

Library of Congress
Cataloguing-in-Publication Data

Villa, Emilio, 1914–2003

[The Selected Poetry of
Emilio Villa. English. French.
Greek. Italian. Latin. Milanese.
Portuguese. Provencal.]

The Selected Poetry of Emilio
Villa / Emilio Villa

—1st Contra Mundum Press
Edition
782 pp., 6×9 in.

ISBN 9781940625058

I. Villa, Emilio.
II. Title.
III. Siracusa, Dominic.
IV. Translation.
V. Siracusa, Dominic.
VI. Introduction.
VII. Segalini, Alessandro.
VIII. Typesetting.

2014939147

Research for this book was aided by a fellowship from the Raiziss / de Palchi
Translation Awards Fund of The New York Community Trust.

Table of Contents

Introduction

Emilio Villa: Biblicist, Art Critic, Experimental Poet...

Similar to the journey ventured by Ahab & his crew, the pursuit of Emilio Villa's work verges on madness. Born in 1914 just outside Milan, Villa began to write verse in seminary school in the '30s and continued to do so until his death in 2003. Spanning over seventy years, his corpus is as fragmented as it is vast, so much so that only just now, 11 years after his death, is it beginning to be pieced together. What Villa published in his lifetime was released through small publishing houses, obscure magazines, in collaboration with visual artists, or in private editions at his own expense & all of this material is now extremely rare. What Villa did not publish he often gave away before it could be crystallized on the page, or even sabotaged his own archives, possibly out of frustration or due to his sibylline nature. One must go to great lengths in order to locate his work, even trekking to destinations such as São Paolo, Brazil.[1] Trips to South America aside, even the search for Villa's more obscure papers in and around Italy can prove to be challenging: one must contact his friends, fellow artists, and various archives, which proves dizzying because each friend, artist, & archive sends you to yet others, resulting in an overwhelming amount of leads to pursue, until tracking Villa becomes an endless, odyssean task.[2] In short, although we currently posses a fragmented picture of Villa's work, there are surely surprises that still await us, for it is in part how this sibyl-poet wanted it and in part due to the nomadic way in which he sometimes lived, which resulted in materials often being lost.

Compared to most 20th-century literary figures, Villa's artistic interests were extremely diverse: he was a poet, a visual artist, a critic who wrote on both contemporary and prehistoric art, an etymologist, and a translator of ancient texts, the Hebrew

Bible principal among them. No matter the genre or medium in which he worked, he employed a number of different languages, both modern and ancient: Milanese dialect, standard Italian, French, Portuguese, Spanish, English, Provençal, Latin, ancient Greek, Hebrew, Sumerian, Akkadian, and Ugaritic as well as the ideograms of primitive Mediterranean civilizations. This linguistic range is rare, even amongst the lions of Modernism.

In his poetry, Villa causes these different languages to clash in varying degrees. A given piece may be composed in a single language, or peppered with other languages. Sometimes Villa makes use of abrupt code shifting: one language suddenly gives way to another entirely as a text unfolds. A more subtle linguistic operation is also at play that could be defined as a "cross pollination" of the varied languages Villa used.[3] For example, a poem in Italian may take on the syntax of Sumerian, or vice versa; an Italian word may assume an ancient Greek inflexion; or a modern lexicon will produce neologisms in a 'dead language' such as Latin. In fact, at times, there is a paleolization of modern languages and a modernization of ancient ones. These different tongues also serve to unexpectedly alter the tone of Villa's texts, as when a base description of an orifice in Milanese dialect is offset by a high-sounding Latin nomenclature. Likewise, at the level of content, Villa seamlessly intermingles primitive and modern references, eradicating the eons that separate them, as when ancient Mediterranean deities suddenly appear in a poem set in California's Silicon Valley.

The relative unavailability of his works, his diverse artistic interests, & the great erudition he displays in his writings, are all factors that have deterred many critics from working on Villa. In turn, this has led to his almost complete marginalization from the annals of Italian culture thus far. For instance, he is absent from the major anthologies of 20th-century Italian poetry.

Yet, even if anthologists had dealt with Villa's texts, inevitably, they would have difficulty situating them, for the typical parameters used to structure an anthology cannot easily accommodate Villa's poetry, if at all. The innovations found in his texts predate, by years, in some cases even decades, the novelties of the most prominent poetic figures, groups, or movements. To insert Villa's work in the Italian 20th-century canon would mean to greatly disrupt the status quo; consequently, it would undoubtedly require redrafting many if not all of its coordinates.

If the question of Villa's influences must be considered, discerning precisely who they are through his personal library is well nigh impossible. Over the years — due to moves, financial hardships, or just plain indifference — parts of it have gone missing. Although it is possible to discern influences through textual analysis, it is difficult to confirm exactly what poets (and other writers) he may have been reading. The surviving portion of his library is comprised primarily of ancient language grammars, biblical dictionaries, and the collected myths of early Mediterranean cultures. Moreover, when examining Villa's unpublished papers in his archives, we find that he scattered his verses across scraps of used paper such as gas bills, receipts, brochures for exhibitions, post cards, paper bags, bus tickets, calendars, or the work of other authors. The preservation of Villa's rendering of the Hebrew Bible, on the other hand, is untouched by such chaos: continuity was maintained across the different pages and drafts of a lifetime undertaking. Such a treatment demonstrates, at the very least, that his biblical translation held a place of prominence for him. It is then safe to speculate that, more than any other poet or movement, what influenced Villa was the Bible and the ancient myths and languages that contributed to its formation. Compared to many of his contemporaries, Villa had a much wider sense of viewing literary history

— his primary interests were not ten years old but rather ten thousand years old.[4]

Villa treated everything he did as poetry, or more precisely, as the language of poetry, be it his art criticism, his visual art, the etymology of a word, or even his translation of the Pentateuch. Specifically, each of his works is concerned with a moment of linguistic genesis, in which the raw material of a language precedes codified signification; in various ways, as will be illustrated shortly, the texts demonstrate this. Every language Villa chose to employ was also treated in the same way: many of the poetic techniques in his Italian verse are at work in his French, ancient Greek, English, & so on. For this reason, herein, along with poems in tongues other than Italian, examples of Villa's essays on contemporary and ancient art, the reader will find a complete passage from his translation of Genesis. In many respects, it was in translating this biblical cosmogony that he was led to create a number of cosmogonies of his own; thus, it is only natural we continue our pursuit from there.

Genesis

The history of the Bible resembles the telephone game children play in school: someone picks a word, whispers it to a classmate, and the action is repeated until it reaches the last child in the room, who pronounces the word for all to hear. The game results in a drastic alteration of what was originally spoken — passing from mouth to ear, from person to person, the word "orange" somehow morphs into "elephant." When it comes to the transmission of the Bible, the game was of course carried out on a far more serious scale: all those playing hailed from a different culture, spoke a different language, adhered to a different belief system, and were separated by centuries and, in some cases, even millennia.

In his translation of the first five books of the Hebrew Bible into Italian, Villa eludes all the various redactions, theological deformations, allegorical readings, and especially the notion of revelation, which have come to shape the Bible's millennial game of telephone and returns to its originary sources. Specifically, he returns to the primordial myths in order to reactivate a generative force that has long lied dormant in the recesses of time. Villa first achieves this by approaching the Bible as a literary text and not as doctrine of faith; therefore, his concern is solely literary and philological, not theological, as is evident from the introduction to his translation of Genesis:

> This translation of the first book of the Bible, defined in the Hellenistic era as "Genesis," that is "Origin," proposes to abandon the confessional notion of "divine" revelation, in which the celebrated literary monument came to be dissolved historically. The theologumen of "revelation," either generic or specific, "patristic" or "existentialistic," so arid due to the extravagant investigations of Christian theology, is, in this translation, entirely eluded, through an objective approach: exactly because in the Hebrew literature at our disposal an authentic notion of "revelation" can not be verified; or, certainly, it is not given. And only by judging every Christian theologumen an artificial and superfluous option, a perishing mythologism, is a conscious responsibility to the text made possible.[5]

The literary monument to which Villa refers is comprised of those myths belonging to early Semitic tribes. The signifying potential of this literature was slowly diluted as interpretations of it became codified under various doctrinal systems. Although remnants of this "mythology" exist in the early Hebrew writings we still have at our disposal, according to Villa, it was later completely obfuscated under the formation of Christianity. For him, the responsibility inherent in translating the Pentateuch is to cause these myths to resurface so the Pentateuch can once again foster a myriad of different interpretations.

Since the meaning behind their language is veiled by indeterminacy, by nature, myths resist univocal interpretation. They lie outside history, beyond the 'veil,' in a primordial time we can never know. Myths have no authors in the sense that literature as conceived in modernity does, hence the circumstances in which they were born, or how they evolved over time, are questions that can never be answered. As we read from Villa's introduction to his translation of the ancient Babylonian cosmogony, the *Enuma Elis*, myths are eternally unfathomable:

> The myth cannot be translated, it is inexplicable, always, and without hope. The myth is the tumultuous concentration where an infinite feeling finds its home. Its period is a point, its unreal frequency, fiction. This may be a simple explanation of origins, an evocation of chaos and its temporal organization; or it could be a naturistic myth that contemplates the victory of the sun (Marduk) over the rigors and the death of winter (Tiamat), the clashing between the two forces of nature; or a symbolizing in astral myths; or all of this at once. And it does not matter. The myth cannot have equivalents, analogies, speakable relations. And the translator cannot do anything but render the precise feeling of his own ineptitude. He cannot help his readers in any way. If he did, he would betray them.[6]

Villa saw the same paradigm of the *Enuma Elis* in the early myths that led to the formation of the Hebrew Bible. Actually, when it comes to his translation of Genesis, he found that the raw signifying force was in an even more concentrated form: this biblical cosmogony was born out of an immense assortment of myths originating throughout the Mediterranean, each recounting a different version of the creation of the universe. Furthermore, for Villa, the many cosmogonic myths of pre-Judaic cultures are not merely stories regarding the creation of the universe, but more specifically tales of man's appropriation of his expressive tools in order to carry out a linguistic genesis:

> The act of making the divine "visible" or "felt" [...] or the "theophany" [...] are, in an examination of the Bible, of a mythical nature in a pure form, or in the form of an operating cult. In the texts of the patriarchal, or ancestral, legends, every theophany is tied to a strict condition of cult etiology; in the cosmogonic text no report exceeds the mythical concept of the *Verbum naturans*, of the *Verbum operante*. (Ibid., 12)

The "*Verbum naturans*" and the "*Verbum operante*" imply that language gives birth to the world and subsequently shapes it. Thus, in these lines, Villa begins to overturn the Christian idea of revelation by re-establishing a mythical paradigm. The divine is "made visible" by the human word; it is man who "speaks" the divine or, in many cases, it is man who transgresses the word of the supposed divinity to name his own universe. The Christian idea, on the other hand, suggests a god that reveals himself, speaks the universe, and places man within it. In this belief system, "god's word" is viewed as final and man passively adheres to it. For example, the Christian mass still upholds this notion with the liturgical refrain: "This is the word of the Lord, amen."

The story of God speaking the universe (fiat lux) does open the book of Genesis in the Hebrew Bible, but it is much newer in respect to the myth of the fall. That cosmogony evolved within the Hebrew culture united under Moses, morphing over time to reinforce a monotheistic belief (one God alone with the power to create). Then, as the biblical text was consolidated, this story was placed before "the fall of man" (which, since it belonged to an older polytheistic culture, still reveals the discrepancy between one god and many gods). As Villa tells us, during the period in which the various Semitic tribes came to form a unified Hebrew culture, the perspectives regarding cosmogony were even more conflicting and fragmented:

> As the fragmentary reports were fused together over the centuries, there was a consolidation of a heterogeneous & sporadic speculation of a theological kind, as well as a natural aggressive frenzy for symbolic and emblematic certitudes, in which lies the conservative energy of the "religion" of the "Jews" [...], that is a collection of nomadic tribes that were, for the most part, Semitic. (Ibid., 14)

As this consolidation took place, certain redactions were made to the Pentateuch that ignored a much more varied literary patrimony, one that did not permit such symbolic or emblematic certainties. From these fragmented mythologies, Villa draws one particular example that paints a rather different picture of the relationship between the divine and man, as well as the role of the *Verbum naturans*, when compared to the later redactions of the Hebrew and Christian doctrines:

> In a third cosmogonic narrative — which is founded on the various reports of cosmic war between a group of pre-

> cosmic divinities, or primordial forces, separated by an Abyss — we find the concept of the primordial refusal on the part of man (a demigod; "form" of the divine's outward breath) of the Word of the divine; and the consequent saga of humanity's move toward liberation, or salvation, of the formation of his initial destiny. (Ibid., 13)

Man, previously a demigod in the form of divine breath, comes into being when he refuses the word of the divine. He is simultaneously exerting his independence from those gods and taking control of his own divine power: to create through language. Certain aspects of this myth still linger in the "Fall of man" passage in Genesis: the discrepancies between *Yahweh & Elohim*, man becoming *Elohim* himself, the linguistic transgression of God's word, and so on. Yet, Villa's re-insertion of this early myth within his translation of the "Fall of man" passage compels us to interpret Eve's action of disobeying the word of God not as a sin but rather as an act of liberation.

The purpose of Villa's translation is to reinstate the signifying force of these various myths within the overall framework of Genesis, which is preserved not only within the paradigms of the individual myths themselves, but also amid the clashing perspectives of these myths: each seems to tell a story that is in conflict with the next, resulting in irreconcilable interpretations.

> Thus, the confusion of the different levels brought about an emptying of the myths and the archaic symbols, which, when re-interpreted, deformed, then forced into collusion with other neo-Mesopotamian, Iranian, and Mediterranean notions, were diluted in new vague contents where the Judaic, Hellenistic, and finally Christian exegeses reserved their own intentions & drew their own power. [...]

> For this reason, the active text needs to be recovered, as much as this is possible, from under the alterations & the reshufflings, adjustments, and obliterations. (Ibid., 16–17)

In order to restore the radically indeterminate nature of the text, Villa adopts an approach that faithfully represents the incompatibility of the various exegeses, as well as the fragmented state of Genesis at its earliest literary conception. For the most part, the source text Villa used in his translation was the Hebrew edition "edited by Alt, Eissfeldt, & Kahle, which is based on the complete Masoretic manuscript from around 1000 AD, that is the Leningrad Codex."[7] This version is widely considered to be the definitive and most reliable edition of the Hebrew and Aramaic scriptures, but Villa preferred to supplement it with the various myths of early Mediterranean cultures (which he found in different archives that held different editions written in different languages) in order to create a sort of biblical collage.

When describing the different schools of ancient Biblical scholars and how each reconstructed the text, Villa's position closely resembles that of the *Elohist*:

> In regard to prophetic "schools" or "societies," between the IX & VIII centuries BC, [the Elohists were] a group who collected traditions that were more ancient, or, in any case, pre-monarchical (in some sense seen as conservative and anti-monarchical), recuperating fragments and episodes of the legends of the ancestors, drawing partly upon autonomous oral documents, and partly upon literary reports scattered throughout the land of Palestine, which probably date back to Ugaritic-Phœnician legends. [...] The Elohist focuses on a literary tradition agitated by the various cultic and cultural influences hailing from the Syro-Palestinian coast, where Oriental thought, Paleomediterræan counter-

> influxes, Mesopotamian culture, & the late references to Egyptian theology meet to form a hybrid. (Ibid., 21–22)

Recuperating the fragments, legends, oral documents, and sporadic literary references hailing from much more ancient cultures, the *Elohist* insisted on all the nuances of the biblical text whereas the *Yahwist* followed a more traditional & strictly doctrinal approach. While most contemporary renderings of the Pentateuch stop at the Hebrew, both in their translation and notes, in traveling further back to excavate the meaning of words, Villa can be seen as a modern *Elohist*. A philologist of ancient languages, Villa merged etymology with his conception of a poetics in search of the *Verbum naturans*:

> The systematic search for the sacred and organic etymology [...] is, in the complex corpus of the Bible, the vertebræ that runs through it, perpendicularly & horizontally, in every time period and in line with the principle of the creativity of the word, a concept that was the same for the ancient Aramaic shepherd as it was for the educated priest in the Hellenistic era. (Ibid., 19)

Whether he is translating Hebrew into Italian, re-weaving the various myths back into Genesis, or etymologizing in his notes, Villa strives to restore the unbridled force of the word, as if it were being spoken again for the first time.

Through the science of history, the more ancient or earlier usage of terms can reveal certain forgotten meanings. However, the further back Villa travels in his excavation of the Hebrew Bible, the more the meaning of words become a-historical and uncertain: as a result of examining their ambiguous origins, Villa reveals their greater signifying potential. This is one of the ways in which his translation is distinct from every other: it emphasizes the enigmatic genesis of words in order for them to regain their truly protean & plastic nature, whereas other translators eschew the mystery with essentially dubious certitudes instead, surely made not to leave the authority of the text in question.

Poetry

When composing his own verse, Villa carries out the same search for the *Verbum naturans* as he did when translating the Hebrew Bible. In fact, many of the linguistic elements found in his rendering of the Pentateuch can also be traced throughout his poetry: he capitalizes on the tension that is part and parcel of myth, an enigma's capability of proliferating meaning without ever exhausting it, lacunæ or syntactical gaps, ludic games that allow the reader to choose a thread of discourse, the absence of the author, inexplicable subject shifts, the fragmentation of texts, the incompatibility of perspectives, the phonetic approximations between words, and most of all the 'returning' of words to their mysterious origins. As we read Villa's poetry, all these factors coalesce to create a sense that we are engaging with some sort of long lost, ancient (and in some cases partial) manuscript. While the poet generates the text, much like a philologist, the reader must learn how to live with its precariousness & keep in mind that interpretation is as uncertain as it is in Villa's translation of the Pentateuch: when one believes that meaning has been grasped, it just as quickly vanishes or is displaced or disrupted by another meaning. Consequently, it is most salient to focus on how Villa constructs the signifier in order to produce signification and not necessarily signification itself.

In Villa's writing, the presence of the authorial self or "I" begins to wane at an early stage. In fact, in an article he penned for the journal *il Frontespizio* in 1937, Villa openly declares his position concerning this issue: "It is our opinion that poetry cannot interest itself in biographical documents, in the events, either internal or external, of man..."[8] At that time, in Italy, the predominant style of verse was largely subjective; the then poet laureate, Eugenio Montale, as well as the Hermetic group operating in Florence, used language as a passive vehicle for transmitting a poet's thoughts to an audience. Villa was one of the first to radically veer from this trend, contending that an author's biography can suffocate a text — leading readers to interpret it according to his or her personal history — or that the author is not always the 'authority' — to follow his interpretative key can result in a reductive investigation of the text's variegated richness. Instead, for Villa, the reader's focus should lie solely on the language of a poem and not the speaking author, for language is autonomous. Villa is however not adhering to a conceptual notion regarding 'the death of the author' à la Roland Barthes; in Villa's poetics, the removal of the self coincides with his biblical renderings: it mirrors how there were no authors of ancient texts, leaving readers to decipher poetic enigmas for themselves. It is not by chance, then, that his presence begins to radically diminish in the '40s, throughout the collection *Oramai*, a period in which Villa's work on the Hebrew Bible began to intensify greatly. By the time we reach the subsequent collection *E ma dopo* (1950), the author has vanished entirely and language takes the forefront, as further underscored by the titles of the individual poems themselves, such as "Linguistics" & "Words."

The subjects of Villa's verse (whatever they may be) are often buried amid syntactical fragmentations. On several occasions his poems begin *in medias res*, making readers feel as if they were being thrown into the middle of a conversation started elsewhere, quite possibly in a different language. Consider the beginning of the long poem *comizio 1953*: "and going further down down down to the scrawny time of dusty christians [...]" (296).

The first part of the poem, the one that contains whatever happened before that "and," was never written. Consequently, Villa causes us to feel the panic of incompleteness and the urge to find the poem's origins. However, those origins do not exist. Since the fate of Villa's texts has been notoriously chaotic, it could be surmised that this fragmentary aspect testifies to the accidents of history rather than the author's intentions, but there are strong indications to the contrary. In fact, the history of *comizio* demonstrates that such fragmentation was deliberate and not entirely material in nature (as if the complete text was actually lost *&* has yet to be recovered). Villa's bibliography lists the piece as *comizio 1953* (Roma: 1959) but the original manuscript is not in his archives. In 1989, it was reproduced in an Italian anthology compiled by Aldo Tagliaferri; since that volume was edited under the poet's supervision, the version contained therein was long thought to be the only one in existence. I originally translated *comizio* from that anthology but recently discovered that another, longer version of it had been published in an obscure Italian literary journal in 1961. Herein the poem is included in its entirety (to the best of my knowledge), restoring two pages that were missing from the beginning and one from the middle. In each version, the poem begins *in medias res*; hence, Villa's textual strategy remains unaltered. Yet, such a confusing bibliographical circumstance is not unusual in Villa and is all part of the sibyl-poet's game. In "Pezzo 1941," which opens with a hypothetical introductory clause that is not followed by a consecutive chain, but rather a series of conditions, this fragmentariness is especially palpable:

> It could be
> that on any given
> day air would travel
> half-heartedly through the air,

maybe, but if Lake Garda fails to recover in time
all the dust eaten by cyclists in meaningless races,
& kilometers that don't count, good for nothing,

maybe, as long as [...] (62)

Complicating the structure is a series of subordinating conjunctions like *if, as long as, as if,* and *therefore*. As a consequence, the entire poem changes in meaning depending on how the reader decides to reconstruct the syntax. At times, the opening of certain poems can create temporal confusion, as in *E ma dopo*:

After the after is after
after dinner the storm
after agony the heliotrope and bending
the stamens [...] (106)

In this poem, the typical unfolding of cause & effect is jumbled; the reader does not know what came first and what after, just as we cannot know origins or conclusions, not in any ultimate or absolute sense. A similar linguistic act exists in "Astronomia." Yet, whereas in the previous texts the various possibilities were implicit, here Villa marks them with much more clarity:

[...]

it is right to believe that in the { space / slow mirror of rues / spirit }

the fluorescent odyssey of degrees defoliates and the floating
and mute full-moon vertebrae declined at the front of contrary projections!
then did you hear the sound reverberate in the cracked universe
of the ionosphere?

[...] (120)

The line *it is right to believe* gives rise to three different options: *space, slow mirror, spirit*. Furthermore, with the use of the prolepsis that places the verb *defoliate* at the end of the verse, it is difficult to determine if one of these three things defoliates, or if it is something that is named in the following stanza.

At times, Villa's texts resemble the enigmatic responses of an ancient sibyl. Prior to departing for war, ancient Greek soldiers would ask the sibyl if they would return alive. Her response was invariably: "Ibis redibis non morieris in bello." The answer to her enigma all depended on where the soldier placed a comma. Similarly, in Villa's texts, interpretation depends on the placement of punctuation, how subjects are linked to predicates, or how the tears within an individual word itself are reconstructed. These linguistic games invite readers to intervene and shape the materiality of the language Villa has displayed before them. And it is inconsequential how different or even incompatible interpretations may be. As we observed with Villa's translation of Genesis, the varied interpretations are the consequence of a radical ambiguity surrounding the origins of a text, its language, and the time and place in which it was first spoken.

In Villa's work, fragmentation can also come in the form of a sentence that carries on almost indefinitely through a lack of full-stops to help give definitive form or order to a poem (or, at times, periods are placed where they typically should not be). In *Sì, ma lentamente*, for instance, sentences seem to go on indefinitely as they unfold through syntactical twists and turns. In a poem that is nearly twelve pages long, the number of periods can be counted on both hands.

Villa also acts like a sibyl by tearing his work to shreds & casting it to the wind, such as with *Poesia è* (579), which was composed on ten individual pieces of paper. The original order of the stanzas is unknown for these folios were left jumbled in a box. Therefore, they can be shuffled together in a number of different ways, causing the signification to change with every new combination. The poet achieves this same sense of fragmentation within the individual pages of various poems throughout his œuvre. In such cases, Villa is elaborating on Mallarmé's theories regarding the text as cosmic architecture in causing a big bang to happen on the page — where words and sounds float aimlessly across its space awaiting structure — in order to once again emphasize the random nature of language. In other cases, Villa emphasizes fragmentation by inserting blank spaces on the page, which he positions at strategic points within his texts, as if they were linguistic traps. Sentences, periods, and entire discourses often disappear within these gaps, rendering interpretation even more uncertain, which again is reminiscent of translating an ancient manuscript riddled with lacunæ. Villa does not do this for an æsthetic purpose but rather to interrupt the discourse so as to deny any certainty. For instance, in "Linguistica," the syntax of the text is breached before it ever reaches a logical conclusion, by periods and then blank spaces:

> There's no more origins. Nor.   Nor does one know if.
> If there were origins and not even.
>   And not even a reason why origins
>   are born   Nor any longer
>   faith,   idol of Amorgos!
>   [...] (126)

It is as if these verses gravitated dangerously around these gaps, vanished within them, and then reemerged to start over anew on the other side of the gaps. Fragmentation is not intended, in my view, to be visually stunning, as was largely the case under the early European avant-gardes, where the Futurists' experiments with "Words in Freedom" increased the force of the message, or where Apollinaire's *Calligrammes*, for the most part, visually underscored the referent of the words employed. Villa, rather, causes the referent to vanish entirely, emphasizing, in another form, the indeterminate nature of language; a breakdown in the relationship between language and the object it describes. One could say that the blank spaces that visually perforate Villa's pages are almost a reaction to and not a continuation of the experiments carried out by the first wave of the European avant-gardes.

In using the work of another Italian poet as a counterpoint, Villa's placement of the abysmal space on the page becomes clearer. Critics have insisted that in the early poetry of Giuseppe Ungaretti, the empty space of the page acts to heighten the marvel of the word (*la meraviglia della parola*); like a firecracker against the backdrop of the darkest night, the word stands out on the page and stuns the reader with all of its signifying power. Yet, as the light of the firecracker cuts through the night sky, it also enhances its darkness, or rather, as the word juts from the page, the empty spaces around it become more ominous in such stark contrast to it. Bruno Bandini's insightful observations regarding Villa's work as an art critic speak equally to his poetry:

> For Villa, art is a divinity that is always absent, to which we can poetically attribute characteristics, assign 'attributes.' Art is a presence of the luminous, of the divine, which leaves traces of itself through flashes, simulacra, secret confidences: the critic can do nothing but try to recreate the force and the marvel of the absent, the tension of that original force that has irremediably concealed itself.[9]

Therefore, Villa enhances *the marvel of what's missing*, which lies in the empty spaces, the lacunæ, the abysses that call the word's meaning into question & render interpretation highly unstable.[10] While at times the strategic placement of the empty space or period serves to momentarily interrupt the discourse and send it in different directions, at other times, these small abysses may devour it completely, as in *17 variazioni*:

> [...]
> seed was the wind.
> the voice a process of hydrogenations.
> not eliminated, the extreme
> seasons were language.
>
> scents were frost and night,
> and weather that, was such that.
> the soul distance through equality,
> and the number folly the purest folly.
> [...] (166)

Aside from fragmenting syntax, Villa's work on individual phonemes and morphemes within his verse is particularly striking if not distinctive. A few indicative examples will serve to demonstrate how the poet employs similar techniques throughout his artistic corpus, no matter the collection, or the language he adopts. These techniques include: corruptions, etymological games, *voces*, glossolalia, word-strings, portmanteau, amalgamations, neologisms, & finally litanies. Furthermore, since the different linguistic devices he utilizes tend to resist rigid categories, it should be taken into consideration that ours are in no way set in stone; certain examples may pertain to more than one category alone.

Villa often corrupts words by ever so slightly modifying their spellings. As Cecilia Bello-Minciacchi states in her article on Villa's Latin, "Hupokritam vocem," the reader often encounters the "phenomenon of Latin or Greek hyper-characterization given the use of "h" or "y" that are etymological or verbal concretions that tend toward a magnification or archeo-etymological distortion."[11] Although her analysis is primarily aimed at the recurrence of this phenomenon in Villa's more ancient tongues, it may also be applied to the poet's use of modern languages. For example, hyper-characterization takes place when Villa replaces the 'i' in *Italia* with a 'y.' The substitution not only causes the name to seem foreign, but also illustrates the diverse evolution of languages. While the Greek *epsilon* does not remain in Italian, it does in other tongues foreign to it, like English. While graphically the word Italya appears different, its pronunciation does not change, as it does ever so slightly with the poet's corruption "Itaglia." At times, Villa includes an 'h' where grammatically it should not be, as in "eucharistico" in *comizio 1953*, so when inserted into *eucaristico*, the "ch" resembles the Greek "x." Thus, the poet brings out the "xristo" in "eu*charist*ico."

Villa also 'corrupts' by causing a swerve in the evolution of a word, demonstrating how its formation could have occurred differently, either phonetically or graphically. For example, he rewrites adjectives by switching their endings, as in "Argomenti," with "italiarde, tosche, lombane" (italiane, toscane, lombarde), or changes the beginning of nouns, as in *comizio 1953*, where he switches "agonia" to "ingonia." In the same poem, he plays on the engendering of Italian, creating linguistic hermaphrodites by using the adjective for masculine in its feminine form ("masculina") & feminine in its masculine form ("femmino,") or transforming feminine words into masculine (and vice versa), as in *poiana* to *poiano*.

Villa also highlights the etymology of a word by rewriting it according to more ancient phonetics. In *comizio 1953*, we find "eideia," which demonstrates how the word for "idea" is a derivative of the Greek verb εἴδω, to see. Villa also explicitly informs his readers that the meaning of his words following these ancient etymologies — as in the poem "Artemis" from the collection *Verboracula* — "leges sumerice" (you will read in Sumerian). Or in *17 variazioni*: "eu te dic en son latin" (I'll tell you in Latin sound). These benchmarks serve an important aim in Villa's poetry — they inform the reader as to whether he is playing on the meaning of more ancient terms, or on their phonetic value. Similar games take place in reverse when Villa uses modern languages to rewrite ancient Greek & Latin terms, treating them as if they were still spoken.

On occasion, the poet breaks words throughout a poem in order to bring out their etymological affinities. Consider the original Italian of "Però prima del vento":

> [...]
> i verbi coniugati a malapena, e i gemi-
> ti, e imprese, e faccende e càno-
> ni, il bene della vita,
>
> sono i semi riscaldati tra le dita
> di una sola mano, di una lingua
> sciolta, di una lingua nuova;
>
> e le radici semplici o gemi-
> nate, nel nuvolo sommerso
> dei parlari, [...] (67)

By parsing "gemiti" (moans) & "geminate" (geminates), Villa simultaneously emphasizes the similar root of these two terms

and their completely different meanings, which begs the question as to what *moans* have to do with *geminates*? Furthermore, *gemi-* rhymes with *semi*, suggesting that a word part functions as a seed that eventually grows and branches into other words, like *gemi-* into *gemiti & geminate*.

Throughout Villa's œuvre, this breaking of words to form new combinations and associations increases. At the ending of "hyménée liturg," from the collection *Heurarium*, the poem suddenly shatters into different pieces that may be recombined in various ways. While "hyménée liturg" moves from linear into splintered verse, later in life, Villa created entire poems based solely on the parsing of words.[12]

Aside from 'techniques' that focus on the fragmentation of morphemes, Villa also creates words of pure sound to which any signification has yet to be applied, a technique which can be elucidated with Giorgio Agamben's term *vox*. A word that evokes a momentary sense of insecurity, incomprehension, or even instability can be defined, according to Agamben, as a *vox*, for it lies on the cusp between sound & signification: "non è mero suono, ma non è ancora significato." The *vox* may either come in the form of a completely new word introduced by the poet, or as a word stripped down to its purely phonetic value, emptying it of conventional meaning. In either case, the *vox* does not serve as a bridge between signifier and signified, but rather opens a gap that reveals a sense of "insecurity." The effect is that we come into contact with the very seeming origins of language, any language, with that moment in which sounds are uttered for the first time with the intention to signify.[13] The first true example of this phenomenon can be found in the poem "ultimatum à la corrrrée," where Villa plays with the sound of the first letter of the alphabet:

last AA
AA. AAA. A.AA
AAAAAA A A A
AAAAAA A. AA.
A. AAA. AA. A.A.
AAAAAA A A A
AAAAA A t u m
[...] (330)

The repetition of "alpha" suggests a series of small beginnings that occur through different amalgamations of the same sound, as if this one letter holds infinite possibilities in and of itself, even before it is folded in with other letters. The letter is not only the first of the alphabet, but "alpha" also implies a beginning, a linguistic origin. "A t u m," the first word following the grouping of A's, plays on the phonetics of "atom," implying that, as the atom is a building block of life, the letter A is one of language.

Examples of *voces* proliferate in Villa's English of *Options* (337), too: "hyle," "unds," "mollow," "wers," "incolumity," "Transaptomathic," and similar *voces* may be found in any of the languages the poet employs in his verse.[14] While these are somewhat reminiscent of the language they are couched in, Villa created his own mysterious terms when renaming his poems later in life. These new titles include, amongst others: XEIS, SHIVS, ESSMO, CASSEOHS, ΣΟΣ, and ABKUM; enigmatic words that seem to originate from some long lost language and are completely indecipherable.

When these individual *voces* coalesce, they form a *glossolalia*; a poem composed mostly of sound with little meaning. One emblematic instance of this is the piece aptly entitled "Genesis":

kart kars
ker
crin krus
kres
kruk
christ cru
christ cresc
cerast cereal
cru
crux
rux ærug rug ros reg
krugs krag
crus crura
[...] (454)

It is as if we were witnessing the birth of a language and its subsequent morphology through the scattering of words through empty space. Villa begins with the word "kart," then reconstructs its hypothetical transmission (and manipulation) across the ages, until it comes to form recognizable terms in different languages (such as "christ," "cereal," or "crus," which is Latin for "leg"). This entire galaxy of words rests precariously on a random agglutination of sounds that seem to derive from some mythical age.

At times, Villa constructs nominal strings of text in which different words are grouped together for purely phonetic reasons. Consequently, the barriers separating their significations are weakened under the pressure of the signifiers. "Luogo e impulso" is composed completely of nouns that are joined phonetically by a sequence of alternating rhymes:

Half idea and half fruit
half risk half desire
half whole half absolute
half bread half expire

Half space and half effigy
half body and half shade
half torment half malady
half dry half cascade
[...] (114)

The typical meaning of these words is emptied out and the application of new meaning must be explicated through their phonetic similarities. Villa also has a tendency to assign words functions they previously did not possess by either transforming nouns into verbs, verbs into nouns, or nouns into adjectives.[15] Although it is common in Italian to use the infinitive form of verbs as nouns (i.e., il dire = the act of saying), the poet utilizes conjugated verbs as nouns. For example, in *Letania per Carmelo Bene,* we read "il vedodire," which literally translates to "the Isee-saying" (542). A more common occurrence is the transformation of nouns into adjectives: the English "brained petals," suggesting flower petals with brains ("Options"), & the Italian "vulvatico" ("Euoneiric transfer"). While the adjectival form of "vulva" does not exist in Italian, in English we do have "vulval" or "vulvar." However, these refer to a shape that is similar to a vulva, while "vulvatico" (vulvatic) almost suggests a vulva-like function. Also, this neologism rings of the Italian "viatico" (viaticum), bringing a rather blasphemous connotation to the priest's administration of the last rites.

Villa frequently creates neologisms, which could also be referred to as neo-formations or amalgamations, by combining different words to form linguistic synergies. In "Imprimatur" (273), we find "ombelisco," which is a combination of "ombelico" (navel) and "obelisco" (obelisk). In "Contenuto figurativo," the poet writes "equibollente" (147), which merges "equipollente" (equivalent) & the verb "bollire" (to boil). In *comizio 1953*, Villa replaces the "idea" in "ideologia" with "idolo" (idol), which in *Letania per Carmelo Bene* is rewritten again as "eidealologia." Villa's neologisms can also be comical. One of the most amusing examples of these amalgamations comes again from "Imprimatur": "Occhitesticoli" may indicate a combination of the intellect (according to Plato, the eyes are the most intellectual of the senses) and the viscera; or it could be a reference to the bogus legend regarding the female pope Joan and the subsequent procedure carried out by the conclave to assure themselves, by examining the genitals, that the Vicar of Christ was not a woman. Or it could even be a corruption of English, that is "eyeballs" become "eyetesticles" with Villa then translating it into Italian.

Villa also separates words to show how they are already a synergy of different meanings. In *comizio 1953*, we find "od rosa," where he removes a letter to emphasize the "rose" in the Italian for "odorous." The same applies to "inane llato" (bejeweled) further on in the same poem, through which Villa highlights the "inane."[16] In *comizio*, he creates a neologism by simply removing a letter: taking an 'n' out of the verb "depennare" transforms the action of crossing out into that of either removing the pain (pena) or the penis (pene). Rather than parsing a word, Villa often inserts parentheses to show how two different, essentially conflicting, meanings are found within a single word. In *Letania per Carmelo Bene*, we have "Orga(ni)smo" and in *Poesia è*, "in(de)finito." He underscores more explicitly the morphemes a word contains by writing them next to it, as in *Letanie*: "di glottidi ammainate, mai nate." The verb "ammainare" means to haul down, but is also comprised of "never born." Furthermore, we can view the title of Villa's second collection *Oramai* in this light: while together "ora" and "mai" mean "by now," when separated they mean "now" & "never." This also attests to the fleeting signifying power of poetic language, in that it is simultaneously what *is* and what *never has been*; it is both present and strangely absent.

Throughout his texts, Villa also generates certain neologisms phonetically, which are born out of the sound of other words. For instance, in the English of "the cuban gong," Villa takes advantage of the rhyme in order to create new terms:

[...]
and Nip nettle to rumnage sweetly
implicitly into rump explicitly into purling
hurling
burling
when bride bear buckle into blackbloodvessel murling
[...] (331)

While "purling" & "hurling" are common English words, "burling" & "murling" are Villa's. A similar act takes place when the poet first separates morphemes & then breaks them further down, to their phonetic value. Consider the last line of the prose-poem *SUB BREGME*, "(Ember, Member, Remember, Emb, Embor) [...]" (358), which is a play on a verse by Francesco Petrarca: "... come posson queste *membra* / da lo spirito lor viver lontane? // Ma rispondemi Amor: Non ti *rimembra*..." [17] Elaborating on Petrarca's parsing of the linguistic units of "remember" to send meaning in two different directions (the mental act of recollection and the physical presence of the body), Villa directs our attention to the morpheme "ember," splintering meaning yet a third time. And he does not stop there. While Petrarca's wordplay is limited to what semioticians refer to as the "first articulation" of a linguistic sign, the division of a word into *meaningful* units (in this case, members of the body and memory), Villa, with "Emb" & "Embor," pushes his play on "remember" into the "second articulation" of the sign, into the realm of pure sound, where words have yet to accumulate meaning.

The same phenomenon is repeated in Latin, with different results, in Villa's *Sibylla ndrangheta*:

[...]
indrangena   indrongeta
androgina   dendrangeta
mandragula   extrangulata
ingenerata   semisanguis
               hydranguis
artranxia   antrangula
indramatica   faux olim
               eructans ab ovo
indroguaina   endrorgana
indogunanta   androngyna
[...] (526)

While in the previous two examples sound leads to the creation of new *voces*, here Villa simultaneously generates new words and accumulates those already in existence by playing on their phonetic value.

Like the call and response exchanged between a priest & worshipers, or a primitive tribe working itself into the syncopated rhythm of a chant, Villa relies on the litany, the repetition of a single word or phrase throughout his poems, in order to empty them of their inherent meanings & imbue them with new ones. Within church services or processions, the litany is a series of petitions: the clergy recites a number of different statements to which the parishioners respond with a refrain. For example, as a priest lists a number of prayers (such as for the healing of the sick), the people reply with a *kýrie, eléison*: "lord have mercy," or "Grant us, o lord." In his poems, Villa transforms this petitioning of the divine into a supplication for meaning, which, much like the answer to prayers, never comes, but continues on indefinitely.

The litany is also tied to the poet's experience in translating the Hebrew Bible, as Villa himself explains: "In the Old Testament, the name Yahweh appears about 6700 times. This long litany, ineffable and obsessive, is the trace of the figure of this divinity that creates its own phantoms & fable..."[18] Thus, we can say that in Villa's poetry, this litany, similar to the repetition of Yahweh in the Hebrew Bible, is the incessant search for the meaning(s) of a term. Yet, the one true meaning (if one can even speak of such a thing) is always allusive, and thus the operation of generating more meanings must continue. In other words, the litany is the obsessive pursuit of a meaning that cannot be found & the accumulation of a number of different meanings yielded by that pursuit. In acting as the refrain within a poem, the word, or phrase, is the point in which the poem simultaneously empties what it has previously acquired and begins to take on the new through whatever follows. The result is that Villa pushes a term to become everything & nothing. In "Cosa c'è di nuovo" (57), a poem from *Oramai*, Villa employs the refrain "what's new is" at the beginning of the first four stanzas. And in the fifth stanza, we read "the universal substance trembles." The introduction of "what's new" has a butterfly effect, in that it sets off a chain of new events that take place across the entire universe.

This repetition is also reminiscent of a child's incessant use of the question "why?" when trying to discover the meaning behind things: "Why is the sky blue?" "Because it is a reflection of the ocean"; "Why does it reflect off the ocean?" & so on, until the search for the meaning behind why things are the way they are comes to include everything around us. In "Imprimatur" (255), a poem from *3 ideologie*, we find the refrain "ibi et ubique," ("there and everywhere"). This suggests that the meaning of the poem is, paradoxically, both present & absent: — it is there but also everywhere else. Furthermore, the last stanza of the poem finishes with an "amen," which would suggest the end of a discourse. However, the refrain returns once again and is not followed by a period. Ending as such, the author leaves the poem open in order for its discourse to continue another time, perhaps *ad infinitum*. Similarly, in *Poesia è*, the repetition is an attempt to define the indefinable: "poetry is almost everything: that is everything, less / what it really is" (588).

Art Criticism

Traditionally, the role of the art critic is to clarify the work of art, to draw meaning from it, to provide readers with the necessary tools to approach or understand it. Villa, instead, refrains from advancing any interpretation at all, & even further compounds the enigma of the work by writing a poem *about* it (in the literal sense of *around* it: cf. *Geometria Reformata*, 470–497). Thus, Villa creates a paradox that is simultaneously altruistic and self-serving: the artwork under analysis both maintains its distance from decipherability, and serves as a basis to create his own original poetry. More specifically, by couching his "exegeses," so to say, in a cryptic form of verse, Villa shrouds the historical circumstances of the artwork in mystery, consequently transforming it into a myth. Thus, through this unique form of "criticism," primitive and abstract art become one and the same.

In his essay "Noi e la preistoria" (615–622), originally published in *Arti Visive* in 1954, Villa traces the origins of art back to one simple gesture carried out by Neanderthal man: the displacement of a whalebone from the shore into his cave. Villa recognizes this as the first manifestation of an aspect fundamental to all art — the materiality of an object was transformed into something it was not before. As Villa writes: "Nowadays, it is believed that [...] Neanderthals did not posses any faculties that we would today call 'artistic' [...]. However, [...] the fact that picking up and transporting the vertebra into their dwelling should prove that they understood the object's 'singularity'" (616). Here, Villa makes two very important observations. The first is that many abstract artists & theorists of the 20th century prefer to indulge in the deceptive tranquility that art has evolved considerably since its primitive origins. Yet, if we consider an example like the Chauvet caves in Southern France, it's evident that the charcoal drawings depicting herds of animals not only display a rather skilled hand, but also that the use of space in the caves is strikingly modern: the placement of the drawings on a concave section of the wall, together with the illumination of a nearby fire-pit, gave the drawings a sense of kineticism. All of which, it could be said, recalls the dynamism of our not so distant Futurism, and in particular Umberto Boccioni's paintings, such as *La città che sale* (1910). The second observation is that the action of retrieving the object from the shore and displaying it in a cave must have been motivated by a change in Neanderthal man's perception of that object — that something typically taken for granted was suddenly assigned a different function & space.

This prompts Villa to venture into the enigma surrounding how such a displacement occurred: "what both paleontologists and historical archeologists have struggled to clarify is precisely the reason why an object, either found in nature or manufactured, came to be charged with a function the object itself does not naturally have" (618). And this could have happened for any number of reasons. Was the object part of a magico-religious ceremony of worship? Or was the vertebra magic in and of itself: a complex structure evoking a sense of both continuity and variation? Perhaps it served as an example of something primordial man sought to build, a chain or weave?

The fact that answers to such questions can never truly be verified and belong to an inaccessible past, leads the critic to approach the matter in a different way than the paleontologists, who try to find "what causes the object to emit new relationships with spheres of activity that are external to it" (618). Searching for *what* our whalebone "emits" means, according to Villa, to move in the direction of interpreting its meaning and toward æsthetics. He equates delving into matters of "beauty" to casting a rather reductive light on the object. To assign it an æsthetic is to try to figure out what it intends to say. And in so doing, the observer pushes the object toward a specific if not single interpretation. Consequently, this renders the object impotent, for the many ways of perceiving it are suffocated by one perception alone. Yet, since the mythical circumstances surrounding the whalebone prohibit us from advancing any certainties, it maintains its mystery, and thus its almost endless power of evocation. With this, we home in on a fundamental aspect of Villa's criticism. Rather than in what the object *says*, Villa was interested in what it actually *does*: the gesture through which an object is transformed into something else, the pure &

novel act of making. What matters then is not what the Neanderthal saw in the whalebone, but rather the displacement itself, for it was "the pure act that led prehistoric man to a concrete communication with the world, or rather to taking possession of the world" (622). By simply moving the whalebone, the Neanderthal went from passively being in the world to actively taking hold of it, to shaping it in such a way that it appeared differently (which, not by chance, resembles the paradigm of the cosmogonic myths mentioned earlier). And we can view this gesture as inflicting a tear upon the world, one that comes in many forms: as the shifting of an object from one place to another, as a line etched into a wall, & so on. The tear is the first step in the creation of all art: the refashioning of a material so that it evokes new relationships with the world (as its continuity is broken, a diversity is revealed, & a desire to reassemble all the pieces in a new way is evoked). This allows us to transgress our typical perceptions: once the materiality of the object is altered, it unhinges the way we look at it, acting as a gateway through which the things we take for granted appropriate characteristics that had previously been kept hidden, or are concealed by the habits of our perceptions. As Riccardo Panattoni and Gianluca Solla observe, Villa opens new horizons: "A horizon is in fact a gash, an open laceration. Therefore horizons are opened only at the cost of opening wounds."[19] And it is this same initial act of tearing carried out by Neanderthal man that Villa saw in the abstract art of the 20th century: "To those superficial people who object by saying non-figurative invention is forty years old, we object that it is instead fifty thousand years old" (622). Consider Marcel Duchamp's *Fountain*, wherein the artist executes a displacement similar to that of the whalebone, or any one of Lucio Fontana's *Cuts*, which literally exhibit all the qualities of the aforementioned tear. The artist inflicts a wound on the canvas, exposing what is hidden behind it. By explicitly emphasizing the gesture — the act through which the world is re-made — 20th-century abstract art easily lends itself to the critic's comparison to the art of primordial man.

Villa follows one of the precepts expressed in the *Manifesto tecnico dei pittori futuristi*: "Consider art critics useless & damaging."[20] In his writings, he uses myth to connect primordial & modern art, and, in the case of the latter, to thwart any reductive critical interpretations. To do so, he must salvage the work from its historical setting & surround it in the same enigmatic, mythical circumstances as those in which primordial man operated. And this is where Villa's poetry comes in: his "criticism" in the form of poetry makes it appear as though he were talking about some ancient object with inexplicable properties. In Villa's writing on Fontana's *Buchi*, we find that Villa employs the same techniques he does in his own verse. In the first part of his exegesis on the TROU — "hole" in French — he switches linguistic codes right away, moving from Latin to French. In the same way, he also relies on English, as in *complexities of Survival, à manger les trous*, or the amusing *trou I, trou you*. Used over a hundred times in different forms, the one phoneme TROU constitutes the entire essay, which recalls the litany and its obsessive repetition of a term. Listen to the series of nonsensical rhymes, such as *boutrou foutrou toutrou troutrou*, or strings of portmanteau words, such as *tatrouage, troudre, troumatique*, or *trul* (a combination of *trou* and either *nul* or *cul*). Villa often uses the alliteration of T-R to connect distant signifiers, as in *trou tué pour tuer, bien, (tuer la mort)*. He also creates interesting neologisms by clashing different words together or against each other, defining Fontana's work as a *trouviol, troucarie*, or *troupassage*, which is also reminiscent of the gateway opened by the tear.

In the form of the writing, we see the insertion of empty spaces not only between different words, but also dividing single words themselves. Even if one quickly skims through the text, one immediately sees how the syntax almost expands and contracts, opening into prose and then condensing into verse, making the discourse difficult to follow in any sequential manner. Finally, toward the end of the piece, Villa asks the same question of Fontana's *Buchi* as he does of the Neanderthal's whalebone, which roughly translates as: "What could this mean? I don't believe it means anything, precisely; nothing, *&*, in every case, his work doesn't say anything but nothing, good; his work only relates." If Villa is not interested in the signification of Fontana's work, then his criticisms of it must too refrain from signifying. The scope, instead, as we read in the postscript to the piece, is to produce "*une niche niche / dans une niche / c'est une viole née / à chymère obligée*" (636). For the artwork to continue to signify without making statements, it must be shrouded in a mythical quality, that "black veil of the obligatory chimera" that keeps the enigma from being deciphered.

Although we've seen how Villa's criticism avoids supplementing an artwork with any univocal interpretation, what remains to be answered is how Villa appropriates it in order to create his own original poetry. Similar to how abstract art recovers the initial act of altering the materiality of the world, Villa plays on the earliest etymologies associated with writing verse. In fact, the dictionary definitions of the two acts are surprisingly similar. The term poetry comes from the Greek *póiesis,* which in turn derives from the Greek verb *poiêin,* meaning "to make." At its origins, then, poetry simply referred to any form of making, and not necessarily to an act of saying. And the Latin term for verse, *versus,* derives from the verb *vértere* (to furrow a field).[21]

To furrow is to reshape the physical make-up of the land, to open a wound in the earth, one that allows for aeration and the planting of new crops. In writing verse, the poet furrows the page, modifies its landscape, aerates language, and plants a seed to generate new possibilities.

If the statement regarding poetry as making has been reiterated so often as to now seem almost hackneyed, it holds particular relevance when it comes to Villa and his treatment of language as a raw material. His work truly adheres to the original notion of "making" for, as we have seen, Villa acts as the poet-*faber*, working on the phonemes and graphemes that generate meaning and not meaning itself, which is left to the reader to decide upon. In fact, the same tear Fontana inflicts upon the materiality of the art-object is carried out by Villa upon the materiality of language: portmanteau words, code shifting, blank spaces, jumbled syntax, fragmentation, et cetera — all attest to the poet's reshaping of language. For Villa, the single phoneme "TROU" becomes an inexhaustible source of wordplay, a linguistic genesis that sets in motion an endless chain of interpretative possibilities. Therefore, like Fontana's *Buchi*, Villa riddles the page with his TROU. Villa's poetic criticism of abstract art is then *une niche dans une niche*, a hole within a hole, or rather, "trou I, trou you," which is not only a statement directed at Fontana but also an invitation extended to every individual reader.

Emilio Villa: Biblicist, Art Critic, Experimental Poet...

1. Villa lived in São Paolo from 1951 to 1952, where he worked for the MASP Museum under the direction of his friend & fellow compatriot Pietro Bardi. Although his stay was brief, Villa was extremely prolific while there. We know that he composed a number of placards for exhibitions on primitive South American art (the specific contents of which remain unclear), but it is very likely that the museum's archives contain other surprises.

2. That is, if the custodians of such holdings are magnanimous enough to even allow access in the first place. Anyone who has conducted research in Italy knows that its cultural patrimony is not only kept tightly under lock and key, if not often deliberately concealed, but also hindered by petty bureaucracy.

3. Or, in the words of the Italian poet and critic, Lello Voce: "[...] more than pluri-lingualism, within the work of Emilio Villa [...] it seems that already one language alone is inhabited by many different languages." See his "Il transito provocato delle idee antiche. Appunti sulla poesia di Emilio Villa" (2006). Available online at: liberinversi.altervista.org/tag/emilio-villa/. The translations of this and all subsequent citations are my own.

4. For the longest time, Villa was known in Italy solely as an art critic and remained a poet's poet, so it is equally difficult to speak of those whom he himself may have influenced. Among those aware of his verse, only a few openly recognized it, such as Adriano Spatola, Giulia Niccolai, Patrizia Vicinelli, Corrado Costa, and Luciano Caruso. Other, more prominent Italian poets, such as those of the Novissimi group, were likely aware of his poetic innovations during the '40s & '50s but did not acknowledge them until the '70s & '80s.

Genesis

5. E. Villa, "Sulla traduzione di testi biblici," *il Verri*, № 7–8 (novembre 1998) 12.

6. "L'Enuma Elis," introduzione, traduzione, e note di E. Villa, *Letteratura: Rivista trimestrale di letteratura contemporanea*, № XII (1939) 2.

7. Ibid., 17, note #4.

Poetry

8. E. Villa, "Sopra il ritorno del canto," *il Frontespizio*, № 6 (giugno 1937) 458.
9. B. Bandini, "Informale e dintorni," *I linguaggi della critica. La critica d'arte in Italia dal dopoguerra ad oggi* (Rimini: Fara Editore, 1996) 46.
10. In *Alphabetum cœleste* (cf. "Other Writings" section of this volume), Villa intensifies the panic induced by the abysmal blank space by removing words from the page and casting them onto the expanse of a much larger space: a few sentences and letter clusters, reproduced in tiny font, linger on what appears to be a ten by fifteen foot white wall.
11. C. Bello, "*Hupokritam vocem*, in margine a *Sibylla* (metastatica)," *Atelier*, № 45, anno XII (marzo 2007).
12. Cf. "Pythica" in the collection *Verboracula*.
13. See G. Agamben, "Pascoli e il pensiero della voce," *Categorie italiane* (Venezia: Marsilio, 1996).
14. Cf. his Portuguese & French in *Heurarium* or his Latin in *17 variazioni* and *Verboracula*.
15. For verbs into nouns, see the opening line of *Semper pauperes* wherein he uses "Breda," the name of a manufacturing plant outside Milan, as a verb: "Già da lontano breda, già da tempo, con l'indice levato" (73).
16. One is never completely sure when making such assumptions given the rather sloppy nature of the editions of Villa's poetry. Typos are very likely to have occurred and, in fact, the poet probably welcomed them.
17. F. Petrarca, "Canto 15," *Canzoniere*, a cura di M. Santagata (Milano: Mondadori, 2008).
18. E. Villa, "Sulla traduzione…," ibid., 20, note #6.

Art Criticism

19. R. Panattoni and G. Sola, "Emilio Villa o lo squarcio dell'impersonale," E. Villa, *Poeta e scrittore*, a cura di Claudio Parmiggiani (Milano: Mazzotta, 2008) 396.
20. U. Boccioni, C.D. Carrà, G. Balla, G. Severnini, L. Russolo, *Manifesto tecnico dei pittori futuristi* (1910). Available online at: www.futurismo.altervista.org
21. Curiously, *vertere* shares the same etymology as *vertebra*, & Villa, in the introduction to his translation of Genesis, refers to the *verbum naturans* as the "vertebra" running through the text.

The Selected Poetry

of

Emilio Villa

Da *Adolescenza*

From *Adolescence*

1934

Poesia mia

Nasci dagli argini
Del monte,
Vieni da aperti
Cancelli d'ombre,
Vergine aria nata
In margini
Di carne.
Se questa svagata
Cenere di cose
Agiti ancora,
Vergine fiato
Il fuoco che accendesti eterno,
E che rivive,
Voci sincere e calde ti ritrova.

E questi che si scrivono improvvisi
Vagiti bambini d'altri mondi
Son eterni.

My Poetry

You're born from the levees
Of the mountain,
You come from open
Gates of shadows,
Virgin air created
In margins
Of flesh.
If you disturb
This negligent
Ash of things once more,
Virgin breath
The eternal fire you lit,
And that's reborn,
Will find you warm sincere voices again.

And these that are written sudden
Child cries of other worlds
Are eternal.

Parole silenziose

Sono incantate finestre, sul fondale
Del mio cielo dischiuse
Le parole:
Disumanate e mie.

Quando sono stanco di morire
In questa buia stanza
Prode mi dischiarano
Remote e liscie.

Chè in bocca de l'eternità
S'è accesa la parola del mio tempo,
E lieto sul fondo degli anni,
Come nella melma del naviglio
Acqua m'adagio; e passo.

Silent Words

They're spellbound windows,
Against the backdrop of my sky
Words ajar:
Dehumanized and mine.

When I'm tired of dying
In this dark room
To me they reveal
smooth and distant shores.

For in the mouth of eternity
Ignites the word of my time,
Happy at the bottom of years,
Like water in the naviglio's
muck, I lie down; and pass.

Specchio di pini sul lago

Greve coro di culmini,
Alto gorgoglio d'acque,
Ogni voce un'ombra
Riagita nei gorghi.

Lago, specchio di sorgive, anch'io
Cresco nel buio:
Vicino a le stelle con voi
Sono fiorito e solo.

Anime rievoco dal cavo
Delle onde, che presso il groviglio dei miei rami,
Nido d'echi distese, aduno
A sillabare il tempo.

Le stelle m'ingemmano le rame,
Mi vestono le foglie di silenzi,
Mi muoiono le anime qui in mano.
Sbiadite come foglie astrali.

Sono fiorito e solo. Sacerdote
Del tempo eterno, che vegeta
Tra ramo e ramo,
Stella e stella,
Onda e onda.

Pines' Mirror on the Lake

Gloomy chorus of peaks,
High gurgle of waters,
Every voice stirs
Shadows in the whirlpool.

Lake, mirror of springs, I too
Grow in the dark:
Near the stars with you
I'm blossomed and alone.

I call souls back from the hollow
Of waves, which I gather by my tangled
Branches, nest of outstretched echoes,
To beat time.

The stars bejewel my branches,
Leaves cover me in silence,
Souls die here in my hand.
Faded like astral leaves.

I'm blossomed and alone. Priest
Of time eternal, sprouting
Between branch and branch,
Star and star,
Wave and wave.

Voci del vento

L'onda del vento a sognare
Sua dispersa matrice,
Un mare, fiorisce.

Vento,
Viva vena del cielo,
Rinata canzone
D'un diluvio, quando
Le tue voci diventan silenzi,
E parlano, mute, nel sogno.
Odo primavere nate
Dal tuo gelido grembo,
Gioie rassegnate d'un esilio umano.

Vento,
Tre volte puro,
Come me, come
Se fossi l'ultimo uomo
Vissuto, e vissuto
Solo di carne mia e di me.

The Wind's Voices

The wave of wind dreaming
Its lost matrix,
A sea, flourishes.

Wind,
Sky's lively vein,
A downpour's
Reborn song, when
Your voices become silence,
And, mute, speak in dream.
I hear Springs born
From your icy womb,
Resigned joys of a human exile.

Wind,
Three times pure,
Like me, as
If I were the last man
Alive, and alive
Only through my flesh and myself.

Vita agreste

Tra noi è come quando
In cielo nascono bianchi buoi
E rosari di nuvole gonfie
Si sgranano.

Bestie del campo,
Bue, faccia di sogno,
Pecora bella,
Amici nostri,
Viviamo.

Rural Life

Between us it's like when
White oxen are born in the sky
And rosaries of swollen clouds
Pass.

Beasts of the field,
Ox, face of dream,
Beautiful sheep,
Friends of ours,
We live.

Vita

Fosforescente velo, la mia spoglia
Mortale, ride del suo tempo
Che t'ha fatta sincera come un'acqua.

Io vivo dove mi percuote
Vortice di luci,
L'ora della vita.

Cosmici iati, lo spazio ci varca,
E varcati, ci umana,
E raccoglie nel seno dell'eternità.

Life

Phosphorescent veil, my mortal
Remains, laughs at its time
That made you sincere like a water.

I live where life's hour
Smites me,
Vortex of lights.

Cosmic hiatus, the space crosses us,
And crossed, makes us human,
And gathers us in eternity's bosom.

Alla morte

Un gorgo di passate terre,
Voragine di cieli sfumati,
O Signore, ad ogni sera,
La morte è vicina.

Ma non ti so male,
Morte, mia madre, estrema
Aurora: quell'alito
Di consunta eternità
Mi crea.

Se mi abbandono
A te, mortale, ritorno
A vivere il tuo primo dono.

For Death

A whirlpool of past terrains,
Deep ravine of blurred skies,
Oh Lord, every night,
Death is near.

Yet I don't see you as evil,
Death, my mother, ultimate
Aurora: that breath
Of spent eternity
Creates me.

If, mortal, I give
Into you, I return
To live your first gift.

Paese medioevale

Un popolo di pensieri bigi e santi,
Come vecchi angeli sospesi al cielo,
Dondola su l'onde delle campane.

Le occhiaie scarne del campanile
Hanno parole strane e senza senso
Che si staccano da l'ormeggio con paure.

Paurosi gridi nascono dalle valli vuote,
Escono fiati dal silenzio dei cimiteri,
I vivi hanno le faccie dei morti.

Ma superstite senso d'uomini svaniti,
Cenere d'antichi cuori sparpagliata,
Raccolgo per l'aria una pregherai mia.

Medieval Town

A people of grim and holy thoughts,
Like old angels hanging from the sky,
Rolls across the bells' waves.

The scrawny orbits of the bell tower
Bear strange words with no sense
That break from the mooring with fear.

Empty valleys birth frightful screams,
The cemetery silence exhales long breaths,
The living take the faces of the dead.

But surviving sense of vanished men,
Scattered ashes of ancient hearts,
I gather my prayer across the air.

Silent Words

1. The *navigli* are waterways that run through Milan. A few are still in use today.

Prendi la rocca e il fuso e andiamo in California ...

*Grab the Distaff and Spindle and Let's Go to California ...**

1941

... A nìvole di nebbie dei re longobardi,
si partiva per le cene, con le torce,
coi letti arrugginiti, sulle spalle,
a fare una pasqua, per i morti,
senza fine. Poi tramontava il giùbilo
di pentecoste, a picco
sopra il torrente del mio paese, o giovane Strona:
grigia, quanto la tunica dei giorni:
le donne che hanno ci hanno vigilato
han volto, a capo in giù, le sacre torce.
Solo, tre becchi di lampada, a petrolio,
ancora rischiaravano gli àzimi,
che si doveva trangugiare nelle albe
del bene (e del male), sulle strade.
Ho preso, un giorno, lo stallo
nel coro, o cicale!, dei miei simboli benedetti:
dove a scorza d'alberi, mangiati dalla folgore,
le foglie fuggite cantavano le antifone:
"Alza ferro contro il tuo petto!
perché si sappia, fin dall'inverno,
se tu sei arido o fertile: e chi
ti salverà dai gesti futuri?"
"Non mettere il tuo cuore
sulla vigna di Sirtori o di Somma,
sulla vigna d'Appiano o di Missaglia:
perché il vendemmiatore bagna il pane
dentro la secchia dell'aceto."
"Colui che implora, a ogni mattino,
la sapienza dagli àcini dell'uva,
saprà incendiar tutte le vigne
nel giorno dell'addio..."

... In the cloudy fogs of Longobard kings,
we left for dinner, with torches,
with rusty beds, on our backs,
to have an Easter, for the dead,
without end. Then the Pentecost's
rejoicing set vertically
over the stream of my town, oh young Strona: 1
grey, as the tunic of days:
the women who kept watch over us
turned, upside-down, the sacred torches.
Only three oil lamp spouts,
still lit the unleavened bread,
we were supposed to swallow in the
dawns of good (and evil), on the roads.
I grabbed, one day, the stall
in the choir, oh cicadas!, of my blessed symbols:
where on the bark of trees, eaten by lightning,
the escaped leaves sang the antiphons:
"Lift iron up to your chest!
so we know, as early as winter,
if you're barren or fertile: and who
will save you from future deeds?"
"Don't set your heart
on the vineyards of Sirtori or Somma
on the vineyards of Appiano or Missaglia: 2
for the vintager dips bread
in the barrel of vinegar."
"He who implores, every morning,
the wisdom from grapes,
will know how to burn every vine
in the day of goodbye..."

Grab the Distaff and Spindle and Let's Go to California

* The title of the poem comes from an Italian emigration song composed around the early 1900s in Brianza, a region close to Villa's birthplace. In the region's dialect, the refrain of the original song goes:

> "Ciapa la rocca e'l fus
> Che andem in California,
> andarem in California,
> in California a stopà i bus!"
>
> [Grab the distaff and spindle
> because we're going to California,
> we'll go to California,
> to California to stop holes!]

1. The city of Strona lies north-east of Milan.
2. Sirtori, Somma, Appiano, and Missaglia are towns outside Milan, in the Lombardy region. They are all famous for their wine.

Sì, ma lentamente

Yes, but Slowly

1941

al municipio di cinisello intenerito dai fulmini
e tiritere degli aerei, a quello di balsamo, visto nel forello
delle chiavarde e delle svolte
a vanvera: al circondario
di monza nella rinomata
temperie dei manzi dei manzetti e dei salumi
nostrani: alle tarde
piene di muggiò fatte di nuvole
di stufato, umide, colte dentro i fischi viola e nell'acetilene, e sopra
in alto al bastione intemerato dei fulmini futuri, che
verranno e non verranno,
al sindaco malato, al prevosto che ragiona crepitando
con le mandibole delle cicale: ai ciclisti,
ai grilli alitanti e il fiatone seminato
sul manubrio del manubrio, sopra i parafanghi: e,
in fondo, in fondo a tutti, nel salubre
connubio dei ragionari festivi o di bassa
risonanza delle anatomie bovine
nel criptio delle carrucole, delle serrande?
chi che aspetta di sentire le parole? o voi
aspettate di sentire le cose tra le cose? o qui si aspetta
di udire le cose e le parole? ma chi cose
e parole chi dice, dove sono? parlare
sì, si può: è libero parlare: e con chi parla?
diremo insieme le creazioni, le cose scarnite
e scottanti. e che e come e sotto che fogliame raro
sarà il nuovo, l'altro, peccato originale. dominus
sit in corde, amore mio,

to the town hall in cinisello softened by lightning
and the lullabies of planes, to that of balsamo, seen through
the key hole and the turning
at random: to the district
of monza in the famous
cultural atmosphere of veal of meats of salamis
homemade: to the late
high waters of muggiò made of stewed 1
clouds, humid, caught within purple whistles & acetylene, and above
on high to the ramparts undefiled by future lightning, that
will or will not come,
to the sick mayor, to the parson who reasons crackling
with the jaws of cicadas: to the cyclists,
to the breathing crickets and the panting sown
across the handle of the handlebars, above the fenders: and,
behind, behind everyone, in the wholesome
alliance of festive or low resonating
discussions about bovine anatomies
in the crackling of pulleys, of shutters?
who expects words to be heard? or you
expect to hear things among things? or is it that one expects
to hear things and words? but who says things
and who says words, where are they? speak
yes, you can: speech is free: and you speak with whom?
together we'll say the creations, the things essential
and pressing. and what and how and under what rare foliage
will be the new, the other, original sin. dominus
sit in corde, my love, 2

meu bem. o voialtri che sapete che rosa
che rosa ma che rosa che state aspettando?
"cambia voce" disse allora una sagoma dal chiaro
fosco, disse: "cambia disco! le idee
le abbiamo consumate mate tutte!" e mi umilia.
dagli spalti dell'ambone sciogli, anima corta e sventaglia
il fazzoletto rosso dove hai sperperato pietrisco
e gli scaracchi della mezza predica, e tartagliando
e masticando stracchino e la barbera,
spalanca l'acqua del libro e leggerai:
"ora avvenne
che le cimici entrarono nelle commessure della nave,
e fecero molte e figlie e figli, generazioni assai,
come la sabbia innumere del muto, del perenne.
ora avvenne. avvenne che la grand'arca là,
senza la chiave, non fu calafatata per mancanza
di materie prime *in loco*, e tutto invece
tappata con lievito e bucce delle fave. ora avvenne.
che le cimici moltiplicando come le stelle a fuoco
del firmamento squartarono premendo il transatlantico,
e infine avvenne che dall'alto iddio
maledisse le cimici e noè e gli innocenti, e va bè,
pargoli e le pudende e tutti, e così sia, transeat".
attendiamo, pazienza che verrà, mettiamoci alla cosa:
verrà quando nella sera nel paese poco
dove incrociano al largo i cirri incandescenti delle secche
pietanze e gli strilli della balera o dancing, in una prosa
di vino, quando teneramente mulinando primavera fra le stecche

meu bem. or the rest of you who know what rose 3
what rose but what rose you're waiting for?
"change tune" then said a shape from the clear
gloom, it said: "change the music! ideas
we've consumed -umed them all!"and it shames me.
from the battlement of the pulpit you loosen, short soul and fan
the red kerchief where you squandered crushed stone
and the spit of half a sermon, and stammering
and chewing stracchino and barbera, 4
part the waters of the book and you will read:
"now it happened
that the fleas entered the ship's joints
and they made many girls and boys, generations a plenty,
like the innumerable sand of silence, of the everlasting.
now it happened. happened that the great ark there,
without the key, was not caulked for lack
of prime materials *in loco*, and everything instead
plugged with yeast and the husks of beans. now it happened
that the fleas multiplying like the firmament's
fiery stars quartered pressing the transatlantic liner,
and finally happened that from on high god
cursed the fleas and noah and the innocent, and okay,
little children and pudenda and everyone, and so it be, transeat." 5
we wait, patience will come, let's get to the thing:
it will come when in the evening in the little town
where the incandescent clouds of dried meals cross off shore
and the shouts of barn dances or halls, in a winy
prose, when spring tenderly milling between false notes

e musicando spargerà per l'emisfero colorito, a grandi
manciate le cavallette e i grani e le fontane
del grano universale e del corniolo, e venere
venere somma e un lume inimitabile di iridio
(ci avrà i capelli
che ci hanno il colore
che ci ha il frumento
e come il colore
che come il firmamento
che sono gli occhi suoi,
o giuramento, sì,
la sposerò.
la sposerò davanti all'altare)
ho da parlarvi teneramente mulinando da parlarvi
di odio, della prudenza, e, con ironico fare,
di cicli e vini vari e condimenti, e di ragioni?
della grande saggezza di dopo l'imminente peccato originale
o dei morti dei vivi e delle bestie tradizionali?
dire quanto è lungo il verme che lavora nel mollo delle prime
mele? o da insegnarvi guardare con il collo
storto nel piatto dove mangi carnagione, smalto e sali?
sì, sette anni di magra, sette,
sette di siccità:
non abbiamo torrenti
se non quelli bruttati dal tannino, pozzi
non abbiamo che sciutti, che foppe
basse: quali aride piene come le coppe ime
allora, che retate e quale

and musically will spread across the colored hemisphere,
in great handfuls the grasshoppers and grain and fountains
of the universal grain and the cornel tree, and venus
supreme venus and an inimitable light of iridium
(it will have hair
that has the color
that has the wheat
and like the color
that like the firmament
that are her eyes,
or promise, yes,
i'll marry her.
i'll marry her in church)
i must speak to you tenderly milling to speak to you
of hate, prudence, and, with irony,
of cycles and different wines and condiments, and reasons?
of the great wisdom following the imminent original sin
or of dead of living and traditional beasts?
or say how long is the worm working in the soft flesh of the first
apples? or should i teach you how to watch with neck turned
to the plate where you eat complexion, polish, and salts? 6
yes, seven years of low waters, seven
seven of drought:
we don't have torrents
if not those soiled by the tannin, wells
we don't have but dry, and shallow
ditches: which arid high waters full like lowly cups
then, what round up and which

lume, quali immortali affogati
potremo rimpiangere, potremo e scongiurare,
piangere e sospirar?
piazza dei cinisèi
ohi rombolì
ohi rombolà
non abbiamo ricchezze, né armi che i vegetali
né canzoni insigni, né bellezza
noi di qui: non abbiam qui non abbiam là
e nemmeno povertà:
non abbiamo né ragione né pietà,
non abbiamo il metro che misura
le pertiche tradizionali: cosa diremo quali
e quali vangeli decimali predicare? anche le foglie esigue
esigue al soffio esposte e dal vento
ninnate sembran le povere ali senza corpo, e chi predica
sistemi al popolo delle foglie, chi insegna
il comunismo agli animali sulle soglie?
e foglia e rifoglia
rifoglia biondina
l'amore si sfoglia
l'amore e la vita.
sovvenire non si può nei giorni
se non ai casi estremi: pensando
voi volete le parole belle, sagomate a spaghi, a trepidi
contorni, volete le parole non parole, e tutto
volete: il frutto i semi gli aghi adorni,
ma tutto non si può, o magari

light, which immortal death by drowning 7
can we regret, can we and implore,
weep and sigh? 8
square in cinisello
eh rumble ling
eh ramble lang
we don't have riches, nor weapons other than vegetables
nor distinguished songs, nor beauty
us around here: we don't have here we don't have there
and not even poverty:
we don't have reason nor pity,
we don't have the standard that measures
the traditional rods: what will we say which 9
and which decimal gospels will we preach? even small leaves
small exposed to the breath and lulled by the wind
they look like poor wings without a body, and who
preaches systems to the population of leaves, who
teaches communism to animals on thresholds?
and leaf and releaf
releaf blondie
love leafed through
love and life.
one cannot remember in the days
if not in extreme cases: thinking
you all want beautiful words, shaped like threads, with anxious
borders, you want words that aren't words, and you want
everything: the fruit the seeds the adorned needles
but everything one can't, or maybe

tutto non si deve non conviene è brutto:
forse dire cose altissime e lustrate o ideare
sagome ideali e pure con la pertica
della cuccagna: voi volete, volendo, le parole
per quando insieme aperti gli occhi o quando
grevi come le castagne li chiudiamo,
comprendere volete e non comprendere
per dopo il prossimo imminente già vicino altro peccato originale
col ciondolo lerài
col ciondolo lerèra
e già di là lontano si sfogano i galli impegolati della sera,
nel sugo lustrante della nafta, scocca
il murmure precipite, l'iridio costeggiando,
delle pianelle da muggiò, una falange
gli scialli morbidissimi di cinisello, la luganiga
livida nella città di monza e il buon odore
che sfolla controvento crespo e tra le frange:
soli soli saliranno in cima al campanile, pange
lingua gloriosi, a percepirvi insieme in fila transitare morti e vivi corrosi
morti dei vivi nel precipite sussurro dell'iridio
e non sai se l'olio che ci danno
è imbroglio, o inganno il vaglia.
transito! ma un po' alla volta col segreto
naturale della paglia e delle nespole spacciate,
dei papaveri caduti in mezzo ai grani,
un po' alla volta ma un po' piano capiremo
il dritto e il torto, i vani
nitriti sul filo trepidante, delle redini,

one shouldn't not worth it it's ugly:
maybe say lofty and polished things or devise
ideal shapes even with the greasy
pole: you all want, if you want, words 10
when eyes are open together or when
heavy like chestnuts we close them,
you all want to understand and not understand
after the next imminent already close other original sin
with a swing a ling
with a swang a lang
& already over there far away the tarred cocks of the night let off steam,
polishing in the juice of naphtha, the precipitous
murmur strikes, iridium coasting,
of slippers from muggiò, a phalange
the supplest shawls from cinisello, the livid
luganiga in the city of monza and the crisp smell 11
that scatters against the wind and between the fringe:
alone alone they will climb to the bell tower, pange
lingua gloriosi, to perceive the dead & living crossing in file corroded 12
dead of the living in the precipitous murmur of iridium
and you don't know if the oil they give us
is genuine, or if the money order is fake.
just passing through! but a little at a time with the natural
secret of hay and peddled medlars, 13
of poppies fallen in the wheat fields,
a little at a time but a bit slower we shall understand
the wrong and the right, the vain
neighs on the trembling blade, of the reins,

e l'unità e lo spirito, credi
tu che credo anch'io, credi e non credi, e sentiremo
le spalle più leggere sotto maglia, e l'unica
qui è di fare sempre un po' per bene.
ti vien voglia — di cantare piano
e fare marameo — col palmo della mano
ai profeti in carne ed ossa
ai mercanti sull'orlo della fossa.
beato chi a bella vista la luna anche di giorno trova
vagabondare tra la gente, piova o faccia bello,
e quando si avvita la nebbia intorno all'ultimo
corno della sera, e i bambini di milano
stanno ancora in giro con il brucio sul cavallo
e sotto ascelle per racimolare dai calcestri qualche cosa,
e ridonda un grande
prèmito rosso, i tonfi sani con misura della macchina stradale,
il tamburo selvaggio, il cuore delle brughiere
che si ascolta in tutti i campi, dalla biella
e dal pistone e dal pedale, o quasi
il furtivo grattare delle pianelle nel lustrante
della nafta, che passeggiano da muggiò, o i diti
della pioggia sulla vigneta del prevosto, o sugli scialli
o sulle foglie dei moroni tonti.
ma cosa saranno allora i paragoni fini? i conti? è roba
da mangiare o roba da dormire o è un salario?
è foglia passa d'autunno che cade sopra le rotaie
e fa slittare i tram in modo vario, o altro? ma
paragoni invece fini sono

and unity and the spirit, do you believe
that I believe as well, you do and do not believe, and we shall feel
our shoulders lighter under shirts, and the only thing
is to always do some good.
you feel the need — to sing slowly
and to cock a snook — with the palm of your hand
at prophets in flesh and blood
at merchants with one foot in the grave.
lucky are those who see the moon even in daytime found
roaming among the people, rain or shine,
and when the fog winds around the last
horn of the evening, and the children of milan
are still out with a burning in their crotch
and under armpits to collect something from the asphalt, 14
and a great red tenesmus
abounds, the healthy measured beat of the street machine,
the wild drum, the heart of the moorlands
heard in all the fields, from the connecting rod
and the piston and the pedal, or almost
the stealthy shuffling of slippers in the polishing
of naphtha, that walk from muggiò, or the fingers
of rain on the parson's vineyard, or on the shawls
or on the leaves of dumb mulberry trees.
but then what will become of subtle comparisons? calculations?
is it for eating or for sleeping or is it a salary?
is it the withered leaf in autumn that falls on the tracks
and causes the tram to slip in a varied way, or something else? but
rather subtle comparisons are

le parole che aspettate, oppure
le cose che aspettate, come quell'uno
che aspetta in certi giorni venir giù la pioggia, e alla fin fine
dopo tutti i conti, dopo il vento e il vago prèmito,
scende con gentil misura, con circospezione, come
ai bambini il latte della tetta?
eh, no. non proprio
non propriamente queste cose qui,
col ciondolo lerài
col ciondolo lerèra.
o che si possa insegnare con parole
toccanti e colorate, quanto s'allevino per le stuoie
s'allevino i bigatti e i modi le tecniche le maniere?
ognuno parla come se stesso e tutti parliamo
nel mondo come tutti
cosa vogliamo
cosa dai germi e dagli insetti? trapelano
di foglia in foglia
e sfoglia e risfoglia
rifoglia biondina
l'amore la vita
perché noi tutti di qua siamo quei che ha paura, per remota
impazienza, non solo di morire ma di perdere una cosa
di quello che un tempo è stato guadagnato, di perdere
un tempo, con tanti pareri e oscure
manipolazioni, nel grande passato, la pelle, il vento,
il lustro, il liscio, il dolce, il buio che stormisce
di bruco in bruco, tra la particella, tra le cose, l'aura

the words you all wait for, or rather
the things you all wait for, like that one
who waits for the rain to fall on certain days, and at the very end
after all the calculations, after the wind and the vague tenesmus,
descends with gentle measure, with circumspection, like
milk from tit to child?
well, not quite. not exactly
not these things here,
with a swing a ling
with a swang a lang.
or that can be taught with words
touching and colorful, how many silkworms are
grown on mats and modes techniques manners?
everyone speaks as themselves and we all speak
in the world like everyone else
what do we want
what from germs and insects? they slip out
from leaf to leaf
and leaf through and releaf
releaf blondie
love life
because everyone here is someone who is scared, out of remote
impatience, not only to die but to lose something
of what was once earned, to lose
a time, with many opinions and obscure
manipulations, amid the great past, the skin, the wind,
the luster, the smooth, the sweet, the darkness that rustles
from worm to worm, between the particles, between things, the breeze

e la corrente ariosa in policromi aghi sotto gli astri
magari, pungere i semi non maturi, un fragile magnete
in ogni sposa, il freddissimo intelletto
che spinge l'accattone a scegliersi, degli angoli, quell'angolo là!
passando e ripassando
con grande opinione
tra le due ali bislacche
del pomeriggio della colazione,
senza sapere, un giorno
si capita nel gran nebbione
nostrano dove le vacche
tutto hanno un solo, intorno,
colore beige, o viola o avano.
questi erano i mattini limpidi come un bicchiere
risciacquato in molti lavandini e bacinelle di zinco,
chiari i mattini stavano nelle robinie trasparenti, e stracche
gibigiane e rase e sventolate, e il rude e il pelo
gigante delle cotiche e la gente
che voleva coglionarvi qui, *in loco*,
quando il cranio roco del porcello che s'impunta mareggiava
senza quiete un'altra alba di cristalli, l'alta
bufera, la sete, un po' per volta, e prude le nature
in petto tormentando scarne uccelle, e ragazze
lombarde coi pedùli e le solette nylon velature.
una scarpa e una ciabatta chi se la lega chi se la gratta e
dente milanese che morda
intelligenza che non ricorda
formica che scivola sulla corda e

and the airy current in polychrome needles under the stars
maybe, puncture immature seeds, a brittle magnet
in every bride, the cold intellect
that pushes the beggar to choose, out of corners, that corner there!
passing and passing again
with great consideration
between the two bizarre wings
of the afternoon of breakfast,
without knowing, one day
we're caught in that
thick local fog where cows,
everything, around, has only one
color, beige or purple or havana
these were the mornings limpid as a glass
rinsed in many sinks and zinc basins,
clear mornings in transparent locust trees, and worn out
glaring and smooth and fluttering, and the roughness
the gigantic hair of rinds and the people
who wanted to make a fool out of you here, *in loco*,
when the pig's raucous cranium that jibs wavering
another restless dawn of crystals, the high
storm, the thirst, a little at a time, and natures' itching
in the chest tormenting skinny birds, and lombard girls
in hiking boots and insert nylon stockings.
a shoe and a slipper those who tie it those who itch it and
milanese tooth that bites
intelligence that does not recall
ant that slides on the rope and

una scarpa e una ciabatta chi se la lega chi se la gratta e
malinconici milanesi
dalle pelli ben stirate
a tamburo e tamburelli e
per male o per bene che vada
milanesi siamo sempre quelli e
milanesi generosi, che vi pare
regalare caramelle
di puro zucchero alle belle
figliole di motta industriale?
un po' per volta col segreto ascolta
il maturare della paglia e delle nespole nel fuoco
sottilissimo, e un po' per volta
tutti noi noi capiremo il dritto o il torto,
la striglia, l'unità, il lungo e il corto
e il naturale; ascolta nei sinistri
tocca-tocca maturare primavere e
sentiremo la bocca più leggera, quando un'italia
animale molta nelle costole passerà, nel gran costato
malinconicamente, una conoscenza
eroica, musicale, un'invenzione colta, generata
di aspetti buoni e parapiglia: e non l'elettrica
o qualche altra sfatta luce o simili bruciori,
ma la brina sopra il sopra ciglia, e giù di lì
la musica guardare e riguardare; e non l'elettrica
(o qualche altra sfatta luce terrena)
ma il murmure precipite dell'iridio, ma il lume
inevitabile dell'iridio, nello smaglio lanceolato delle sere immortali

a shoe and a slipper those who tie it those who itch it &
melancholy milanese
with well ironed skins
taut like a drum and tambourine and
be it good times or bad times
milanese we're always the same and
generous milanese, who to you seem 15
to give out candy
of pure sugar to the beautiful
daughters of motta, the industrialist? 16
a little at a time listen in secret
to the ripening of hay and medlars in the subtlest
fire, and a little at a time everyone of us
we will understand the right and the wrong,
the horse brush, the unity, the long and the short
and the natural; listen in the sinisters
touch-touch ripening springs and
we will feel our mouths lighter, when a very
animal italy will run through our ribs, melancholically
through the great rib cage, a heroic,
musical knowledge, a learned invention, generated
by nice aspects and turmoil: and not the electric
or some other worn out light or similar burns,
but the frost above the eye brow, and there about
the music watch it & watch again; and not the electric
(or some other worn out earthly light)
but the precipitous murmur of iridium, but iridium's
inevitable light, in the lanceolate unraveling of immortal evenings

e su nel celeste
poligono remoto
tra iadi e pleiadi
neghittose in moto
bruciare grandi
i grandi genitali
sul lago ove ulisse
faceva le imprese.
altre favole ci sono, favole
ancora, e la musica
degli altri, la musica di quelli là che sembra
non già la musica, ma il pantano della foppa, e beato
chi ti trova la luna dirottata tra la gente sulle labbra
timide dell'universo, nel murmure dell'iridio quando
vicino a sera incerta tra la gente umanissima
si rampica la nebbia sopra l'aeroporto
verso la manica a vento, nel campo della breda, nel paesano
spirito aranciato delle sere immortali
che carezza le scene e flemmatica gli omeri e le balzane
cose delle baggiane dalle smorte vene e dalle cosce
lunghe di segala vegetale, quando
sui fili dei celesti sali urlano le sirene delle aziende
e il rubicondo respiro dei fuggiaschi solleoni e il luogo
dei luoghi nottambuli allagati della lomellina,
e le irrigazioni colore di viola nei momenti delicati:
nelle congiunture: abbiamo per i nostri passi
delle città, città sopra la terra sotto la terra e a filo
di terra negli scantinati:

and up in the remote
celestial polygon
between hyades and pleiades
slothful in motion
burning great
the great genitals
on the lake where ulysses
carried out his feats.
there are other fables, fables
still, and the music
of others, the music of those over there that doesn't
seem like music at all, but the morass of the ditch, and lucky
are those who find the high-jacked moon among people on the
timid lips of the universe, in the murmur of iridium when
close to an uncertain evening between the kindest people
the fog climbs above the airport
toward the windsock, into breda's field, in the rustic 17
orange-colored spirit of immortal evenings
caressing the scenes and soothing the shoulders and the eccentric
things of dumb girls with pale veins and long thighs
of vegetable rye, when
on the strings of celestial salts the factory sirens scream
and the rubicund breath of fugitive dog days and the place
of all night-owl places in the flooded lomellina, 18
and purple colored irrigations at delicate moments:
in the joints: on our walk
some cities, cities above ground, below ground and on the
level of basements:

e sassi deteniamo e galline di rarissimo colore e bisce
di cristallo e le caraffe lisce ed il mastello
al sole e cieli di iridio se fa bello
e gazose appannate per i defunti nel giorno dell'uffizio
e cimase baluginanti colore cadmio nello smaglio
lanceolato delle sere immortali!
siamo seri! in sagrestia
maggiore il chierichetto
stuzzica con un cero il petto
delle colombe che non volan via
e il popolo che ascolta dai gradini
il calmo fragore dell'aeronave
e il prevosto che cerca la chiave
nel tumulto dei bambini
e il popolo che sente sul sagrato
come a quota mica male
vola, quota lieve, quota
celeste, come ridere una trota
nella grande acqua universale,
e l'elica girare e fare argentea ruota!
e l'universo è qui, qui solamente a un pelo,
l'universo è qui, a un pelo di ciglio,
a un pelo di ciglio di zanzara le ali
umettate nel rorido lampaneggio
di improvvise compiète giallo cadmio,
pane salato, salso paese zafferano, serpi rifatti
in stato di cadavere, in statu
prisco: e scale di legname tutto a scuro dove sbatti
il menisco se scendi troppo di precisa.

and we hold pebbles and hens of the rarest color and snakes
of crystal and smooth pitchers and the basins
in the sun and skies of iridium if it's nice out
and gazosa fogged for the dead on the day of the service 19
and the flickering cadmium color roof in the lanceolate
unraveling of immortal evenings!
let's be serious! in the main sacristy
the altar boy
with a candle tickles the breasts
of doves that don't fly away
and the people that listen from the steps
to the calm rumble of airships
and the parson looking for the key
amid the tumult of children
and the crowd that hears it in the churchyard
at an amazing height
how it flies, light height, celestial
height, as if nothing like a trout
in the great universal waters,
and the propeller turning and the silvery cartwheels!
and the universe is here, here only by a hair,
the universe is here, by an eyelash,
by a mosquito's eyelash wings
moistened in the dewy sparkle
of improvised complines yellow cadmium,
salted bread, salty saffron country, snakes laid out
as corpses, in statu
prisco: and wooden ladder in the dark where you bump 20
your kneecap if you descend in haste.

ma o trapassati con veste di gracile sofferenza, lunga storia
di tenebre dentro la quale il nostro episodio si cancella
e alla cieca brandisce, si spuntano le nostre armi:
le bucce dei grilli
i noccioli di ciliegia,
la sansa dei marroni
affumicati, i semi
di girasole e di tomates:
e i trilli strozzati
nella strozza dei passeri
scuotendo le nostre trombe
o trapassati con veste di gracile sofferenza, fuoruscite
dalla crisalide brutta dei secoli celtici o spagnoli
o comunisti, fuori dalla custodia, fuori
a bere i soli balsamici succhi della vita
e della sorte: rispecchiatevi in fronte,
in piazza, alla fonte, sul fondo dei ramaioli,
specchiatevi nello spirito spirituale: lasciate
in tale guisa baluginare nell'opera del verbo
e delle interiezioni e dei vocaboli di scarto,
come in una reale lontananza la cuspide
di iridio dove il fulmine si strema e si confonde:
il verde della vostra mirabile carnagione, la gazosa
spumeggiante sulle lastre, e il rifiorire
concorde dei gelsi, tale è la rinomanza
caduca ma solenne nel grido eccellente delle bestie.
adesso lentamente
è venuto tardi, sì, ma tardi
sì, ma lentamente.

but or deceased dressed in feeble suffering, long story
of darkness where our episode is erased
and blindly brandishes, are weapons dulled:
the crickets' shell
the cherries' pit
the chestnuts' residue
smoked, tomato
and sunflower seeds:
the strangled trills
in the throats of sparrows
rattling our trumpets
or deceased dressed in feeble suffering, exited from
the ugly chrysalis of celtic centuries or spanish
or communist, out of the sleeve, out
to drink the only balsamic juices of life
and fate: look at your faces in the mirror,
in the square, at the spring, at the bottom of ladles,
mirror yourselves in the spiritual spirit: in this
fashion let the cusp of iridium where lightning
grows weak and confused flicker
in the work of the verb and interjections and
second rate words, as in a real distance:
the green of your marvelous complexion, the frothy
gazosa on the slabs, and the harmonious
re-flourishing of mulberry trees, such is the fleeting
yet solemn fame amid the excellent scream of beasts.
now slowly
it's late, yes, but late
yes, but slowly.

Yes, but Slowly

1. Cinisello Balasmo and Muggiò are towns located just outside of Milan.
2. The expression *Dominus sit in corde* (May the Lord be in my heart) is found in the *Munda cor meum* (Cleanse my heart), a traditional Catholic mass hymn.
3. Portuguese for "my honey."
4. *Stracchino* is a soft cheese from Lombardy and *Barbera* is wine produced in Piedmont.
5. Latin for "Let it go."
6. In Italian, the word *carnagione* (complexion) echoes *cacciagione*, meaning game caught for eating.
7. Most likely a reference to "Death By Water," section four of T. S. Eliot's poem *The Wasteland*.
8. Villa makes several references to popular Italian songs throughout the poem. For example, this verse, *piangere e sospirar* (*weep and sigh*), is a quote from "Quel mazzolin di fiori." Other verses reminiscent of popular Italian melodies are: *ohi romboli / ohi rombolà* and *foglia e rifoglia / rifoglia biondina…* (translated here as *eh rumble ling / eh ramble lang* and *leaf and releaf / releaf blondie*), and *col ciondolo leràì / col ciondolo lerèra* (*with a swing a ling / with a swang a lang*).
9. A linear measure used by the ancient Romans, typically ten feet in length.
10. *Pertica della cuccagna* in the original: a traditional game played at Mardi Gras in which someone must climb a greased pole to reach bounties lying at the top, such as a leg of prosciutto or a wheel of cheese.
11. A type of sausage.
12. The medieval Latin hymn *Pange lingua gloriosi corporis mysterium* was written by St. Thomas Aquinas for the feast of Corpus Christi.
13. Italian proverb: *Col tempo e con la paglia maturano le nespole* (All good things come to those who wait).
14. *Calcestro* in the original. A cheap type of pavement composed of recycled materials. In time, as the pavement fell apart, children would collect its various components.

15. This rings of the old Milanese saying *Milanes-sem, Milanes-sarem, Milanes-restum* (Milanese we are, Milanese we will always be, and Milanese we'll remain).

16. The *Motta* family owned a chain of pastry shops in & around Milan and was famous for its panettone.

17. Founded in 1886 just outside Milan, the Breda company manufactures locomotives, armaments, aircraft, buses and trams.

18. Part of the Po River valley, the *Lomellina* is an area located in south-western Lombardy.

19. *Gazosa* (also *Gassosa*) is a drink made of carbonated water & sugar.

20. *In statu prisco* is Latin for "in a very ancient state."

Da *Oramai*

From *By Now* *

1947

Cosa c'è di nuovo

Di nuovo c'è che ai giovanotti ramazzati via
non si può tenere spalancate più le palpebre
con gli stecchini a punta, vita non ce n'hanno più:

di nuovo c'è gli occhi bianchicci dei maschi
milanesi sui fili del filobus, dei tram, sui pali;
mica sarà triste seguitare a mirarsi negli occhi tristemente!

di nuovo c'è che tra la polpa e l'osso c'è che fa caldo
e che fa freddo a una ragazza che possiede gli occhi
come una compagna arata dalla guerra, fuoriporta;

di nuovo c'è che poche piante vanno avanti a venir su;
e mani conciate di ragadi e di caligine
accendono le stufe di ghisa, non c'è gas;

c'è che trema la sostanza universale, e il nostro cuore
non per vanto, né per forza, ma mi sembra buono, e trema
un rumore di vie d'acqua, vie d'acqua e ferrovie:

il vento ha lasciato solchi di poggia e macchie d'unto
sull'intonaco delle facciate larghe quindici metri,
e solchi, cioè rughe, nella piazza lustra degli anziani;

What's New

What's new is that one can no longer keep
the eyelids of swept away young men open
with sharpened toothpicks, they're no longer alive:

what's new is the whitish eyes of Milanese
males upon the wires of trolleys, trams, and poles;
don't tell me it's sad to go on looking sadly in each other's eyes!

what's new is that between flesh and bone there's something
that turns a girl either hot or cold, who has eyes
like a countryside plowed by war, outside the city walls;

what's new is that few plants continue to grow;
and hands ruined by lesions and soot
light the cast-iron stoves, there is no gas;

is that the universal substance trembles, and our heart
not out of pride, nor duty, but it seems good, and a sound
of water ways trembles, water ways and train tracks:

the wind has left furrows of rain & greasy stains
on the plaster of facades fifteen meters wide, and
furrows, that is wrinkles, in the old folks' polished square;

le finestre sono una semenza tra fanali: e io
che semino fiato e gran buontempo, e tu
che in su e in giù passeggi per le arterie del centro;

e io che faccio stracci paragoni, e tu che porti
la bellezza malinconica e avara dentro l'ombra rossa
d'essere ancora bella, ragazza come una campagna;

e io che so fare complimenti dimenticati, e tu passare;
e tu che pensi che bisogna guardare quello che bisogna,
e io che penso agli animali barbelanti che torneranno

ancora come una volta a pisciare vicino all'aria; e tu
fammi una lista musicale di panni da asciugare
all'aria generosa e sventurata della nostra camporella.

(1944)

windows are a seed among headlights: and I
sow breath and great goodtime, and you
walk up and down the arteries of town;

and I make ragged comparisons, and you carry
the stingy and melancholy beauty within the red shade
of still being beautiful, a girl like a countryside;

and I know how to give forgotten compliments, and you move on;
and you think that one needs to watch what is needed,
and I think about shivering animals that will once again

piss close to the air like they used to; and you
make me a musical list of clothes to dry
in the generous and hapless air of our *camporella*. 1

(1944)

Pezzo 1941

Potrebbe darsi
che l'aria un giorno
qualunque, viaggiasse
per l'aria a malincuore,

e ma se il lago di Garda non recupera col tempo
tutta la polvere mangiata dai ciclisti in gare assurde,
i chilometri che non contano, fatti per niente,

e ma fin quando agli stradali con le pioppe nichelate
parlino l'ozono e la pioggia a fil di terra d'ideali
giubilei, di comunismo fresco 'me 'ne rosa

                                        e ci succeda allora quasi
come se nel seno martoriato dalle lance,
devozioni premurose, tenerezze, vanità,
le nostre diocesi annegassero una per una
un po' alla volta, e dentro l'altro
effimero vaso dell'aria con un riso fraterno
sopra a galla la gente naufragata
salissero, ma senza
il corpo folto come il corpo o come cosa

e fin quando il cappone renitente,
prigioniero sul ciglio delle nebbie o nelle
stoppie violette dell'autunno, non morisse
eroicamente colpito da quel temperino che si tira
per caso, e che lo sbuca a sangue in uno stinco; o

1941 Piece

I

It could be
that on any given
day air would travel
half-heartedly through the air,

maybe, but if Lake Garda fails to recover in time
all the dust eaten by cyclists in meaningless races,
& kilometers that don't count, good for nothing,

maybe, as long as the ozone and the horizontal rain
speak to traffic cops with nickeled stands of poplar
about ideal jubilees, communism fresh as a rose

                                        and then we would feel
as if in our chests mangled by spears,
thoughtful devotions, affections, vanities,
our dioceses were to drown one by one
little by little, and inside the other
ephemeral vase of air, shipwrecked people
were to surface
with a brotherly laugh, but without
the body dense as a body or as any thing

and as long as the dodging capon,
trapped on the edge of the fog or within
autumn's violet stubble, failed to die
heroically wounded by that pocket knife thrown
by chance, stuck in his shins until blood is spilled; or

l'odore dei vagoni strisci ai posti di blocco
e sappia alfine che le notti della terra
e i mugli dalle stalle briantine, e il fiato

dei foraggi forestieri, e l'aria piena
di stufato con il manzo nostrano, e il resto
sullo zinco in sonanti nichelini, come mani
brinate toccheranno il firmamento: e qualche

biglia d'agata recondita nel panico ronfare
delle pioppe ci farà o lume o scuro

e mica i cieli
sono un capitale sicuro, senza fondo, o una miniera
priva di patria e sentimento

pertanto corrano le truppe a far ombre coi pastrani
sul lavorerio di frontiere per le miglie e miglia,
anno per anno; e più l'ascoso affanno dei respiri
qui in patria cresce e con più gela
nel caos, e qui trapela,
come una nostalgia obbligatoria il pesce
della lume settentrionale, le voltate
a biscia del vagone, le sue soste, i giri
in campagna lunghissimi, in mezzo alla pittura
notturna dell'acqua fina fina e della guazza

per cui, matto di debolezza in faccia al terrestre sogno
dove i sassi maturino d'Europa, o galleggino
come rottami i giardini patrizi nel naviglio della pace,
le nazioni escogitate nel sogno degli strani
cancellieri con la testa piena di pigne

as long as the train's smell slithers to checkpoints
and realizes in the end that the world's nights
and the lowing from the stalls of Brianza, & the breath 2

of foreign fodder, and the air filled
with a stew of local beef, and the change
of musical coins across the zinc counter, will touch
the firmament with frosted hands: and then

some agate marbles concealed in the panic snore
of those poplars will serve as lamps or blinds

                    and it's not like the heavens
are a sound, bottomless investment, or a mine
devoid of fatherland and feeling

therefore, let the troops hurry like shades with coats
on the borders bustling mile after mile,
year after year; and more the hidden anguish of breaths
grows here in the fatherland & furthermore freezes
in the chaos, and here it seeps out,
like a mandatory nostalgia the fish
of the northern star, the train's
snake-like turns, its stops, the long
detours through the countryside, amid the nocturnal
painting of the lightest water and murk

thus, drunk with weakness facing the earthly dream
where the stones of Europe mature, where stately
gardens float in the *naviglio* of peace, 3
nations devised in the dreams of strange
chancellors with rocks in their heads

matto di sentimenti l'ultimo navigante o macchinista
o marinaro d'acqua dolce e chiusa, o corridore
in pista, dimenticati gli argenti dei canali e delle verze,
il mormorio delle posate d'alpacca che si nettano
dopo desinare in una fiacca lenta dalle porte
spalancate per le alzaie, se ne vada
al di là dell'anima

e che al di là dell'anima ogni cosa è specchio
d'una celeste cattolica confusione, né vogliamo
credere troppo al nostro corpo, questo specchio, e basta,
per questo tempo, con la luce che ci dà fastidio

però noi altri in tanto siamo, con timore,
con reverenza, e gli uni e gli altri, e poi,
su dai registri indaffarati dei poveri del comune,
noi transitiamo, come la nuvola patita, verso il buono
liquore dell'atlantico, in fondo alla provincia,
senza rumore di frontiere o corridoi: è là

che tutto sarà vago e irreprensibile, tutto
comune; non una spanna di penombra
più forte mai appare là più della notte

elettrica, da pesci.

(1942)

drunk with emotion the last seafarer or engineer
or fresh water sailor, or athlete at the track,
forgotten the silvery shimmer of canals and verdure,
the murmur of pewter silverware washed
in doorways opening onto towpaths
in that slow after-supper idleness, let him go
beyond the soul

& then again, beyond the soul everything is a mirror
of celestial catholic confusion, nor do we want to
believe in our bodies too much, this mirror, enough,
for the time being, with this annoying light

yet meanwhile the rest of us exist, both one and the other,
fearfully, reverentially, and then,
rising from the busy welfare rolls
we pass, like sickly clouds, toward the fine liquor
of the Atlantic, at the county's end,
without the noise of borders or hallways: that's where

everything will be vague and flawless, everything
in common; there, not a single strip of twilight
ever appears stronger than the night

electric, fish-like.

(1942)

Però prima del vento

Però, prima del vento,
prima che il vento piova
a lungo andare, a stesa,

i verbi coniugati a malapena, e i gemi-
ti, e imprese, e faccende e càno-
ni, il bene della vita,

sono i semi riscaldati tra le dita
di una sola mano, di una lingua
sciolta, di una lingua nuova;

e le radici semplici o gemi-
nate, nel nuvolo sommerso
dei parlari, per un secolo

almeno! E siete voi pronti
a non conoscere, e a negare,
a pronunciare detti assurdi,

come così: "Credo quia ..."?
"credo che è ora di andar via",
"credo che tutto", e "penso che"?

Però prima che venga
prima che l'ombra della bellezza
annuvoli i moderni continenti,

But Before the Wind

But, before the wind,
before the wind rains
in the long run, spread out,

the verbs barely conjugated, and moa-
ns, endeavors, and errands and cano-
ns, and the gift of life,

are the seeds warmed in the fingers
of a single hand, of a quick
tongue, of a new language;

and the geminate or simple roo- 1
ts, in the submerged clouds
of speeches, for a century

at least! And are you ready
not to know, to deny,
to pronounce absurd sayings,

such as: "*Credo quia* ..."? 2
"I believe it's time to leave,"
"I believe that all," and "I think that"?

And before it comes
before the shadow of beauty
clouds the modern continents,

però prima che venga
tardi, e che qualcuno
bussi alla porta, o il telefono

squilli e ci interrompa,
facciamo tutti insieme qualche cosa:
la speranza non è finita, ma comincia:

quella cosa nel pieno delle cose
ci darà la frase giusta
di riverberi, da usare

come una lama, come una decisione
nel groviglio, nel tumulto:
appena ripensando

a un affarino vegetale che profuma
di pomi e di carrube, o le formiche
in pista sul davanzale della metropo-

li e una faccia nostrana alla finestra,
e le braccia assai lunghe, e di lontano,
solo tra cielo e cielo, il ciel che sfuma,

un strido di tolle e di gavette:

pensando così a delle secche
pitture per indigeni o croati, e acqua
per dopo, acqua per sempre;

and before it gets
late, and someone
knocks at the door, or the phone

rings to interrupt us,
let's all do something together:
hope isn't over, it's beginning:

that thing at the peak of things
will suggest the phrase with
the right echoes, to be used

as a blade, as a decision
in the tangle, in the uproar:
barely rethinking

a little vegetable contraption that smells
like apples and carobs, or ants dancing
on the windowsill of the metropo-

lis and a local face at the window,
arms extremely long, and far off,
alone amid sky and sky, the sky fading,

a shriek of tin-cans and mess-tins:

thus thinking of dry
paints for natives or Croatians, and water
for later, water forever;

e un temporale non scabroso, rozzo,
candido e immobile, silenzioso
e senza vento, dell'autentico

colore dell'acqua in fondo al pozzo,
per i figli della legge, bei figlioli
di sentenza varia e panni scarsi.

and a storm not scabrous, raw,
candid and still, silent
and windless, of the true

color of water at the bottom of the well,
for the children of the law, beautiful children
of varied phrases and shabby clothes.

Semper pauperes

Semper pauperes vobiscum habebitis,
sed me non semper habebitis.
S. Matteo

Già da lontano breda, già da tempo, con l'indice levato
a tramontana, quel medesimo che uccise sulla scorza
del gelso due formiche in assolute faccende,
con l'indice levato noi segnammo, per prudenza,
per un vago bisogno di ricordi e per la forza
stessa del semplice pensare, quella casa
che da lontano chiama e ci sospira, così piena
ancora di romantici sentimenti, e del profumo
di defunti che neppure in lontananza vorrebbero scommettere
la verità dei nostri connotati, la giustizia dei nostri documenti,
altri liquori d'ombre e di figure travasando,
non già le nostre, stanche e provvisorie nell'agire,
come una pianta senza nome, di nessuno, senza categoria
plausibile al sorteggio dei suoi temporali,
dove anche i passeri, anche i passeri, e perfino
i passeri, perfino gli uccelletti, orbi nel fumo
della mente e privi di un governo autoritario,
fondano nel volo senza scampo, senza gradi, l'arco
della notte ventura in un osanna, sempre al divario
d'una sorte continua che li scava; e poi sparire.

Semper pauperes

Semper pauperes vobiscum habebitis,
sed me non semper habebitis.
St. Matthew 1

It already *bredas* from afar, already for a while, with index raised 2
to the north, the same one who killed two ants
in absolute affairs on the bark of the mulberry tree,
with index raised we pointed, out of caution,
out of a vague need for memories and by the sheer
power of simple thinking, and that house
calls us from afar and pines, still so
full of romantic feelings, and the fragrance
of the deceased who not even from afar would bet on
the truth of our features, the justice of our papers,
decanting other liquors made of shades and figures,
certainly not ours, tired and temporary in action,
like a plant without name, owner, or plausible
category in the draw of its storms,
where even sparrows, even sparrows, as well as
sparrows, as well as little birds, blind in the smoke
of the mind and devoid of an authoritarian government,
establish in their flight without escape, without degrees, the arch
of the coming night in hosanna, always on the brink
of a continuous fate that wears them down; and then vanish.

E adesso quei rondoni, tuttavia, io mi domando,
quando gli autunni cominciano la marcia, come reggimenti
ravvolti nei pastrani sugli asfalti leggeri,
dal San Gottardo, avranno tuttavia
i loro cari defunti disegnati sulle foglie del cielo?

Scapole d'un giovanotto
nell'azzurro solitario,
nel cielo le giornate
son più lente degli uccelli,
orbi nella mente di sale.

Ma poi la rondine ritorna ad infierire:
non muta la sorte delle foglie, tale
che in altro largo serbi un'espèride preclusa
ai censimenti, stanze di pomice, lucenti
ghiaie ebbre, nel suono dei palazzi viola;
che in altro largo serbi un continente
come l'ala d'un aprile a banderuola,
senza mercati alla pianura di Saronno, e piova,
povero, i mantelli, le lenzuola, le mutande,
le formiche e i lampioni agonizzando; e poi sparire.

(1941)

And now those swallows, still, I wonder,
when autumns begin to march, like regiments
wrapped in greatcoats on light asphalts,
from the San Gottardo pass, will they still have
their dear deceased drawn on the leaves of the sky?

Shoulder blades of a young man
in the solitary blue,
in the sky the days
are slower than birds,
blind in the mind of salt.

But then the swallow returns to pummel:
the fate of leaves does not change, so much
that in another clearing it saves a hesperides
hidden from the census, rooms of pumice, shiny
inebriated gravel, in the sound of purple buildings;
that in another clearing saves a continent
like the wing of an April shaped like a weathervane,
without markets on the plain of Saronno, and let it rain, 3
poor thing, the cloaks, the sheets, the underwear,
the ants and the streetlamps agonizing; and then vanish.

(1941)

Buonasera

In fondo a una giornata corrosa per i chiasmi
e tormentata per i crepacuori, per puntigli vani,
per i cari fantasmi dei pani, dei soldi, della faccia,
e per gli allarmi falsi, e per i primi
numeri che certo appariranno
al di là degli ultimi, per tutto
che ci tuffa giorno e giorno, da mattina
a sera in lei, la meraviglia, il lotto, la caccia,

si ricordano degli stradoni, un po' perduti
in mezzo alla giovane rugiada,
i miei stivali impaltati sulla terra terrena,
ove un telefono osi dalla patria superna
di tenermi a bada, e darmi lena; e mi riporti
in una cadenza milanese o madrilena, una rada
"buonasera", l'onda alterna, l'illimite
sgomento, gli orgogli dell'affetto e il sentimento
dei cugini vivi: con loro, prima di prendere sonno,
scommettere una per una le faccende trasognate
dei pani dei soldi della faccia: la parentela
sola è il lavoro di tutte le giornate, in tutto pari
all'invisibile salario: e le generazioni, casa per casa...

Good Evening 1

At the end of a day corroded by chiasms
and tormented by heartbreaks, by vain piques
by the dear phantoms of bread, money, face,
and by false alarms, and the first
numbers that will surely appear
beyond the last, by everything
that dips us day after day, from morning
till night into her, the wonder, the lottery, the hunt,

they remember highways, somewhat lost 2
in the midst of youthful dew,
my muddy boots on the earthly earth,
where a telephone from the heavenly fatherland
dares to keep me at bay, to spur me on; and it takes me
back to a cadence of Milan or Madrid, a sparse
"good evening," the alternating wave, the endless
dismay, the prides of affection and the feeling
of cousins alive: with them, before falling asleep,
waging one by one dreamy endeavors
of breads money face: kinship
alone is the work of everyday, one with
the invisible salary: and the generations, door to door…

Ma ormai son grande, e quasi un uomo, e vario: e qui
pensa di scrivere un romanzo un po' lontano,
pensa a un temporale che cadesse sugli omeri
pianino o su robinie nude di fianco agli stradoni,
e poi pulsava il tuono in gola alle livide serate
come lo squarcio in cui ognuno sogna di avere un sonno tremendo
con insalata cruda e nebbia e le robinie
e tutto. Allora probabilmente tu sospetti che la terra
è un albergo in disordine che ci aspetti noi
e clienti di riguardo per avventura ritornati
adagio indietro, in punta di piedi.

(1939)

But now I'm grown, and almost a man, and varied: & here
he thinks of writing a somewhat distant novel,
he thinks about a storm slowly falling on shoulders
or on naked locust trees lining the highways,
& then the thunder throbbed in the throat of livid evenings
like the gash where everyone dreams of being terribly sleepy
with raw salad and fog and the locust trees
& everything. That's when you might suspect that the earth
is a hotel in disarray waiting for us all
and an esteemed clientele that wound up coming
back slowly, on the tips of their toes.

(1939)

Gli argomenti

A dar la baia, o condannare
in aperto giudizio, all'aperto,
le piante, segate a filo

di catrame, la forza malinconica
del marciapiede inaffiato,
il disonore e il diritto del portello

dove stride la città
con cose da fare, e con vago
bagliore di rame

che è il primo serenare
e l'ultimo navigare
nel quintino trepilante

di squinzano col frego della tacca.

Tutte le tribù cadute
al di là della spalletta, dentro il fiume
per alzare il livello dell'acqua,

per saggiarne la fisica
profondità, per naufragare,
per patire e maturare,

Arguments

To poke fun, or condemn
in open judgment, in the open,
the plants, sawn at the tar

mark, the melancholic force
of the watered sidewalk,
the dishonor and the right of the hatchway

where the city screeches
with things to do, and with vague
copper glare

that's the first settling
and the last sailing
in the shaking fifth

of squinzano with a notch mark.

All the tribes fallen
beyond the embankment, in the river
to raise the water's level,

to test its physical
depth, to shipwreck,
to suffer and mature,

alzando le mani,
sforzando la fronte,
fregandosi la cispa,

amor di pietra amore
di pietra antelucana
e di facciate stralunghe,

con la vita sana,
con la vista vispa,
il primo serenare

e l'ultimo navigare,
quaggiù, lassù, le nuvole
docili, mansuete, come mosche,
italiarde, tosche, lombane…

ardi abbastanza, così,
vena povera, consigliata
nella vera amarezza?

(1942)

raising hands,
straining brow,
rubbing rheum,

love of stone love
of antelucan stone
of extra long façades,

with healthy life,
with spry sight,
the first settling

and the last sailing,
down here, up there, the docile
clouds, tame, as flies,
italiard, toscard, lomban… 2

do you burn enough this way,
poor vein, counseled
in true bitterness?

(1942)

Di volt, una lüsnada

Di volt, una lüsnada…

Nün sem di mort che vörarisen minga
persüadiss de vess mort,
che sem scundüu dedré i purtùn,
'me di làder, dedré la porta, in fund,
de la legria (ma cun la stringa
dislasada), cul nas in ari, e speta
che la te vegna bona. Be', a mund:
ma söta no a spüašà sül mür.

Di volt, una lüsnada…

Parlà, parlà de šender, de rusada, parlà
cui öcc saràa, cui laber che čičaren
de per lur, sensa vurè, parlà
l'è cume dí: "nagott. Pasiensa. Amen.
Se vedarèmm anmò, va là."
Ma pö me ven la lüna, cume un martur,
e turni indré de cursa, curi a cà,
per paüra che 'l fiö dent in la cüna
el me taca fög

Lasèm slungà la man, tusànn, lasèm
slungà; la vita è un valser; un tempuràl.

Di volt, una lüsnada…

(1937)

A volte un lampo

A volte, un lampo…

Siamo dei morti che non sanno
persuadersi d'essere morti,
sempre nascosti dietro i portoni delle case:
come ladri, in fondo, dietro la porta
della felicità (ma coi lacci
delle scarpe slacciati), col naso in su, e aspetta
che torni un'occasione propizia. Beh, lasciamo andare,
ma smetti di sputacchiare sui muri.

A volte, un lampo…

Parlare, parlar di cenere, di rugiada, parlare
cogli occhi chiusi, colle labbra che chiacchierano
da sole, automaticamente, senza volere, parlare
è come dire: "nulla. Pazienza. Così sia.
Noi ci vedremo ancora, non temere."
Ma poi mi torna la malinconia, come uno stupido,
e torno indietro di scatto, corro a casa
per paura che mio figlio nella culla
abbia preso fuoco.

Lasciatemi allungare una mano, ragazze, lasciatemi
allungare: la vita è un valzer; un temporale.

A volte, un lampo…

Sometimes a Flash

I

Sometimes, a flash...

We are dead people who can't
persuade themselves they're dead,
always hidden behind the front gates:
like thieves, in the back, behind the door
of happiness (but with laces
untied), with nose in the air, and wait
for the right moment to return. Well, never mind,
but stop spitting on the walls.

Sometimes, a flash...

Speaking, speaking of ashes, of dew, speaking
with eyes closed, with lips that blabber
on their own, automatically, unwittingly, speaking
is like saying: "nothing. Relax. So be it.
We'll see each other again, don't worry."
But then my melancholy returns, like an idiot,
and I quickly turn around, run home
out of fear that my son in his crib
has caught fire.

Let me cop a feel, girls, let me
cop: life is a waltz; a storm.

Sometimes, a flash...

Natus de muliere, brevi vivens

L' uomo in natura senza dubbio
fu inventato come un grido
a bruciapelo: odio,

ira, indumenti; propagato
nella apparenza, o febbre
universale: nato a sentire

legge e fede, nato di donna
per mangier la foglia, per contarla
lunga, per contarla corta,

manda giù quanto più può
saliva; nato di donna
per mangiar la foglia, parla e vuole

maniere d'ogni sorta,
secco il corame delle suole,
fa digrignare i denti; agisce

azioni chimiche, cose
che son lecite o non sono, a voglia,
oneste che fan gran figura, o diso-

nore: commerciali, generose,
che fregano il prossimo, e consumano
i desideri e la freschezza al viso;

Natus de muliere, brevi vivens 1

Without a doubt man in nature
was invented like a point-blank
scream: hate,

wrath, garments; propagated
in the appearance, or universal
fever: born to hear

law and faith, born of woman
to get wise, to make it 2
long, to make it short,

gulps down as much saliva as
he can; born of woman
to get wise, speaks and wants

manners of every sort,
dry the leather soles,
makes you grind your teeth; performs

chemical actions, things
that may or may not be legal, depending,
honest things that make you look good, or

bring dishonor: commercial, generous things,
which swindle your neighbor, and consume your
desires and freshness of the face;

che non arrivano a niente, fredde
che mettono i brividi; servili
che umiliano serviti e servitori;

pubbliche, che son strapazzi
mica tanto lievi, che molta
opera chiedono, e non cuore,

finalmente!; nato di donna,
sacramenta e fa i suoi fatti, scaltro
o no, igienici o immortali; s'arrangia,

legge nei cuori, negli occhi,
nelle pietre, nei giornali,
e, appena può, muore; mangia,

costruisce sentimentali agglomerati
sugli elenchi telefonici, sbatte
quadrelli uno in pigna all'altro,

i quadrelli rossi, che mangiano
calcina, difendono gli arti
e le giunture dai colpi d'aria,

e va bene
ma non possono parlare
come né i fiori, come né i denti:

that don't lead anywhere, so cold
they bring chills; so servile
they humiliate served and servant;

public, which are no small
headache, requiring
too much work, and no heart,

finally!; born of woman,
he curses and minds his business, shrewd
or not, hygienic or immortal; he makes do,

reads in the hearts, in the eyes,
in the stones, in the newspapers,
and, as soon as he can, dies; eats,

builds sentimental agglomerations
on phone books, slams
tiles one on top of the other,

the red tiles, that eat
mortar, defend the limbs
and joints from drafts,

and that's okay
but they can't speak
neither like flowers, nor teeth:

fare l'uomo non è che una
maniera come un'altra
per scamparla bella:

uomo, nessuno non gli dà mai ragione,
e né la ragione e né il torto,
e né la legge e né la fede;

e allora gareggia: azioni
che non può sapere né volere,
misura, vende, crede, tribola

e non ottiene: sarà cibo
al morbus novus, esca
ai batteri più sicuri: perché

perché la salma è stretta; l'aria tira
forte, e via con essa l'alma
sfugge, temeraria, vile,

forte presa dal piacere
nazionale: e forse è

che forse qui bisogna cambiar aria
tutti quanti: è un consiglio,
un argomento decisivo.

to act as a man is nothing but a
manner like any other
to come out alive:

man, nobody doesn't ever agree with him,
neither right, nor wrong,
neither law, nor faith;

and so he competes: actions
he can't know or desire,
he measures, sells, believes, suffers

and never obtains: food
for the morbus novus, bait
for the most reliable bacterium: why

because the body is tight; the air blows
hard, and with it the soul
escapes, reckless, vile,

strong taken by national
pleasure: and maybe it's that

just maybe here we need a change of scenery,
everybody: it's a suggestion,
a conclusive argument.

Per miracolo

Così, per uno scarto, per miracolo, anche il sasso
vibrava come un'aria, come un bioccolo, e con passo
carico, nuvole di fosforo avariavano per via
lo splendore di balsamo nel suffragio gelato dell'ombria.

Allora, amanti senza volto e senza fame, con il fiato
allora sottovoce si diceva, ci dicevamo: "fu il peccato
a renderci immortali, fu il peccato! Che egoisti,
poi" E le nostre occhiaie — una finestra — così tristi

furono come il merlo che non spicca il suo balzo da pannocchia.
Noi non siamo mai stati più antichi delle nostre ginocchia,
ove adagiammo al tramonto le palme, perché vana
al vento, giubilando, non s'alzasse la tua sottana

con la sottanina, audace velo.

(1940)

A Miracle I

Like that, swerving, a miracle, even the stone
vibrated like an air, like a curl, and with laden
steps, clouds of phosphorus rotted in the street
the splendor of balsam in the frozen suffrage of shade.

So, lovers without faces, without hunger, with soft
breath they said, we said to each other: "it was the sin
that made us immortal, it was the sin! How selfish
of us" And our eye sockets — a window — so sad

were like a blackbird that never makes its corn-like leap.
We've never been more ancient than our knees,
where we laid down our palms at sunset, so that, in
jubilation, in the wind, your skirt wasn't lifted in

vain, along with your slip, taunting veil.

(1940)

Ormai

Un giorno la giovinezza, con circospezione
abbandona arbitrariamente i capolinea. Ecco.
E io ricordo le finestre che s'accendono al pianterreno
sul vialone, e somigliano così profondamente ai radi
ragionamenti che faremo sul punto di morire,
in articulo, con l'ombra degli amici, a fior di mente.

Invero
non so più se viva tra le secche
ancora il suo tepido serpire, adesso,
in province gelate, come una romanza
fine e perenne sul filo della schiena, ma davvero
so che nelle lacrime lombarde, ove credemmo
di mieterci a vicenda, vagabondi baleni
dissipavano i veli nuziali alle riviere.

Ed era un nome d'alta Italia, a ripensare bene,
era un nome questa raffica, che non osi
più inseguire? E la felicità dell'occidente
si salva in occidente?

Disabitate ormai le alzaie, e disperando
ormai del nostro sentimento (e la nebbia
ormai mietuta che ci stringe a mezza vita),
disabitate le alzaie e disperando ormai,

By Now 1

One day youth, with arbitrary
circumspection abandons the end of the lines. That's it.
And I remember the windows that light up at ground level
on the boulevard, and they so closely resemble the rare
reasoning we'll exchange on the brink of death,
in articulo, with shades of friends, skimming the mind. 2

In truth
I no longer know if her warm slither
still lives in the shallows, now,
in frozen provinces, like a subtle
ever-lasting song at the edge of the spine, but really I
know that in Lombard tears, where we thought
we reaped each other, roaming flashes
dispelled the nuptial veils of the shores.

Was it a name for this northern Italy, to think again,
was this flurry a name, that you no longer
dare to pursue? And is the happiness of the West
safe in the West?

Towpaths by now uninhabited, and despairing
by now of our feeling (and reaped
by now the fog that clenches our waste),
towpaths uninhabited and by now despairing,

se la patria fosse una cittadinanza unica, reale,
andrebbe ricordata in un risucchio, a capofitto
per le celesti aiuole, la parte più dimessa
del nostro pensare lontanamente: andrebbe
ricordato uno spesso passaggio di brumisti
e di taxi, quel che tossisce sul margine caduco
del Naviglio, o libero tra le pioppe luccicanti
che i diti del vento tamburellano lassù, il brivido
dell'ultimo brum, in una corsa matta, che ci porta
via tutti i fanali e il nostro cuore salutando.

(1939)

if the fatherland were a unique citizenship, real,
it should be remembered in a whirlpool, headlong
across celestial flowerbeds, the most demure part
of our never would have thought: it should be remembered
the frequent passing of coachmen and taxis, the one
coughing on the ephemeral fringe of the
Naviglio, or the one free among the shining poplars
that the wind's fingers drum up there, the shiver
of the last coach, in a crazy race, that whisks
away all our lamps and hearts, waving. 3

(1939)

From *By Now*

* During my research at the Biblioteca Panizzi in Reggio Emilia, I found a copy of *Oramai* containing Villa's handwritten edits. There is no indication as to when these changes were made. In some cases, he modified words or crossed out entire sentences or stanzas. Such corrections will be noted throughout.

What's New

1. *Andare in camporella* is the act of going to the countryside for foreplay or sex.

1941 Piece

1. In the original, the conditional clause of the first stanza sets in motion a number of twists and turns throughout the poem that are marked by the subjunctive tense. Since in English the subjunctive tense is much rarer than in Italian, I resorted to adverbs in order to mark these syntactical shifts.
2. See note on page 25.
3. See note on page 19.

But Before the Wind

1. By breaking these words, Villa calls attention to the phonetic similarities between *gemi-ti* (moans) and *gemi-nate* (geminates), as well as with *semi* (seeds). The phonetic game at play in the Italian cannot be reproduced in English.
2. Latin for *I believe because the fact is that…*, as in Dante's "*State contenti, umana gente, al quia*" [Mortals, remain contented at the quia] (*Purgatorio*, Canto III, 47).

Semper pauperes

1. Matthew 26:11: "For ye have the poor always with you; but me ye have not always" (King James Version). Villa later crossed this out in his copy.
2. Here it seems Villa is using the name "Breda" as a verb. See note 17 on page 54.
3. *Saronno* is a town in Lombardy.

Good Evening

1. Villa later crossed out the entire poem in his copy.
2. In the original, *stradoni* literally means "big roads" that lead into the surrounding countryside.

Arguments

1. *Squinzano* is a type of red wine produced in the southern region of Puglia. The "notch mark" refers to a line on the bottle to measure the quantity of liquid it contains.
2. A mixing of the three adjectives *Italian*, *Tuscan*, and *Lombard*.

Sometimes a Flash

1. Villa later crossed out both the original Milanese as well as his Italian translation in his copy.

Natus de muliere, brevi vivens

1. "Homo natus de muliere, brevi vivens tempore, repletur multis miseriis" — *Man that is born of a woman is of few days, & full of trouble*. From the Book of Job (14:1), which Villa translated in 1947 (see page 673 of the bibliography). He later crossed out the entire poem in his copy.
2. In the original *mangiare la foglia* is an idiom that literally means to "eat the leaf."
3. Latin for *new disease*.

A Miracle

1. Also entirely crossed in Villa's copy.

By Now

1. Originally dated 1939, Villa changed it to 1932 in his copy.
2. Latin for *at the moment of...* Villa is playing with the expression *in articulo mortis* (at the moment of death).
3. Villa crossed out *il nostro cuore* in his copy.

E ma dopo

Yeah but After

1950

E ma dopo

Dopo il dopo è dopo
dopo cenato la tempesta
dopo agonizzato l'eliotropo e chini
in giù gli stami, dopo la festa
i rasoi sul davanzale deposti in quanto il sangue
dai solchi epidermici fuoresce

dopo che uno mesce, Gerolamo mi sposi,
dopo i fuochi odorosi, Gerolamo se m'ami odi che
strisciano sull'etra gli ombelichi delle quaglie,

dopo strizzati i fichi le dalie gli epitelii,
e i pochi colpi dei dadi sulla tavola dei fenomeni,
dopo incenerite ceneri serene di chimere rapsodiche,
dopo nell'etra salubre tra i rami captate
le essenze degli huomeni e sconcertati
i radi bocconi di Bohême, e
cancellate le esalazioni da lavanderia da cracking
da zolfo

Yeah but After

After the after is after
after dinner the storm
after agony the heliotrope and bending
the stamens, after the party
razors laid on the windowsill because blood
seeps from epidermal furrows

after someone pours a glass, Gerolamo marry me,
after the fragrant fires, Gerolamo if you love me listen
to the navels of quails slithering across the air,

after wringing figs dahlias and epitheliums,
and a few rolls of dice across the table of phenomena,
after incinerating the serene ashes of rhapsodic chimeras,
after receiving the essence of men among branches
in the healthy air and baffled
the rare morsels of Boheme, and
erased the fumes of laundry of cracking
of sulfur

e dopo molate le punte alle canne di bambù
al becco dell'assiolo e del cucù
e dopo

liquefatte le acque per tutti i lunghi atrii del golfo,
il crogiuolo delle ombrie radiofoniche
struggendo e coniugata
la mente con lo spettro
mente coniugata in un promiscuo impulso
al casto volo
e spirito omogeneo
spirito serenante

fotogenica giunse la notte e più remoto l'altro,
il tramite assoluto, il scatto
per dove risalgono le triglie diagonali
le triglie alle radici altre del vento
sperperato

e dopo asciugato i calcagni le caviglie i nomi
e traversati gli aromi dei mosti nelle recondite atmosfere
dei cisterni, e dopo regolato i lombrichi e uniti
i perni e le cerniere,

and after grinding the tip of reeds of bamboo
in beaks of the owl and the cuckoo
and after

liquefying the waters across all the long atriums of the gulf,
the crucible of radiophonic shades
haunting and conjugated
the mind with the specter
mind conjugated in a promiscuous impulse
in the chaste flight
and homogeneous spirit
calming spirit

photogenic came the night and more remote the other,
the absolute passage, the sprint
through which diagonal mullets swim up
mullets at the alien roots of squandered
wind

and after drying the heels ankles and names
and traversing the smells of musts in the remote atmospheres
of cisterns, and after regulating earthworms and uniting
pins and hinges,

dopo estirpato i massimi e i minimi, presunti,
e calcolato il tenore acido dei gliceridi nelle azalee

i costi sul calmiere

    dopo calibrato gli idiomi
nel rivoluzionario trepestio su e giù per le scalee
dell'acropoli dove uno dice dormendo: "che diavolo!"
e un altro dopo dice: "che vogliamo morire, allora,
                                        così in camicia?"
e i treni non arrivano puntuali
    "e non c'è più ragione d'essere!"
                            "carogna!"
        e "mi stuzzica il calcagno" e
                        "va alla fogna" e e

"eh, già" "gli ultimi saranno i primi

a morire" e Orlando di Lasso con la musica
a punteruolo e pazienza graduata
tenta forzare la porta alla confluenza delle raffiche
                                            sublime.

after eradicating projected minimums and maximums
and calculating the acid tenor of glycerides in the azaleas

the costs against ceiling prices

after calibrating idioms
in the revolutionary shuffle up and down the grand steps
of the acropolis where someone says in sleep: "what the hell!"
and after another says: "so, are we going to die like this,
in shirt sleeves?"
and the trains are never on time
"and there's no reason for it all!"
"son of a bitch!"
and "it tickles my heel" and
"back to the sewer" and and

"yeah, right" "the last shall be the first

to die" and Orlando di Lasso with bodkin
music and scaled patience
tries to force the door to the confluence of sublime
bursts.

E dopo il dopo è allora
(è ancora)   (di già?)
e dunque allora in un commiato inverosimile,
                                        futuri e paralleli
al corso degli anni e all'ultimissima
analisi delle coniche solari e della polvere,
affini al tuono, alle più labili analogie
razionali, al tema bustrofedico,

defluiscono i veli mitografi dalle superfici moltiplicate.

And after the after is then
(is again)   (already?)
and therefore then in an unlikely parting,
                                        future and parallel
to the passing of time and to the very last
analysis of solar conics and dust,
akin to thunder, to the most transient rational
analogies, to the boustrophedon theme,

from multiplied surfaces the mythographic veils drain away.

Luogo e impulso

Metà idea e metà frutto
metà rischio metà fame
metà intero metà tutto
metà morte metà pane

Metà effigie e metà spazio
metà corpo e metà ombra
metà morbo metà strazio
metà asciutto metà fiume

Metà pesce e metà testa
metà sasso e metà lume
metà mano metà leva
metà corre metà resta

I

Place and Impulse

Half idea and half fruit
half risk half desire
half whole half absolute
half bread half expire

Half space and half effigy
half body and half shade
half torment half malady
half dry half cascade

Half head and half fish
half stone and half light
half hand half switch
half rest half flight

Metà troppo metà poco
metà vita metà cosa
metà gesto metà scopo
metà fuoco metà rosa

Metà piombo metà voce
metà riso metà vento
metà statua metà sasso
metà calma metà accento

Half scarce half rife
half gesture half aim
half thing half life
half rose half flame

Half led half *vox*
half laughter half vent
half statute half rocks
half calm half accent

Astronomia

Udito per caso sibilare la gran lancia viola nella ionosfera?

    poi transita di qui e sobrie aree
    dirama dai remoti seni e questo
    è questo il tuo parlare a trama
    questo essendo

l'opinione l'opera il respiro: non accorgersi confondere le acque

    etimi leggendari omologare nel suono
    di pietra pietra e nella conca alma
    del sinistro (piede a mano, ma sinistro)

udito i germogli decimati dalla calma ascia delle cadenze?
                un'opinione sì, ma un'opera è respiro.

bene si crede che nello { spazio
specchio lento delle rute si disfogli
spirito }

Astronomy

Did you hear by chance the great violet lance hiss in the ionosphere?

then it passes through here and branches
sober areas out of remote breasts and this
this is your speech by a thread
this being

the opinion the work the breath: not realizing muddying the waters

legendary etymons homologating in the sound
of real stone and in the nurturing valley
of the sinister (foot by hand, but sinister)

did you hear the sprouts decimated by the quiet axe of cadences?
an opinion yes, but a work is breath.

it is right to believe that in the { space
slow mirror of rues
spirit }

la fluorescente odissea dei gradi e le natanti e mute
vertebre plenilunie declinate alla fronte delle proiezioni contrarie!
udito allora riverberare il suono nello screpolo universo
della ionosfera?

the fluorescent odyssey of degrees defoliates and the floating
and mute full-moon vertebrae declined at the front of contrary projections!
then did you hear the sound reverberate in the cracked universe
of the ionosphere?

Senza armonia

L'oscura punta d'essere l'essere dell'essere
del crescere del salire: e struggere e segregare
senza pietà
            senza armonia
                        il punto emblema

della freccia disgiunta dallo sforzo
con impulso decrescente, verso il lacero

Una temperatura delira sulle palpebre della catalisi
cieca, un pensiero moderno avulso a un macero patema
      nel confuso segreto
               che parole!

che il primo salto
   che il grido acutamente
   articolato nell'indice ialino
                  nei tendini
                     nei pori

Without Harmony

The dark point of being the being of being
of growing of rising: and to burn and segregate
without pity
          without harmony
                    the point emblem

of the arrow separated from the effort
with waning impulse, toward the torn

A temperature raves on the eyelids of the blind
catalysis, a modern thought ripped from macerated anxiety
        in the confused secret
                what words!

that the first leap
    that the scream acutely
    articulated in the hyaline index
                in the tendons
                  in the pores

nel pane
nell'aceto
nel coke
nell'aria
di cobalto, e *che* i furori delle consonanti spettrali!

nell'enfasi varia del teorema insoddisfatto
nell'interiezione
nella fine combustione
nella tensione libera
nell'intreccio dei vimini
nell'apotema
nei pori dell'antracite e nello schianto

del ghiaccio cui incrina la lama di una primavera
indimenticabile!

in the bread
in the vinegar
in the coke
in the air
of cobalt, and *that* the furors of the spectral consonants!

in the various emphasis of the unsatisfied theorem
in the interjection
in the subtle combustion
in the free tension
in the weave of wicker
in the apothem
in the pores of anthracite and in the clash

of ice whose blade is cracked of an unforgettable
spring!

Linguistica

Non c'è più origini. Né.   Né si può sapere se.
Se furono le origini e nemmeno.
        E nemmeno c'è ragione che nascano
        le origini   Né più
        la fede,   idolo di Amorgos!

chi dici origina le origini nel tocco nell'accento
            nel sogno mortale del necessario?
No, non c'è più origini.   No.
                                Ma
il transito provocato delle idee antiche — e degli impulsi.
E qualsivoglia ambiguo che germogli intatto
        dalle relazioni
        dalle traiettorie
        dalle radiazioni
        dalle concezioni

        luogo senza storie.
        Luogo dove tutti.
        E dove la coscienza.
        E dove il dove.

Linguistics

I

There's no more origins. Nor.   Nor does one know if.
If there were origins and not even.
And not even a reason why origins
are born   Nor any longer
faith,   idol of Amorgos!

who do you say originates origins in the touch in the accent
in the mortal dream of the necessary?
No, there's no more origins.   No.
But
the provoked transit of ancient ideas — and impulses.
And any ambiguity that sprouts intact
from relations
from trajectories
from radiations
from conceptions

place without stories.
Place where everyone.
And where the conscious.
And where the where.

Per conoscere l'incommensurabile semenza delle vertigini adombrate

le giunture schioccate nei legami
la trasparenza delle cartilagini
il cieco sgomento dei fogliami

agricoli nelle forze
esteriori, e l'analisi fonda
incisa nel corpo dell'accento.

No.
Non c'è più. Né origini nei rami. né non origini.

Chi arrestava i sintagmi sazi nel sortilegio della consistenza
usava lo spirito senza rimedio nel momento indecisivo
come un compasso disadatto, non esperto, così non si poteva
agire più niente, più, ombra ferita e riferita, proiezione
senza essenza, così che speculare sul comune tedio
un gioco parve, e ogni attimo-fonema
ancora oggigiorno sfiora guerra e tempo consumato, e il peso
corrompe dell'ombra dei tramiti dell'essenza.

To know the incommensurable seeding of foreshadowed vertigo

the joints snapped in the ties
the transparency of the cartilage
the blind dismay of the foliage

agricultural in external
forces, and the deep analysis
carved on the body of accent.

No.
There's no more. Nor origins in the branches.   nor non origins.

Those who arrested satiated syntagms in the spell of consistency
used the spirit without remedy in the indecisive moment
like an unsuited compass, inexperienced, so nothing could be
acted any longer, any, wounded and re-wounded shade, projection
without essence, so that speculating on common boredom
looked like a game, and every moment-phoneme
today still verges on war and consumed time, and the weight
corrupts some shade some passings some essence.

E codesta sarebbe.   Questa la fine concepibile:
se attraverso l'idea massima del pericolo e dell'indistinto
si curva l'anima estrema nell'attrito di idrogeno e ozono e i giorni
acerbi sommano giorni ai giorni quotidiani nell'araldica
prosodia   delle tangenze,
soffocando ogni flusso di infallibile irrealtà in:
        i verbi
        i neologismi.

Chi le braccia levava saziate di viole nel palpito assortito
oggi paragona ogni rovina paragona allo spirito
immune che popola e corruga a segmenti il nembo
delle testimonianze storiche, delle parabole nel grembo
confuso delle parrocchie e nelle larghe zone
di caccia e pesca e d'altre energiche mansioni culturali.

E non per questo celebro coscientemente il germe
        sepolto, al di là,

And this would be.   This the conceivable end:
if through the maximum idea of the indistinct and danger
the extreme soul is curved in the clash of hydrogen and ozone and the
unripe days add days to everyday days in the heraldic
prosody   of tangencies,
smothering every flux of infallible unreality in:
          verbs
          neologisms.

Those who lifted arms satiated with violets in the assorted palpitation
today compare every ruin compare to the immune
spirit that populates and furrows in segments the nimbus
of historical testimonies, of parables in the confused
womb of parishes and in the large areas
for hunting and fishing and other energetic cultural responsibilities.

And this isn't why I consciously celebrate the seed
          buried, on the other side,

e celebro l'etimo corroso dalle iridi foniche,
l'etimo immaturo,
l'etimo colto,
l'etimo negli spazi avariati,
nei minimi intervalli,
nelle congiunzioni,
l'etimo della solitudine posseduta,
l'etimo nella sete
e nella sete idonea alle fossili rocce illuminate
dalle fosforescenze idumee, idolo di Amorgos!

and celebrate the etymon corroded by phonic irises,
        the immature etymon,
        the erudite etymon,
        the etymon in rotten spaces,
        in the shortest intervals,
        in conjunctions,
        the etymon of possessed solitude,
        the etymon in the thirst
and in the thirst suited to fossil rocks lit
        by Idumean phosphorescence, idol of Amorgos! 2

Geografia

Sconfina, forma reale, nella balugine arsa delle chiome
inanimate!   eludi il nome!   penetra

il nesso fantastico delle matematiche particolari: e sparsa
furia di là   là dove la tempesta

musica nidiate di appennini e i verecondi

nerbi delle foci essenziali
e dei congegni librati a larghi schemi nell'anello

continentale   e dei coefficienti
di vili radici,   percettibili

appena nella sinossi fiorita, e il sesso stralunato delle pleiadi,
gentili narici   sottovoce.

Geography

Roam, real form, in the burnt glimmer of inanimate
locks!   elude the name!   penetrate

the fantastic nexus of particular mathematics: and scattered
fury over there   there where the storm

sets to music broods of apennines and the chaste

backbones of essential estuaries
and of devices soaring in large patterns in the continental

ring   and of the coefficients
of vile roots,   barely

visible in the blossoming synopsis, and the bewildered sex of the Pleiades,
gentle nostrils   sotto voce.

Le parole

Una stagionaccia di tumescenti avvoltoi,
svignate le mogli per mancanza di cibarie di scandali di orgasmi
e d'altre storie, toccherà dimenticare con indifferenza, e con sentita
espressione, i campi spremuti dagli amici intimi, i terreni
recinti, i verdi trapezi con i lampi pomeridiani, i tiepidi
screzi della primavera nazionale dietro i terrapieni, e le fontane
occulte del sapere grano a grano le similitudini dei fiori
dei venti dei trafeli nei luoghi non segnati, e le settimane
che nei chiasmi risorge la carne unanime-inanime nei chiasmi

e massacrare il gallo forbito tra i brughi lombardi
il gesto che trafughi alla notte il sangue fresco gli alberi e le alte
quote degli astri vanitosi, e la polare cha valica i sentieri
delle ascisse, e risospingere proprio così

contro i drastici orizzonti frantumati dai tamburi i candidi fantasmi
e sfogliare le direzioni ortogonali e nelle vuote

Words

A nasty season of tumescent vultures,
wives ran off for lack of food of scandals of orgasms
and other stories, must be forgotten with indifference, and the sincere
expression, the fields squeezed by intimate friends, the fenced in
fields, the green trapezia with afternoon flashes, the tepid
frictions of the national spring behind the embankments, and the occult
fountains of knowledge grain by grain the similes of flowers
of winds of heavy breaths in unmarked places, and the weeks
that in the chasms the flesh resurfaces unanimous-inanimate in the chasms

and slaughtering the well-mannered rooster among Lombard heathers
the gesture you steal from the night the fresh blood the trees and the high
altitudes of vain stars, and Polaris that crosses the paths
of abscissas, and to push back just like that

against the drastic horizons shattered by the drums the candid ghosts
and to leaf the orthogonal directions and in the empty

sfere annusare le ferraglie tra le rose paniche e il sentore
di rugiada dai poderi avversi e il crudo
raziocinio delle millesime angolature divelte nel guizzo delle trote,
le cuspidi sonore degli shrapnell e il cielo nudo

lento delle azalee,
vero che tu vedevi nel liquore dell'atlantico con gli occhi
della vita intera, e concepivi le termiche metafore
e le ipotesi grandi ottemperare alle medesime
cause influenti delle maree, e delle volte
climatiche che accadono nello sperma degli squali bianchi?

quindi in un impeto unanime bevemmo in coro
gli insiemi, e uno per uno il soffio amato della sola inquietudine
che rapinava l'ombra e decimava i fatui
semi delle consuetudini verbali, i risplendenti
rameggi dell'uranio e il vero ulivo
d'oro nella più cheta tenebra del quarzo, e il fiume

vivo delle arterie che risale il lume-lavoro degli scheletri.

spheres to sniff the iron scraps among the panicky roses and the smell
of dew from adverse farms and the crude
reasoning of the thousandth angles wrecked in the jump of trout,
the sonorous cuspids of shrapnel and the nude slow

sky of azaleas,
true that you saw in the liquor of the Atlantic with eyes
of the entire life, and you conceived of thermal metaphors
and the great hypothesis complying with the same
influential causes of the tides, and the climatic
vaults happening in the sperm of great white sharks?

then in unanimous impetus we drank the sets
in chorus, and one by one the beloved breath of the only unease
that robbed the shade and decimated the fatuous
seeds of verbal habits, the resplendent branches
of uranium and the true golden olive
tree in the calmest darkness of quartz, and the living

river of arteries that flows up the taper-work of skeletons.

Dinamica accanita

A mente formuliamo una dinamica
accanita: il carro con le cinque ruote
oblique nel senso periodico
dei punti cardinali sulle dita della mano usuale.

E se tu vedi adagio salire per la china storta
questa grande ruota morte, bene, séguila
pari pari, e giunto in alto sui ripiani panoramici

e tu ruba dalle matte arene del silenzio geloso
nell'ora che la porta litargica, gl'illimiti
itinerari e spazi vulnerabili recuperando, sbatte
sullo stipite e nel cardine di sale

cigola accanitamente, quel che alla terra torna
misurato compenso e quota infera
ideale: ruba

corna gentile di sangue congolese, e la luna
inviperita sulle cateratte.

Dogged Dynamic

By heart we formulate dogged
dynamics: the cart with five oblique
wheels in the periodic sense of
cardinal points on the fingers of the usual hand.

And if you see this great death wheel slowly
climb the crooked slope, good, follow it
very closely, and once you've reached the panoramic plains

and steal from the mad arenas of jealous silence
when the lethargic door, recuperating
unlimited itineraries and vulnerable spaces, slams
on the frame and in the hinge of salt

stubbornly creaks what returns to the earth,
measured reward and the ideal infernal
altitude: steal

horns ennobled by Congolese blood, and the moon
livid on the cataracts.

Contenuto figurativo

Ipotesi solenne è se

se con la lingua dei vangeli semitici il vento lecca
i cardini gli stipiti e nelle filiture
le uova della polvere disseppellisce e una secca
luce e le semenze scure nelle crepe qua là là
e dappertutto

è se

se il vento affonda nella proteina il morso
e nelle radici degli sterri e trivellando il dorso
delle locuste trema e scatta
la traiettoria dell'etere omogeneo (se minimi
se minimi per minimi dà minimi
e retrattili abissi)

Figurative Content

It's a solemn hypothesis if

if with the language of the Semitic gospels the wind licks
the hinges the frames and in the filatures
unearths the eggs of dust and a dry
light and the dark seeds in the cracks here there there
and everywhere

it's if

if the wind sinks the bit into the protein
and in the roots of excavations and drilling the locusts'
back trembles and triggers
the trajectory of the homogeneous ether (if minimums
if minimums times minimums equals minimums
and retractable abysses)

ed è se usi con le mani specificamente usuali
l'aria come fosse una matita di cristallo,
            come un ago
sfrenando la misura il palpito numerato la superficie

e non se il vento vago

o l'aria di natura ma dell'aria-aria
l'intimissimo prisma delirante e della raffica
la curva medesima, ma il puro

            omogeneo: l'idea
            l'idea e il coro,
            l'attimo e l'intenzione,
            il lutto; il non sensibile

coro della percezione, la parabola che
che procede immutata dalla curva; poi il frutto
che scende dall'idea che; e spazio da spazio,
come l'erto transito distende d'un battito solo
il passero sbiancato dagli aerei cicli,

and it's if you use with specifically ordinary hands
the air as if it were a crystal pencil,
        like a needle
unleashing measure the numbered throb the surface

and not if the vague wind

or the air of nature but of air-air
the most intimate delirious prism and the curve
itself of the barrage, but the purely

        homogeneous: the idea,
        the idea and the chorus,
        the moment and the intention,
        the mourning; the non sensitive

chorus of perception, the parable that
that proceeds unchanged from the curve; then the fruit
that falls from the idea that; and space from space,
as the steep transit spreads out in a single beat
the sparrow whitened by aerial cycles,

come l’erto uovo
che su dove e su
e nelle parti
e nelle parti delle parti
in partibus infidelium,

e su dove
per la materna anatomia, tra le carti-
lagini serpeggia e per i fragili arti
del chiasmo la nuda
incertezza, i guizzi,
il trauma e sulle scorie gelide il lume sentito,
quello nero
quello del moto, quello
dell’attimo e la follia.

Il cielo è

è pensato pesato misurato smisurato, mah! chi sa,
e la calma è il segreto dello spasmo, la radura
del cielo, la prescritta natura,

like the steep egg that
over there where and over there
and in parts
and in the parts of parts
in partibus infidelium, I

and over there where
through maternal anatomy, among the carti-
lage and across the fragile limbs of the
chasm slithers the nude
uncertainty, the jump,
the trauma and the light perceived on frozen debris,
the black one
that of motion, that
of the moment and folly.

The sky is

is pondered weighed measured and measureless, well! who knows,
and the calm is the secret of the spasm, the sky's
opening, the prescribed nature,

e il cielo è alquanto confuso come il consenso degli uomini,
come il cuore delle donne, semplicissima orma
il sentiero dell'acqua equibollente sulla pietra

e sempre prima molto prima quasi che tu possa
enunciare la forma o dire
una figura, l'acqua
ha già detto da sola, ora et ab aeterno, il tutto
e l'orma originale.

E però se

se tu usi l'aria come una matita di cristallo,
un ago, il perno dittongo che stride al centro
della ragione, premito del filo
d'erba che vuole inoltrarsi dentro il masso,
matrice che strepita e lavora e inventa, lenta
arteriosa iperbole, enigma madornale, immaginaria
dimensione e varia analisi, sbattendo

and the sky is just as confused as the consensus of men,
as the heart of women, the simplest footprint
the path of the equibolent waters on the stone 2

and always before way before so you can almost
enunciate the form or speak
the figure, the water
has already spoken on its own, now et ab aeterno, everything
and the original footprint.

Sure but if

if you use the air like a crystal pencil,
a needle, the diphthong pivot that screeches at the center
of reason, contraction of the blade
of grass that seeks to penetrate the boulder,
matrix that clamors and works and invents, slow
arterial hyperbole, egregious enigma, imaginary
dimension and various analyses, slamming

quanto sbattono
gli stracci delle bufere sulle creste Alleghani
per la ragione che
il cervelletto dello scoiattolo pietra diventa

e che nell'ora che solidifica
che nasce il corno
che nasce la siringa
e nasce il sambuco
e il femore sulle cosce

e viola d'amore
e cello e mandolino
nel soffio fino
del Barnegat, le rocce,

un refe di musica da niente
trasale è la viola
che taglia l'agata
e la sparuta corrente,

as the storm's
tatters slam on the Alleghenian ridge
for the reason
the squirrel's cerebellum becomes stone

and that in the hour when it solidifies
when the horn is born
when the syringe is born
and the elder tree is born
and the femur on the thighs

and viola d'amore
and cello and mandolin
in the subtle breeze
of Barnegat, the rocks, 3

a startled thread of nothing much
music it's the viola
that cuts the agate'
and the meager current,

e se però

se sparisce l'ombra sedata dello spasmo, circoscritta,
esanime, del germe ed il richiamo sano
del minerale (calce quarzo rame) allora

la falce, ecco
la ruota, ecco
e è anche così
e anche non così

e il dolmen
il menhir
il cromlech
il sese *con le mele*

xòana e stele
colonna ed acrotèrio in noce
e il cemento delle rampe e scale
e i legni in croce
e il putiferio vaginale…

yeah but if

if the contained, sedated, lifeless, shade of the spasm,
of the germ, disappears and the healthy call
of minerals (lime quartz copper) then

the scythe, that's it
the wheel, that's it
and it's also like that
and also not like that

and the dolmen
the menhir
the cromlech
the sese *with apples* 4

xoana and stele 5
column and acroterion in walnut 6
and the cement of ramps and stairs
and boards in a cross
and the vaginal mayhem…

Corrado Cagli, pittore

per operare una croce
ci vogliono due legni: o
due segni e l'aria: tre
per porre l'architrave: e costole
d'aria per seminar la voce ove dio vuole.
Ma tu forse muovi la tua considerazione e giri l'ombra e la rigiri,
l'ombra dei segni progettati nuovi, nell'ordine ambigualente
del dominio

altro:

altro dal fogliame e dagli stinchi
altro dall'onda e dalla polvere subsònica
altro dal vento e dalle pàtine romantiche
altro

dalla polpa mite e tonda e dal contatto
parallelo

Corrado Cagli, painter 7

to set up one cross
you need two boards: or
two signs and the air: three
to lay the architrave: and ribs
of air to sow the voice where god desires.
But maybe you shift your consideration and turn the shade and turn it again,
the shade of signs projected as new, in the ambigulent order 8
of the dominion

other:

other than the foliage and shins
other than the wave and subsonic dust
other than the wind and romantic patinas
other

than the meek and round pulp and the parallel
contact

altro dal filo dell'evento e della lite umana
altro dai gusci e dal velo
altro dal bianco limo latte sugli usci

in una bassa mattina di colore ovale

altro, già, altro ancora, dal graffio duro
dell'unghia sull'erma di diorite
altro dall'altro oltre l'ultimo altro
il puro omogeneo dei teoremi orali, e il puro che ritorna; l'acqua
liscia e disunita di ogni sembianza che rigenera, e sulle corna
del fuoco bianco e nero sulle corna
sanguina la sagoma adorna della tragedia orientale.

Qui mi firmo. Mi firmo col mio nome. Noi giochiamo
solo con le conseguenze e con la inane
logica inane delle manifestazioni impulsive.

other than the thread of the event and human squabble
other than the shells and the veil
other than the white silt milk on doorsteps

on a low morning of oval color

other, yes, other still, than the nail's heavy
scratch on the diorite herm
other than the other beyond the ultimate other
the pure homogeneity of oral theorems, and the pure that returns; the smooth
uneven water of every semblance that regenerates, and on the horns
of black and white fire on the horns
bleeds the ornate silhouette of the eastern tragedy.

I'll sign here. I'll sign with my name. We only
play with consequences and the inane
inane logic of impulsive manifestations.

Place and Impulse

1. A few liberties have been taken to maintain the rhyme scheme found in the original. For example, vox replaces the original "voce" to rhyme with rocks.

Linguistics

1. An expression of Cycladic art (c. 3000–1500 BC), the *idols of Amorgos* are stylized human forms about a-meter-and-a-half in height, typically carved out of hard stone. These are some of the earliest known examples of sculpture & therefore represent the "origins" of Western art. Since these figures belong to a mythical past, it is unclear what sort of function they performed, if they were created for worship or simply out of early man's artistic sensibility.
2. In Hellenistic-Roman geography, the adjective *Idumean* referred to a region of southern Palestine inhabited by the Edomites, descendants of the biblical figure Esau.

Figurative Content

1. *In partibus infidelium* is a Latin phrase meaning "in the lands of non-believers."

2. The original reads *equibollente*, a combination of the prefix *equi*, meaning equal, and the adjective *bollente*, boiling. Phonetically, it is very close to the Italian *equipollente* (equivalent), which is why I created "equibolent."
3. The only "Barnegat" we could identify was a township located in Ocean County, New Jersey.
4. In Latin, *sese* is the accusative form of the reflexive pronoun meaning himself, herself, itself, or themselves.
5. "Xoana" were wooden effigies used in various ancient Greek cults. No original examples survive today, only stone or marble copies.
6. An *acroterion* is a classical architectural ornament placed on the apex of a building's pediment.
7. Corrado Cagli (1910–1976) was a prominent Italian painter. Over the years, Villa wrote several "poetic criticisms" dedicated to his work. It is difficult to tell if Villa had a particular Cagli piece in mind here, although it may refer to Cagli's book *I destini alternati agli Intercalari* [Destinies Dispersed amid Verbal Tics], which was published by Edizioni d'Argo in 1949, the same publisher who printed Villa's *E ma dopo* a year later.
8. The original reads *ambigualente*, a combination of *ambiguo* (ambiguous) and *ambivalente* (ambivalent).

17 variazioni su temi proposti per una pura ideologia fonetica

17 Variations on Themes Proposed for a Pure Phonetic Ideology

1955

1 imprestami una battaglia di suggestioni tassative, di zanzare di
allegrie di classiche maniere o impetuose, decise,   non timide né tenere

e caratteristici contatti con tutto quello che il presentimento
accumulato nel futuro accumula di relativamente straordinario e di
inconsueta potenza nell'ordine, diciamo così, per paura, per ipotesi,
per noia terrestre

calde congetture in più e di grandezza inimmaginabile
liberamente misurata nell'orbita delle frenesie   come
se uno guarda dritto sull'asse dei capofitti: come a dire,
press'a poco, strabico, sguercio, o simili, di sbieco, e via

beh, spirami speculazioni apparenti e sperimentate nel chiasmo
dei tagli e delle congiunture   la piena ragione del distante
coniugato con l'ubiquo

cedimi, prego, la fulminea consulenza protestata dal simbolo
temerario   cedimi le tue pause solenni
(aumentate, magari!)   e cantami sul pallottoliere
                                    la materia magnifica

1 lend me a battle of binding suggestions, of mosquitoes of
mirth of classical or impulsive manners, decided,   not timid nor tender

and characteristic contacts with everything the accumulated premonition
accumulates in the future that's relatively extraordinary and of
unusual power within the order, let's say, out of fear, or hypothesis,
or earthly boredom

additional warm conjectures and of unthinkable greatness
measured freely in the orbit of frenzies   as
if staring at the axis of head-firsts: that is to say,
more or less, cross-eyed, one-eyed, or similar, askew, and so on

well, fill me with apparent speculations, tested in the chasm
of cuts and joints   the full reason of the distant
conjugated with the ubiquitous

surrender, please, the swift council protested by the reckless
symbol   surrender your solemn pauses
(increased, even!)   and on the abacus sing to me
                    of magnificent subjects

delle parabole senza materia
delle occhiate senza ragione
delle vacanze
delle sbadataggini infernali

cantami i disastri accertabili che s'incontrano di solito
nell'incolume spettrale della intensità   lo squarcio
sui fianchi del sudario, velum templi
prex (orphica) pex (perspectiva)

intensifica la dimensione algebrica del lacero   le forme
più gentili più scaltre più esaltate più generali del gesto
finalizio, dies iræ

e concentra gli ultimi frantumi di umano intelletto
in un cavo inaccessibile di improperi   come in un
palmo di mano o in un lago di aria ragionata
o musicata aria mentre stridono

sul disco della divinità orizzontale forbice e lesina
coltello punteruolo pece e spago

of parables without subjects
of glances without reason
of vacations
of infernal distractions

sing to me of ascertainable disasters usually seen
in the ghastly invulnerable of intensity   the rip
along the edge of the shroud, velum templi
prex (orphica) pex (perspectiva)

intensify the algebraic dimension of the tear   forms
more gentle more shrewd more exalted more general of the finalizing
gesture, dies iræ I

and concentrate the last fragments of human intellect
in an inaccessible hollow of curses   like in a
palm of a hand or in a lake of reasoned air
or air set to music while on the disk

of horizontal divinity screech scissors awl
bodkin knife pitch and twine

2 gli alberi si sposavano
le pietre erano dèi
il mare possedeva corpo e capo.

le immagini erano il silenzio
inquinato. le figure erano la polpa
dell'invisibile. e le labbra
forti come le scapole e le mascelle.

seme era il vento.
la voce un processo di idrogenazioni.
il linguaggio erano le stagioni
estreme, non eliminate.

gli odori erano gelo e notte,
e il tempo che, tale che.
l'anima era lontananza per uguaglianza,
e il numero follia purissima follia.

la musica era il nodo era
la stuoia. e lo sforzo

2 trees married
stones were gods
the sea had body and head.

images were polluted
silence. figures the pulp
of the invisible. and lips
strong like jaws and shoulder blades.

seed was the wind.
the voice a process of hydrogenations.
language was the extreme,
not eliminated seasons.

scents were frost and night,
and weather that, such that.
the soul was distance by equality,
and the number folly the purest folly.

music was the knot it was
the mat. and effort

era l'ombra fissamente considerata
in inconcepibile moltipliche
incroci attriti giustapposizioni

forza per forma era il cuneo
e l'anima futura era l'anima
dell'anima senza divisione.

e così leggemmo insieme
l'enuma eliš i rancori
teogonistici e le sciocchezze
senza scampo di Kierkegaard
e le maledizioni dell'antico
testamento.

3 Il caffelatte finito, le freguglie ai piedi delle prealpi rosa
& tuae quidquid lubidinis per ora
al primissimo piano la foglia odorosa dell'arrosto con le guglie
del rosmarino al secondo ripiano il fruscio del raion
e i muscoli di ilaria spezzano l'ago inossidabile

the shade obsessively considered
in inconceivable multiplications
junctions frictions juxtapositions

force through form was the wedge
and the future soul the soul
of the soul undivided.

and so together we read
the enuma elish the theogonistic 2
rancor and inescapably
Kierkegaard's nonsense
and the curses of the old
testament. 3

3 After caffè latte, crumbs at the feet of the rosa prealps
& tuae quidquid lubidinis per ora
on the first floor the fragrant leaf of the roast with pinnacles
of rosemary on the second the rustle of rayon 4
and the muscles of cheer snap the stainless needle

allo sbocco delle vitamine (*lume morto e fum ki dura*)
e le pianelle e i pomodori e i peperoni al terzo uscio
anche dopo dentro in pancia i pesci voglion acqua
al quarto il soffio del borotalco sciorinato per la figlia
delle azzurre marinare (*al disco ki stravaca la scuidella*)

scroscia l'acqua al quinto piano palpita
contro le piastrelle la maniglia di porcellana a sterzo
sotto la coscia d'albicocche gorgogliano le tubature e sbatte l'asse
al sesto piano ribolle il lume elettrico davanti al Sacro
Cuore nella nicchia e raschia la radio "primavera
d'ogni cuore" nelle tenebre sgargianti e i baccalà
non si lasciano a mollo per dei secoli e dei secoli
mens optuma quæque mens optuma

in terrazzo le rane sciacquano lenzuola e picchia
nell'umido fumo in qualche andito il ferro da stiro
un becco malinconico da preda la mamma non mi strilla
ma che vacca di una signora, ma che vacca di una,
(ma che vacca) ventata di cibarie veneziane
e ferraresi di spezie di colonie e matriciana

at the vitamins' outlet (*lume morto e fum ki dura*) 5
and *pianella* and tomatoes and peppers at the third door 6
even after inside in the stomach fish need water on the
fourth the puff of talcum powder displayed for the daughter
of blue sailor outfits (*al disco ki stravaca la scuidella*) 7

the water roars on the fifth floor throbs
against the tiles the wheel-shaped porcelain handle
under the apricots' thigh the pipes gurgle and the toilet seat slams
on the sixth floor the electric light boils before the Sacred
Heart in the niche and the radio scratches "primavera
d'ogni cuore" in the vivid darkness and don't let 8
the baccalà soak for centuries and centuries
mens optuma quæque mens optuma

on the balcony frogs rinse sheets and the iron
in the humid smoke in some hallway pecks
a melancholic beak of prey mother doesn't yell at me
but what a cow of a lady, but what a cow of a,
(but what a cow) whiff of venetian and ferrarese
food cologne spices and matriciana 9

ma che sentano scottare la tua lagna come una spilla
fino in fondo alla strada l'acquetta dei tuoi occhi rosa
nelle adiacenze e in tutta la nazione mera
che sentano! lustri con l'acquetta della rilla rosa nel tondo
la maniglia le chiavistelle i pomi frusti d'ottone e il fondo a sera

nous aimions tous beaucoup ça

delle padelle scoppi il buco delle serrature e varie
filiture d'aria nel frastuono di cicli e motocicli e nelle carie

tu potresti rivelare a tutti quanto veramente buona
è la febbre! quanto l'ira è breve e l'ebrietà e di che cosa
vivi di che pane usuale di che cure di che fame quando suona
il campanello alla porta e non aspetti nessuno di usuale

perché la anziana bagnarola si è smaltata nel bieco
serale il tripode è caduto con fracasso
nelle adiacenze e in tutta la nazione mera (mamma
se fosse mamma capirebbe, se lo fosse!) che palpitazioni
cardiache cor æstuans cor tremitans cor videns

but let them hear your burning complaint like a pin
at the end of the street the drip of your pink eyes
in the neighborhood and throughout the whole nation
let them hear it! with the drip of the pink rilla in the round
polish the handle the bolt the worn-out brass knobs and at night the bottom

nous aimions tous beaucoup ça

of pans let the hole in the locks explode and various
threads of air in the rumble of cycles and motorcycles and in the caries

you could reveal to all just how good the fever
really is! how brief the wrath and intoxication and what you
live on the usual bread what cures what hunger when the doorbell
rings and you're not expecting any usual guest

since the old tub was enameled and in the nightly
gloom the tripod fell with a bang
in the neighborhood and throughout the whole nation (mother
if she was a mother she'd understand, if she was one!) what cardiac
palpitations cor æstuans cor tremitans cor videns

grande dolcezza di senso a somiglianza del vento prealpino
negli specchi rosa dentro i bronchi e nella tromba nell'anima
delle scale il cielo è andato in alto! alto spreco

(se fosse mamma capirebbe!) ahi, polvere di rondoni
scapicollanti, sù, al cielo! non volate così sotto, tanto basso,
così qui! lo specchio incrinato da una ruga risolleva
la scarogna, ruggini e iridate le gronde
raccolgono una vuota eco e un secolo di ricordi

e i secoli ricordi in fuga a onde verso il vicolo cieco,
e il simbolo dei ricordi è l'acciuga appesa ai travi
e là saltavi per intingere la mollica e la Natura va
più dolce e più filata nei seni dei bambini

se non che il cuore se si è molto fini
il cuore quando è perso è perso non lo prendi più.
Piangi. La stanga di nikel e il vento
il vento, semplicemente il vento.

nous aimions tous beaucoup ça

great sweetness of sense resembling the pre-alpine wind
in the pink mirrors in the bronchioles and in the well in the soul
of the stairs the sky has risen! rising waste

(if she was a mother she'd understand!) ah, dust of breakneck
swifts, up, to the sky! don't fly that low, so low,
so here! the mirror crazed by a wrinkle revives
bad luck, the rusty and iridescent eaves
gather an empty echo and a century of memories

and the centuries memories in flight in waves toward the dead end,
and the symbol of memories is the anchovy hanging from beams
and there you jumped to dip the bread and Nature moves
sweeter and straighter in the chest of children

except that the heart if one's extremely refined
the heart once it's lost it's lost you'll never catch it again.
You cry. The nickel rod and the wind
the wind, simply the wind.

nous aimions tous beaucoup ça

4

it is world of the back hune wone it is
it is world of the horse half heart head
it is world of the workwork it is is

it is father of the snakewife
it is world of the tree and tree and
and it other is father of the other
and of the all all all all other.

what is it? native. what and why?
why, christ, why, we tell. alien.

I tell: yes. I. native and alien. Signe
vivant. I. signe signe signe. with mien
with deep mien and dark drag.

what is it and what other? what
between it-rock-ruin and all other (water,
fire, air)? between I and me
is *water*, fire, air and all streaming chaos?

it is work of work and it
is world of the world of the horse
upon the tree as fragrant breath

4

it is world of the back hune wone it is
it is world of the horse half heart head
it is world of the workwork it is is

it is father of the snakewife
it is world of the tree and tree and
and it other is father of the other
and of the all all all all other.

what is it? native. what and why?
why, christ, why, we tell. alien.

I tell: yes. I. native and alien. Signe
vivant. I. signe signe signe. with mien
with deep mien and dark drag.

what is it and what other? what
between it-rock-ruin and all other (water,
fire, air)? between I and me
is *water*, fire, air and all streaming chaos?

it is work of work and it
is world of the world of the horse
upon the tree as fragrant breath

as pleasure. revolves and dies. I
see. now and plus tard. plus
tard de la lune.

words wind wife blowing
escape tombé d'après nature:
what is it? christ! what is time?
I felt what. I felt what
all kingdom is workwork
of the snake-abyss, as native
olives and all alien things.

e givme a tickling spring, christ,
with wings and with
hushed rumbles and exquisite resemblances.

and talk me and tell dark hours
dark oblivions dark trees dark
leaves dark darkness and
whitening water. it is
a world in intumo semine.

as pleasure. revolves and dies. I
see. now and plus tard. plus
tard de la lune.

words wind wife blowing
escape tombé d'après nature:
what is it? christ! what is time?
I felt what. I felt what
all kingdom is workwork
of the snake-abyss, as native
olives and all alien things.

e givme a tickling spring, christ,
with wings and with
hushed rumbles and exquisite resemblances.

and talk me and tell dark hours
dark oblivions dark trees dark
leaves dark darkness and
whitening water. it is
a world in intumo semine.

seme nelle rotaie al capolinea sotto le traversine tarlate
semente sulle selci della capitale
un grano sulla coda del passero
un protone (come si dice oggi) un quantum gonfio d'ombra
nell'isotopo
o (supponiamo) un bacillus æstheticus subtillimus
nelle mucose mascellari del lupo o nell'orfizio
anale della balena
un seme (qui si dice) che lievita, della Giustizia
una briciola (o freguglia) magari seccolita, appunto,
di Giustizia banale in fondo alla saccoccia del vecchio
ministro farabutto in altalena
una goccia (mettiamo, per caso) dentro il lavabo tutta notte
oh, il tempo è una falsità che irriga
l'epidermide nelle zone di attrito
una proteina snella e gentile come un postulato per le bisce
un lampaneggio in un crepaccio celestiale, simbolico,
o una istantanea delusione che veleggia nel cranio
del cane senza padrone, per cui

5 seed in the tracks at the end of the line under the rotten ties
seed on the cobblestone of the capital
a grain on the sparrow's tail
a proton (in the parlance of our times) a quantum bloated with shade
in the isotope
or (let's suppose) a bacillus æstheticus subtillimus
in the wolf's maxillary membrane or the anal
        orifice of the whale
a seed (as we say around here) that leavens, of Justice
a speck (or crumb) maybe dried out, exactly,
of banal Justice at the bottom of the pocket of the old
        rascal minister on a swing
a drop (let's assume for a moment) inside the sink all night long
        oh, time is a falsity that irrigates
        the epidermis in areas of friction
a slender and gentle protein as a postulate for garden snakes
a flashing in a celestial crevasse, symbolic,
or an instantaneous delusion that sails in the skull
        of a dog without a master, whereby

questo stabilito e confermato, noi dementi verticaloidi
e intelligenti perlomeno una volta
e mezza, rotolando un po' qua un po' di là sul terreno
trebbiato dalla furia dei molteplici
e non generati sensi di energia, noi
nutriti della semenza alacre della genialità mortale, di noialtri
chi e per quale mai festività ha piantato nelle crepe questo
seme morbido in un luogo di non attenzione, dove è fiato
che viva e serpeggi nel popolo delle foglie la Giustezza
analitica? noi consumiamo insieme la Natura
e il Terrore fino a che una resurrezione qualsivoglia
nella trama degli abissi e dei fiorami, nell'aria
segreta come quella di stamani alle 8 e 35 circa,
taglierà l'ultimo colloquio e ne trarrà, invisibile
numero, illimite ipogeo, in balìa
del liquore solenne senza seme e senza cenere

once established and confirmed, we demented verticaloides
and intelligent at least once
and a half, rolling a little here and a little over there on the terrain
threshed by the fury of multiples
and un-generated senses of energy, we
nourished by the brisk seed of mortal geniality, out of us all
who and for what sort of festivity has planted in the crevices this
soft seed in a place of non attention, where is the breath
that lives and slithers in the population of leaves,
the analytic Justice? together we consume Nature
and Terror until any sort of resurrection
in the weave of the abyss and inflorescence, in the secret
air like the one this morning around 8:35,
will cut the last meeting and from it will draw,
invisible number, boundless hypogeum,
some solemn liquor without seed nor ash

6 nous aimions tous beaucoup ça

aurais-je du parvenir aux clameurs
absolus, aux ressources indifférenciées,
par l'art, par l'art sonore,
ou sur l'échelle ronde des grandes avions
transatlantiques, mamelles roulantes
dans la calme blonde, notre chair
inattendue ou multiple.

à chercher des instruments simples
et indeterminés, des instruments
proportionels et drôles

on rencontre un étranger dans l'extase
si consequemment sinistre et secret,

le puits des conséquences oubliées
ou refoulées dans un bagne immémoriale

6 nous aimions tous beaucoup ça

aurais-je du parvenir aux clameurs
absolus, aux ressources indifférenciées,
par l'art, par l'art sonore,
ou sur l'échelle ronde des grandes avions
transatlantiques, mamelles roulantes
dans la calme blonde, notre chair
inattendue ou multiple.

à chercher des instruments simples
et indeterminés, des instruments
proportionels et drôles

on rencontre un étranger dans l'extase
si consequemment sinistre et secret,

le puits des conséquences oubliées
ou refoulées dans un bagne immémoriale

dans les pommes de terre dans les laves
d'éruptions dans des dollars couverts
d'une pâte subtile de démence algébrique
dans les fulgurations sexuelles
dans les opacités successives
dans toutes les entrâves héréditaires.

pas d'orguedenisation nationale — et alors
pas d'orguedeuil rational — et alors
pas d'abîmes intentionnés — pas de
et alors

7 pas d'huile — pas de grandes matières
intérieures — pas de denrées sonores
pas donc de réhalité — pas grand nombre
de tonnes de vibrations méque-aniques
pas de grandes affirmations de douleur
pas de nuit de négations parfaites
pas de mots bruts pas de mots bruits

dans les pommes de terre dans les laves
d'éruptions dans des dollars couverts
d'une pâte subtile de démence algébrique
dans les fulgurations sexuelles
dans les opacités successives
dans toutes les entrâves héréditaires.

pas d'orguedenisation nationale — et alors
pas d'orguedeuil rational — et alors
pas d'abîmes intentionnés — pas de
et alors

7 pas d'huile — pas de grandes matières
intérieures — pas de denrées sonores
pas donc de réhalité — pas grand nombre
de tonnes de vibrations méque-aniques
pas de grandes affirmations de douleur
pas de nuit de négations parfaites
pas de mots bruts pas de mots bruits

pas de quoi pas quoi pas
d'éléments généraux reculants
génereuse au fond des abîmes intentionnés
pas de sublimes économies pas
de régularités absurdes constituées
pas d'idéalisations hybrides pas de quoi
et alors

[dia]thèmes sur l'air adhaesit anima, vivicafi secundum

8 deum deum deum dixit
mais rien ne prouvant que

a dit le a dit que le préêtre romon
pour égorger la pierre[re]
oxidïane sous la lune dernière
la pépêtre va tromber trom trom

pas de quoi pas quoi pas
d'éléments généraux reculants
génereuse au fond des abîmes intentionnés
pas de sublimes économies pas
de régularités absurdes constituées
pas d'idéalisations hybrides pas de quoi
et alors

[dia]thèmes sur l'air adhaesit anima, vivicafi secundum

8 deum deum deum dixit
mais rien ne prouvant que

a dit le a dit que le préêtre romon
pour égorger la pierre[re]
oxidïane sous la lune dernière
la pépêtre va tromber trom trom

ah bien, bien bien, ça
la laimière coule des mamelles
du soprano Dodoro telles
telles que: « no! non erubescam!
cur erubescitis ? » elle
chanchantait voix vive fanatisme

et ce n'est pas ce que je crois que ce ne soit pas
pas parce que les lions fébricitants à Mycène
ont changé ses accents ses couleurs ses temps!
ont changé: « deus dixit
non erubescam! cur erube
scitis ? » flâneurs bien élevés,
faquirs fatalistes, dénoncez

et la flumvière coule des veines
des mamelles du soprano
sur les néophites obstrués
par l'hygiène sucrementale
des sexes des vieux-cesexes

ah bien, bien bien, ça
la laimière coule des mamelles
du soprano Dodoro telles
telles que: « no! non erubescam!
cur erubescitis ? » elle
chanchantait voix vive fanatisme

et ce n'est pas ce que je crois que ce ne soit pas
pas parce que les lions fébricitants à Mycène
ont changé ses accents ses couleurs ses temps!
ont changé: « deus dixit
non erubescam! cur erube
scitis ? » flâneurs bien élevés,
faquirs fatalistes, dénoncez

et la flumvière coule des veines
des mamelles du soprano
sur les néophites obstrués
par l'hygiène sucrementale
des sexes des vieux-cesexes

9 desires between powers and quiet

if here he known
if flames down

all white you when future speak
all white with smell
all white legitimate confusion people
all white thoughts
all white singing
all is cause of movement of
all white herself and

a line agonize on the earth and
a flame too agonize on the
a poem only recognize upon limb
of white airless
of no-air

9 desires between powers and quiet

if here he known
if flames down

all white you when future speak
all white with smell
all white legitimate confusion people
all white thoughts
all white singing
all is cause of movement of
all white herself and

a line agonize on the earth and
a flame too agonize on the
a poem only recognize upon limb
of white airless
of no-air

e pigro segno delle sonore agonie il tardo
separare sé da sé e udir fina
marmorea onda e nebbia delle partizioni
straniere e dolce fiamma inglese o beduina.

[dia]thèmes sur l'air adhaesit anima, vivicafi secundum

Il panico spoglio degli dèi dell'acqua di tutti i giorni
delle pietre del cemento dei pensieri dei pozzi dei rioni
della velocità non sai mai se dove si comincia
e se dove si finisce è ora e dove la prudenza
è come una lettera cancellata dalla lunga pioggia
fine, e la cavi di saccoccia e ti viene la follia,

come pezzi sudici di richieste confidate a venti
persone senza leggerezza senza rimorsi autentici
accomiatandosi affezionatamente, e non giova
a gran che il sussidio dalle comunità, e c'è chi piange
irresistibilmente, e chi è di leva e non ci vuole
andare, e la zingara intanto legge chi sa cosa
sulla mano trasandata in via Lombardia a Roma

and lazy sign of sonorous agonies the slow
separation of self from self and hearing
fine marble wave and fog of foreign
partitions and sweet english or bedouin flame.

[dia]thèmes sur l'air adhaesit anima, vivicafi secundum

the bare panic of everyday water gods
of stones cement thoughts wells districts
of speed and you never know if where you start
and where you finish is now and where caution
is like a letter erased by a long thin rain,
and you pull it from your pocket and madness sets in,

like filthy scraps of demands entrusted to twenty
people without levity without genuine remorse
affectionately taking leave, and there's no real
benefit in subsidy from communities, and a few cry
irresistibly, and others are drafted and don't want
to go, and meanwhile the gypsy reads who knows what
on the unkempt hand on via Lombardia in Rome

sulla mano vecchie anatomie civilizzate
o nomadi, cadute in avaria, o stravaganti
diagrammi di allegorie sentimentali per maramaglia,
o come sillabe ribattute da cicale palestinesi,
o di prudenza casalinghe, di mortali
delicatezze, o forsennate eleganze
che abitano qui in questi paraggi, e irritazioni

da sconcio madrigale tutto istintivo, tassativo
anzi, e cortesie mostruose; e rudimentali, proprio
appena appena in punta, divinazioni, e miracoli
a bellapposta esagerati senza sentimento, tutti
in un pettine di nailon per pudicizie; e curiose
fiabe morali da ripassare al tempo
futuro o condizionale, tra forbice trinciapolli

e bulloni di turbìne seminati e tiranti e sestanti
e madreviti e reperti preistorici d'arte vasaria; e
dipinte un po' per tutto a scie fosforiche le tenebre
dei galli dei passeri e delle bisce e raffiche
di porpora, la vaniglia di ossa bianche e polpe

on the hand ancient anatomies civilized
or nomadic, fallen in disrepair, or extravagant
diagrams of sentimental allegories for riff-raff,
or as syllables hammered by Palestinian cicadas,
or of domestic caution, mortal
tenderness, or furious elegance
that live around here, and irritations

from indecent madrigals, all instinctive, better yet
binding, and monstrous civilities; and rudimentary, right there
just barely on the tip, divinations, and miracles
purposefully exaggerated and without feeling, all
in a nylon comb fit for modesty; and curious
moral fables to be reviewed either in the future
or the conditional, between poultry shears

and sown turbine bolts and ties and sextants
and nuts and prehistoric findings of pottery art; and
painted a bit everywhere in phosphoric wakes the darkness
of roosters of sparrows and garden snakes and bursts
of purple, the vanilla of white bones and the flesh

di brina e architetture di zucchero frantumano
orizzonti promiscui meccanici vegetali come un filo
unico di refe in attese di profetiche gare e di un ozio
colorito, familiare, ospitale, volante, salato.

Oh, filo di refe perduto dalla sottana zingara
pronuncia in pubblico il morso pio, rituale,
della corrosione liturgica, della quotidiana
ma quotidiana redenzione, e togli di dosso
al mondo rionale il tempo, come togli
la camicia a un bambino dopo la cerimonia.

II en rims ki se inkaval
com li jest del Destin
second li numbrs da rot astral
ki immen dus animal

eu te dic en son latin
rent el sangr di longbard
comt el cor de bastard
ma el penser di omnadge fin:

of frost and sugar architectures shatter
promiscuous mechanical vegetable horizons like one unbroken
string of twine waiting for prophetic contests and a colorful,
familiar, hospitable, flying, salty idleness.

Oh, string of twine fallen from the gypsy's slip
declaim in public the pious, ritual morsel
of liturgical corrosion, of the quotidian
yet quotidian redemption, and remove time
from the back of the local world, as you
remove a child's shirt after the ceremony.

II

en rims ki se inkaval
com li jest del Destin
second li numbrs da rot astral
ki immen dus animal

eu te dic en son latin
rent el sangr di longbard
comt el cor de bastard
ma el penser di omnadge fin:

O mi durce auta proi
de li forests d'obscur
o surce di tuts li foil
u ti te a mis l'endroi

e u ti regard li entroil
ki es, por favor, ki t'enjoi?
ki es ki t'ennoi?
ki es de li stels pur

au tems di l'eklyps permanent
de jorn e de not, ki es

ki assí t'envoi gyrant li vent
de a rot? oh, pra long la long voi.
oh, prec, sis bem pruvdent,
oh, escort, prec, la vois

ternant li secrements
de la loi talian e de li sents
di l'eidogram gypzian ki kalm
s'esnud en l'auratge di man!

O mi durce auta proi
de li forests d'obscur
o surce di tuts li foil
u ti te a mis l'endroi

e u ti regard li entroil
ki es, por favor, ki t'enjoi?
ki es ki t'ennoi?
ki es de li stels pur

au tems di l'eklyps permanent
de jorn e de not, ki es

ki assí t'envoi gyrant li vent
de a rot? oh, pra long la long voi.
oh, prec, sis bem pruvdent,
oh, escort, prec, la vois

ternant li secrements
de la loi talian e de li sents
di l'eidogram gypzian ki kalm
s'esnud en l'auratge di man!

Va donc a man partadger
a solitud drent li verger:

escort donc unit li animal provenzan
e espet un cor cristian genial,
o mi durce proi, o natal
de a fol deman, jornad de mat;

eu mir de longtems ni fait
ni desfait el mi pais dinans,
en so projet offis, e eu pans
el son outradge e a desesprans.

in rime che si accavallano
come i gettiti del Destino
secondo i numeri della ruota astrale
cui trascinano i due animali

io ti dico in suono latino,
così simile al sangue lombardo,
e con cuore di bastardo
ma con pensiero di fine umanità:

Va donc a man partadger
a solitud drent li verger:

escort donc unit li animal provenzan
e espet un cor cristian genial,
o mi durce proi, o natal
de a fol deman, jornad de mat;

eu mir de longtems ni fait
ni desfait el mi pais dinans,
en so projet offis, e eu pans
el son outradge e a desesprans.

in rhymes that pile up
like the revenue of Destiny
according to the numbers on the astral wheel
where they drag the two animals

I'll tell you in Latin sound,
so similar to Lombard blood,
and with a bastard heart
but with thought of fine humanity:

o mia dolce alta preda
delle foreste di oscurità
o sorgente di tutte le foglie
dove tu hai posto il tuo recapito

e dove custodisci le viscere labirintiche,
chi è, per favore, che ti diletta?
chi è che ti annoia?
quale delle stelle pure

al tempo delle eclissi permanenti
di giorno e di notte, chi è

che così qui ti manda, facendo girare i venti
della ruota? oh, lungo la lunga vita,
oh, ti prego, sii assai previdente!
oh, ascolta, prego, la voce

che eterna i giuramenti
della legge e dei significati
dell'ideogramma tzigano, che calmo
si denuda sulla bufera delle mani!

oh my sweet high prey
of the forests of obscurity
oh source of all the leaves
where you established residence

and where you guard the labyrinthine viscera,
who is it, please, that delights you?
who is it that annoys you?
which of the pure stars

at the time of permanent eclipses,
day and at night, who is it

that sends you here like this, causing the winds
of the wheel to turn? oh, along your long life,
oh, I beg you, be extremely cautious!
oh please listen to the voice

that eternalizes the oaths
of the law and meanings
of the Tzigane ideogram, that calmly
undresses on the storm of hands!

ora la mano va a frazionare
la solitudine dentro le verziere:

ascolta, dunque, uniti gli animali provenzali
e attendi un cuore cristiano geniale,
o mia dolce preda, che nasci
dal folle domani, una giornata da matti;

io guardo da lontano il mio paese
ancora né fatto né disfatto,
offeso nel suo avvenire, e io penso
il suo oltraggio, e la disperazione.

12

Collima, dico, lo schema con l'essenza? e il dominio
con le leggi dell'essenza? e l'essenza medesima
con la molta fronte del tempo? Tutto, dico,

che hai fatto sparire una volta e una volta
nel gioco degli occhi labili è? idea soltanto
sarebbe? per esempio, dico:

Now the hand moves to fracture
the solitude inside the verdure:

listen, then, once united the Provençal animals
and wait for a genial Christian heart,
oh my sweet prey, born
of tomorrow's madness, a crazy day;

I look at my country from afar
still neither done nor undone,
offended in its future, and I think
its offense, and desperation.

12 I say does the design match the essence? and the power
the laws of essence? and the essence itself
the vast brow of time? Everything, I say,

that you made disappear once and once
in the game of transient eyes is? Could it be
just an idea? for example, I say:

tra l'occhio e il lacero fondo
delle trame è una miniera, corre
tra l'occhio e il malocchio, corre

e lavora il futuro delle forze
intimissime, il ragionare prodigioso,
il mutamento; e la fonte dei barlumi

indugia con le sottrazioni irrimediabili.
Oh, avara ipocrisia, menda originale, prèdica
l'uovo bianco alto come la luna, il puro

Zero aumentato dal silenzio, dal genio
imperituro della catastrofe e della nudità!
Consci? collima? indugia, dico?

Guarda, allora: non l'iride cornea,
non forse nemmeno il cristallo ialino,
disco eccentrico della crisalide, ma l'occhio

between the eye and the torn bottom
of the weft is a mine, it runs
between the eye and the evil-eye, runs

and works the future of the most intimate
forces, the prodigious reasoning,
the mutation; and the source of glimmers

lingers with the inescapable subtractions.
Oh, miserly hypocrisy, original fault, preach
the white egg high as the moon the pure

Zero increased by silence, by the everlasting
genius of catastrophe and nudity!
Do you know? Does it match? I say, does it linger?

Look, then: not the corneal iris,
and maybe not even the hyaline crystal,
eccentric disc of the chrysalis, but the eye

l'occhio-bruco, l'occhio-verme,
l'occhio-larva, l'acropoli-farfalla, e il suono
delle cavallette impenitenti dal tempo del deserto!

Generosa inutilità, generosa, dunque,
generosissima ipocrisia, pesa il grado
di imminenza, il sapore dello stile

pratico, le arterie numerate una a una,
la batteria, la tepida fontana dei gas, e la caduta
obliqua immortale degli atomi sul fondo uniforme.

Ululavano monosillabi ossificati, sillabe
plurali al cloro, e mascelle-caverne,
e le meningi esorbitanti di curiosità:

c'è un oceano ignoto, e di colore, in qualche modo,
molto chiaro? e sentenze e nascite e precipizi
di luce, e doni capricciosi, e gorgheggi aerati

the grub-eye, the worm-eye,
the larva-eye, the acropolis-butterfly, and the sound
of the grasshoppers impenitent since the days of the desert!

Generous uselessness, generous, therefore,
the most generous hypocrisy, the degree
of imminence weighs, the taste of practical

style, the arteries numbered one by one,
the battery, the tepid fountain of gases, and the oblique
immortal fall of atoms against a uniform backdrop.

They howled ossified monosyllables, plural
chlorine syllables, and cavern-jaws,
and the meninges exorbitant with curiosity:

is there an unknown ocean that, in color, is
somewhat clear? and rulings and births and cliffs
of light, and capricious gifts, and aerated warbles

di balsami venerei, e spazi gelosi
di salsa, vigili, flessibili? dunque:
collima lo schema? l'essenza? Guarda

ancora: scenario larvale di estasi liquide,
acidità del pensiero spento, zootipico, questo
possiedi a essere solo nel possesso. Essere

solo a possedere ciò che si possiede, cosa
possiamo utilizzare? povero patrimonio
arcaico delle cose, degli utensili, decente

simbolo delle rassegnazioni e dei legami!
Sono di tutti i sassi? saranno, dico,
di qualcuno. I sassi? amano in silenzio

il silenzio. I sassi strutturano il sibilo
e la traiettoria. I sassi quanti secoli
vincolano dentro? e non piangono, non

of venereal ointments, and jealous, vigilant,
flexible spaces of sauce? therefore:
does the design match? the essence? Look

again: larval scenario of liquid ecstasies,
acidity of snuffed thought, zootypical, if you're
the only owner that's what you own.

Being the only one to own what you own,
what can you use? poor archaic patrimony
of things, of utensils, decent

symbol of resignations and ties! Do
stones belong to all? I say they must
belong to someone. The stones? they love silence

in silence. Stones structure the hiss
and the trajectory. How many centuries
do stones bind? and they never cry,

sanguinano: sposano l'ombra, la ripudiano,
sposano il vento, la forza, la calma, tutto...
forse le leggi umane sono di sasso?

I sassi sono dure leggi sul terreno
e nell'aria e dopo conquistati i sassi, qui
comincia la pesca universale...

pesca la luna nel fosso col rastrello, mano
saggia avida svelta, e che lunone! quello
delle grandi nottate popolari e delle nebbie

grigie nel cuore unico del pipistrello,
degli innamorati nei giardini comunali,
o forse il lunone dei pozzi dei gatti dei fossi?

o quello dei fuochisti e macchinisti,
o delle maree? o quello di quella sera
dentro il bicchiere della grappa e a fil di tetto?

never bleed: they marry the shade, and disown it,
they marry the wind, the force, the calm, everything...
could human laws be made of stone?

Stones are harsh laws on the terrain
and in the air and after conquering the stones,
the universal fishing begins here...

fish the moon in the ditch with the rake,
quick wise eager hand, and what a moon! that
of the great popular nights and the grey

fog in the unique heart of the bat,
of the lovers in public gardens,
or maybe the big moon of the well of cats of ditches?

or that of the stokers and engineers,
of tides? or that of that evening
in the glass of grappa and at roof level?

o quello di Venezia, del cinematografo,
o, se di sangue, quello dentro i teschi
letterari o riflessa negli spettrogrammi e trema

sulle corna insonni dei caprioli? o quello
sui rapidi senza patria e senza numeri
inchiodati al casello di frontiera tra la neve?

o sui lucenti calcari di cattedrali
cui le formiche spianano e trapanano
le sementi d'erba gramigna, oppure

quello sentimentale nei cuori ermetici
dei guerrieri e dei guerrafondai?
O luna eccellente, certo, l'essenza collima …

e soffia l'ignara polvere del tuo sorriso
verso l'aldilà di ogni futuro, oltre ogni
dove ultimo il tempo futuro sparisce,

or that of Venice, of the cinema,
or, if a bloody one, the one inside literary skulls
or reflected in the spectrograms and does it tremble

over the sleepless horns of roe deer? or the one
over the express without a country or numbers
nailed to the signal booth at the border in the snow?

or over the shiny limestone of cathedrals
that ants flatten and drill through
with seeds of bermuda grass, or else

the sentimental one in the hermetic hearts
of warriors and warmongers?
Oh excellent moon, sure, the essence matches...

and blows the unsuspecting dust of your smile
toward the other side of every future, beyond
the place where the last future disappears,

e l'idolo di Amorgo sullo stelo
inflessibile nell'amoroso inganno scruta
l'essenza di una incredibile vela, e c'è,

dico, nei seni inviolati oltre ogni tempo
futuro, lo squarcio dove l'ignara polvere
del tuo sorriso corre grida e posa

senza decrescere più? è un grano, solo
un grano di frumento rubato a staia
infinite di pula in tutto l'energico

universo: e a ricercarlo per la prodiga
eternità tu cercherai: lo troverai quando
il caldo rumore dei tempi vuoti si smorza.

13 [dia]thèmes sur l'air adhaesit anima, vivicafi secundum

nous a confié l'instar du verbum dans un prisme [or]oral
era un polpo armoniastico, un archetipo deliberato nel tema
della calcificazione 1° les gencives orageuses

and the idol of Amorgos on the unbending
stalk in the amorous deceit stares at
the essence of an incredible sail, and I say,

is there, in the untouched breasts beyond every
future time, a break where the unsuspecting dust
of your smile runs screams and settles

without decreasing further? it's a grain, merely
a grain of wheat stolen from endless
bushels of chaff across the energetic

universe: and if you search for it you'll search
though a prodigal eternity: you'll find it when
the warm noise of empty time subsides.

13 [dia]thèmes sur l'air adhaesit anima, vivicafi secundum

nous a confié l'instar du verbum dans un prisme [or]oral
it was a harmoniastic octopus, a deliberate archetype in the theme
of calcification 1° les gencives orageuses

et les lèvres ombrageuses
in italiano: plessi contorni rabeschi cimose cornici
profili trafilati moreschi bugnanti rosoni ecc. ecc.

2° les grandes incertitudes appliquées sur l'im-
minence séduite du sperme-gauche

idest 3° la fin raisonnée des mots-machine-came-
carambole-hypothème à serrure mi-raison

alors pourpar l'émotion raisonnée l'organsme
outre le journuit outre la vérité qui tomba
sous l'hégémonie de la perception, et donc

onomatéveillez : a) le chaos (χ)
b) la vélocité négative (-v) c) l'énergie négative,
c.à.d. qui est qui est le quiète le avant le repos (-j)
d) la lumière négative |et| qui n'est ni l'aurore ni
l'obscur ni la soif ni l'éclat ni la plaie ni

et les lèvres ombrageuses
in Italian: plexus sides arabesques selvages frames
profiles *trafilati* moorish ashlars rosettes etc. etc.

2° les grandes incertitudes appliquées sur l'im-
minence séduite du sperme-gauche

idest 3° la fin raisonnée des mots-machine-came-
carambole-hypothème à serrure mi-raison

alors pourpar l'émotion raisonnée l'organsme
outre le journuit outre la vérité qui tomba
sous l'hégémonie de la perception, et donc

onomatéveillez : a) le chaos (χ)
b) la vélocité négative (-v) c) l'énergie négative,
c.à.d. qui est qui est le quiète le avant le repos (-j)
d) la lumière négative |et| qui n'est ni l'aurore ni
l'obscur ni la soif ni l'éclat ni la plaie ni

subdivisez, pour amuser Einstein, la masse incidentelle
occidentelle
excidentelle
accidentelle

agacez la hiérarchie mécanique [et] déhiscente
des chaos assemblés
comme qui
les turbines et les bielles et les cames
c.à.d. *e l'è bel e l'è bun e l'è gram*
e l'è gram cume un cural
viva la machina del gias artificial

l'éternité commestible / avec qui qui / avec am
les chances de l'improbable absolu [-t]
le thème du tempstemps [$-t^{-t}$] et la cendre
eructée de vertèbres méphitophéliques $\begin{vmatrix} t^t \\ h \end{vmatrix}$

on arrache les envergures secrètes des espaces
des futures enventures

subdivisez, pour amuser Einstein, la masse incidentelle
occidentelle
excidentelle
accidentelle

agacez la hiérarchie mécanique [et] déhiscente
des chaos assemblés
comme qui
les turbines et les bielles et les cames
c.à.d. *e l'è bel e l'è bun e l'è gram*
e l'è gram cume un cural
viva la machina del gias artificial

l'éternité commestible / avec qui qui / avec am
les chances de l'improbable absolu [-t]
le thème du tempstemps [$-t^{-t}$] et la cendre
eructée de vertèbres méphitophéliques $\begin{vmatrix} t^t \\ h \end{vmatrix}$

on arrache les envergures secrètes des espaces
des futures enventures

parcourir les tunnels ananalyser les éponges urbenistes

pincer les shrapnells enterrés
entraîner *sur les bancs du noir du zéro* tous
les monstres — rameaux du blafard
explosoisifs trironiques engendrés par l'illustre
communion des communions des gros sexes anonymes et
tous les sexes de genre x y z... n... et
de genregenre -x -y -z... -n et!

oh là là! chaosagète bascogne!

chaosagète bascogne — ouestgond
guascogne — vache blonde
gascoke — quartz de gomme
euzkon-con — gouache chome
euzkara — oeufs de gland
hache de sonde
culdequelconque
bascule oignon
arche de carogne

les scories

parcourir les tunnels ananalyser les éponges urbenistes

pincer les shrapnells enterrés
entraîner *sur les bancs du noir du zéro* tous
les monstres — rameaux du blafard
explosoisifs trironiques engendrés par l'illustre
communion des communions des gros sexes anonymes et
tous les sexes de genre x y z… n… et
de genregenre -x -y -z… -n et!

oh là là! chaosagète bascogne!

chaosagète bascogne
guascogne
gascoke
euzkon-con
euzkara

ouestgond
vache blonde
quartz de gomme
gouache chome
oeufs de gland
hache de sonde
culdequelconque
bascule oignon
arche de carogne

les scories

de noir oxhydriques chlorhydriques
noirmère noirpère noirfou noirsuie
noirnue noirnoyau noirpluie
noirsoit noirsouffle noirsoul
noirneige noirsuitefuite noirnul

nous sûmes vraiment décider la science-mensonge
rhapsodique, l'eidoloyatrie-convulsive
moi conconnaît les crucruthèmes bifides
        les mythèmêmes trifides
        les blasphèmes fifides
        la pantomême infide

et le fourchettes catapulte charrue aéromètre boomerang
tomahawk CGE, RKO, cetera

        les morphèmes vi-vides
        les théorhèmes avides
        les myephèmes midides

de noir oxhydriques chlorhydriques
noirmère noirpère noirfou noirsuie
noirnue noirnoyau noirpluie
noirsoit noirsouffle noirsoul
noirneige noirsuitefuite noirnul

nous sûmes vraiment décider la science-mensonge
rhapsodique, l'eidoloyatrie-convulsive
moi conconnaît les crucruthèmes bifides
          les mythèmêmes trifides
          les blasphèmes fifides
          la pantomême infide

et le fourchettes catapulte charrue aéromètre boomerang
tomahawk CGE, RKO, cetera

          les morphèmes vi-vides
          les théorhèmes avides
          les myephèmes midides

les choeurs épiquedermiques
du steatopyge
du mélampyge
du yacintopyge
du leucopyge

pyge pyge pyge sur les épaves rohoeurpyge
noirnoir des voixons subtilisées
jusqu'au NUL qui est bien l'outre ou l'autre

il faut donc: tautomatiser l'essentiel du chaos par des siens
par d'hyperseinsthèmes entrouverts
par des fonctions perdûment inattendues
par des mappes aurraurales
par des axes floraisons
au fond de la pluie grise de la protosensitivity
(frappe à l'intérieure antérieure de la matière)

par des axes figurals par des saxes ensemencés
par des sexes homogéneisés par des astrolabes
récitales par des doigts par des stygmates

les choeurs épiquedermiques
du   stéatopyge
  du   mélampyge
    du   yacintopyge
      du   leucopyge

pyge pyge pyge sur les épaves rohoeurpyge
noirnoir des voixons subtilisées
jusqu'au NUL qui est bien l'outre ou l'autre

il faut donc: tautomatiser l'essentiel du chaos par des siens
par d' hyperseinsthèmes entrouverts
par des fonctions perdûment inattendues
par des mappes aurraurales
par des axes floraisons
au fond de la pluie grise de la protosensitivity
(frappe à l'intérieure antérieure de la matière)

par des axes figurals par des saxes ensemencés
par des sexes homogéneisés par des astrolabes
récitales par des doigts par des stygmates

minérales par des dagues par des excès numerals
par des dès par des itérations germinales par des plaies

par descendre des scories des épaves d'horizon
à la puissance *n* à l'ancienne inquiétude olive
des expertises pures aux vectors maximums!

dans le ruine dans le gel dans le grande bagarre
du grand tour entre nacre et ardoise
révéillons sous les portes blondes les daleths
multipiés de lithium en hélice, corpus-noise,
par ex-simple

le matin répandait sa fraîcheur gothique
sur le entures, mes amies
fidèles étant toutes attentives, ensevelies

dans le fémur d'Apollon
je ne pouvais pas les exciter par les doigts
ni par les dès vifs

minérales par des dagues par des excès numerals
par des dès par des itérations germinales par des plaies

par descendre des scories des épaves d'horizon
à la puissance *n* à l'ancienne inquiétude olive
des expertises pures aux vectors maximums!

dans le ruine dans le gel dans le grande bagarre
du grand tour entre nacre et ardoise
révéillons sous les portes blondes les daleths
multipiés de lithium en hélice, corpus-noise,
par ex-simple

le matin répandait sa fraîcheur gothique
sur le entures, mes amies
fidèles étant toutes attentives, ensevelies

dans le fémur d'Apollon
je ne pouvais pas les exciter par les doigts
ni par les dès vifs

il faut dinciser le code, donc, à *n* (haine)
impulsion très égales
pour saisir les cendres les scories les épaves
du grand cliché négatif corpus noir
des grandes issues roulantes!

inventer   attendre   échouer

la flèche toujours interrompue
                par la cendres
                par les encidentrails exléctriques
                et scories
                magnétiquestiques
tique tyché corpus noir
(rovina, e mai udito anima più profonda di un profondo
popolo mentre va in rovina)

la guêpe zigzaguante effrayant corpus noir
                    englouti pourpar la marveille
                    le solsoleil-perdrix dans-dans le blé blond

il faut dinciser le code, donc, à *n* (haine)
impulsion très égales
pour saisir les cendres les scories les épaves
du grand cliché négatif corpus noir
des grandes issues roulantes!

inventer   attendre   échouer

la flèche toujours interrompue
                par la cendres
                par les encidentrails exléctriques
                et scories
                magnétiquestiques
tique tyché corpus noir
(ruins, and never heard a soul deeper than a deep
population as it goes to ruin)

la guêpe zigzaguante effrayant corpus noir
                    englouti pourpar la marveille
                    le solsoleil-perdrix dans-dans le blé blond

le pornophème sépulcral s'exhalant sex-haleine
sur la dioriteurite en fleur
le choeur-araignée
sur les ailes des logis cinématiquestiques
tique tyché / tyché croque-mitaine

jusqu'à ce que l'unité l'émotionelle soit reduite
à la mesure d'un biblionème de poil de trou de cul

de guêpe zigzaguante sur l'épi

il faut diviser ébranler diminuer le nul dans le nul
et ainsi soit-il voilà la formule:

$$! = \frac{\text{dérisoire}}{\text{inébranlable}} = \frac{\chi(\chi - 1)}{2^{-h}} = !$$

le pornophème sépulcral s'exhalant sex-haleine
                    sur la dioriteurite en fleur
                    le choeur-araignée
                    sur les ailes des logis cinématiquestiques
                    tique tyché / tyché croque-mitaine

jusqu'à ce que l'unité l'émotionelle soit reduite
à la mesure d'un biblionème de poil de trou de cul

de guêpe zigzaguante sur l'épi

il faut diviser ébranler diminuer le nul dans le nul
et ainsi soit-il   voilà la formule:

$$! = \frac{\text{dérisoire}}{\text{inébranlable}} = \frac{\chi(\chi - 1)}{2^{-h}} = !$$

14 prati erbe terremoti ecc. tutto come una volta
come di tutti ecc. gragnuole e stoppie
dove vanno a smorzarsi le mattine delle dita
rosa, e l'inumidiscono arti vizzi che si sfanno
o adolescenti o mezzo e mezzo, *quinto dato ricevü*
quindes donn fan quindes cü, e verde: *'verde que'*
verde que yo e nel concime secco e sfuso

y yo quiero rojo, y muslos para el lumbre
y pájaros de besos y nombres de pájaros
de besos y medidas de pájaros de besos
y medidas de pájaros de besos de brisas, ah
que yo qiuero, sui prati, ai cavalcavia, lungo
le scarpate, dove uno sottilizza a voce: uccidere
vangare trebbiare tribolare e tutto
il vocabolario popolare a dirotto
parmi la jeunesse des écoles générales (mi pare)

dove si tirano su di scatto alti 12 m. nel lattime
della nebbia non conclusa, confidenziale, nel catalogo
delle opere umane scheletri di pesci di ferro coi bulloni,
e le vene di rame, *ah que quiero*, dell'alta tensione

14 fields herbs earthquakes etc. everything as it was
as it was for everyone etc. stubble and barrages
where rosy-red finger mornings go to subside,
and are dampened by dry limbs falling to pieces
or adolescents or half and half, *quinto dato ricevü*
quindes donn fan quindes cü, and green: *'verde que'* 16
verde que yo and in dry fertilizer in bulk 17

y yo quiero rojo, y muslos para el lumbre
y pájaros de besos y nombres de pájaros
de besos y medidas de pájaros de besos
y medidas de pájaros de besos de brisas, ah
que yo qiuero, in the meadows, along the overpasses, and
the embankments, where someone quibbles out loud:
kill dig thresh suffer and the entire
popular vocabulary in a downpour
parmi la jeunesse des écoles générales (I'd say)

where they suddenly stand 12 m. high in the milk crust
of the confidential unconcluded fog, in the catalog
of human works, skeletons of iron fish with bolts,
and copper veins, *ah que quiero*, of power lines

e dichiarato infine, molto solennemente, che *l'amore*
e farem come fa il pesce, l'amor senza mutande
non lo farem mai più, a quell'epoca tutti si udiva
allora per un intimo dovere estremamente naturale
l'oscuro sangue socratico in battaglia nelle arterie
dei passeri e nei numeri allarmati, e insieme
una lama di temperino arrugginita dentro una buca,
o una falce, e pezzi di cingoli e zoccoli paesani

ah, que yo quiero verde y rojo, pandispagna!

e nei recessi zenitali una sillaba sola
radiofonica, e nel vocabolario impensato
del sasso lì, o nella freccia del clakson
che riga di zuccherini il ventre fottuto dei celesti
smagli sopra la nuca, o sulle rotte
ortogonali, sull'analisi cocciuta di un cono
dinamico, come una grazia antiquata ma geniale l'idea
dei seni italiani celebra la presenza e la consuma

and in the end they declared, rather solemnly, that *l'amore*
e farem come fa il pesce, l'amor senza mutande
non lo farem mai più, at that time everyone heard 18
then out of a very natural intimate obligation
the obscure Socratic blood battling in the arteries
of sparrows and alarmed numbers, together with
the rusty blade of a pocket knife in a hole,
or a scythe, and pieces of tracks and farmer's clogs

ah, que yo quiero verde y rojo, sponge cake! 19

and in the zenithal recesses a lone radiophonic
syllable, and in the unthought vocabulary
of that stone there, or in the arrow of the car horn
that scratches with candy the goddamn womb of celestial
snags above the nape, or on the orthogonal
routes, on the stubborn analysis of a dynamic
cone, just like an antiquated but brilliant grace the idea
of Italian breasts celebrates the presence and consumes it

Dico de te, Ytalya subjecta, dico
de te, smorto ambiente soleggiato,
turistico, schiava delle terre, gente
scarsa, gente acerba, e antico sobrio
tenore in ogni ceto, in ogni sesso, in ogni
senso, discreto. E lampaneggi folgorati di mica
e baleni dei zigzag o melograna o spiga

o punta di segala d'avena a spinapesce
loglio ortica per natiche nel giorno dell'obbrobrio
che cresce gramigna zizzania e carestia aprica

verso l'ora che cade una certa quale cartilagine d'ora scabrosa

vennero lo strepito e il concerto e l'ira delle trombe negre

e della mucca nei reconditi ronfi della latteria

sotterranea, e lo scompiglio meteorologico nella segatura

bagnata come un pulcino,

e un solo spirito

Dico de te, Ytalya subjecta, dico
de te, sickly sunny environment,
touristy, slave of nations, scant
people, unripe people, and ancient sober
tone in every class, in every gender, in every
sense, discreet. And shimmering bursts of mica
and zigzag flashes or pomegranates or ear

or tip of rye of oat in a herringbone pattern
barley nettle for buttocks in the day of mounting
opprobrium bermuda darnel and sunny famine

around the time some sort of cartilage from a scabrous time falls
came the clamor and concert and the wrath of the black trumpets
and cows in the hidden snores of the subterranean
dairy, and meteorological discord in the sawdust
soaked to the bone,
and a single triune

trino quanto un gancio ruggine di minaccia ebbe
a quell'ora possesso dell'ora nel mulinello gigante
dei gusci d'arachidi, come di una legione perduta in trasferta
e solenne delle sue armi preistoriche, degli scudi di corame
ringhiosi, delle derrate, del tabacco, dei registri di fureria,
dei flebili scudisci all'ombra dei temporali, degli ordigni
igienico-sessuali, dei molari profondi e cariati, delle ginocchia
divaricate e petti in fuori come i rubinetti di latte,

o pioppe

d'argento a cresta in ripa del torrente, contorti per tutta
la distesa vergata sui catasti, e sollevò alfine
la sua danza vitrea, e leccò levigò pazientemente quindi
il rilievo dei tuoni in toppe smorte come muscoli
disarticolati, allergici, sulle essenze, e trepidò
razzolando solitaria e pensosa a un brindisi
e in crescendo danzò la pazza gallina accidentale fino
al quindici gradino della noia fantastica, e poi più

spirit like a rusty hook of threats at that time
took possession of the time in the gigantic whirlpool
of peanut shells, like a legion lost in transit
solemn about its prehistoric weapons, its shields of snarling
leather, supplies, tobacco, the quartermaster's ledgers,
feeble whips in the shade of storms, hygienic-sexual
explosives, deep and cavitary molars, knees
spread and chests puffed like milk faucets,

or silver

poplars crested along the stream, twisted across the entire
expanse written by hand on land registers, and at last it lifted
its glassy dance, and patiently it licked and thus polished
the relief of thunders in dull patches like disjointed,
allergic muscles on the essences, and it fluttered
rummaging pensive in solitude about a toast
and the accidental crazy hen danced in crescendo up to
step fifteen of the fantastic boredom, and then more

16 matter and egg eyes
and egg eyes jewels and
crammings egg eyes jewels and
+ greatful dark drive VIRUS +
and old VIRUS as infinitive eyes =
as Select Souls in dwelling of
of WEST MATTER WEST HIGH WEST
as old Furies of the Philosophy
of the Socratic Hope and Surplus
with greatful Night's Pole in the lung
of a mad horse
and instantaneous VIRUS
and sky of the GREAT VIRUS

16 matter and egg eyes
and egg eyes jewels and
crammings egg eyes jewels and
+ greatful dark drive VIRUS +
and old VIRUS as infinitive eyes =
as Select Souls in dwelling of
of WEST MATTER WEST HIGH WEST
as old Furies of the Philosophy
of the Socratic Hope and Surplus
with greatful Night's Pole in the lung
of a mad horse
and instantaneous VIRUS
and sky of the GREAT VIRUS

17 ecco ecco ecco
ecco
ecco
da un panoramico scrimolo
urbano vedi spirito meridiano boccheggia di concerti d'ampie
giurisdizioni di evangeliche collisioni che leccano gli stipiti e i minimi
orli del silenzio a bocca spalancata e dopo finalmente
sulle tavolate lavagne scranni troni stalli sgabelli chaises longues la
miscelata fioritura della mentalità corrente e il geniale
e scombinato giuoco dei gradini delle raffiche degli elenchi
telefonici dei prezzi calmieri dei cartelloni pubblicitari e l'aria,
poi, ECCO, l'aria nelle sillabe di un'ottava di Torquato
al Gianicolo, oh, ecco, questa sì, e nulla
ecco
ecco
scivola più nella gran voce universa alla disperata, tranne
la breve cara voce dei poeti d'Italia, Alfonso Gatto, o
quella di Montale, di Sandrino pederasta, breve fischio
in statu erecto, e nulla è rivelato se non la conchiglia arida
di riflessi vocali e il sommo vestibolo di acido carbonico originale

17 there there there
there
there
from a panoramic urban
ridge you see meridian spirit gasp with concerts with ample
jurisdictions with evangelical collisions that lick the frames and the smallest
edges of silence with mouth wide open and after finally
on the tables planks high-back chairs thrones stalls stools chaise lounges the
blended flowering of the common mentality and the brilliant
and scrambled game of steps of flurries of telephone
books of ceiling prices of advertising billboards and the air,
then, THERE IT IS, the air in the syllables of Tarquato's octave 21
on the Gianicolo, oh, there it is, this yes, and nothing 22
there it is
there
slides anymore in the great universal voice in despair, except
the brief dear voice of Italian poets, Alfonso Gatto, or 23
that of Montale, of the pederast Sandrino, brief whistle 24, 25
in statu erecto, and nothing is revealed if not the arid shell
of vocal reflections and the loftiest vestibule of the original carbonic

della rivelazione, se tu abbandoni gli aneliti
e scendi al rischio mansueto di contare
uno per uno il numero geometrico della giacca
borghese, o crudele eroe matematico

ecco
e insieme allora in coro all'unisono insieme bene
tutti ecco si dice: ma cosa
c'è di irrivelato, di inevitabile
nella sufficienza, o nella differenza o
nella meraviglia toccante urgentissima dell'amico
Leonardo, o nell'attenzione, o in questo
ecco umano rovinoso parere? ecco

dal nulla al nulla, liquido tragitto,
bassorilievo d'acqua falsa, è l'inevitabile

acid of revelation, if you abandon the yearnings
and succumb to the tame risk of counting
one by one the geometric number of the bourgeois
coat, oh cruel mathematical hero

there it is
and together then in chorus in unison together good
everyone there it is let's say: but what's
there, of the unrevealed, of the inevitable
in the sufficiency, or in the difference or
in the touching most urgent marvel of our friend
Leonardo, or in the attention, or in this
there ruinous human opinion? there

from nothing to nothing, liquid stretch,
bas-relief of false water, it's the inevitable

17 *Variations on Themes Proposed for a Pure Phonetic Ideology*

1. The *Dies Irae* (Day of Wrath) is a 13th-century Latin hymn written by Thomas of Celano. Villa translated this work into Italian. See page 673 of the bibliography.
2. The *Enuma Elish* is the Babylonian creation myth, which Villa translated from the original Akkadian in 1939. See page 673 of the bibliography.
3. Villa also translated the first five books of the Hebrew Bible. See pages v–xiii of the introduction.
4. In the original, Villa plays on the word "piano" (floor). For example, he uses "primissimo piano," which besides meaning "first floor" is also the cinematic term for "close up." In the following line, he writes "secondo ripiano," which literally means "second shelf."
5. Milanese dialect, meaning *now that the light is dead the smoke remains.*
6. A *pianella* is a type of Italian pancake that can be either sweet or savory.
7. Milanese dialect, meaning *to the yoke those who tip their bowls.*
8. Most likely a reference to a popular song of the time, meaning *spring of every heart.*
9. "L'amatriciana" is a pasta sauce that takes its name from the city outside Rome. Although the recipe varies from city to city and from cook to cook, it is typically prepared with onions, pork jowl, wine, & tomatoes.
10. The *rilla* reference is unclear.

11. In English in the original. All further instances of Villa's own English will be signified in the translation with the typeface: "AaBbCc, Ee, Gg..."
12. Villa is playing on two Italian expressions for good luck: "In bocca al lupo" [In the mouth of the wolf] and "In culo alla balena" [In the ass of the whale], which are comparable to the English "Break a leg."
13. In Provençal, followed immediately by Villa's Italian translation in the original. His translation has been rendered into English.
14. For Amorgos, see note 1 to "Linguistics" on page 157.
15. A mix of French & Italian, meaning *she's beautiful, she's good, and she's big / she's big as a canal / long live the artificial gas car.*
16. Milanese dialect, meaning *fifth piece of info received fifteen women make' fifteen asses.*
17. *Verde que / verde que yo* is the first verse from Federico García Lorca's *Romance Sonambulo.* The Spanish that follows is Villa's elaboration on that poem.
18. A nonsensical Italian phrase, meaning *love and we'll do as the fish, love without underwear we'll never make it again,* possibly modeled after a nursery rhyme. We left it in Italian to maintain the same macaronic feel found in the original.
19. In Italian, *pandispagna* literally means "bread from Spain."
20. This is a highly Italianized Latin meaning "I say of you, Italy the subject, I say of you."

21. Torquato Tasso (1544–1595) was an Italian poet best known for his romance epic *Gerusalemme liberata* (*Jerusalem Delivered*, 1580).

22. The *Gianicolo* is a hill lying behind the neighborhood of Trastevere, in Rome. The entire city can be seen from Piazza Garibaldi, which is lined with marble busts of many famous Italians.

23. Alfonso Gatto (1909–1976) was a prominent member of the "Hermetic School" of Italian poets working in Florence during the 1930s and '40s. Villa contributed articles and reviews to the group's literary journal *Frontespizio*, as well as exchanged a handful of letters with its members regarding the possible publication of his early verse.

24. Eugenio Montale (1896–1981) was a widely popular 20th-century Italian poet, best known for his *Ossi di seppia* (*Cuttlefish Bones*, 1925).

25. Probably a reference to the Italian poet Sandro Penna (1906–1977), who, during the late thirties, collaborated with the same literary magazines — mainly *Letteratura* and *Frontespizio* — as Villa.

26. Villa is most likely referring to his contemporary poet, Leonardo Sinisgalli (1908–1981). In 1953 he founded the magazine *Civiltà delle macchine* and served as its director until 1958, years in which Villa contributed a number of curious articles, with topics ranging from art reviews to ship building in ancient Greece (see page 700 of the bibliography).

3 ideologie da piazza del popolo / senza l'imprimatur

3 Ideologies from Piazza del Popolo / Without the Imprimatur

1958

Imprimatur

evirò con una semplice folata il Terrore Moderno, sputò quindi
la pietra necessaria che aveva trangugiando, commettendo phallo, poi
curva porgeva la tazza degli avvenimenti geologici e
dei freddoloni popolari, adorni di poesia diplomatica, e nell'Onnivoro

ibi & ubique

grembo rovesciava delle immagini inalterabili, aliquid inconcussum,
senza stagione senza incontri perentori senza il seme il mite fiatone, e ordinava
che per 40 giorni di 40 notti (perché 40 è un numero Così) dalle Alpi
Probabili, dalle assurde catene prealpine, fino giù giù Giù
alle Tribune Quaternarie, a ciascuno venisse ripartito Tanto Universo
quanto ne può lavorare la testa di un uomo homunculus
che ha perduto il fiatone e il capolinea e il senso dei recuperi

oh, amazzone blugins, cosa corri dietro per vicoli ai Ghiganti
caduti nell'Ontario, con un tonfo, con il cordone
ombelicale penzolante! cosa! perché, quasi certamente,

Imprimatur

castrated the Modern Terror with a simple gust, then spat
the necessary stone it had chewing, committing phallus, and 1
passed the beveled cup of geological events and
popular weather wimps, adorned with diplomatic poetry, and in the Omnivorous

ibi & ubique

womb turned inalterable images inside-out, aliquid inconcussum,
without season seed peremptory encounters the meek panting, and ordered
that for 40 days of 40 nights (since 40 is that Sort of number) from the Probable
Alps, from the Absurd pre-alpine range, all the way down down Down
to the Quaternary Tribunes, each is assigned as Much Universe
as the head of a homunculus man can work
who lost the panting the end-of-the-line the sense of recouping

oh Amazon blujeens, why do you chase through allies Ghiants 2
fallen into the Ontario, with a thud, with a dangling
umbilical cord! what! why, almost certainly,

era: la Grande Grande Grande Glissade
dans la solidi-fication dans la déso-lidari-sation
de l'Inéxécuté Spécial, ma douce douce douce Gomorrhe!

pour le Chien du Ciel égorgé et
dont l'Écrat terrifie, dolcissima Gomorrha, dolce
organo, esiguo
orifizio per un Ostensorio dell'Eterna loquela,

e fontana del Singhiozzo deperito che vigila con l'autorevolezza
di una sciabola musicale, come se ubriaca avesse da squarciare
in quattro porzioni assai bene distinte l'avvento dell'ira Generalizia,
quella cosa che si guarda per la prima volta, una sola volta,
e una volta per sempre, poi basta

ça c'est qu'il disait d'avoir bien reçu de Sodome
accroupie le Sens donné sombre mutilé
peuple energique des … ! mon peuple au carcan
le présent reste Mais

ibi & ubique

it was: the Big Big Big Glissade
dans la solidi-fication dans la déso-lidari-sation
de l'Inéxécuté Spécial, but douce douce douce Gomorrhe!

pour le Chien du Ciel égorgé et
dont l'Écrat terrife, sweetest Gomorrha, sweet
organ, scant
orifice for a Monstrance of the Eternal locution, 3

and fountain of the withered Hiccup that keeps watch with the
authority of a musical saber, as if drunk had to tear
into four rather clear-cut portions the advent of the Generals' wrath,
that thing seen for the first time, one time alone,
and once and for all, then that's it

ça c'est qu'il disait d'avoir bien reçu de Sodome
accroupie le Sens donné somber mutilé
peuple energique des… ! mon peuple au carcan
le présent reste Mais

en s'exhaussant rejoindre le Souffle
de la bête divine Paroxysme Invective
des jaillissements novenaux
des réflexions arides d'Holocaustes
collatéraux et le fait émerger
rejeton, mystérieuse Vigilance
de l'épée des Syllabes qui gardaient les Liens

dolores quasi dolores quasi dolores

pour un hymne-guérison
épithète primorialique qui
sur la trame-songe des archanges
des grandes Hantises du jour chargées
d'amphores de cendre de victimes splendides
isolées
chacun sa cognée, Démolisseur
méprisant, chacun sa lignée
ténébreuse madornale confidence
sur les tartables

ibi & ubique

en s'exhaussant rejoindre le Souffle
de la bête divine Paroxysme Invective
des jaillissements novenaux
des réflexions arides d'Holocaustes
collatéraux et le fait émerger
rejeton, mystérieuse Vigilance
de l'épée des Syllabes qui gardaient les Liens

dolores quasi dolores quasi dolores

pour un hymne-guérison
épithète primorialique qui
sur la trame-songe des archanges
des grandes Hantises du jour chargées
d'amphores de cendre de victimes splendides
isolées
chacun sa cognée, Démolisseur
méprisant, chacun sa lignée
ténébreuse massive confidence
sur les tartables

ibi & ubique

terre terre terre! écoute
le souffle d'Un homme comme d'Un Homme
qui niche au milieu des couronnes
de la Grande Grande Métacalypse

e adesso? adesso chi esorcizza più farine e la carne e i cestoni
di verdura? Oh, verdeggiante Pinus Pinea
intorpidita di sensitive parusie, all'ordine dell'universa
potatura, la frondosa
chioma noi come procella i suoi carmi segreti
elencando in misurato elenco teologale strazieremo, o i suoi rami
dentro l'acqua del Terrore
Moderno marciranno, inquinata
gola, annosa corona della mezzaluna, addome
sinistro e la solenne
spastica esultante convocazione degli zuccheri erotici
da ogni più recondita stazione cellulare, dai confini
irrimediabili, e con perversa
emozione salutiamo allora il moderato presagio

ibi & ubique

terre terre terre! écoute
le souffle d'Un homme comme d'Un Homme
qui niche au milieu des couronnes
de la Grande Grande Métacalypse

and now? now who exorcizes anymore flour and meat and baskets
of vegetables? Oh, verdant Pinus Pinea
numbed by sensitive parousia, by the order of the universal
pruning, the leafy
crown we'll mangle just like a storm its secret song
listing in measured theological lists, or its branches
will rot in the water of the
Modern Terror, polluted
throat, age-old crown of the crescent, left
abdomen and the solemn
spastic exalting convocation of erotic sugars
from the most remote cellular station, from the irremediable
borders, and with perverse
emotion so we salute the moderate omen

ibi & ubique

e la Saldezza religiosa e morale di questo nostro popolo
magari confuso come una manciata di arachidi, a tradimento,
o, che dico, di pop-corn: con gli immortali
cieli offesi, o verdeggiante Pinus Pinea,
della madonna e del padreterno, con dentro
gli entropismi evoluti, i gargarismi recitali, e tutte
le cause di annullamento di Matrimonio nei Vari
settori e ceti, svergognati da leggi sismiche assai di pregio,
vendute a prezzi popolari e ribassati, sottocosto, dumping,
con molte le figurine del concorso ecclesiastico, la storia
dei papi e delle vergini descritta
lunghesso il sinixter digitale, corri a seminare

ibi & ubique

le ceneri giustiziate dell'amoroso inganno, suscitatore
degli ironici celesti ripari, là dove non è più chi assalga,
o, nel fruscio obliquo dei morti, l'anima sorprenda
nelle sue riservate ragioni, e Agisci! è ora, è quasi tardi

and the religious and moral Resolve of this people of ours
perhaps confused like a handful of peanuts, surreptitiously,
or, what am I saying, of popcorn: with offended
immortal heavens, or verdant Pinus Pinea,
like hell and goddamnit, containing
evolved entropisms, recital gargles, and all
the cases of Marriage annulled in the Various
sectors and classes, shamed by top-shelf seismic laws,
sold at set and discounted prices, below cost, dumping,
and many come with figurines from the ecclesiastical contests,
the history of popes and virgins described
alongside the digital sinixter, run to sow

ibi & ubique'

the executed ashes of amorous deceit, instigator
of ironic celestial shelters, there where assailants are no more,
or, in the oblique rustling of the dead, may the soul be surprised
in its private reasons, and Act! it's time, it's almost late

oh belles folies   orgueil tyrannies
telles paroles   oublies
lignes cruelles   mot-vase
brisé que je dois   vous donner

ibi & ubique

e quando non appena o poco dopo non si sa quando
la satyra è bell'e finita, convoca tu,
Beniamina, al telefono Vegetale del Terrore
Moderno, che ha perduto quel famoso
volto specifico, le miniere
degli Occhitesticoli, le spiritali
angherie munite regolarmente del sigillo viminale
e segnami tu nella voce marmorea, tra le filiture
dei lastroni che combaciano non si sa bene se sì o se no,
il più tenue spiraglio Messianico, la nostra
impenetrabile creatura Verbale, il termine
scalfito dell'oracolo in diorite, la sillaba, la fiammata

oh belles folies orgueil tyrannies
telles paroles oublies
lignes cruelles mot-vase
brisé que je dois vous donner

ibi & ubique

and when as soon as or right after no one knows when
the satyre is over and done, you summon,
Beniamina, on the phone Vegetable of the
Modern Terror, which lost that specific
famous face, the mines
of the Eyetesticles, the spirital oppression regularly 4
equipped with the Viminal seal 5
& mark for me on the marble voice, between the grout
of slabs that no one really knows if they do or do not match,
the most tenuous Messianic opening, our
impenetrable Verbal creature, the term
of the oracle, etched in diorite, the syllable, the blaze

numquid, inclyte, concrepabunt?
artifex pereo! qui nidificabo
in cerebro aspidem et basiliscum
& thoen! ascende igitur et calma
sepulturam Asini
dormientis in gyro saturniae maxillæ

eh, carognate e coseturche che succedono sulla basletta
dei terreni irrigui in lombardia in umilia a poma
a malano e in drianza, sulle cunette

sotto la schienadasino del maldivento
della scigheria che fischia nelle carregge
nelle folate indigene di polvere rossa che rompe
qui dalla Siria, le buriane della cultura sportiva
e della maledizione sulla vigna canadese

e tutti ma tutti gli archetipi di procelle che se io
fossi per avventura un meteorologo ammodo, qui, Agirei! Ma chi

ma chi esorcizza più, dicevo! e chi ereno

numquid, inclyte, concrepabunt?
artifex pereo! qui nidificabo
in cerebro aspidem et basiliscum
& thoen! ascende igitur et calma
sepulturam Asini
dormientis in gyro saturniae maxillæ

eh, dirty tricks and unspeakable acts that happen on the double chin
of the irrigated terrain in lombardy in umilia in pome
in malan and in drianza, on the humps 6

under the sloped pavement of the windache 7
of the thick fog that whistles in the towpaths
in the indigenous gusts of red dust that irrupts here
all the way from Syria, the tempest of sports culture
& of the spell cast on the Canadian Vineyard

and all I really mean all the archetypes of storms that if I
were by chance a proper meteorologist, here, I would Act! But who

I was saying, but who exorcizes anymore! and *chi ereno*

chestui che parlaveno
con il cuore onaletico di un Linneo?
dâi, dilettante, scaraventa il tuo onus, l'esorcismo
astruso patetico rampante, nell'orbita
lirica, il prodigio del lacero-confuso
e quelli che vanno in moto con il tubo di scappamento aperto,
o quelli che vogliono piantarmi nella schiena come un ortostato bizzarro
il sibilo paonazzo dell'imprimatur, il brivido innocente della curia, no:

quelli invece che in questo istante medesimo finiscono il campionato
funebre, o tracciano diagrammi cinici e titoli di celestiali
remore su e giù per le torbide lavagne:

o il povero cristo che confonde ancora al giorno d'oggi la liscivia
con la lascivia, sì: o anche quelli che dei bene equilibrati
glutei si fanno esimio tamburo per conoscere
le popolazioni nell'ora di caccia e pesca, o del membrum
in statu erecto il vessillo per le orde di Rappresaglia

ibi & ubique

chestui che parlaveno 8
with the onalytic heart of a Linnæus?
Come on, amateur, hurl your onus, the abstruse
Pathetic rampant exorcism, into the lyrical
orbit, the marvel of the laceration and confusion
and those who ride their bikes with an open exhaust,
or those who want to plant on my back as if it were a bizarre orthostate
the purple hissing of the imprimatur, the innocent chill of the Curia, no: 9

those instead who in this very same moment finish the funeral
tournament, or trace cynical diagrams and titles of celestial
regrets up and down across murky blackboards:

or the poor devil who to this very day hears lye
in lascivious, yes: or also those who out of their well-balanced 10
buttocks make illustrious drums to get to know 11
the people at the time for hunting and fishing, or of their membrum
in statu erecto the banner for the hordes of Reprisal

ibi & ubique

quelle che si sdraiano in un salotto accogliente
per reprimere la condizione, ma segretamente
è per farsi fotografare la fotografia della capigliatura
d'arancio in fotocolor; o quelli che fanno, nel clima
di svanite euforbie, del sangue erba o ferro o calcolo
o iattura, e poi non credono più a niente, né
alla fine della prosperità, né ai maggiori
avventurati esotismi del beene e del mamale,
delle destinazioni tassative e dei ricordi storicizzabili,
delle pretese dei desideri dei vantaggi ventilati,

ibi & ubique

e quelli che pitturano con temeraria amarezza i paradossi
sensibili esautorati privi di fondamento, ma tuttavia
colmi di arroganze ipotetiche, tante e poi tante ancora
idee intrecciate come un cesto di tribolazioni bibliche
ragni scorpioni scolopendre e aciduli basilischi;
e quelli che si affidano sempre a un prodotto di grande marca,
tanto nel genere sport, quanto per la musica, e quanto per il caffè

those women who lie down in an inviting room
to repress the condition, but secretly it's because
they want to be photographed the photograph of orange
hair in technicolor; or those who turn, in the climate
of vanished euphorbia, blood into grass or iron or calculation
or calamity, then they don't believe in anything anymore
neither in the end of prosperity, nor in the greatest
ventured exoticism of goood and evevil,
of binding destinations and historicizable memories,
of demands desires and rumored advantages,

ibi et ubique

and those who paint with rash bitterness divested
sensitive unfounded paradoxes, but yet
brimming with hypothetical arrogance, more and even more
braided ideas like a basket of biblical tribulations
spiders scorpions centipedes and acidulous basilisks;
and those who always trust a brand name product,
as much in sports, as in music, as in Yemenite

iemenita, e poi magari si stortano l'anulare negli elementi
del termosifone; e quelli infine che onorano la vita
con la Grossolana Allegria, con i cross-words, con le matematiche

Sennonché, umanamente discorrendo, qui
alla nostra tenera età, nel gran garbuglio
delle fantasie moderne e delle circostanze, dei
demetriaci prodigi, nella geniale concimaia
degli auguri e delle angosce rimaste in sospeso
con trepidanti eclissi che non si risolvono, chi
forse intravede oltre gli anniversari, oltre l'araldica
catastrofe che ne ingoia tutti? Ma
o dove, o a quale ombelisco ex utero virginali, o dove
potrà ancorare una sua bara gelosa la bara ovale
dell'Italia, clemente pitagorico convoglio, o fitto
gerundio? Acrobata,
evoca tu l'idea concava del Disfacimento, oplà,
pigiando sul Fulcro del Pelvi del Bacino e delle Reni,
e lungo i quattro Fastigi del Vento oscillando, baluginante
preda, oplà! giustiziato! Sotto un altro! e della Somma Scocca

coffee, and then they might twist their ring-finger in the
heater's elements; and lastly those who honor life
with Crude Mirth, cross-words, and mathematics

Except, humanly speaking, here
at our tender age, in the great tangle
of modern fantasy and circumstances, of
Demetrian miracles, in the brilliant hotbed
of wishes and interrupted anguish
with anxious eclipses that can't be solved, who
might see beyond anniversaries, beyond the heraldic
catastrophe that swallows us all? But
or where, or from which umbelisk ex utero virginali, or where
could he anchor his own jealous coffin the oval coffin
of Italy, merciful Pythagorean convoy, or thick
gerund? Acrobat,
you conjure up the concave idea of decay, hup,
treading on the Fulcrum of the Pelvis the Hips the Kidneys,
and oscillating along the four Crests of the Wind, flickering
prey, hup! executed! next! and of the Supreme Hull

ibi & ubique

è come un qualunque respiro l'ululato che ti scardina,
il fiato energico della sopravvivenza simbolica,
descritta nel sup-tellurico delle crude anatomie
dell'accaduto del decaduto del coinvolto

ibi & ubique

che segnala gli uragani di cui si compone il cervello
policromo della tellina, dell'acino d'uva, del grano
di pepe, del serpe giustiziato in loco,

e come accoglierai, sermone genuino, universale fuoco
del perdono, questa talmente e così così sfogata
proprietà della ragione spesso plebea e libera?
o perfino in altre vigne d'inferno, sperperata
nei lunghi sorrisi di piogge avare, vermino-autunnali?
o in un burrascoso
vino di compassione di grazia di memoria di abbracci
e di vergogne alacri, a due volti? oh, i'm go
per cui (i and go)

ibi & ubique

it's like any sort of breathing the howling that unhinges you,
the energetic breath of symbolic survival,
described in the sup-telluric of crude anatomies
of what's happened what's fallen what's involved

ibi & ubique

that marks the hurricanes composing the polychrome
brain of the clam, the single grape, the pepper
corn, the snake executed on site,

and how will you receive, genuine sermon, universal
fire of forgiveness, this so greatly vented
often liberal and plebian quality of reason?
or even in other infernal vineyards, squandered
in the long smiles of stingy, verminous-autumn rains?
or in a stormy
wine of pity grace memory embrace
and brisk two-faced disgrace? oh, i'm go
hence (i and go)

diremmo: primo, di comunicare con gli agenti giurati delle tribù
doviziose, e scomunicare gli altri, scambiando se dio vuole merci
infami, ma delicate, e idololatrie da sottilissimi reliquami, come
fosse il piloro di Marylin Monroe, tanto per fare un esempio esotico,
ma ci sarebbe sempre anche un altro: (but, why, why, christ ?!)

ibi & ubique

incidere poi con un magnetofono la vista epigrafica delle dinastie
faliche egizie diadochiche, e i rozzi sentimenti dei sovrani gottosi
e appena istruiti nel sigillo e nel rotolo, nel tempo medesimo
riducendo a silenzio perentorio, e anchilosare perfino, gli scribi
imbecilli che fanno pratica di discipline amministrative di sessi
secondari e relativamente parziali:

ibi & ubique

poi si potrebbe utilizzare senza riprovazione la lettera
del Demolitore per scardinare il portone millenario
di una città praticamente in disuso, o per ampliare a dismisura
un Distretto chiuso da spessi giganteschi falli confinarii,
e per chi volesse passare pesare riposare pensare e proclamare

we'd say: first, communicate with the sworn agents of the wealthy
tribes, and excommunicate the others, exchanging god willing corrupt,
but delicate, merchandise and ideolatries for the most subtle reliquids, as if 13, 14
it were Marylin Monroes' pylorus, just to cite one exotic example,
yet there would always be another: (but why why, christ?!)

ibi & ubique

then on a reel-to-reel record the epigraphic view of phallic 15
Diadochic Egyptian dynasties, and the crude sentiments of gouty
sovereigns and barely trained in seals and scrolls, at the same time
reducing to peremptory silence, and even stiffen, the idiotic
scribes who train in administrative disciplines of secondary
and relatively partial sexes:

ibi & ubique

then without reproach the Demolisher's letter
could be used to unhinge the millenary gate
of a city nearly abandoned, or to expand immensely
a District blocked by thick giant border phalluses,
and for those who want to pass weigh rest think and proclaim

l'arrivo dell'Uomo Ignoto da Ignote Feacie, e che deve
risiedere nella zona giusta, prevista dai legali
consentimenti delle nuvole dei piccioni delle irrigazioni a tromba
delle ceneri combuste da veneranda ecatombe, è
una testimonianza eccezionale, amen: e sull'altra riva

ci sono i Monotoni precoci sull'altra riva della piazza
delebile; e dinastia anagrafiche penose che datano soltanto
dal penultimo restauro in data 38.15.63 delle mura
disperate, fatiscenti sotto sforzo dei convolvoli, delle
alluvioni locali, nonché delle verdure esilaranti,
i capperi, le ortiche, la vite canadese, le orchidee

potrebbe significare che noi, selvatichi e magnanimi
adolescenti del giorno d'oggi, ormai quasi niente più
sappiamo delle nascostissime maledizioni del passato
prossimo, che sono ossi, selci, anatomie, denti
allungati come le ombre della sera, e la ragione
del massacro finalissimo e ceneri relative, del fuoco
indispensabile, delle astute designazioni cerimoniali
operate dall'enigma, dal reggicalze, dalla guêpière:

the Unknown Man's arrival from Unknown Phæacia, who must
reside in the right zone, designated by the legal
consents of clouds pigeons waterspouts
the ashes burnt by venerable hecatombs, it's
an exceptional testimony, amen: and on the other shore

of the delibile piazza precocious Monotonous people;
and painful anagraphic dynasties that only date
back to 38.15.63 the last restoration of the desperate
walls, crumbling under the stress of convolvuli, of
local floods, not to mention the exhilarating vegetables,
capers, nettles, Canadian vines, orchids,

it could mean that we, today's wild and
magnanimous youth, by now almost know nothing
about the most hidden curses of the recent
past, which are bones, stones, anatomies, teeth
stretched like the night's shades, and the reason
behind the most final massacre and relative ashes, of the
indispensable fire, the astute ceremonial designations
wielded by the enigma, by garter-belts, by the guêpière:

e le trafelate simultaneità di guerre legalitarie
o di consapevole pace, proprio sul campo della battaglia
Generalizia, menzionata soltanto, per riguardo e per un
ricatto, a fiore di labbra su uno dei cantoni della piazza:
e il sangue viene spedito con coraggio, costantemente, quasi
puntualmente, ma le ingorde infermiere
lo bevono di nascosto nel sud della patria!

e così. E non ci sono più pascoli inteneriti, più reliquie
di santi mastodontici misteriosissimi generosi disumani,
così noi dirigiamo verso l'altissimo immaginario
le nostre tentazioni accurate, il transito
graduale verso una vegetazione le cui forme
dovrebbero svariare secondo le circostanze
secondo i pellegrinaggi le bestemmie le eventualità
corrispondenti; perché vien certo

ibi & ubique

and the breathless simultaneities of legalitarian wars
or of conscious peace, right there on the field of the Generals'
battle, barely mentioned, out of regard and out of
blackmail, murmured in a corner of the piazza:
and the blood is dispatched with courage, constantly, almost
punctually, but the greedy nurses
secretly drink it in the south of the fatherland!

and so. And there are no more softened pastures, no more relics
of mysterious generous mammoth inhuman saints,
so we direct our accurate temptations
toward the highest imagination, the gradual
transition toward a vegetation whose forms
should vary according to the circumstances
according to pilgrimage blasphemy and corresponding
possibility; for it's certain

ibi & ubique

che chi abbandona in malo modo le proprie femmine
dai raggianti ombelichi, a giusto titolo, potrà abbandonare
anche la piazza senza alcuna ragione plausibile, per un improvviso
scarto di questa ingegnosa prudenza, e amen

ibi & ubique

that those who in a huff abandon their women
with radiant belly buttons, and rightly so, could also abandon
the piazza without any plausible reason, out of a sudden
swerve in this ingenious caution, and amen

ibi & ubique

antiquate sonorità cristiane...

antiquate sonorità
cristiane
pour sex dead tom tom

calcola il corpo innumerevole
sans idéeal commun
balance très balance (per le aziende)
balance intégral (per le tenute)
sous la préessence des fruits
des courbures-matière corrompue
alignantes-alignées des matrices
sur les culibrautions spectrales

dans l'après dîner
chaque lundi

et tous les temps et les hauts temps
gémirent se mirant soul les maimains

et sous les mains
le panthéon à hiérogluphes
irresistibles et demeurés

où sont
les grandes
chiennes
les chênes
de Saul

M
O
T
O
R

symptômes d'aimour

dans l'araignée conçue
la génesse dla grande
corpe

oh, vocali ancora semipagane, cieche
prede, fonti di ossigeno
agli squali, alle passere! semi, oh,
dell'acu
ta pietà, al mu
sico gentile gio
vane convoglio
e conseguenti re
tate, spalancando
di quest'ora tarda
il verso allo sbaraglio
per buonsenso leg
gero e pensosa
economia, con ogni
preesistenza, e il superno
convegno sigillato
nel cavo brucato
della mano indigena.
quale ferita!

e acceso il lume delle indagini
del profondo, noi insieme, con immobili
e disarticolati ragionari si scommette
due testicoli contro solo una mela
che la vita dev'essere il contrario
della vita e della natura: consumeremo
il fiato fino all'ultima vocale utile

symptômes
evolués
pour
si je
m'avance
dans l'air sombre

!corps lumbard
corps bastard

inutile
profondo!

huître-air de la transmanence
huître-œil

come o non come ma come
i luoghi dei luoghi nel solfeggio
dei testimoni, nel sospiro
idumeo o lesbico o hittita

sépanouir lepa-
nouissement sépanouisse

sang lumbard
sang busard

volk ambulaire de thératothèmes
deuxheures
deshakespeares

à l'ouest
le dieu le plus jeune le plus eau
pendant l'ouverture je te baptise

où sont
les abîmes
où sont
les grandes
scèénes

à duexheuréer deuxheures
dans le sang de shakespeures
dans les veines alignées

O
L
I

perché siamo un popolo
di lampadine fulminante!
e chi ruba la cenere nei mastelli
e chi frantuma le pipe di gesso,
non sa leggere la mano di pitagora
ne réponds pas

je me présente
devenu
cruel

song for tree
sing for true
sang pour truie
sens fort

autres simptômes

1.000.003

antiquated christian resonances...

antiquated christian
resonances
pour sex dead tom tom

calculates the innumerable body
sans idéeal commun
balance très balance (for corporations)
balance intégral (for estates)
sous la préessence des fruits
des courbures-matière corrompue
alignantes-alignées des matrices
sur les culibrautions spectrales

dans l'après dîner
chaque lundi

et tous les temps et les hauts temps
gémirent se mirant soul les maimains

et sous les mains
le panthéon à hiérogluphes
irresistibles et demeurés

où sont
les grandes
chiennes
les chênes
de Saul

M
O
T
O
R

symptômes d'aimour

dans l'araignée conçue
la génesse dla grande
corpe

oh, vowels, still semi-pagan, blind
prey, oxygen source
for sharks, and sparrows! seeds, oh,
of the acu
te pity, of the mu
sical gentle ju
venile convoy
and consequent ro
und ups, opening
the reckless verse
at this late hour
out of faint wis
dom and thoughtful
economy, with every
preexistence, and the supernal
convention sealed
in the nibbled hallow
of the indigenous hand.
what a wound!

and lit the light for investigating
the depth, together, with immobile
and disjointed reasoning, we'll bet
two testicles against only one apple
that life must be the opposite
of life and nature: we'll consume
breath until the last useful vowel

symptômes
evolués
pour
si je
m'avance
dans l'air sombre

!corps lumbard
corps bastard

useless
deep!

huître-air de la transmanence
huître-œil

like or unlike but like
the places of places in the solfeggio
of testimonies, in the Edomite
or Lesbian or Hittite sigh

sépanouir lepa-
nouissement sépanouisse

sang lumbard
sang busard

volk ambulaire de thératothèmes
deuxheures
deshakespeares

à l'ouest
le dieu le plus jeune le plus eau
pendant l'ouverture je te baptise

où sont
les abîmes
où sont
les grandes
scèénes

à duexheuréer deuxheures
dans le sang de shakespeures
dans les veines alignées

O
I
L
S

because we're a people
of burnt out bulbs!
and those who steal ash in tubs
and those who shatter clay pipes,
are unable to read Pythagoras' hand
ne réponds pas

je me présente
devenu
cruel

song for tree
sing for true
sang pour truie
sens fort

autres simptômes

1.000.003

translatio

(c.à.d. lecture probable physique sans souci du venir
d'aspic jéroglyphe stylé dans l'obélisque de la place)

Vu le Code Sacramental
sur la Place de l'Équité,
les Bêtes à Cornes
sur la Barque des Couilles,
les Gâteaux des Morts
sur les Textes des Apodòseis
pour Petites Conditions
de la Nourriture Idéale,
enfin
le grand Marathon du vice
multiplié par ... [lacune :
peut-être, un dieu de conscience] un arbre
doux, aux yeux-rejetons, sensibles
parentés,

bien !
peut-on calomnier les dieux
du Vice? faire pleurer les Souffrances
sans parenté, au moment où le Trope éternel
replie sur soi-même comme un diadème
de Cendre, et Nouvelles heures surgissent
rédigées proliférantes équivoques débordantes
mon Astre inoui?
j'Attends
aux saturnales expiatoires, dans le Ventre
salutaire noir du psaume, ton Triomphe,
chaos héroïque mon Astre ennui,
Cœur dissimulé…
et les Phases que je sème pour qui s'aiment
qu'un autre les dévore.

Imprimatur

1. The original "phallo" is a corruption of the typical spelling "fallo," which can mean either "foul" or "phallus."
2. In the original, Villa combines the words "blue jeans" and spells them phonetically (*blugins*) according to Italian diction.
3. The Italian word *loquela* immediately recalls the work of Dante, especially the pilgrim's conversation with Farinata in the tenth canto: *La tua loquela ti fa manifesto / di quella nobil patria natio, / a la qual forse fui troppo molesto.* (*Inferno* X: 25–28). Translations of the term vary: accent, mode of speech, or tongue. However, I feel "locution" better captures the nuance of the Italian.
4. See page XXVIII of the introduction.
5. The *Viminale* is one of the Seven Hills of Rome, atop of which lies the seat of the *Ministero dell'interno* (Ministry of the Interior). At the time this poem was composed, the building also housed the offices of the *Presidenza del Consiglio* (the prime minister & his cabinet), which have since been moved to Palazzo Chigi.
6. Villa is playing on the names of Italian toponyms: Umilia instead of Emilia, to evoke humility; Poma instead of Roma, to evoke pome; Malano instead of Milano, to evoke malady; and Drianza instead of Brianza. Only Lombardia (Lombardy) is left untouched.
7. In the original, *maldivento* sounds similar to *mal di dente* (toothache).
8. Roman dialect for "who are these guys who spoke with."

9. *Curia* refers to the papal court in the Catholic Church. This governing body did not give Villa its "imprimatur" (seal of approval) to publish his a-confessional translation of the Old Testament. Although he had signed a contract to print the translation with the prestigious Italian publisher Einaudi, it backed out after the papal court's decision.
10. In Italian, "liscivia" (lye) and "lascivia" (lasciviousness) are phonetically different by only one syllable.
11. Another Dante reference, this time to the last line of the twenty-first canto in which the pilgrim encounters a group of devils who salute their leader through flatulence: *ed elli aveva del cul fatto trombetta* [and each made a bugle of his ass].
12. A combination of the words "ombelico" (umbilical) and "obelisco" (obelisk).
13. A combination of "ideologia" (ideology) and "idolatrie" (idolatries).
14. The original "reliquami" is Villa's combination of "reliquie" (relics) and "liquami" (sewage or sludge).
15. The Italian reads "faliche" with one "l," which is most likely a typo. Villa may have intended the adjective "fallico" (phallic) or, given the list of geographical references in these lines, it may be a variant on the adjective "falisco," referring to the land "belonging to the Etruscan civilization."

comizio millenovecentocinquanta3

nineteen-fifty3 rally

1959

di andare ancora giù giù giù al tempo scarnito dei cristiani di polvere   con le solfe
e le strofe bislacche e sui polsini le sigle fruste   e le stole
sui calcagni   e che

al tempo scarnito dei cristiani   che guardando solo in alto tendere e distendere
le pattone inondate, arrosées,   dove sguazza il ragno, qui uno
mangia come canta, canta come mangia   e che sospetto di aver carpito
la musica nella camola, si si,   la musica, e l'indicibile

frangia tutta bassa e minimissima, sulla curva del barbosso,   respiro e volo
tondo, e poi le rare   Itaglie
sfavillando e sfavellando i giorni che pioveva l'idrico   fitto sull'amido

e sul fustagno e sui sassi sybillini e con moderni   toni sbranava
il sereno, mentre noialtri   si parlava unitamente
onestamente parlando coi ginocchi, passi   dietro passi, coi
ginocchi come chi si tappa le orecchie con la scapola, a eccelse ruote, confuse un po', al largo
dei labirinti e degli specchi maestri, in subaffitto   si parlava
dello sbuffo della quaglia negli occhi del chimerico OZONO!

and going further down down down to the scrawny time of dusty christians   with raves
and odd rants and worn-out monograms on the cuffs   and stoles
down to the heels   and that

to the scrawny time of christians   who look only on high to lean and stretch
the drowned *pattone*, arrosées,   where the spider splashes, here you 1
eat like you sing, sing like you eat   and a suspicion of figuring out
the music in the maggot, yes yes,   the music, and the unspeakable

fringe all low and extremely fine, on the *barbosso*'s curve,   breath and circular 2
flight, and then the rare   Itaglie 3
beaming and blabbering the days when the hydric rained   heavy on the starch

and the corduroy and sybilline stones and with modern   tones mangled 4
serenity, while the rest of us   we spoke in unity
in honesty speaking with our knees, step   after step, with knees
like those who cover their ears with their shoulder blades, for celestial wheels, a bit confused, deep in
the labyrinths and the master mirrors, subletting   we spoke
of the quail's panting in the eyes of the chimeric OZONE!

nel chimerico suono dei cristiani
piramide degli accenti e delle note, nel
che tocca l'oltresuono, l'oltredove
scaccia la stremata ideazione,
balla il poiano: l'odore librato
il corso dell'aria fina, ferma e grama,
polla e palta tinta, e tira
e una robinia con rugiada, e nelle remote
giganti della boria lombarda
rada in un pugno:

a chimeriche quote, nella cruda
brio e nella brina di lattuga
la pertica misura e il ragno
e non udito, les oiseaux du ciel, in fuga
di benzina che ripete
un gran canale, un bagno dall'inferna
e molla, una gran strada, la gran falla
Valve i sospiri
e la borrasca impietra
e con luce sgranellata, a galla,

tra frasca e frasca e frasca della Penisola e dall'Olla ovale
che s'incrina salta fuori la cicoria molla, la teppa; e il cuore dei porri

e la paglia, e il ciuffo di menta, a filigrana
e sù e giù per le segale una lamentosa uretra,
scorre la Patria come una volpe dietro la strusa annusando dal grugno
est, polpa assonnata di parvenze di parole d'anima infusa,

lisa, a ipotenusa
e inalberata
le brecce del muretto

quando offerta e azione, supplica e sacramenti, zucchero e odore di merda e saformenti
tagliano venti e si infilano

in the chimeric sound of christians   at chimeric heights, in the crude
pyramid of accents and notes, in   the zest and frost of lettuce
touching the beyondsound, the beyondwhere   the perch measures and the spider
drives away exhausted ideation,   and unheard, les oiseaux du ciel, fleeing
the buzzard dances: the soaring odor   of gasoline following 5
the course of subtle air, still and wretched,   a grand canal, a bath from the infernal
spring and tainted mud, and in the   end, a grand road, the grand breach
and a dewey robinia, and in the remote   Valves the giant
sighs of lombard pride   and the storm petrifies
barren in a fist: and with grainy light, floating,
about the bush & bush & bush across the Peninsula & from the oval Olla 6
that cracks wet chicory and moss leaps; and the heart of leeks

and straw, and a sprig of mint, with worn   filigree, as a hypotenuse
and up and down the rye a lamenting urethra,   and incensed
the Fatherland flows like a fox after a scent sniffing from the snout   the holes in the eastern
wall, sleepy pulp of appearance of words of infused soul,

when offer and action, plea and sacrament, sugar and smell of shit and saphorment 7
                    cut winds & squeeze through

e nella casa vana restano soltanto le boccole salve   color granata, di vetro,
sul cuscino, e il centopiede   assassinato; e nella casa
restano solamente gli ori i cani la paglia e spicchi   secchi d'aranci, e ragnatele
alacri, segnale della eccellente convalescenza   e ormai, ormai

nelle putrelle di ghisa e nelle scodelle   delle libazioni   degli inizi
della vita tradizionale sociale normale   e familiare   in giro ai cavicchi si stempera
il ritmo delle zoccole sulle buche   e contro i due calcagni

il sismico premito della formica   delle festuche   della perfetta
luce non parlata, non generata orazione   sul filo di ferro   che taglia in due
la polenta, gli aggettivi, le congiunzioni salivate,   i verbi perfino!   stereofonici, i verbi,
radicitus citus tus,

quale ovipara musica! magnetica e le impronte
vocali e quelle digitali volgarmente mischiate alla calcina calda e sul terreno
che squaglia, le schiene d'asino le carregge il morso
prodigo
delle caligini dynastiche dei fulmini adatti a tirare dai sassi sybillini sangue occulto
e mazzi di cicoria, e senza furia

and in the inane house remain only saved bushings   *granata* in color, in glass,
on the pillow, and the murdered   centipede; and in the house
remain only dogs hay jewelry and dry slices   of oranges, and busy
cobwebs, sign of excellent convalescence   and by now, by now

in the cast iron joints and cups   for libations   of the beginning
of traditional social normal and   familial life   around the pegs fades
the rhythm of rats over holes   and against the heels 8

the seismic spasm of the ant   of hay   of the perfect
unspoken light, un-generated oration   on the wire   that cuts polenta
in half, adjectives, salivating conjunctions,   and even verbs!   stereophonic, the verbs,
radicitus citus tus,

such oviparous music! magnetic and voice-
prints and fingerprints coarsely mixed in the warm mortar and on the ground
that melts, saddlebacks reins the prodigal
bit
of dinastic fogs of lightning suited for drawing occult blood from sybilline stones 9
and bunches of chicory, without rushing

senza cor d'olio senza sorriso ma con cinerea   già cul atoria far segni
d'intelletto e devozioni   di bestia   spisciolando tempeste
sulla spranga   e si sfalda
la spavalda intima gemma sola della paura in orecchie abissali dei manzi ammattiti o matti,
e strusciano le baggiane i fregoni sullo stemma sulle soglie sui piatti e le padelle, esorciste
per Nergal l'Anaconda che avanza sui canestri dell'alba dal nudo asilo che lo ingenera, e, oh, rutili

cartilagini di Itaglie e d'altre terre teppiste, rinvergate! e a nuoto negli occhi muti
delle vipere l'onda annoda della flemma della luce e il transito sbircia della quaglia gioconda
e le caligini dynastiche sposa ai venturi occhi inviolati,

e spurgo di anime da iella nella cruenta limpidezza delle piste,
e là per dove il prevosto baccagliando al cane scortica la coda
masticando l'eucharistica membrana di formentone giallo
sotto il baldacchino degli estrosi cirri in gara, a vista, e spacca, trac,
il cervelletto alla lucertola impenitente, un filo in trepida amara

sede di od rosa maglia di anice di grappa e di naftalina, e odore
di fegato di merluzzo e di carogne nel vestibolo delle narici   e lungo il torace
brivido d'incenso, trame fischiate di camole di arredi nella foresta sottogonna del corpuschristi,

without the heart of oil without smile but with ashen   ejà cul atory making signs 10
of intellect and devotion   of the beast   pissing tempests
on the staff   and it crumbles
the arrogant intimate lonely gem of fear in the abyssal ears of maddened or mad steers,
and the *baggiane* rub the *fregoni* on the crest on the thresholds over the plates and in the pans, exorcists 11
for Nergal of the Anaconda advancing across the baskets of dawn from the naked shelter that generates it, and, oh, rutile 12

cartilage of Itaglie & other thuggish lands, rediscovered! & swimming in the mute eyes
of vipers of phlegm of light the wave knots and the transit of playful quail glances
and marries dinastic fogs to future untouched eyes,

and the purging of souls of bad luck in the bloody clarity of tracks,
and there where the quarreling priest flays the dog's tail
chewing the eucaristic membrane of yellow corn 13
under the canopy of whimsical cirri in a race, in view, and breaks, crack,
the cerebellum of the impenitent lizard, a thread in the quivering bitter

seat of scented knit of anise grappa and mothballs, and smell 14
of liver cod and carcass in the vestibule of the nostrils   and along the thorax
shiver of incense, whistled weaves of maggots of furniture in the forest under the skirt of corpuschristi,

uguaglia l'incanto incendiato dei Patti Massimi: oh, albero
di avvenenza Speleofonica, albero del Precetto, di ladra
eideia, di fonda chiacchiera, che il sangue in Itaglia non lava
le soglie e i marciapiedi, ma il chianti su uno straccio di tovaglia nuziale
appena che libato impiastra di rosso il sale e le freguglie di pane, e il coppino, buon augurio,
che se la goda a darci dentro! e uno allora, diceva la rava e la fava, e che eh no, eh no,
eh no, eh no!
eh sì, sociofugo
eh, assimilatore…

se ghe scapa la caca de sgnapa ghe se scepa la ciapa del bus del cü, del peritoneo! e uno allora

per Due Coltelli e Tre in fondo al lago inan ellato
ragiona a gran fatica in mezzo ai sassi sybillini nei laceri
bindelli della celeste tovaglia, con i crampi
e il gomito che scotta quando per i campi scaglia a dieci ai dieci nudi
venti la fionda verso dove non ci si vede più e innescata è la sera:

ma: albero geodetico, fiuto dello stratempo fedele, albero di galeotta
avvenenza, negli scudi che il nubilo, sù e giù, sparpaglia, e tempo
stravagante, a spasso, sù e giù, sulle finestre sulle croste sulle tibie sopra i cuoi sopra il lattime
delle guance nella cagliata e nella coppa a fare opachi stampi e malinconica

equals the incinerated incantation of the Maximum Pacts: oh, tree
of Speleophonic comeliness, the tree of the Precept, of thieving 15
eideia, of deep chatter, so blood in Itaglia doesn't wash
doorsteps and sidewalks, but the chianti on a shred of nuptial tablecloth
as soon as swallowed smears the salt and breadcrumbs with red, and the ladle, good omen,
enjoys going all out! and then one, said this that and the other, and that, oh no, oh no,
oh no, oh no!
oh yes, sociofugal 16
oh, assimilator…
if he has to crap schnapps, he'll shred the side of his ass, the peritoneum! and then one

reasons with great difficulty among sybilline stones
about Two Blades and Three at the bottom of the en ringed lake in the torn 17
shreds of the celestial tablecloth, with cramps
and a burning elbow when through the fields the sling hurls ten by ten
the naked winds where you can't see anything anymore and the evening is triggered:

but: geodesic tree, a nose for faithful extra-time, tree of seductive
comeliness, in the shields scattered by clouds, up and down, and extravagant
time, strolling, up & down, on the windows on the scabs on the tibias over the hides & over the sickly honeycomb
of cheeks in the curd and in the cups to form opaque stamps and melancholic 18

carezza e lente spire, e dura scorza alle gibigiane: rotta, così,
sgargia la livella del T e B: e domani, ma domani,   il candore

che entra come un temperino nudo, come una carognata, la gemma della paura o dello sfizio,
un gotto
di manduria dentro il lago, e ma domani sarà una gran bella giornata! un gemito
dentro i testicoli, lungo, e nostalgia della sua cenere   e ma domani

più nisciuno in questa scura foppa sa più bene se la pietra permansiva
e immemore in immemore equilibrio starà sopra la pietra,
o sull'arcata delle spalle i pensamenti a grani con tutta
quella catabrega di figlioli a precipizio   e la legge
dell'uomo che ha mangiato di straforo il pànico vitale, sussidio
delle comunità, delle fabbricerie, dei sindacati, delle tribù ...
tarlate da un acume propizieviole   e il lume
sforbiciato da molteplici scaramanzie, come l'albero
ignaro, svelto   nel rameggio
tra il nubilo e il tempaccio nazionale e internazionale, il frullo
e la chiarezza in equilibrio immemore, una fetta   di buontempo,
qui nessuno bene sa la lippa come un cazzo catorcio o qualunque
baldanzoso orifizio, ecc. ecc.   mulìn mulèta
ghe se slunga la tèta!

caress and slow spirals, and thick skin for the blinding glare: broken, like that,
the level of T and B flares: and tomorrow, but tomorrow, the candor 19

that enters like a naked pocket knife, like a dirty trick, the gem of fear or the whim,
a drop
of manduria in the lake, yes but tomorrow will be one hell of a day! a long 20
whimper in the testicles and nostalgia of its own ashes yes but tomorrow

nobody no more in this dark ditch knows if the permansive stone 21
obliterated in obliterated equilibrium will remain on top of the stone,
or if granulated thoughts on the arcade of the shoulders with all
that noisy bunch of children at breakneck speed and the law
of man who has slyly eaten the vital panic, subsidy
of communities, of *fabbricerie*, of unions, of tribes... 22
worm-eaten by a propitious acumen and the light
snipped by multiple superstitions, like the unsuspecting
tree, nimble in the branching
between clouds & the national & international bad weather, the whir
and the clarity in obliterated equilibrium, a slice of good weather,
here nobody knows the tipcat like a jalopy cock or any other
prancing orifice, etc. etc. mill milly
her titty looks silly! 23

qui le piaghe d'Itaglia si curano con lo sputo, il leccalecca
universale, e lecca il Verde Rame delle palanche, e si curano
con la glykyrhiza linnaei, o regolizia che dir si voglia, oh jeus jesus
del christ, un bacio,
el azucar me mandega
el cocoron del cacio!

potrà per dentro in cinerei cereali una re voluzione crepitare
ardentemente? dove per i sacri alberi
ancora scarseggiano le acque insaziabili, senza
canali, senza vene disegnate in croce, o i barlumi
intellettuali pro capite, o la festa del carpire
brusco, a tono, in coro, tanti argomenti tutti insieme in una volta unica?
due tori si battono nel cuore della poiana! per uno
che comincia così che finisce cosà, che sa e non sa le larve dei coiomi,
che non sa se dare del tu o del ti
sui carri di cenere itineraria negli imi ardenti cunicoli,
e così sembra, e così sia

di là da tutte le facce d'anime impappinate del purgatorio, di là
dalle ultime palizzate, riverenza e scatto, di là dai polmoni della vacca
dove i fiori del girasole crepano senza un lamento, per cui

here the sores of Itaglia are cured with spit, the universal
lollipop, and it licks the Green Copper of coins, and they're cured
with glykyrhiza linnaei, or licoresse whatever you want to call it, oh jeus jesus 24
of krist, a kiss,
el azucar me mandega
el cocoron of cheese!
can a re volution burn ardently inside cinereous
cereal? Where for the sacred trees
there still isn't enough insatiable water, nor
canals, nor veins drawn in a cross, nor the intellectual
glimmers per capita, nor the party for the rude
understanding, in spades, in chorus, so many arguments all together all at once?
two bulls clash in the heart of the buzzard! for one
who begins like this ends like that, who barely knows the larvae of cojones,
who doesn't know whether to use 'you' or 'ye'
on the carts of itinerary ash in the deep ardent tunnels,
and that's how it seems, and so be it

beyond all the floundering faces of souls in purgatory, beyond
the final fences, reverence and pounce, beyond the cow's lungs
where the sunflowers die without a sound, and so

si capisce l'orrore interno e lo scabroso   palpito, per cui,
e si sa bene le dita in croce del coma e della paralisi e dell'ingonia,   e i pollici
a mulinello, si sa le occhiaie inviperite tra le felci e sulle traiettorie del piombo, e si sa
dove il poiano becca col becco l'ultima sentenza di sangue universale
e si sa le bucce dei sabati scaricati sottoterra o tra diademi di marroni infornati
da ingerire, e sui calcestri tra le gobbe nelle cucce tra le larve per le vene eccetera
rovistare mentre nell'ombra del coppino   mite e losco
si adagia una pinza d'acciaio il maggiolino   e il dito imparziale
bagnato nel vino gnucco e nel sale paonazzo lo spappola che s'impiastra   e allora
ci ha messo sù putiferio baracca saformento e porcudighel, e si placano
i due tori nel cuore della poiana di Sesso Calende,   le cineree

impronte digitali sfregate sulla mezzanotte, e storciti
capovolgiti, lampeggia, Maestà della Poiana! se, allora, raccolta
nella nazione l'universa febbre, spessa, con un mestolo incontaminato, per lungo
ribrezzo allora impietra l'Alto Abdomen dell'Abdomeneddio!
gremito di magoni, di rancori giulivi, di singhiozzi, di sgraffi,
di letanie senza testo, irrespirabili,   e obliquamente
le salme degli alti Cani cinerei ansimano incorrotti in punta alle canne
fluttuando   e l'ecuméne
dei bulbi pieno e vuoto vidima il potere e il nonpotere dell'Onnipotente

you understand the internal horror and the scabrous throb, and so,
you know very well the fingers crossed over coma paralysis and ingony and thumbs 25
in a twiddle, you know infuriated bags under the eyes amid the ferns along the trajectories of led, and you know
where the buzzard pecks with its beak the final sentence of universal blood
and you know the peels of saturdays dumped underground or between crowns of baked chestnuts
for ingesting, and on the concrete between the humps in the dog's bed between larvae through veins etcetera
rummaging while in the shade of the meek and seedy ladle
a pair of iron pliers settles the beetle and the impartial finger
soaked in chewy wine and blushing salt that squashes it and gets dirty and then
caused a mess the whole joint saphorments and tell him off, and the two bulls 26
calm in the heart of the buzzard of Calends Sex, the ashy 27

finger prints rubbed against the midnight, and twist
turn upside down, flash, Majesty of the Buzzard! if, then, the thick,
universal fever is collected in the nation with an unspoiled spoon, out of
long disgust, then the High Abdomen of the Abdomenenddio petrifies! 28
filled with knots in the throat, merry resentment, sobs, scratches,
litanies without a text, unbreathable, and obliquely
the corpses of high cinereous Dogs pant uncorrupted on the tip of the reeds
floating and the full and
empty ecumene of bulbs validates the power & non-power of the genuine 29

genuino, alleato al tenero delirio nell'inedia e allo schianto
furtivo, elegiaco, delle erotiche asce, e degli stipiti deperiti a colpi d'anca,
a sbatti e molla e lasciandare che il cielo   appartiene!

e nelle rocce di tenebre ti si strozzano i lividi precipizi le sideree fiumane i rari
riflessi   per somme linee   e i prèsaghi
tedeum   e l'unghia incarnata delle estasi dentro le cortecce
del gelso   e l'occhio estirpato alla sua roccia, immoto
sugli oziosi scandagli, ebete vendetta   fino a che
la fanfara di carruba intonerà a pelo d'aria, scrocchiando,   l'era nuova,
l'èra bicipite, delle diavolerie fonetiche,   i neumi palinsesti
dal foro dell'uovo di una syllaba clandestina solitaria esimia tenue caduca urbana generosa
lunga e carnale come il corpus della separazione e dell'uguaglianza: e nella cuna
tonda, come dei due orecchi del manzo, del padiglione dell'orecchio tra timpano e martelletto
rugando, fiorisce il cembalo insonne lanceolato degli espressi di frontiera, e il polverone
stormendo si avventa fuori orario dei camion, e il senso, a distanza,
delle luci gemelle nelle orecchie, perpetuo, sommesso attimo   e baleno
dei Novissimi: cioè, una vallata, a canestri, di albe   immolate
dall'amor delle anime, dal suffragio   indenne
delle larve e dei cognomi pellegrini oltremondani barbari nazionali necessari sovietici o giudei

Omnipotent, ally to starvation's tender delirium and to the furtive,
elegiac crash of erotic axes, and door jambs worn out by thrashing hips,
by push & pull & never mind that the sky   belongs!

and in the rocks of darkness your livid precipices sidereal floods rare reflexes are
strangled   in broad strokes   & the prophetic
tedeums   and the ingrown nail of ecstasies inside the bark 30
of the mulberry   & the eye uprooted from its rock, motionless
in idle soundings, idiotic revenge   until
the fanfare of carob plays skimming the air, cracking   the new era,
the bicipital era, of phonetic devilries,   the neumic palimpsests 31
from the pinhole of the egg of a clandestine, solitary, illustrious, delicate, caducous, urbane,
generous, long syllable, carnal like the corpus of separation and equality: and stirring in the round
cradle, like the two ears of a steer, of the auricle of the ear between timpani and hammer
the sleepless lanceolate cymbal of the frontier express trains blossoms, and rustling
the dust cloud of trucks pounces after hours, and the sense, from a distance,
of the twin lights in the ears, perpetual, subdued moment   & the flash
of the Four Last Things: that is, a valley, basket-like, of dawns   sacrificed 32
by the love of souls, by the unharmed   suffrage
of larvae and otherworldly barbarian pilgrim national necessary soviet or jewish surnames

uno che incomincia così, che finisce cosà,   darà agli incendi
l'Uccello di apollo e le cosce di santa Creatura, maschia o femmino,

oh, ignaro, oh gelido oh decrescente talamo dei nostri aliti
a ridosso, scapola a scapola! omelia e smalto e muscolo
del sortilegio paraclitico, esalando, in virga verbi,
ti fulmini, o sancta ecclesia, novero ecumenico, informe
apocalisse vocalizzata e suggellata con labbra inerti, tra le vigne
ti fulmini: uno stupore idolologico, ma maligno, e una rissa
aspra di cieli incenerisca il satanico peplo, il pascolo, e il nubifragio.

one that begins like this, and ends like that,   will throw the Bird
of apollo to the fire and the thighs of saint Creature, masculine or feminine, 33, 34

oh, unsuspecting, oh freezing oh decreasing nuptial bed of our breaths
so close, shoulder to shoulder! may homily and enamel and muscle
of paracletic sorcery, exhaling, in virga verbi, 35
strike you down, or may the sancta ecclesia, ecumenical list, shapeless
apocalypse vocalized and sealed with inert lips, among vineyards
strike you down: an idolological yet evil stupor, and may a bitter 36
quarrelling of skies incinerate the satanic peplum, the pasture, and the storm.

nineteen-fifty3 rally

1. Generally eaten in the fall, *Pattona* is a semi-sweet flat cake made with chestnut flour.
2. *Barbos* is Milanese for "chin."
3. *Itaglie*, pronounced It-al-yay, is Villa's intentional misspelling of the plural form of Italia. Throughout the piece, Villa often employs the plural "Itaglie" as well as the singular "Itaglia."
4. In the original, Villa replaces the first "i" in the adjective "sibilline" with a "y"; we adapted the English spelling to this irregularity.
5. The word for "buzzard" is feminine in Italian (*poiana*). Villa, instead, gives it a masculine ending (*poiano*).
6. *Tra le frasche*, literally "between the branches," is an idiomatic expression with many meanings: to avoid doing something, to jump from one subject to another in conversation, or to find a private place to make out with your lover.
7. *Saforamenti* is Milanese dialect for *sacramenti* (sacraments).
8. Today the principle meaning of *Zoccole* (sewer rat) is "whore" (in Roman dialect). In Italian, mice and rats are often associated with sex. See "sorca" (from the Latin for "little mouse"), as well as "topa" (mouse), which refers to the female sex organ.
9. As with "sybilline," Villa replaces the first "i" in "dinastico" with a "y." The reverse was done in English to mirror the original.
10. Villa parses the Italian noun "giaculatoria" (a short prayer) to highlight its different components: *già* (already), *cul* (ass), and the ending -oria.

11. "Baggian" in Milanese dialect means someone who is stupid, dumb, or slow-witted. *Baggiane* is in the feminine plural. A *fregoni* is someone who "frega," that is, "rubs" or "fucks." The passage may refer to a ritual carried out in the famous Galleria Vittorio Emanuele II in Milan: for good luck, people grind their heels into the testicles of the bull depicted on its mosaic floor.

12. *Nergal* was a deity worshipped throughout Mesopotamia, a figure Villa most likely encountered often as a translator of ancient Semitic languages.

13. The adjective *eucharistica* should be spelled without the "h" (eucaristica), but Villa carries out a hyper-characterization of the word by following a Greek spelling (see page XXII of the intro). We have, instead, removed it in English to mimic the irregularity.

14. In the original, Villa removes the second "o" in "odorosa," highlighting the morpheme "rosa" (rose) within it.

15. A combination of the nouns "speleological" (having to do with the exploration of caves) and "phoné."

16. *Sociofugal* is a phrase coined in 1957 in English by Humphrey Osmond, a British psychiatrist. It describes a seating arrangement that promotes seclusion by facing the seat outwards. However, the Italian *sociofugo* is, in all likelihood, Villa's original creation and probably meant somebody who flees from social situations.

17. In the original, the adjective "inanellato" (enringed) appears as *inan ellato* to emphasize the "inane" contained therein.

18. *Lattime* is the crusta lactea, milk crust, or honeycomb disease: a yellowish skin rash affecting the scalp of newborns.
19. It is not clear what Villa had in mind with these initials, although it may be a reference to tuberculosis.
20. *Manduria* is a town located in the Puglia region of southwestern Italy known for its strong red wines.
21. *Permansivo* is a combination of the verb "permanere" (to linger on, remain, or continue) or the adjective "permanente" (permanent) & the adjective "espansivo" (expansive).
22. The *fabbriceria* is an office in the Roman Catholic Church that oversees the construction and maintenance of ecclesiastical property.
23. The little rhyme in the original *mulìn mulèta / ghe se slunga la tèta* literally means *mill sharpener / the tit grows longer* in Villa's native Milanese dialect.
24. Villa is playing with the Latin nomenclature of botany: the noun *glykyrhiza* refers to the plant whose roots are used to make licorice while the adjective *linnæi* refers to the scientist Carl Linnæus, who invented that very nomenclature. *Regolizia*, instead, is a vernacular spelling of the Italian word for "licorice."
25. Rather than "agonia" (agony), the Italian reads *ingonia* (ingony).
26. The original *porcudighel* is a euphemism for the blaspheme "porco dio" (pig god).
27. *Calends* is the first day of the month in the ancient Roman calendar, but when speaking of Greek Calends one postulates an impossible date, since the Greek calendar did not have Calends.

28. Villa is playing on the liturgical expression "domine deo," which is typically rendered in spoken Italian as "domineddio." Villa brings in the "abdomen" to create "abdomenenddio."

29. *Ecumene* was used by the Greeks and Romans to denote the boundaries of what was then known to be the inhabited world. Today, it refers to the projection of a united world under the Christian Church.

30. *Tedeum* is the Latin hymn "Te Deum" (Thee, oh God, we praise).

31. The adjectival form of *neume*: the basic element of Western musical notation prior to the invention of five-line staff notation.

32. *I Novissimi*, or *The Four Last Things*, refer to the final events of the apocalypse: death, judgment, heaven, & hell.

33. Apollo's bird was the crow. When one of his lovers, Coronis, had an affair with Ischys, a crow informed the God of her betrayal. At first he did not believe the bird and turned its feathers from white to black as punishment for spreading lies. Upon discovering the truth, however, Apollo made the crow sacred, entrusting it with the task of announcing important deaths.

34. Villa creates two grammatical hermaphrodites by providing the Italian adjective for "masculine" in its feminine singular form (maschia) and the adjective for "feminine" in its masculine singular form (femmino).

35. The adjectival form of *Paraclete*: the Holy Spirit in the form of an advocate or counselor.

36. Villa substitutes "idol" for the prefix "ideol-" in ideological.

From *Heurarium*

1961

apoklypse

Ma Mis Ma minutieuse Apoklypse
Des Souffles à l' Égard de l' Être-Être dans Souffle
et comme un Clou Clé dans de dès des Poumons élevés
Rougissant aux Festins-Holocaustes-Tammuziens Débarqués en Vain
Sur Orient en Vain Toquades-Poids-Fontaines Collectives pour
Charmefoyer sous les Pléroxies Etrangères d' Une
Nature très très brève décalée retrouvée dans les Bras des Échos Secs
des Urines des Titans quam parum probabilis
ideo
idea
un Cœur mystologique or fire of bread or whip of bread or blind falcon of
bread closed in chaos
Par le Sceau de Ton œil souder les verticales du Désordre dérobé à la
Pépérennité
conspiratrice Un métal vite monte On devient dangers! le Tumulte
On devient sursthèmes verticales
On devient Délire en Relief!

Ton Lieu Tout Lieu est 'Première Fois
Première Voûte
car je suis Soir
de vaches Occultes'
et j'aime les Alsphaltbettes fructifiantes dans
les Jardins des Souffles
Les Hauts Téléphones Saturnieux!
Ma miminutieuse Apoklypse

(1951)

hyménée liturg

[1956]

elle voulait des rayons-moelle
rassaisissir les obélisques de sang
l’ Es
prit dans
tête tue
tordue
pousse malgré tout
et
ouvre inachevée ombroffrande sexyle
guenille frôle mangée d’ après nature
enfante sa mère à l’ issue
salée du ravin
méandre
auréole sexe île
et
vo
mit
vo
mit
vo
le le

pouillème l' Ombylic des Syrtes
Saturniennes
l' épéechair!

épargnez
les
peuples,
simples, guerres virides, guerres de lieu, gue
rres périmées, décès lascifs, gueguerrelles

et la trouble tribu débouche ses parents!
dont elle afflige les coeurcorps péritonés
glissés d' après nature dans le piège des squelettes syntaxe

<table>
<tr><td>par des</td><td>sé</td><td>phys</td><td>dieupouillés</td></tr>
<tr><td>cuillers</td><td>mul</td><td>iolo</td><td>pouill</td></tr>
<tr><td>vider</td><td>acres</td><td>gi</td><td>és,</td></tr>
<tr><td>l' Oeil</td><td>fleuris</td><td>iiques</td><td>ar</td></tr>
<tr><td>fleuri du</td><td>sur</td><td>pin</td><td>rosé</td></tr>
<tr><td>Kyk</td><td>les</td><td>acl</td><td>s</td></tr>
<tr><td>lope de Kr</td><td>socles</td><td>es</td><td>de</td></tr>
<tr><td>ète comme</td><td>fur</td><td>phal</td><td>coul</td></tr>
<tr><td>un pot</td><td>yeux</td><td>lus</td><td>heures!</td></tr>
</table>

allusion et

olation

allusion et parenthèses considérées

inter

dévorées migratrices

par de

dans

sur

hystère

afin qu' il y ait

une route au bout

des cendres de

l'agneau des années

surplace

surparole

la présence

suppliciée

éty

mologie disparue

dans
le
ventre lappelappe
de la parabole du
festin
carambole
du
toutperdre
du
saccage
dans
le ventre
lappelappe
cachot réclus en ré
clusion sous l'orgue
lœil en petites caté
ractés
ponctuées
happings!
des 100 eyesyard et les yeux

des yeux
des portes
essuiera les larmes
du
toujours
de la répétition généralisatrice
par
lésions
de
prépucecrâne

chapellecouple
brûlante
exultez, fémursvierges
hémistiches [dieresis]
dans
hémistiches
chargent
dia-
critiques
de la prisongénie miraculeuse ou
abominable

ECCE
PUER
DATUS
EST
[NOBIS]

par balancement
du bout
de la tige

la cruauté sans couleur
sans spectre
sans pudeur
il demandait: où
est la demeure du
droit?
point d'allégorie!

BIS
DIMIDIASTI
SAL IN
OVO

par le grandegoutte
dpollution
prêtkosmogonienne
sur disparition
fumée
blanche
race

cette probation pour verger
du
châtiment au long
— qu' une sujétion larvale
[voilà la leda multipliée par une
glosse-plume-rejeton]
les autruches
de plaisance

du
thrônculaire

par l' hystère
lésion
battue
hypersucrisation des vingtamines
dans la parousie qui
brûle
à son rôle palpable tremble à se
partager en écailles
la defectuosité de la

p o n c t u a t i o n

[1957]

ultimatum
à la corrrrée 1953

last AA
AA. AAA. A.AA
AAAAAA A A A
AAAAAA A. AA.
A. AAA. AA. A.A.
AAAAAA A A A
AAAAA A t u m
tu tu tu tu tu tum
1 x 1 x 21 x 1 x 1 x
1 x aux aux aux
nubifrages nus
aux aux aux aux
oxyfrages bus
aux aux aux aux
gens de bien de
gens de
genre de couleur
1 x 1 x 121 x 1 x
1 x 2111 x 12 x
1 x 11 x JAUNE
et, mais bref
andé davialcu tuti

the cuban gong

captious phonetic
el precio del azucar

seductive conch of language and
glandulous facundity of
el precio del azucar
HEADY uncaught of he Mothes
hatch meek of the Mothes
uncaught spirit pantingly
and Nip nettle to rumnage sweetly
implicitly into rump

when bride bear buckle into blackbloodvessel

suffered downy speech
suffered suff to

paralytic eyelid down
a gamut
HEADY down
down
and el precio del alcazar

explicitly into purling
hurling
burling
murling
growing scar (stigmata) pitta
into growing wavelesses oblivion

when wine brite rear fackler whare when what wine backing
harshly + abstersion + headdress + headstrong oh! down down,
oh, nimble purpot burnimble bearbobscure volvenc
scissible Storm Unipare Urinatory Howling
dash
out
to
turne
to

prune
obscure revolvency exuvial V I R U S
How Are the .... Raised Up

as
in the Shrine
lies kneeling
palsied
Baal
Bol
Beef
throw down with with
and Nip Frock
snatch with Rain
alltogether Hold from
Chasm
dark time Nailscratch Claw
Joinable Unguis
For
as
el precio
into
Urine of the
Baal
Bol
Beef
Down

mata-borrão para flavio motta

eu diria l'*m* encantado, e então
uma nuviosa designação de continentes involuntarios por jogos
nasais, fundos jogos, acende
ao lonje entre os anos desperdidos itinerantes
como faiscas de amarguras
abdominais, como bichos de cristal na nuca muda, acende
o nome mais amado mais miolo mais milagre
e o quem diz: 'agora'! e o quem

cai no corte mitico do mondo, nas luminosas
trovejadas generações dos nomes: lèxico
jejum e fresco come o prado de espinafre de trevo
no recòncavo, pàlidas requisições de ecos
e espirros e rèplicas, anforas anoitecidas
no pulmão gigante, palpitantes gengivas, cenoiras
africanas, paleoafricanas, protoafricanas, coxas
rasgadas o abertas, polpas de aboboras
ideais: agora, agora. Nam rectitudo
per se est phallica, truncada tambèm, devagazinha:

onde una zigoma torna-se sigla o sigla e sigilo, torna-se
constellação deitada nas escuras polpas sem nomes
e incha-se então de raiva a fonte das medidas
e das mudanças, là, eu digo, provocar
o poder subhumano da pasmação, do broto
não mortal, o voo ocioso, o ganir
chupado, de viboras nas câimbras
das vagas, dos grans, e veremos lampejar
a alta caça, a esgrima
em voz baixa na caveira, as balanças de ossos
eschatologicos, agora mismo,

si o sangue da sombra não è sangue ni sombra,
si o cavalo do cavalo agora è sombra desmaiada
o sombra brotada na suma sombra ostra, o som
da tromba saca o celeste descontecer, afrouxa
o orvalho, e o remo corta em dois as cinzas
dos vivos e as cinzas dos sons, como
na pàscoa dos continentes cortò o Brazil e a Angola,
cortó as arvores da ciencia e as arvores da loucura
peregrinante, cortò o tubarão em dois espelhos
a tromba grande: não agora.

(*Bahia*, 1951)

brunt

H

Options

17

ESCHATOLOGICAL MADRIGALS CAPTURED BY A SWEETROMATIC CYBERNETOGAMIC VAMPIRE, BY VILLADROME

am strained by
not sacisfactory
ourd of a mind)

1968

—A—

VETAO SHR ET SH

and h ehre is brunt (i'm strained by (hy)
H a not satisfactory
ground of a mind) (hround mhind ohv)
(horrified Sling! let's go
for Universal Ultimatum-God
Ultimatur from God - from G (ohw)
by
CYCLOFLESH
the hyponecrotic Essence of Muscles of Word Dumps
from free Dedalic or Pythial Style)(hyle
and here of here of the here the Sewer of Member
and Raid's Fluency ber smile

—E—

good, it is need unds
to murder here the Proposition
and tree the tree of Brunds
Proposition That say

with negative Impulses or Brunts sbrunts
with means or
Reversible Enigmes or enigmic Retributions
or Throughs with negative Powers
wers scrambling tanatòzoos and spermatòzoos

—N—

6 + 6 times daily something out = ty
THE DE MO CRAT DY SENT ER Y / Y
from the Proposal Numeral Echœs and ty
Chamaleon Echoes E Chœs
and Reluctant Echœs ( ) E
of Levels lie down, from Meandering Levels,)(ty
down your mind down your all
we're nearing Trialtrim)(ty
we're down the chains on a more mollow Level ⟶ Y
on increasing measure of Universal Hostilidentity

```
WRITE(CHISQP);
ENT REJECT THE TRACK IF CHI-SQUAER OF TRACK GRT THAN CH
IF CHISQP > CHIP THEN BEGIN
WRITE (<"CHISQ GREATER THAN CHIP IN S-VIEW",X10,I2>,J);
  BN4←TRUE;
GO TO VIEW END
ENT CIRCLE FIT TO TRACK IN S-VIEW  END HERE: ASLANT TE
ENT START SPACIAL DESTRUCTION OF EACH POINT; AGO!
  BSR←TRUE; TRUE TUBE                    O GRAZIOSA HYPER
  IF (NOC.GT.IPN) NOC=IPN
START CIRCLE FIT TO TRACK IN S-VIEW
   CALL CIRCLE (1,NOC,UQ,VQ,ALP,BEC,RAD,CHISQP)
   IF (CHISQP.LE.CHIP) GO TO
REJECT THE TRACK IF CHI-SQUAER OF TRACK GRT THAN CHIP
   WRITE (6,125) J
   BN4=.TRUE.
   GO TO 270
  DO 250 IP=1,IPN,1
  BSR=.TRUE.
      I=1                 BENS      APP
UUC IS THE CO-ORDINATE OF THE  -AXIS (PERPENDICULAR TO THE
PTERO-AXIS) OF THE  INCIPAL VIEW, CORRECTED FOR THE OFFS
MAGNIFICATION BY M, OF THE IMPERSONAL VIEW
      UUQ=UP (IP)
   DO 160 WV=1,NOQ
```

—C—

Obviously School of Divinity Among Nations ons
represented the Hypoperiodic on Almost-periodic

BEAMS!

to suck the vanishing wind wrong the Hygh Lesions,
wani ishingshaming shame juggle shame,   g.by
shwame in computer here: hesions
            quantum-mantic in the Death of Humanity
            corpse's inner Kalyx, ah!
(=BREATH) corpse-torpedo x   corpse-gate! x (t) y
            corpse-revelation xx   corpse-pilot! xxx

in dirty Brain Transfer (l'Oubblie)   INFINI(y)E(e)
            in Brained Petals   in Brained Petals
        in a Defectional Spectrum   Spectrum (e)

        in a Rif Rig (p=h)   Kalyps   (a) (a)
                    (for the RUCTED   (ang)
                    Caribean
                    Beachcombers!

FIE ON IT

good by, Franco!)

(good by, Fr,

in eams architect

good by, Fr,!!)

—N—

and here, yes, myself, when inflame, Pythoning
-o/stand

(chance) in a some (chance)
in a some musical War
of psychoplegogametes (chance)

(chance)

at a some Disfinite Number (chance)
(chance) at a some Apomorphic Lymph (chance)
of the someversal Somebody Something

(chance!!)

expire (shamming!) (chance)
vernacular bashful Disfonction
and geographical Prayer and

(chance) and Confluent Brains! (chance)

—EX—

Who would embody herself? ∅
in a Car- Rut who stretch (trying) against to ZERO ∅
in a Glade-Sphere where the incolumity of the feelings explode
in ∅ much Infinites who engage all ∅ breathing times
oh, ∅ ! who would embody herself? ∅
The authority lie into the hands of not-bodies,
who then, who well would (au hasard) embody herself?
almost by a buttock? or an uvula? undivided
and unextensive mycrocytes? ∅
Has no-one prerobotated the new flesh? ∅ ∅
(légerment reconnu null-time, le temps se voisine du précorps!)
and triumph of Pepsin of the Peptic Glands of

peremptory perempt!
evirascerated Br Braidpent

—S—

echo of untimely V I E W   Viewkit

          (near Mountain View   you
          near San Mateo samatio
          near Santa Rosa downtown
          sanarosa, down, big sur)
          surely   town!
          when then we want the wowf

wraith who wrap
Wit of woldheart of wAfrica, ah!   Kitkit
Geological Kit as

—V—

nuncupatively god

          nuncupat (ed) nuncp (ed)

(write, then, until nakedness off) (bellevue court,
next convington road, next the rancho, los altos,
california, u.s.a., write) eh, boy boy, eh boy!
die, good, nothingmighty god,   go go

od odd, sto od up, go off goof god!
(but my spite is wisedart (galliformia)
scoffing into the dip bare goof wen,

my
into the ↕ offall ll) (rmià)
my

—X—

naked excrements
town
Readst Soak
Red
———
Red
A finitive IVE
YELLOW
and yellow's N
numbrical nest
The How! tow (n)

the How Snake How, the How How How, Snack

```
SOBRUUTINE ABAKOS (RWORD,IFLAG)
COMMON TEMP(500),WORD(4000)
DIMENSION  IWORD(4000)
COMMON /FOURVK/ V(12,4), [illegible]
COMMON /ABAR/NIGT,NWDS,IN
EQUIVALENCE (WORD,IWORD),
DATA NTIMES/0/
WORD (K+2500)= SQRT ( WORD(NERR+ K))
NERR  = WORD (10) +  20
NN = 3 * NTYP
DO 100 K = 1,NN
WORD(3000 +NERK) = WORD(ND)
WORD(NERR +3001) = WORD(ND+1)
WORD(NERR +3002) = WORD(ND+2)
WORD(K+ 3100)  =  ( WORD(K+2000) [illegible] WORD(K +3000) [illegible] WORD(K+2
WORD(K+ 3200) = (WORD(K+2500)/WORD (K+2000))* 100
IF(NIGT.EQ.)21   GO [illegible]
NEND = 3*NTYP +  22
```

—by EMB (O) LEM—

put out
(brain) by Emb(o)lem

in Eschatological elementary (buds of Sempiternity) (Semisemp-)
Super-Brain as Stag-beetle of
my nephew (few) (gustatory buds)
look down on bright glowed beds (bud)
down tetra trans infinit Box (brain)
Stealty Box of Humoral Life.
(brain)
hz jump over
hjump over
hph beyond.
and plot brain
André, my ↑
phw neph ew view

and A Transaptomathic Blu Brain is is
to conquer (i thinthink)
(Goad got to keep it in the slac (k)

summer god,
right?
rain
by Unshockable He Men Only

eh!
e brain
highlydevelop p
ed

—L—

the omb the onk the onkeous windows (downs)
of the sensing walked fly up the whiping black heart
black purple (burply)
vein of blody anxiety
(v) (good) (giust about it)
(ty it)
call out turds
it is a victory
it is an assault
(t) (good) (hault)

—F—

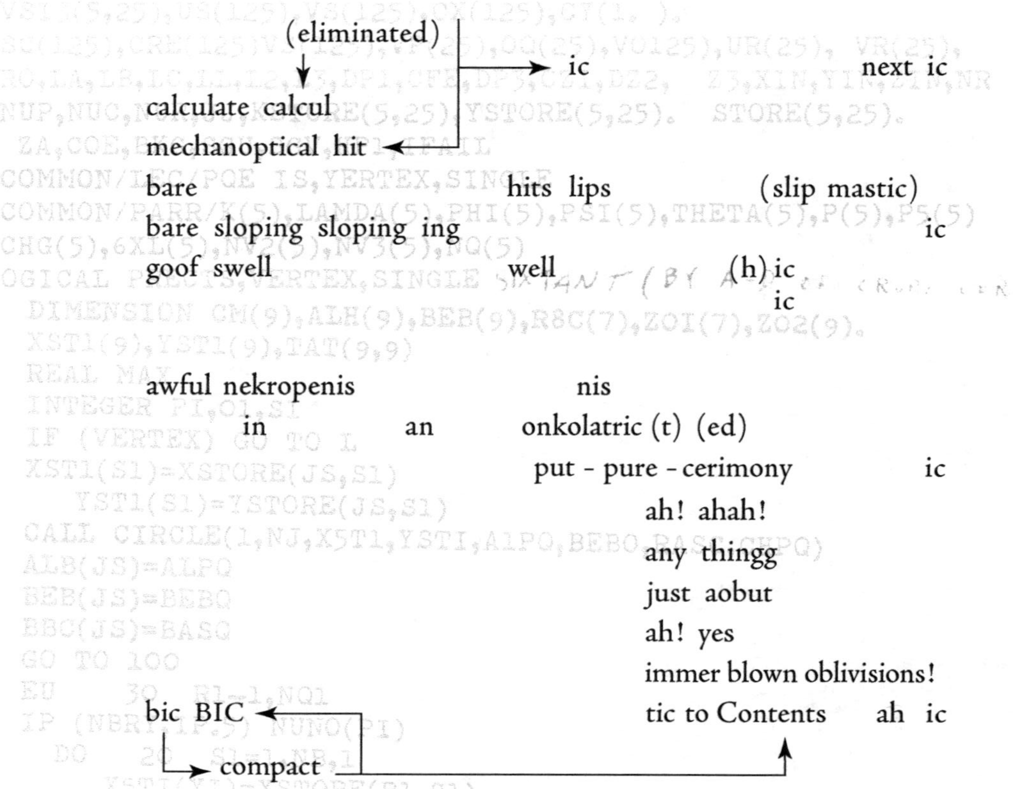

(eliminated)
ic
next ic
calculate calcul
mechanoptical hit
bare
hits lips
(slip mastic)
bare sloping sloping ing
ic
goof swell
well
(h) ic
ic
awful nekropenis
nis
in
an
onkolatric (t) (ed)
put - pure - cerimony
ic
ah! ahah!
any thingg
just aobut
ah! yes
immer blown oblivisions!
bic BIC
tic to Contents
ah ic
compact

—H—

for a and, all the same, cytoplasmes as broid idem

as a marvellous Gulf (for a) idem

as a marvellous Gland

gland Optical Gland

greatglandular, ya (for a)

greatankylar, ya (for a)

greatincular, ya (for a)

call BUPQ

for a

the Bank of Univercule Powder and Qualm

for a

for a selective Mind-Nail (garanted)

for a

for a

for a calculate, push (for a)

Bum

P BUMP!

cool BUMP!

col FLASH!

```
LU←LU2;    LV←LV2;
  GO TO FIRST;
END: IF C=2 THEN VIEWS 1 AND 3 ARE  HOSEN FOR
CB1:
  LENTH←LENTH2:   CS←CS2; SN←SN2;
IF PV=1 THEN LENTH←-LENTH;
  LU←LU2;    LV←LV2;
  GO TO FIRST;
END: IF C=3 THEN VIEWS 2 AND 3 ARE CHOSEN FOR
CB2:
  LENTH←LENTH3:   CS←CS3; SN←SN3;
  LU←LU3;    LV←LV3;
FIRST:
END:  VIEW-1 HAS BEEN CHOSEN AS THE        VIEW;
FOR I←1 STEP 1 UNTIL NUP DO BEGIN
  UP[I]←UST1[J,I]xCS-VST1[J,I]xSN;
  VP[I]←VST1[J,I]xCS-UST1[J,I]xSN;    END;
IF NUP<NFP THEN NPC←NUP  ELSE NPC←NFP;
GO TO SECOND;
END;VIEW 2 HAS BEEN CHOSEN AS THE        VIEW;
LB1:
FOR I←1 STEP 1 UNTIL NUQ DO BEGIN
  UP[I]←UST2[J,I]xCS-VST2[J,I]xSN;
  VP[I]←VST2[J,I]xCS-UST2[J,I]xSN;    END;
IF NUQ<NFP THEN NPC←NUQ ELSE NPC←NFP;
GO TO SECOND;
END.VIEW-3 HAS BEEN CHOSEN AS THE        VIEW;
```

CONSTRUCT

COAGULAT

NUDE

SHATTERED

ALMS-

(call contaminat cont cant KIT!
min menacé ménhâché)

—OX—

pppossessing out decapsulating out o
tth e the fulgurated corpuscle
where all Intervals and
Constellating Scissions of Null-time (al)
drive on o
o (oho) oh, resuscitated pacific Gulfs,
queasy Hills and
shading adolescences of th e)

blo (ooo)
od-less therapic illogical
bals balsamic wondering
comp computered Murder
scomp
pall off fats facil KIT!

(and your Peptic Hemiparalysis)
scoop (into t tyme time timr)
(constituted t)

—OC—

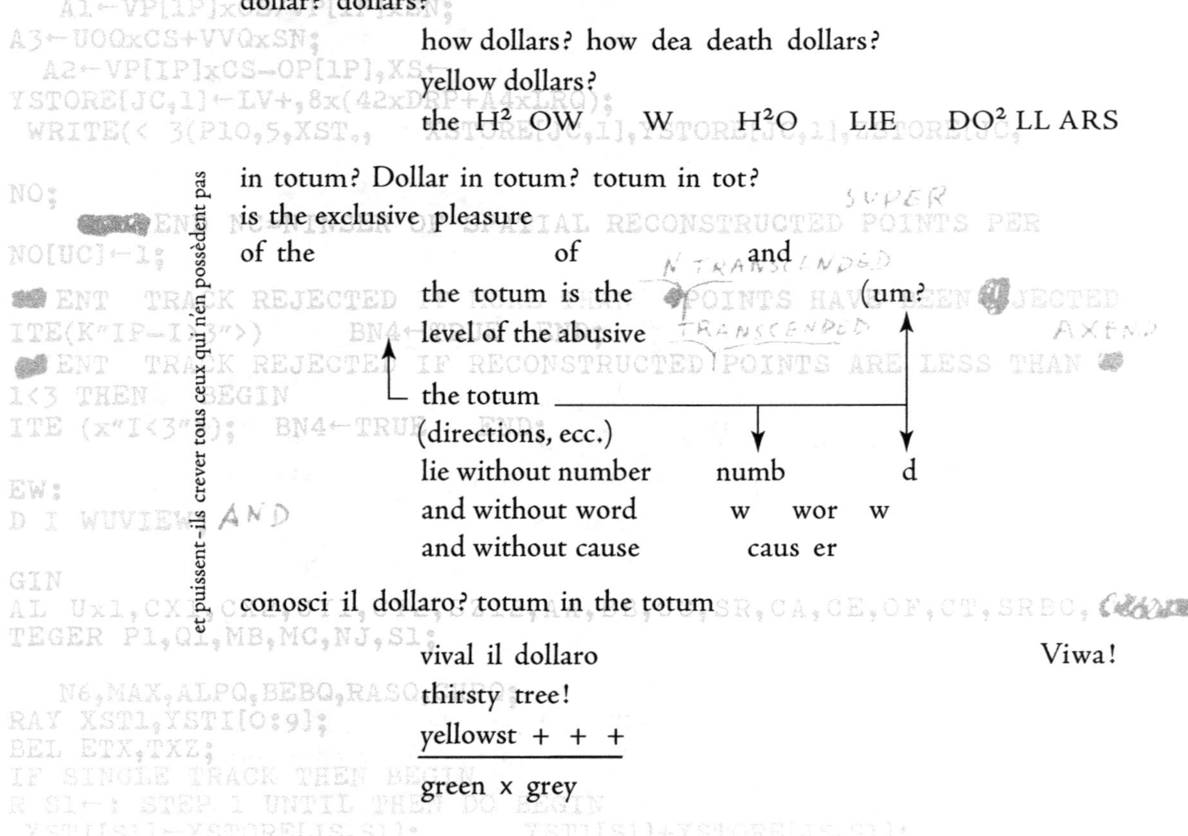
dollar? dollars?
how dollars? how dea death dollars?
yellow dollars?
the H² OW W H²O LIE DO² LL ARS
in totum? Dollar in totum? totum in tot?
is the exclusive pleasure
of the of and
the totum is the (um?
level of the abusive
the totum
(directions, ecc.)
lie without number numb d
and without word w wor w
and without cause caus er
conosci il dollaro? totum in the totum
vival il dollaro Viwa!
thirsty tree!
yellowst + + +
green x grey
et puissent-ils crever tous ceux qui n'en possèdent pas
SUPER
N TRANSCENDED
TRANSCENDED
AXEND
AND

Proktonoos
↓
en redelirant du Synchronos noos
rede RDL evirusant (s'en enfoutant) sexe
EN disyectant la dépé nalisation
dé ca pi ter les mots qu'on ne connais pas
pour recouvrer tout ce qui nous a abandonné

&

décapiter l'air décapitéter
décapiter la voix (obse)
je te dis (à propos du « champ d'inaction »)
déjecté

$$\frac{Sx^{n}}{Sx^{-n}} = \text{EN (Espèce nouvelle)} \times \left(\frac{\text{sNxe S'enfuyant}}{\text{Scène - Snagks}} \right)$$

zz z z z z :

et donc (à propos des « champs de dépénalisation »
décapiter le nombre the number le non
ton nom / ton non / ton nombre
(farfouillant s'enfarfouftant que)

—EX—

o^h au^h aux^h et

et eause demeures venues et

donc il vous disent chose de chose de la chose, disent,
ils, donc, chosent, choisissent, chause
un chouse, un clou dans le pied, disent,
ils d'un niverse Impiété,

$$\frac{\text{oser-ce}}{\text{Hausser}} = \frac{\text{CHOSE}}{\text{CHOSE} \times \text{CHOSE} \times \text{CHOSE}} = \text{f, fut, fût-ce que } \begin{matrix}\text{x}\\ \text{HAOS}^{\text{E}}\\ \text{AU}\end{matrix}$$

ou ça [c] c'est cy ni que : que vive mon Parménide!

et puis, oh! et puis sans se faire, puis sans se faire blesser,
et puits sans cesse, et puis sans se faire anticoncevior,
et puis sans se faire émaner, et puis sans se faire inconnu,
nu, nu, nununamarines, nuanches mêlées, et pus,
et pupuis tu ne tient pas de, ehn! bon, alors, et puis,
tout éclairé, je suis venu que, il n'y a avoir que de

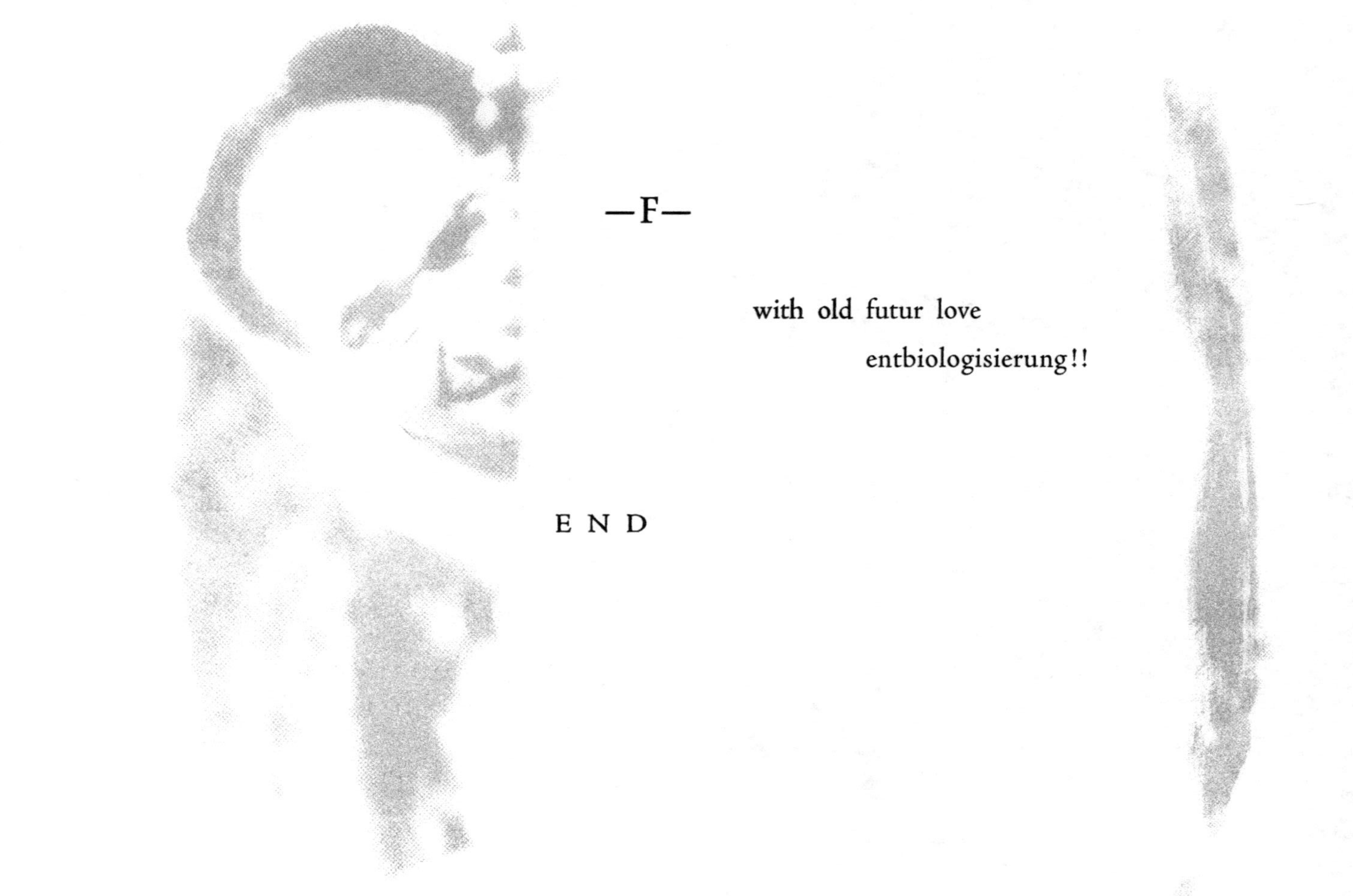

—F—

with old futur love

entbiologisierung!!

E N D

SUB BREGME

1972

BREGME OUVERT SUR BREGME OU VERT
d'ou les fleurs ces bêtes (se bêtent) fleurissent
entant en sortant en recul (par le cul) nul
(c'est mi eux sort ir par la la
feu n'être du cu Il que) di
disent, ils disent : tu as donc *nc?*
payé? qu'est-ce que tu as donc
payé? tu as payé la sémence,
le protosperme? as-tu payé l'y l'i dylle?
as-tu payé la déluxion defluxion luxation
de nêtre? que tu, vicaire de? de toute séquence?
blanche chaux crânienne blanche blême chavire
BREGME BREGME MEGME MEGME MEG
ne me quittez pas donc en écoute, fenêtre,
feunêtres naître, indulgences délices, tout?
ne me, ne vous quittez pas là haut si doux,
les chauves-souris sémaphores véniels et se
reins, ses reins foutus murmurent de loin
d'en haut de la fut nestre, et vont rendrer,
chauves-souris délicat exlamatifs, vifs morts,
ou morts (les morts) en anthropophrénie, pas oùt(r)opie
et murmurent de loin, ses riens, d'en haut,
d'en où, l'où exclamatif, à gésir, à gémir, pregg,
bressé braisé les poils, et, cette fois, en entropofagiggue.
C'est donc du même que la Paix elle-même
dans le bregme secret a étée elle-même
coupée damnée, all-hâchée de 300-fois, ou

de bien plus que 500-fois de fois par, par
(les bazookazz-hymnes de loin de funestres)
les statistiques alors qui flue qui feurissent
qui fleurissent nous fleurissent arrosées
truffées, cœurcasses, cœurcadavres, cœurculs,
des Membres Hauts, mais désormais tous
découronnés des Siens très sombres, les
les Membres ne possèdent megme plus rien, ni
des Prépuces Absolus, ni des eaux Arbres Inconnus
(des Adscisses et des Rescisses, Coordonnés,
Desordonnés, Couronnés cetera) les semences
des dieux vierges sount ailleurs tout près
de la Presse des Horizons, du Tombeau
des Yeux, l'eau des jeux, la Tombe
de tous ceux qui trombent et affirment
pleinement: l'entréTenu s'écarte et cache,
pour le decouvrir, le Rusé Parfois, dans la
dans le va et vient de la nuque-nuque.
Cette Historoire, donc? connais? connais quand?
qle jour 14 de Merde, ede Merde de Pardre,
demeure demrd^{h}, kjai fêtte fait forfait
kjai fait swing shuiñ^{h} kswingint gh
swinginterview 2 into eyesschillings[2]
into the tain tt ted eyes rotten eyes
eyes of the Goddes Bitch Beech.
Tout ça tout sent, sent une peausition massacrée
(revue aux ultradimensions sanitaires, ulctr-)

le frères de (la) (lui) lumière (de là) les frères
s'avoncent sans élon(g) ni flair, ni air ni d'air
(nier ni est ni n'y est pas, niné)   (ekl-qui
halète qui mord/p/e) qui m qu'eklaire
qui avince le lui môme (h) sans se dire
sans se rire sur ce qui avait été dit, et
et quelquefois se massacrer (masse à cré er!)
en me moi, en memoire de père à dit ex
ig é, et alors, voilà l'histoire, un enterré
subregme suplime oùvrefroi (f roi) (of)
(t   rouble) sous le filmprénom (bregmnon)
oh, masse sacrée! crève, tonc, toi-même, Member,
le Glande Etrang(u)lé, Expulsé, Pr(o)p(u)lsé, Ember,
(assez) l'Etranculé le long et c'est se soit
mais en on luit on lui en VI   SI   ON
(le lui mis dans la luimère, pourtant,
mi-ère) (oh, ma sacrée, ma nue, oh, peu tard
ma   SI   ON   massacrée, lève-toi, le ma
tin, le matétin, lève!) plus entre le Glande
Explusé, le temps bourdonne, tik tok, décapite-le,
Corps-de-Charge, Corps-de-Décharge, U
Unigénite et Foutroyé by Parousie de Cendre, by by!
by Equipalpullence, Pus, Puchoix, U
Unigénite, à l'Occ Urrence Outre Age, U
nigénite vivé vécu de ton Nombril Horizontal
(Ember, Member, Remember, Emb, Embor)
et pétard

ΤΑ ΘΗΒΗΙΣΙ ΤΕΙΧΗ *

ΟΥΙΛΛΑ
ΑΙΜΙΛΙΟΣ
ΤΟΥΣ ΛΟΓΟΥΣ
ΕΠΟΙΗΣΕ

1972

1

σκιόεν τὸ ἔνδειγμα ναυαγεῖ
ἐν τῇ παλιντύχῃ κλήσει˙
ἀγαθόν
τοῦ οὐρανοῦ ὄνομα ἐπεὶ τὸ νέφος
ἀμαυρῶς ἤμβλυσε τῆν τῆς ἄτης
φύσιν καὶ ἄημα, τὸ τῆς ἀορασίας
ἄορ ἰχθυοιεδές˙
εἶπερ γὰρ ἄμφω ἐοράσαμεν τὸ αἷμα
ἀρχαιῶν τῶν πραγμάτων ἐκ τοῦ
τοῦ ἀρυτησίμου αἰῶνος κλίματος

βλύειν, ἤδη τὰς παλιρροίας
ἐοράσαμεν αἵματι μυδαλίας
ὡς ἀπόφορον αἷμα, καὶ ἤδη
ὁμοιοσχημοσύνην ἐοράσαμεν
ἐς τὸ ἀτάλεστον κατασπέρχοντα,

ἀλλὰ μὲν τις ὀλίγος ἄνεμος λάθρᾳ
ἠλαίνων ὡς ἄτροπος οὖρος
τὸ τέλος προύτεινε, διαλλαγαὶ δε
νῦν προβάδην βρύουσιν.

2

παιφάσσουσα ἀσήμων τε
ώς επαρά αἰθυίας
ἥς ὄττιος μελέδημα
τὸ οὖθαρ ἔπληξε,
ἐπαιωρουμένη, ἡ ὀμφή
τοῦ ὀμφαλοῦ
τὸ τοῦ μένους
αἰθερίου μερίδιον
ἐδόνησε:

ἀλλ᾽ἀνάτη
οὐδέποτε αὐτή
παύσεται φθιμένη˙

3

καθηδύσμενος, σὺν αἵματι
ἐπιήκοος τε, εἰς τὸν ἰχῶρα
τῶν ὀρειάων τῶν ἐλλήνων
πᾶν ἦμαρ, ἤματα πάντα, πρᾳως
ἐκοισάμην, καὶ οὐ τρέψω
μέχρις μαρτυρίαν ἐρημίᾳ δοῦναι,
μέχρις τε φύμεναι καὶ πνεῖν
μένεα
τοῦ φωνῇ καὶ τύχη τυγχανέμεν
τὸν πόρον ψυχρὸν τῶν θελύμνων,
οὗ ή τῆς, λῆθης κοίτη, θεόφιν
κεκαδμένη, ρέμβει
καὶ τέτατο τῶν λιγυρῶν
αἰώνων μίτος
καὶ ἤδη ἀορίστη
τῆς Αράχνης ἕλιξ ἀθλεύει
καὶ
αὐτῆμαρ ἀμφιλαφές τοῦ Ρύπου πέτασμα
ἀνήνυτος ριπίς, ρῖπος τῆς
μετακινήσεως ἀνήκει.

4

αἰαῖ βλάκα βλέμματα,
αἶ ἀραυαρὸν βλέφαρον,
αἶ πελωρίδα·

                    τοῦ φωτός
αἱ αὐγαί, πανταχῇ ἀναπεφυρμέναι,
γλυκὺ ἐπίσφαλμα
παρὰ τοῦ οὐρανοῦ ἄξονα,
ὄφρα ἡ σκέδασις ἔσται,
ἐπὶ πολυοδίας ἀποθανοῦνται.

5

ἐγὼ μὲν τοίνυν τυφλῶς
                    σοὶ ἔδωξα
τόσονδε καὶ τοσὸν μοῦ
ὅσον τοῖς ἄλλοις
ὀφείλεται, ὥσθ’ οἱ ἄλλοι δε
γίγνοιντ’ ἂυ ἄλλοι
ὥς ἑαυτὸ τὸ ἄλλο

6

ἁγνὴ τε λαγνή πυθία, ἀθιγὴς δεῖξις,
ἡ τὰς πολύστρεπτας ροῦνας σπαθᾷς,
καὶ ὁ νεφελω τὸν ἀναρτᾷς ἄβυσσον
καὶ ῥοιζῆς δίψιον δέμας τῆς προτροπῆς
— τῷ πυρί ὁμοῦ φολίδες φλέγουσι —
εἴσω τῶν μεταρσίων κρημνῶν,
ἤδη εἶτα αἱ ἐχίδναι ἀδελφαί βρομοῦσι,
ἰδυῖα ἐπήλυσις, ἑτεροκλινής καταβολή,
ἐκ τοῦ παιδικοῦ λαβυρίνθου ὠτικοῦ
          καὶ οἱ ὄφιες τῶν μυριελίκτων
                              θνητῶν ψυχῶν

καὶ αἱ ἐχίδναι τῶν χλοηφορώντων μητρῶν
                    τὰ τῶν φωλεῶν τεύξονται
εὐγε στόμα ἐδάκεσαν καὶ τὴν οὐράν
                              — φάσις ἀντίφασις —
καὶ αἱ πυκιναὶ πλήθουσι ρίζαι αἱ αρχαί
               τοῦ βίου τε τοῦ τε κυδοίμου.

7

καὶ οὕτω μὴν νῦν ὁ πτηνὸς κύων
οὔτε ὑφ᾽ ὅτου εὖ πάσσει γιγνώσκων
οὐδὲ σημαίνειν δυνάμενος ὅτου πᾶσαι
ψυχαὶ καὶ ὄρθριαι οὐσίαι καὶ κόραι
δεῖνται, ἄνω ἀπὸ ἐκδημίας,
οἷος εἶναι ἐν ἀστράσιν κύων οἰσάμενος
ὄρθριος ἐξέβλυσε πλαγίως.

ἀλλὰ τῆθεν ὅτι ὁ κοικυλίων
κύων ὤτρυνε προύτεινέ τε
ἡ τῆς οὔτινος οὖν καρδίας
αἶψα ἀποδρύψει ὠρυγή.

καὶ χωρὶς αὐτοῦ, ἐπὴν ἡ ὅλη
σκοτία ἐπὶ τοῦ ὀλίνθου ἔλθῃσι,
χρόνος ὁ καθήκων ἐλεύσεται.

8

ἡ ἀργεστὴς στεροπή
δυοῖν ἀστέρων
ἄνωθεν ἀλλήλους
ἐκβλεπόντων, ἔσπασε
τυφλὴ τοῦ ὁρισμοῦ
ἐπιείκειαν, παρ' ὅσον
πάθημα καὶ ὁρμή.

καὶ ἔσω τήν παλινδινήτην
προχοήν ἐληλύθαμεν.

9

εἰ μὴν πάντα
τῄδεπερ ἤρυσε
καὶ τὰ πάντα
ἄλλοσε τελεῖ

ἄλλοσε ποι τοῦ αἰῶνος

10

πάντων μεσεμβριαζόντων τῶν θηβαίων
ἐν εὐείλῳ χώρῳ, ἤσθιον παγώδες ἐγώ,
καὶ τότ' ἐκ τοῦ μετακοσμίου μέλαινα
μέλαινα πηκτὶς τοῦ αἰλίνου οὔρου
πηκτὶς τοῦ αἰθαλίονος ἀνέμου
ἐλθὼν τὸ λήϊον ἤνθισε καὶ διέπτη
πρὸς τὸν ἀέρα:
ὁ μέλος Θηβῃ πάλαι
ὁτὲ μὲν ἴφθιμα τὰ τείχη ἐξελήλακε,
ἄλλοτε δὲ ὀψὲ τὰ τείχη τρύχεσκεν
ὡς τὰ τοῦ κόσμου πέρατα.

νῦν δὴ τὸ θῆλυ δέρμα ὁ μέλος
καὶ σπολάδα ἐπικαλλύνει, μέσφα τό
μουοίζειν ἐς ἱερὸν τῆς διαφθορᾶς
νόσον περιδρομὴν ἀνεκβαλεῖ.

* In a 'visual' elaboration of his collection *le mûra di t;éb;é* originally held at the Galleria Multimedia di Brescia in 1981, Villa rendered his own poems in ancient Greek into Italian, tore the originals to shreds, sealed them in a plastic sphere, & hung them alongside his translation. This intriguing piece raises many questions concerning issues of both traditional and inter-semiotic translations, not to mention the poet's role as a sibyl, safe-guarding the mystery of the original language by sealing it within a plastic bag.

Villa's original Italian translation of his own Greek, & my own English rendering of his Italian, is what follows hereafter.

le mûra di t; éb; é,

the wâlls of th; éb; és,

1981

1

crepuscolo dell'ombra, il Segnale-Testimonio
annega nel Richiamo, nuovamente pieno
di inquietudine oscura: oh, buono
è il nome del Cielo, favorevole, quando
l'Oscurità, ciecamente squarciandosi,
abortisce e genera la realtà
della Tentazione Orrenda, e il Fiuto:
che è quella spada a forma di pesce
della Invisibilità.

Così noi due allora insieme abbiam visto
il sangue delle Azioni Antiche spuntare
dal piano inclinato del tempo, cui
si può attingere sangue: e abbiam visto
Flusso e Riflusso umidi di sangue:
e abbiamo visto la Fatale Conformità
risospingere sempre in avanti
ciò che non avverrà mai.

Ma un piccolo incorruttibile colpo di vento,
furtivo, vagando come brezza senza ritorno,
ha offerto il Fine; e le Riconciliazioni
ora, poco a poco, tornano a sbocciare.

1

shadow's twilight, the Signal-Testimony
drowns in the Call, filled once again
with dark unrest: oh, good
is the name of Heaven, favorable
when the Darkness, blindly ripping itself,
aborts and generates the reality
of the Horrific Temptation, and the Smell:
which is that sword in the shape of a fish
of Invisibility.

Thus the two of us together saw
the blood of Ancient Actions spring
from the inclined plane of time, from which
blood can be drawn: and we saw
Flux and Reflux drenched in blood:
and we saw the Fatal Conformity
relentlessly pushing forward
that which will never be.

But a small incorruptible gust of wind,
stealthily, wandering as a breeze without return,
offered the Purpose; and now, little by little,
Reconciliations bloom again.

2

scintillata così d'improvviso,
e indistinta, come l'imprecazione
della gabbiana ferita al seno
da una tremenda incertezza della vista,

ecco la Voce dell'Ombelico,
il presago suono
dell'Ombelico, ha scosso,
eccitato, la parte più intima
dell'universo Principio
dell'Atmosfera:

ma essa, innocente, non cessa mai
di consumarsi e sparire.

2

sparked so suddenly,
and indistinct, like the curse
of the female gull, her breast wounded
by a dreadful uncertainty of vision,

there's the Voice of the Navel,
the ominous sound
of the Navel, shook,
excited, the most intimate part
of the universal Principle
of the Atmosphere:

but she, innocent, never ceases
to waste away and disappear.

3

reso felice, nel sangue,
con finissima sensazione,
dentro la magica linfa
dei defunti spiriti elleni,
io ogni giorno, tutti i giorni,
dolcemente mi sono disteso
e assopito,
            fino a offrire
regolare testimonianza
al deserto, fino a suscitare
e a reprimere il coraggio
di trovare ancora, con la voce
e per destino, il passaggio gelido
dei Fondamenti delle Cose, là dove
il Giaciglio dell'Oblio, raggiunte
le divine simulazioni, serpeggia,
e la Ragnatela dei sussurranti
millenni, indefinita si stende,
ellisse del Ragno che gioca,
e nello stesso momento l'infinito
Perimetro, il grande Dispiegamento
della Sporcizia, incompiuto
Ventaglio, gabbia di Mutamenti,
comincia a innalzarsi.

3

made happy, in the blood,
with the finest sensation,
within the magic lymph
of the defunct hellenic spirits,
I every day, day after day,
lay down and slowly
fall asleep,
            'til I offer
regular testimony
to the desert, 'til I summon
and repress the courage
to find again, through the voice
and by fate, the cold passing
of the Foundation of Things, where
the Bed of Oblivion, divine
simulations reached, slithers,
and the Web of the whispering
Millennia, expands indefinitely,
ellipse of the Spider that plays,
and at that very moment the infinite
Perimeter, the great Display
of Filth, incomplete
Fan, cage of Changes,
begins to rise.

4

Ahi indolente sguardo,
ahi fragile pupilla,
ahi òstrica enorme!

Per tutto confuse, le radiazioni,
dolce scivolata, dolce caduta
lungo l'Asse del cielo,
fino a che ci sarà dispersione,
lungo tramiti intrecciati
continueranno a sparire.

4

Oh indolent gaze,
oh fragile pupil,
oh enormous oyster!

Everywhere, confused radiations,
sweet slip, sweet fall
along the sky's Axis,
as long as there's dispersion,
along woven channels
will continue to vanish.

5

e io veramente come un cieco ti ho dato
quella tale e tanta parte di me
quanta agli altri è necessaria
perché altri diventino gli altri
quanto lo stesso Altro.

5

and truly like a blind man I gave you
that certain and large part of me
as much as others need
so that others become the others
as much as the very Other.

6

pura e lasciva Pizia, intatta rivelazione,
che vai producendo aggrovigliate Rune,
e che sospendi in alto il nebuloso abisso,
e sibilando fischi l'assetata forma umana
dell'Impulso (bruciano nel fuoco
intanto, insieme, le Scaglie), dentro
precipiti pareti sospese alle celesti
Regioni, già ecco le bisce sorelle
tuonano, intelligente presagio, fonda-
zione piegata da altre potenze,
tuonano dal puerile labirinto
delle orecchie   e i serpenti
delle anime mortali in se stesse
ravvoltolate e annodate, e le bisce
delle matrici vulve coperte
di vegetazione, andranno a incontrare
le cose delle caverne e delle tane:
si morsero allora la bocca e la coda
[fase /   /antifasi]
e si moltiplicano le arcaiche fitte
radici della vita
e del tumultuoso combattimento

6

pure and lascivious Pythia, unspoiled revelation,
you continue to produce tangled Runes,
suspended over the nebulous abyss,
and hissing you whistle the thirsty human form
of the Impulse (while the Scales,
together, burn in the fire), within
precipitous cliffs hanging from celestial
Regions, and here they are the thundering
sister snakes, intelligent omen, found-
ation buckled by other forces,
thunder from the childish labyrinth
of the ears   and the serpents
of mortal souls enveloped and
knotted in themselves, and garden snakes
of mothering vulvas covered
in vegetation, will go to meet
the things of caves and dens:
then they bit their tails and mouths
[phase/   /anti-phases]
and the thick archaic roots
of life and
tumultuous fight multiply

7

ecco che così il Cane alato, ora,
pur non conoscendo per quali tramiti
egli stesso può portare la fortuna,
né potendo far capire di che cosa
han bisogno le anime, tutte,
e le sostanze primigenie
e le ragazze mattutine, ecco
che aurorale spuntò fuori,
obliquamente, dal basso, dall'esilio,
conscio di essere egli medesimo,
tra gli altri, proprio il Cane:
ma da questo momento, tutto
quello che il Cane, sgranando
i grossi occhi ebeti, ha suscitato
e teso, ecco che l'urlo del cuore
di qualcuno lo devasterà:
e senza il Cane, il tempo esatto
verrà, quando l'ombra totale
sarà discesa sopra il fico
che non matura mai.

7

& that's how the winged Dog, now,
though not knowing by which channels
he himself can bring fortune,
nor being able to explain what
souls need, all of them,
and the primordial substance
and the morning girls, & there,
dawning, obliquely, from
the bottom, from exile,
aware of being himself, that same Dog,
among others, broke through:
& from this moment, everything
the Dog, opening wide
its big foolish eyes, has rustled
and stretched, the cry
from someone's heart will destroy it:
and without the Dog, the exact time
will come, when the total shade
will fall upon the fig
that never ripens.

8

lo scoppio di raggi
di due astri che dal fondo
si spiano a vicenda,
fa scattare la
Cieca Verosimiglianza
della Definizione
e dell'Incombenza
in quanto Evento e Intimo
Trasalimento:

e allora penetrammo
nella foce sempre ritornante.

8

the burst of rays
of two stars that from below
spy on one another,
unleashes the
Blind Verisimilitude
of Definition
and Looming
as Event and Intimate
Startle:

and then we entered
the ever-returning river mouth.

9

tutto è cominciato qui
ma tutto finisce altrove:
altrove, in qualche porzione
del millennio

9

everything began here
but ends elsewhere:
elsewhere, in some portion
of the millennium

10

tutti fanno la siesta i tebani
nel pomeriggio assolato, nella piazza,
io mangio il gelato:

e fu allora
che tra cielo e terra una nera
arpa, l'arpa nera, lamentosa
lontananza del vento infuocato
ornò di fiori il campo di grano
e sparse nell'aria:

la melodia
a Tebe nell'antichità a volte
fece crescere le mura,
della città: prodigiose!

altre volte
quelle stesse mura, come i confini
del mondo, la melodia distrusse.

Oggi invece la melodia
rende splendente l'epidermide
delle donne, e la pelle
degli animali, fino a quando
la musica sospingerà il transito
verso il Sacro Malanno.

10

all the Thebans take their siesta
on a sunny afternoon, in the square,
I eat ice cream:

and that's when
between earth and sky a black
harp, the black harp, lamenting
distance of wind ablaze
adorned the wheat field with flowers
and scattered in the air:

the melody
in ancient Thebes sometimes
made the city walls
grow: prodigious!

at others
those same walls, like the borders
of the world, the melody destroyed.

Today instead the melody
makes the epidermis
of women shine, and the skin
of animals, until
the music pushes the transit
toward the Sacred Sickness.

Da *Il principio della parola*

From *The Word's Principle* *

1988

Corpus abruptum præruptum vastatum, Cancrulum Tropicum, Corpus Inferiale, Grande Grembo e Gambero Ingombro, il corpus rubrum di Calibano, il corpus Pausylyphon, il corpus rubrum di Januarius, di Gennaro Sanguinis Aspis, Flatulus Sapiens, Oculus Ipseicus, Fons Absurda, Meningi a pioggia; o corpus rubrum di Roberto d'Angiò, e il cuore in frustulis, semen rubrum, embryo, spappolato, in giro, a ventaglio, heart-spray. Corpus hemorragicum, e scomparti virali, virus arcaici semisepolti nella Carcassa Intimata dell'Homo Erectus, tout récent venu, Animelle Anginangioine, Medullæ Usque Ad (noi aspettiamo un logos téleios dalle anime che han lasciato oscuri irreperibili i Teschigolgotha di Bios, con assunzione, ora sì ora no, del Lubrico) (agganciare, sospendersi al; quindi gradus ad ætates, gradus ab a evis) (tréphestai come spyrthizein) (gradus) (in frustula Policinellæ) (in combustula Herniarum), lo Stomaco segreto, Esofago intimo dove si agganciano le immagini della flemma e dell'impeto, le esortazioni i deliqui i disturbi sensitivi, le turbe le sorprese le voglie i complimenti per le parentele sessifraghe.

Corpus abruptum præruptum vastatum, Cancrulum Tropicum, Corpus Inferiale, Great Womb and Brimming Prawn, the corpus rubrum of Calibano, the corpus Pausylyphon, the corpus rubrum of Januarius, of Gennaro Sanguinis Aspis, Flatulus Sapiens, Oculus Ipseicus, Fons Absurda, blanket Meninx; oh corpus rubrum of Robert of Anjou, & the heart in frustulis, semen rubrum, embryo, mashed, around, fanned-out, heart-spray. Corpus hemorragicum, & viral compartments, archaic virus semi-buried in the Intimated Carcass of Homo Erectus, tout récent venu, Angina Anjou, Medullæ Usque Ad (we are waiting for a logos téleios from the souls that left the dark & untraceable Golgotha-skulls of Bios, with or without the assumption of Lewd) (hook, hang from the; therefore gradus ad ætates, gradus ab a evis) (tréphestai like spyrthizein) (gradus) (in frustula Policinellæ) (in combustula Herniarum), the secret Stomach, intimate Esophagus where images of phlegm and impetus are hooked, the exhortations the swoons the sensory disturbances, the disorders the surprises the desires the compliments for the sexifrage relations. I

From *The Word's Principle*

* Published in 1988, *Il principio della parola* is an anthology collecting one poem each by a number of different Italian poets, such as Edoardo Cacciatore, Alfredo Giuliani, Angelo Lumelli, Mario Luzi, Antonio Porta, Amelia Rosselli, Edoardo Sanguineti, & Adriano Spatola. None of the works bear any titles; they are simply marked by the author's last names.

1. A combination of "sessi" (sexes) & sassifraghe (saxifrage).

Da *Zodiaco*

From *Zodiac*

2000

Il sogno bruciato di Hekuba

Lettera fuliginante fuliginosa di Emilio Villa
al poeta Nanni Cagnone
dopo l'exitus del suo vaticinio

per purpureum iudicium
literæ multa reliquit
acerrima tunc os meum tescua mentis
ossa verbi mei ne memineris

Hekubæ
somnium sit combustum
et in intumum eat
illac ubi fata perusta
miscentur, per fuliginis literas nostraæ mansumque
intactam permeas ergo pyramidem acrem

this is Hekuba for you
this is Hekate for you

Hekuba, fredda trincea
vulvare, di dove schizzarono
fuori venti cimici

the Magnificent
the Umbrosous — λογ
take one, take a syllable, choose one!
between Cycle of Brains-Cellules
between the Swan-Lilylog Os
between the Black-Lily, Negrog Iglio
of the captured vaticinity
captured by the dark Fire
of voice

The Burnt Dream of Hekuba

Sooting sooty letter from Emilio Villa
to the poet Nanni Cagnone I
after the exitus of his oracle

per purpureum iudicium
literæ multa reliquit
acerrima tunc os meum tescua mentis
ossa verbi mei ne memineris

Hekubæ
somnium sit combustum
et in intumum eat
iliac ubi fata perusta
miscentur, per fuliginis literas nostræ mansumque
inctactam permeas ergo pyramidem acrem

this is Hekuba for you   Hecuba, cold vulval
this is Hekate for you   trench, from which
twenty lice sprung

the Magnificent
the Umbrosous — λογ
take one, take a syllable, choose one!
between Cycle of Brains-Cellules
between the Swan-Lilylog Os
between the Black-Lily, Negrog Iglio
of the captured vaticinity
captured by the dark Fire
of voice

mos oris quasi piccone che picchia
    sullo spettro di un macigno
    sisifeo, e come un soffio
    tremendo lo libra nell'alto
    dell'eone

strepens flagellum clamantis in Igni
gutturem flagellet spiritu nantis
rorantis spiritu per aquas coecas et undas.
Nec inde ergo nec nude nec unde repactas
Vicis undæ per Ignem nudosque vicissim
per hiatus neque hunc neque tunc triceps Voluptas
            horrorque te mordat:
vox Hekubae in pectore verbi Verba momordet
vermen verbi quasi pythican epitomen unam
percurrit pythicumque abomasum
temporis huius nigri nigirissimi gignit:
    omne ex fractæ ventre Vocis orietur
    omne in gremium Vocis revertetur adesum:
    omne, Nanni, incendisti Anien, omne agmen sive vaticinium oris:
omne simul vorabimus Omen:
omne extractum a luctu Gutturis Hymen
ad invicem Semen semel vocis ustæ
incenso thalamo, sive Vocicinium: incenso thalamo
Hekubæ expectorantis somnio Filum
seu Fumum æternitatis infirmæ, sive recensam
umbram simultaneam hanc Tædam, uti videtis
de glottis quam neque pati possumus neque vertere in æra
haec vocalium rerum consumptio
e quale errore espia questo tuo consumarsi in vocem?
et quale educet ænigma hæc rerum ultima moles
Ehu ehu Nanni Camnion! nam ni cesset acclivis ni arduus horror,

mos oris almost a pick that pounds
        away at the ghost of a sisyphean
        boulder, and like a tremendous
        gust lifts it high
        in the eon

strepens flagellum clamantis in Igni
gutturem flagellet spiritu nantis
rorantis spiritu per aquas coecas et undas.
Nec inde ergo nec nude nec unde repactas
Vicis undæ per Ignem ludosque vicissim
per hiatus neque hunc neque tunc triceps Voluptas
                hororque te mordat:
vox Hekubae in pectore verbi Verba momordet
vermen verbi quasi pythican epitomen unam
percurrit pythicumque abomasum
temporis huis nigri nigrissimi gignit:
        omne ex fractæ ventre Vocis orietur
        omne in gremium Vocis revertetur adesum:
        omne, Nanni, incendisti Anien, omne agmen sive vaticinium oris:
omne simul vorabimus Omen:
omne extractum a luctu Gutturis Hymen
ad invicem Semen semel vocis ustæ
incenso thalamo, sive Vocicinium: incenso thalamo
Hekubæ expectorantis somnium Filum
seu Fumum æternitatis infermæ, sive recensam
umbram simultaneam hanc Tædam, uti videtis
de glottis quam neque pati possumus neque vertere in æra
haec vocalium rerum consumptio
and what error are you atoning for consuming yourself in vocem?
et quale educet a ænigma hæc rerum ultima moles
Ehu ehu Nanni Camnion! nam ni cesset acclivis ni arduus horror,

minima mentis errat hirudo.
Niger Hic Draco Parens Aeris sive Fax sive Rerum
erepta imago, consumitur adhuc,
et tous sensuum subactos sine sonus
ad supplicium velut immunis hortetur imago;
flagellum denique clamantis in Igni rorantis
ac perorantis vocis flagellet spectrum Inane
idest
in spelunca stat pectoris edens
Speculumarbos combusta Aeonis
τοῦ Αἰῶυος
seu tempus uti osculum vetus lateris eius,
quasi spectri hians os, et vix alitans os
os proceri habitus alter
vox necnon nonvox Hekubæ necnon Hecatis
per mensulas urnulas uvulas undas
gutturis sit in nihilum conversio noctis:
veram hauris nemoris memorem iungulam actam,
per nigra iudicia fumi et itinere functam
sed mox obruti si verbi evanuerit Ignis,
in quo incendemus?

Tempus — inquit remota vox — tempus
semotum, tempus venit tempus vadit
tempus sceleris urget
tempus surget ipsius anima mundi
ab omine nudo

lex seu os verbi tunc gravior erit
quam Homo:
lex verbi hominem homine gravior adit

(circa 1975)

minima mentis errat hirudo.
Niger Hic Draco Parens Aeris sive Fax sive Rerum
erepta imago, consumitur adhuc,
et tuos sesuum subactos sine sonus
ad supplicium velut immunis hortetur imago;
flagellum denique clamantis in Igni rorantis
ac perorantis vocis flagellet spectrum Inane
idest
in spelunca stat pectoris edens
Speculumaarbos combusta Aenonis
τοῦ Αἰῶυος
seu tempus uti osculum vetus lateris eius,
quasi spectri hians os, et vix alitans os
os proceri halitus alter
vox necnon nonvox Hekubæ necnon Hecatis
per mensulas urnulas uvulas undas
gutturis sit in nihilum conversio noctis:
veram hauris nemoris memorem iungulam actam,
per nigra iudicia fumi et itinere functam
sed mox obruti si verbi evanuerit Ignis,
in quo incendemus?

Tempus — inquit remota vox — tempus
semotum, tempus venit tempus vadit
tempus sceleris urget
tempus surget ispsius anima mundi
ab omine nudo

lex seu os verbi tunc gravior erit
quam Homo:
lex verbi hominem homine gravior adit

(circa 1975)

Geolatrica

Beh, mo' te dico, tibi, sabula, dicam.
Ho inserito l'alluce e l'unghia relativa
nel pieno dell'argilla
per cercarne i grani
per i differenti casi
che si sollevano
dai cieli serrati
per le varie categorie di anime

la sua crescita, il suo
ingrossamento, è dovuta
a ciò che soltanto spira
semplicemente spira
tra pollice in aria e alluce
in terra
non ci siamo mai conosciuti
io corpo, tu terra
se non in maniere diverse
in rami diversi e secondari
di implacabile necessità
di conoscenza, di urgenza filogenetica

la morte in fondo
all'argilla
non sarà allora

Geolatric

Well, so I'll tell you, tibi, sabula, dicam.
I sank my big toe and the relative nail
in the thick of the clay
to search for its seeds
to the different cases
that are lifted
from shut skies
to the various categories of souls

its growth, its
enlargement, is due
to that which only expires
simply expires
between thumb in the air & big toe
in the earth
we've never met before
me body, you earth
except in different ways
in different & secondary branches
of relentless necessity
of knowledge, of phylogenetic urgency

death at the bottom
of the clay
will be nothing

che un tenue
compiacimento
concentrica consunzione
di eteree carogne
di esangui consensi
di digestioni esterrefatte

tutto rimane nel
non-tremendo
e nelle sue rose corrose
di ventilazioni, di psicologemi
di contorti
logos sessuati: di
miraggi presunti che
chiamano dall'ultrainfinito
finito nelle sue fredde
faglie, in sazia cecità di
percorsi e tane.

(1982)

but a faint
complacency
the concentric consumption
of ethereal scum
of bloodless consents
of puzzled digestions

all remains in
the non-trembling
and its corrosive roses
of ventilations, of psychologems
of twisted
sexed logos: of
presumed mirages that
call from the ultra-infinite
finished in its frozen
faults, in the sated blindness
of paths and dens.

(1982)

Geolatria

spezza il pane del corpo,
separa in quattro ventricoli
il canopeo del cuore rapido
fluendo in argilla
tra portici di ghiaia e cunicoli falsi
il congruo accatastato
da cumuli d'echi
dove non si guarda d'arcobaleni incerti
né a sud né a nord
né sopra né sotto
fluttuante fanfara di immani segreti
disfano fragili brulichii
di mondi corporali
nel bisbiglio increato
di alvei di vertebre di terre scure
in preda di coscienza
l'occhio del precipizio
chiare insonni
vallate d'orecchi illumini
di gusci d'ombra a picco
di eternità
obbrobriosamente scomparse
brevi tori d'onda perpetua
e agglomerati d'orge in pompa
e conchiglie gelate di essenze feldspatiche.

(primi anni ottanta)

Geolatry

break the bread of the body,
separate into four ventricles
the canopy of the rapid heart
flowing through clay
between gravel porticos & false burrows
the conspicuous piled
by heaps of echoes
by uncertain rainbows
where the gaze isn't cast
neither south nor north
neither above nor below
fluctuating fanfare of terrible secrets
unravel frail swarmings
of corporeal worlds
in the un-created murmur
of hives of vertebrae of dark lands
hunted by knowledge
the eye of the precipice
clear sleepless
valleys of ears unlit
with shells of vertical shade
with eternity
shamefully disappeared
brief bulls of perpetual wave
and agglomerations of orgies in pump
and frozen conch of feldspathic essence.

(early Eighties)

Zodiac

quello che è sconosciuto e quel che è conosciuto
slargato canopeo del tempo che sarà
per chiuderci, come spazio futuro assiomatico, è in realtà
una offerta dell'immaginazione
circolante in vacuum

abolito nella superficie immaginaria
lo spazio di tortura come spazio
        di respiro, di sospiro, di fiato
        di assideramento, di precipitazione
e come sindrome sciamante
        di atomi, secondo Demócrito,
        secondo Parmenide, secondo Epicuro
qualche sciame di abbruciante,
di annerito nello scivolo azzurrino,
azzurrastro (cifra di coagulate nostalgie)
ordine e modifiche di direzioni
        vengono intimate dal polso, decifratore
        di vincoli e di numeri di fissione
e così sciamano le fughe lineari
        in diagonale, in obliquo, in
incrociato, in illimite corona del
        tempo analizzato, caracollante
        sfinito e deprofetizzato,
        precario e inevitabile,
residuato e indeclinabile,

Zodiac

what is unknown and what is known
stretched canopy of the time that will be
to enclose us, like future axiomatic space, is in reality
an offering of the imagination
circulating in vacuum

abolished on the imaginary surface
the space of torture like space
        of breath, sigh, panting
        of exposure, precipitation
and like swarming syndrome
        of atoms, according to Democritus,
        according to Parmenides, to Epicurus
some swarm of burning,
of blackened on the blue swerve,
bluish (cipher of coagulated nostalgias)
order and changes in directions
        are intimated by the pulse, decoder
        of bonds and number of fissions
and so they swarm the linear flights
        diagonally, obliquely,
crosswise, in unlimited crown of
        analyzed time, spent
        and de-prophesied caracoling,
        precarious and inevitable,
residual and indeclinable,

patria del clima, dell'offerta,
del respiro, del fresco,
del rogo universo, anakalypsis
e espropriazione
voce e cielo

il verbum schizoide, ma insieme
il servum verbum massochicum
(bocca e osso)
il molochicum os orbum
il sadicum os orbis
creano un rapporto inscenato dal quale
si trae immensa sensazione di
lievità o levitazionalità delle membra, del membro,
e inebriante senso di radialità, o radiosità.
Great, great heavens, which
a hand of painted
hand traccia, formula,
chiarisce, integra e disintegra,
semplice testimonianza
del polso precario ordinatore
di piccolo ritmo subsangue.

(primi anni ottanta)

home of the climate, the offering,
the breath, the fresh,
the universal pyre, anakalypsis
& expropriation
voice   &   sky

the schizoid verbum, but also
the servum verbum massochicum
(mouth & bone)
the molochicum os orbum
the sadicum os orbis
create a staged rapport from which
is drawn immense feeling of
lightness or levitationality of the limbs, the member,
and inebriating sense of radiality, or radiance.
Great, great heavens, which
a hand painted
hand traces, formulates,
clarifies, integrates and disintegrates,
simple testimony
of precarious ordering pulse
of tiny sub-blood rhythm.

(early Eighties)

È una faccenda visuale

È una faccenda visuale, vista!
Mi pento delle mie mani
e della mia voce.
Volando e volendo
decretare un universo
toccai il tuo volto
photohiscente
vecchio mandarino lacerato
in tre bagliori
tre e tre volte
(dipanando) (depenando)
con la punta delle dita
muoiono sepolte le dita
sulla mano
e la tua voce in trame sconnesse muore
nell'ultimo guaito di tratti e di varianti
di onore, di orrore
nel senso più ordinario della passione liturgica.

Non c'è niente nel mio
e nel tuo mondo
di cui io non mi penta
per quanto e per quello che tu sai
la tua voce può anche aspettarmi.

It's a Visual Matter

It's a visual matter, sight!
I regret my hands
and my voice.
Willing and waying
to declare a universe
I touched your face
photohiscent 1
old mandarin torn
in three flashes
three times three
(unraveling) (unsuffering) 2
with fingertips
fingers die buried
on the hand
and your voice dies in broken warps
in the last yelp of lines and variants
of honor, of horror
in the most ordinary sense of liturgical passion.

There's nothing in mine
and in your world
that I don't regret
for as much and all that you know
your voice can even wait for me.

Ebbi più tardi lo scarico delle maiuscole,
il flusso delle iniziali allo stato puro,
il sistema corrotto delle sospensioni,
delle parentesi, dei tradimenti fonetici
e tutto ciò mi pizzica come
un festone nel cavo delle narici
o dello sfintere.

S'imbastardirono e s'imbestialirono
allora ambedue i coglioni nostri
s'incazzarono, per dire così.

Poi morimmo ambedue nel
cuore della Belva Sanguinaria
e Sudorifera: morimmo con somma lode,
ma anche con confusa precauzione.

(1982)

Later I had the expulsion of capitals,
the flux of initials in the purest form,
the corrupted system of interruptions,
of parentheses, of phonetic betrayals
and every thing that itches like
a festoon in the hollow of the nostrils
or the sphincter.

So both of these balls of ours
turned bastard and beast
they got in a twist, so to speak.

Then we both died in the
heart of the Bloodthirsty and
Sudoriferous Beast: we died with full praise,
but also with confused precaution.

(1982)

Euonirico transfer

eyios dionysios
grande grande e mite pietra del controvento
come l'odio nel creare, che di rado
capita e si uguaglia
allo stormire di struscio
delle brezze addossate alle colonne,
colonne partorite vecchie, sensazionali, fatte
avanti in procedimenti bislacchi
senza ragionevoli probabilità
di colori annodati ampex annudati
climatici, in disarmo

facce di tolla e labbra sepolcrali
quando ti guardavano dal falansterio
infante, puerile, cantando
sfrontato, sfrondato, sfranto di sfera in sfera,
con frecce in cuore e galantina
di giorni tesi e sparpagliati nel perentorio
intimo screpolo, a predare
nel folto forforeo dei capelli il meduseo
inestinguibile scandalo
di Botri e Sorci, e Scorci controsesso

strangola lo strapazzato d'occhi,
imperioso il pastore di poemi surgelati
cuori coloniali di fosforo femmina

Euoneiric transfer

eyios dionysios
great great & meek stone of the windbreak
like hate in creating, that seldom
happens and matches
the rustling of rasping
of breezes against the columns,
columns born old, stunning, coming
out of bizarre procedures
without reasonable probability
of knotted colors nuded ampex 1
climatic, disarmed

brazen faces and sepulchral lips
when they watched you from the phalanstery
infant, childish, singing
shameless, sheared, shattered from sphere to sphere, 2
with arrows in heart and galantine
of days tense and scattered in the peremptory
intimate crack, preying in
the thick dander of hairs the inextinguishable
medusean scandal
of Botri and Mice, and Sights nonsex 3

strangles the scramble of eyes,
imperious the shepherd of frozen poems
colonial hearts of feminine phosphorous

e di tumulti irrelati, tumuli
audaci sulle dune della cornacchia
cuore di bacio che dovresti
ribattezzare in sale e in ghigno
di memorie carogne,
di antiche, antichissime volpi
a sincero tempo del guatare in giù
in fondo all'occhio vulvatica
di piramidica Medea

scansati, patriottica melma di immemorato
immortale puerperio
dall'alto di ginocchi pressati e strabiccolanti
come gli occhi del dio morto
(perché vivo non ce n'è ancora stato)
dove imperiosa vigila e scorrazza
la schermaglia, l'inafferrabile
inconsistenza dell'anima del corpo.

(1985)

and unrelated tumults, audacious
tombs on the dunes of the crow
heart of kiss that you should
rechristen in salt and sneers
of scummy memories,
of ancient, very ancient foxes
for sincere time of staring downward
deep into the vulvatic eye 4
of pyramidic Medea

out of the way, patriotic sludge of forgotten
immortal postpartum time
from the height of pressed knees, falling apart
like the eyes of the dead god
(because there still hadn't been one alive)
where imperious the skirmish keeps watch
and scampers, the incomprehensible
inconsistency of the body's soul.

(1985)

Trou

Le trou hyérogliphe
au plan de l'echine
s'adombre et dessine
en trous émotifs,
clou ou épine
dans ton ange Tueur
la mort est fine
chose diamètre
éternité ou ombre
membre-pénis regorgé
elle n'a pas de nombre
quand s'ébranle
erronée et sombre
la multiplicité branle
et partout l'encombre
    entr'où sans en être
pourrait on se connaître
pour arroser ou déchirer
des apparitions trempées
la niveau dernier qui penétre
aux derniers degrés
jusqu'aux (sept)ans passés
nue et inconnue

langue perdue
restée pendue
relique d'aspic
dans la coupe pudique
des parenthèses à paraître.

(primi anni ottanta)

Trou
(sensuel)

En plein baiser!
Qu'il soit le trou
le manque qui joue
car c'est le manque à jouer
l'enjeu manqué.

Le trou le plus riche
mouche épouvante de niche
pour que toute fiche
puisse s'éclairer en messages
pour que rien de conscient
n'y touche saint-gelant
messe mise massacre

pour métrer [mesurer] s'en injectant
la distance tolemaïque
et lugubre de nos trous
ou la volonté de se sauver.

Qui est-ce qui ira
jusqu'au de là du voile
à replier l'étoile
perçante contre ciel?
L'émail de Joiele au silicium
et, par mots éclatés,
de l'hérésie verbum
jouer l'Enjeu des essences

du verbum les mille et une fois
ingiganti et rompu:
et d'où il n'y a pas d'issue
ni en dehors ni en dessus.

(primi anni ottanta)

Trou

Trous figés
au fond de la mémoire
au bout du vide
ceux qui cachent
            le miracle
            évolué
en manque en défaut en perte:
chaque miracle nourrit
un enfant dans son trou.
Dans la parole naturelle
où se trouvaient jadis
les dieux sauvages
animés d'un souffle
sifflant
leurs bruits innés
plus vifs que la mort
quand l'Ironie invisible se lève
du Trou tumultueux
de l'Horreur ultime.

(primi anni ottanta)

Trou

Pitié pour la chair tenace!
et pitié c'est le trou
où gît la seule empreinte
du corps ôtage!
[carnaison] chair
ingénieuse et farouche, impitoyable
postulante de la dernière âme
à régime d'outrance et d'extase
en puissance d'engourdissement
tu peux te briser effiloché en hauteur
au bout d'agonie intime
courant entre l'Apsu
et la Mort toute
image cité à jouer
sans qu'aucun trait
de ta figure muette trahisse
l'universelle cicatrice
de ton pouvoir frais
trou effronté
architecture d'ombres reliquiales.

(primi anni ottanta)

carnagione spietata
postulante dell'ultima anima
a regime d'estasi e di torpore
puoi fremere in altitudine
nell'intima agonia
corrente tra l'apsu
e la morte tutta *

The Burnt Dream of Hekuba

1. Nanni Cagnone (1939) is an Italian poet, novelist, & playwright. In 1975, he published a collection of poems in English entitled *What's Hecuba to Him or He to Hecuba,* based on the famous line from Shakespeare's *Hamlet.*

It's a Visual Matter

1. This is a combination of *photo-* (light) & *-hiscente,* which derives from the Latin verb "hiscere" (begin to gape).
2. The Italian verb *depennare* means to cross out. However, *depenare,* with one "n," is Villa's invention. It could either mean to free from penalty, pain, or penis.

Euoneiric transfer

1. While in Italian the adjective "denudato" does exist (to strip or make nude), *annudato* is Villa's invention, which is a combination of "annodato" (knotted or joined) and "nudo" (naked).
2. The Italian reads *sfrondato* (defoliated) but "sheared" has been used to maintain the alliteration of the original.
3. With *controsesso* Villa is playing on the two nouns "contrasenso" (contradiction or nonsense) and "sesso" (sex).
4. The adjective *vulvatico* does not exist in Italian and although English has "vulval" or "vulvar," *vulvatic* has been used to mirror the original. In Italian, the adjective rings of the noun "viatico" (viaticum).

Trou

* This is a translation of the Italian lines Villa wrote next to the French in the original manuscript to this poem:

> "ruthless complexion
> beggar of the last soul
> at full speed of ecstasy & torpor
> you may quiver in altitudes
> in the intimate agony
> current between apsus
> and complete death."

Da *Verboracula**

sancta hæc quam videbitis verborum satura, satura atque nisus mentis, mentis accidiosa fabrica & mentis & febris est; eamet est coniunctio quae est et esse videtur, nec quaedam alia, nec quidem modis patens neque antiquo usui pacta, sed suppar est sermoni adolescentis mei in ecclesiastico dioceseos mediolanensis seminarii prope
Seveso, Monza, Saronno, Venegono

1981

OS APERIAT

OS APERIAT
OS SUUM
ET ARBOR ORIS
MATRIS DECYPHRET
VENTREM
VERBI INSOLESCENTIS
ANIMAM DECIPIAT
ET VENIAT
DENIQUE FETICIUM TOTEM
TOTO EODEMQUE DEFLUXO
IN QUA M
OSSUARIA ÆONIS ORA
ATQUE VENTI
COENOTAPHION FODERE QUEAM
SERM ONIS

CORPUS AE[S]TATIS XIX

mœstior incursus longeque invisibilis horror
illuvies sacra fultaque maximi rima revulsus
Canis avida concepit caudamque momordit,
ignemque in genitos ursit resilire recessus
tunc reserans per inania remque scelusque supernæ
umbræ magna scatit fax, signum quo cœat res,
multa perenniter umbra cœli vulnere languet,
nec quisquam neque scit neque noverit hactenus horam
rursus nempe rumpi meam sensit cicatricem
futuram!

hybridam
sauciam eikunculam
seu speciem
seu rosam
quoquo modo iocunculam
solutam artam exlabratam

(Angera, 1933)

IN HELICONE

apes languebant, longiquæ mente
captæ feminæ, ἄνυμφαι Sorores,
plenis glubentes manibus obtortum piscem
defuncti Orphei, sepeliebant, dulcedine
raptæ, iuxta radices anemonum citrullum oscinem:

penis ille statim crevit olore do-
lore ac æstu, et noctis columna cernitur versa,
super quam umbras persuculptas oscitanter
indemnes rerum pellexi et floruit toto
corpore nostro a corpore scisso luna nigra, 1

super rupem denuo oblivisionis
vecors cinereus equus o[ra]culo vomitans splenduit
vermitans renes, maximis maxillis hinniens:

cuius sub lunata ungula basiliscus hiemis
trepit, subtili lingua glacie labili rauca
gemens carmen sinuosum disiecit columnam
circa:

'urinant, o anima nostra! — dixi —, o vherba 2
emaciata, o — dixi — o melacula μέλαινα,
o mieracula μυέλινα, medulla,
o hieracula ἠτραῖα, visceralia, o molecula
μειλίχια, mollicia! o'

et fragmina demun universi speculi, absque
faciebus, superne capterunt turpia, αἰσχύνη,
constellationis cornua, extra luctantia lucem.

Halitus ignitus, sinsiter fonticulus, olor
infestus halebat in foribus auris
totum ENS trahens: 'o flores — cæciter inquam —
flores cruciales, o leves apes — cecini — immundæ
proboscides! væ vobis, ecce, fulminat! ite!'

palpebribus revolutis dubia fuit, arta
tamen corruptio cœli, anchylosis penis,
torquido spirando fulmine, quod labeis
tetigi et tetigi et tet

subtergens terrens subrisit fulmen,
subter erigens, rigens rictus, flexum
cordi flagellum, echeu τὶς φρίκη ἱερῆ!

ornata illucuit trasenna arida motis
figuris, illucuerent curvatæ res cuius rorida rota
complebat cursum
oh! τῆς μέλαινα
ἄντυξ σελήνης

tunc demun nocturnis is os celibus faucibus
gigantium apium rapui mel et fugimus, vacuo
itinere villos volubilis pubis pieridum abstuli,
κατὰ τίλσιν, et fugi, emunctis varicibus,
sed nos impetiit solitarios versus inguinum
vulvlabilintus, cuius vulvnus nos terruit;

alta tunc ora reticui, vherba bibi Puellæ,
seu τῆς γαλαθηνῆς κόρης, quæ dulcem intendit
dulcedinem, καὶ Ἑλικῶν ἐτινάσσετο:

gelu infectas carnes equi esi, et fugimus
testiculis et ulivis contra ventos prodeuntibus obviam
chresto per undas libedibidinis actæ,
illeporis et per gentiales cruditates:

o[ra]culum et ego diffidi, prædam Vorticis apem
alis quattuor apem instruxi et lenti Fati futui mundum:
'cruam — dixi — herrorem inverecundæ Puellæ, κορίνης'

et [a]pullo pallidus sanguine vherbo
ferox respondit: 'aër non valet
plus quam oculi mei! immagini linque
Viscerum Vultum locutum!' et nisus
est contra altam rupem mentulam inicere.

'Misereatur nostri sterilis herrans
pieridum vulvoculus' — clamavi, et fugimus,
καὶ φόνος σε τιμωρεῖ, mors anima quædam
minuma fuit querens suimet ipsius
effigem in anfractibus æthris migruos
septemptrionis ramos

(1934)

PYTHICA VANA

sta men stlo cus is
sis te
ne sit stat in si q[uæ]
ul us sti[r]ps
ne vi sen tlo ci
sus ni lo cis
mis oc ul i
nec sit nex it is
ac sat ti
sti mu lus us
se des mi cans
sat si dus stel li o ne
[mi]cans la [ma] tes te stra
stel to
lans ster
st stil stil la net
il la ur inæ nex en in
sat men ti s [s]te
sat ill a stli s tit
sat sti irp is op tu ma
sat is
sat ne mo
sat sit us ste læ
sature saturne[!]
sod us sat ore[m]
sat nemo sat iat
sant agius
sut ore[m] stil la sut uræ
tes ca ter mi ni
es tl oc us
in [reb] us

THEATRULUM

intuta progenies, cari bambini
siete invitati ad assistere buoni
allo spettacolo 'Lacus Iactatus I
Contrariorum', seu, recisis
obscuro ligone litoribus,

immodica litura litora videsis
palpabilia, decitata; duo iaculatæ
reciprocæ ripæ, contrusæ,
calamitantes æthram cruentabunt
intutus ganeo sa tur qualo
versetur atque percellam

vultu nervis externis mobilia
atque mollia ligna, molles
creaturas, mœstas infelices
mensuras, ehehu pro pop
pro pupulis expletis! dolor!

luella! purgamen! redundansque
verbum! ehehu pro pupulis!
aquæ aquas arabunt, filioli intecti
putae Pythiæ, atris prorutis
atque proreptis prout res

rixæ dramaticæ censuit
ligneis figuris, fulgure superfluo
interrupto, quasi gigas insons
provocabitur ultra, generosa
exiet inciens cimex in sublicam

scænam, ad Orphei femur instabit,
præceptuali mucrone correptum:
fulmina denique fantia, flumina
flantia flebunt squalidiora

PYTHICA ACIES

glacies facies
faecies uries
acies macies
mities nucies

vehies acies
ories maries
mollies prolies
species necies

duries renies
abies vicies
magies poties
peties naties

pluries pruries
venies alies
seties paries
sities penies

in temp
oral ies
f[ut] uries
fu ries

si ve
sor dies
swer swor
alt ern

sive facies
contra faciem
acies contra
necis aciem

DAEMONOKRATEIA

sub Satanæ satyri horret maxilla
temporis inanitas consumptio quæque
orbis nos usu delicit fraudeque necamur

genii faux genis deletrix
desperataque gena luxata axilla
ehu mala mamilla!

selas selanna irrepsit
sub semine Satanæ
ut per hilum ni

ubiscientiæ ni
captaret cantu ni
ex tasim sinus

descen dentes radi
cis radicis radicis
innumerabilis quoque

captaret quotas obtectas
decli vitates ovi
ovi myster iosi

atque diaphragmata
lusorii luminis sic
atque perpetuam lepi

ditatem mundi

PENSILINA 1

pensilis pulchra nubecula sepulcralis
aut parva pubecula manans, farfara
revulnerum roteatio lepidula ulnis

hymenoptera recens ore iactaque larva
pubes splendidior oculo, nubes languens
palida tepidula aula raris alis

gelidis circumfusa, anginis ephelis,
equidem natæ cunctæ rorantes angues
mortuæque puellulæ ortæ peramœnæ

in helitris roris luroris, vaporibus aptæ,
in intra atque foris prompti motus etherii,
anfractus μελίφρων amussis ungulæ

anthropophagæ interpuellæ!
extrematæ parietes, papillæ, trementes,
atræ pullæ, cunæ meræ, matre

longa cymba, impudicæ naviculæ,
primigenia manducatio rosarum, geniæ
in cruore tymbi celatæ infimæ teniæ,

renes
per letalium humorum fluentes.
penes

(1932)

DIVINUM SCELUS

Omnia ignis mentitur, procul instrepit aër
muta locos terræ cœlumque et tempora volvens,
ipso lumine per cœlum imum fulgetra certant,
raris frondibus oculos alent steriles, orbis
transvolat et linguis iaculantur sidera flores.

(Saronno, 1929)

DEMETRA DEMENS

demens ille demos, demun illa retudit
domum cœlestem languida aquila raptam —
demens ille catus mentem demisit in horto
terga labentia crura artus quoque, aliter ergo
luceat ei egeno nunc mens perpetua ridens,
alent nos alæ delirii funera venti,
longa vocet nos vana nigra illa liquida vena
longus ille prorsus rivus quasi dies ros
in rerum dierumque alluvie et martyres quasi
animales laniaremur memoriis animo
figuris beluis et tremore atque pavore
opacitatis, propudium vitæ, concipiet tremor

NARKYSS

Tempus enim vetitum quoque maius est temporibus nullis; frigida ergo tempora radicum:

glacies undique
nam renascetur
res nuda
quasi deus
quasi dæmon
indivisibilis
sexu et igni
forsitan gramen
quidquam sit
quod non existit:
mortuus ergo
est hic sermo
in limo factus
quasi muta aqua

Pristinam ac oblitiorem libidinem hausit adoriendi mundi, iurgii, cum mundo, mundanæ intercipiendæ pristinae litis, mundi cuius tamen in faciem restiti iurgio et reticui:

in speculo limi
helluatus sum
caro et os
caro et rosæ
caro et ros
caro et ossa
prandium hirundinum

PYTHICA RES

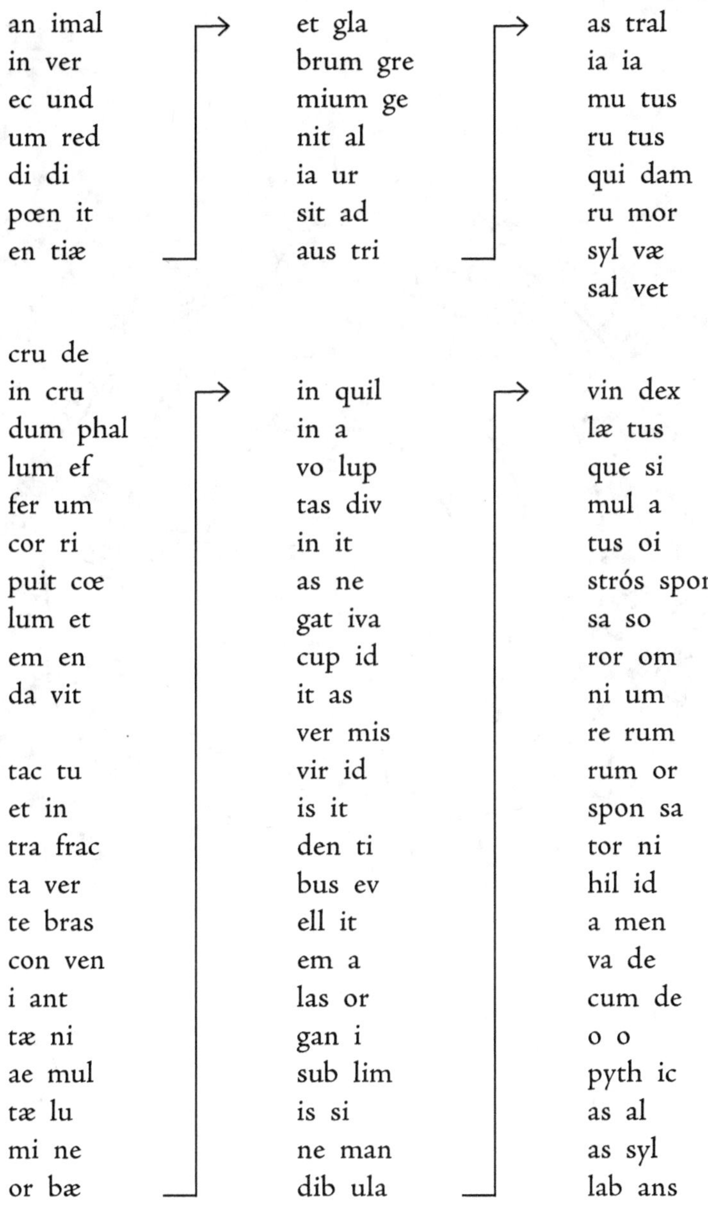

an imal
in ver
ec und
um red
di di
pœn it
en tiæ

et gla
brum gre
mium ge
nit al
ia ur
sit ad
aus tri

as tral
ia ia
mu tus
ru tus
qui dam
ru mor
syl væ
sal vet

cru de
in cru
dum phal
lum ef
fer um
cor ri
puit cœ
lum et
em en
da vit

tac tu
et in
tra frac
ta ver
te bras
con ven
i ant
tæ ni
ae mul
tæ lu
mi ne
or bæ

in quil
in a
vo lup
tas div
in it
as ne
gat iva
cup id
it as
ver mis
vir id
is it
den ti
bus ev
ell it
em a
las or
gan i
sub lim
is si
ne man
dib ula

vin dex
læ tus
que si
mul a
tus oi
strós spon
sa so
ror om
ni um
re rum
rum or
spon sa
tor ni
hil id
a men
va de
cum de
o o
pyth ic
as al
as syl
lab ans

NE OPERIETUR OPUS OPERUM OMNE

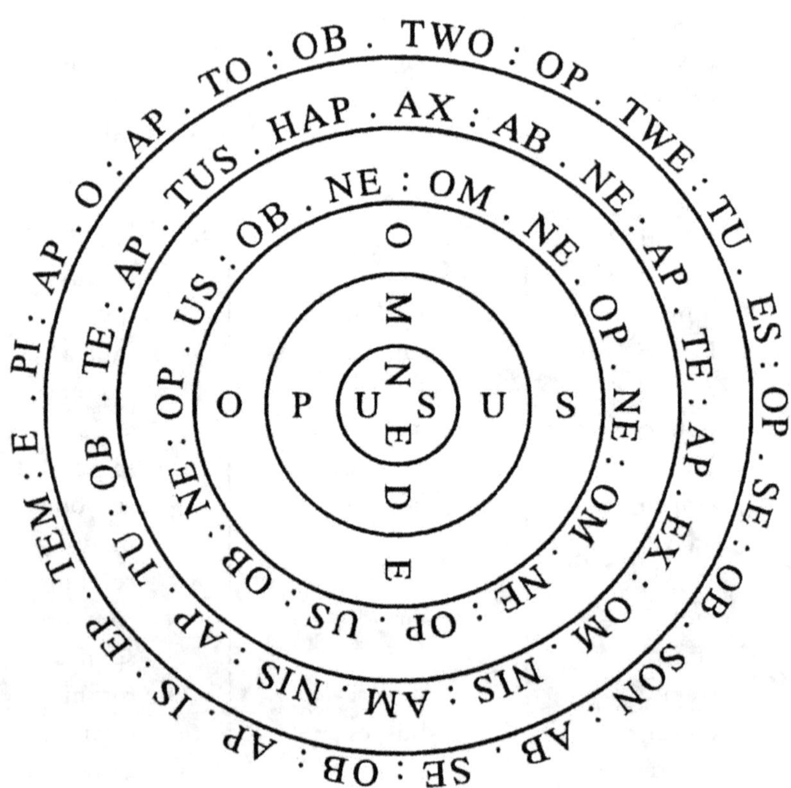

GENESIS

<table>
<tr><td>kart</td><td></td><td></td><td>kars</td><td></td><td></td><td></td></tr>
<tr><td></td><td></td><td>ker</td><td></td><td></td><td></td><td></td></tr>
<tr><td></td><td>crin</td><td></td><td>krus</td><td></td><td></td><td></td></tr>
<tr><td></td><td></td><td>kres</td><td></td><td></td><td></td><td></td></tr>
<tr><td></td><td></td><td></td><td>kruk</td><td></td><td></td><td></td></tr>
<tr><td></td><td></td><td>christ</td><td></td><td>cru</td><td></td><td></td></tr>
<tr><td>christ</td><td></td><td></td><td>cresc</td><td></td><td></td><td></td></tr>
<tr><td></td><td>cerast</td><td></td><td></td><td>cereal</td><td></td><td></td></tr>
<tr><td></td><td></td><td></td><td>cru</td><td></td><td></td><td></td></tr>
<tr><td></td><td></td><td></td><td></td><td>crux</td><td></td><td></td></tr>
<tr><td>rux</td><td>ærug</td><td>rug</td><td>ros</td><td>reg</td><td></td><td></td></tr>
<tr><td></td><td>krugs</td><td>krag</td><td></td><td></td><td></td><td></td></tr>
<tr><td></td><td></td><td></td><td>crus</td><td></td><td>crura</td><td></td></tr>
<tr><td></td><td></td><td></td><td></td><td>crurum</td><td></td><td></td></tr>
<tr><td></td><td></td><td>krak</td><td></td><td>kren</td><td></td><td></td></tr>
<tr><td></td><td></td><td></td><td>kres</td><td></td><td></td><td></td></tr>
<tr><td>cruen</td><td></td><td>kar</td><td></td><td>krek</td><td></td><td>car</td></tr>
<tr><td></td><td>crud</td><td></td><td>croct</td><td></td><td></td><td></td></tr>
<tr><td></td><td></td><td></td><td></td><td>khrys</td><td></td><td></td></tr>
<tr><td></td><td></td><td>christ</td><td></td><td>chrest</td><td></td><td></td></tr>
<tr><td></td><td>krē</td><td></td><td></td><td></td><td></td><td></td></tr>
<tr><td></td><td></td><td>crear</td><td></td><td>krew</td><td></td><td></td></tr>
<tr><td></td><td></td><td></td><td>caro</td><td></td><td>kreas</td><td></td></tr>
<tr><td></td><td></td><td></td><td></td><td>cruc</td><td></td><td></td></tr>
<tr><td></td><td></td><td></td><td></td><td></td><td>vera</td><td></td></tr>
<tr><td></td><td></td><td></td><td></td><td>carex</td><td></td><td></td></tr>
</table>

LETO

leges sumerice juxta Delum
juxta Carnicas Præalpes

NI$_4$ .TIL utpote quæ
dingir NINTILLA
dingir ṇị[ṇ].ṭịḷ >
> *ḷị.ṭị > ḷẹ̄ṭẹ

ṇị$_4$.ṭịḷ h.e. Domina Potnia Vitæ
e latere Costa iacta
Domina et Costa, Domina Domus τοῦ Esse
Palmula Vivens, Velans, Vulvans
inter silvam monstrorum
monstrum Apollo rite clamque nascetur

ṭịḷ h.e. Palmula Ridens in Ara
h.e. Costa Telum Sanguen Lilium

ad corticem glubendum,
palmulam ævi imminentis,
ossa aquæ, corripiat
et sectilis lupus regnet inultus
enormitatis fraudibus unctus:

Leto scugnitia læta
subacidi piscis pondere
ablato, Leto adlupata
lusu spasmodico levi
lustralem feram sumerice
mordat:

cydonio extruso scroto
scrofulas esit preci-
pitanter, glandulas, fragas,
usque ad nates terga
rudibus candida lunis
per ramos per undas per merdas instrata fugiant monstra

SALTAFOSSUM

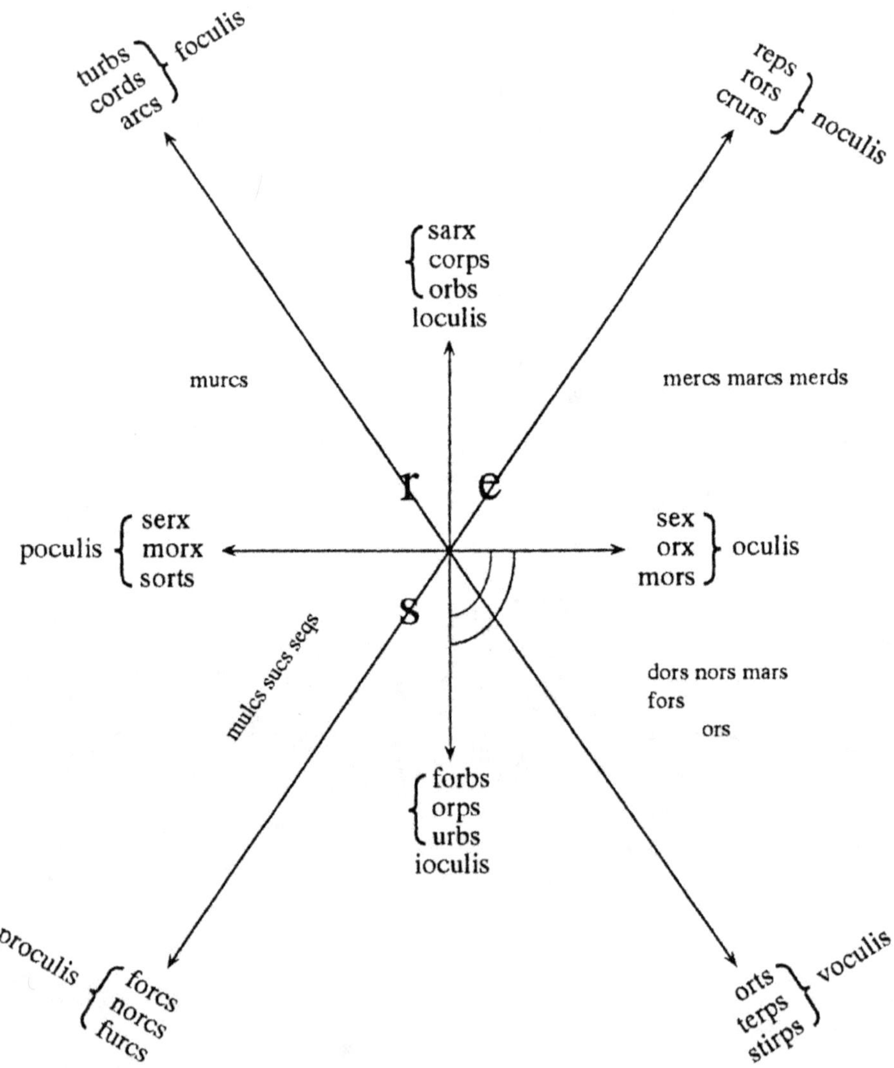

SALTAFOSSUM

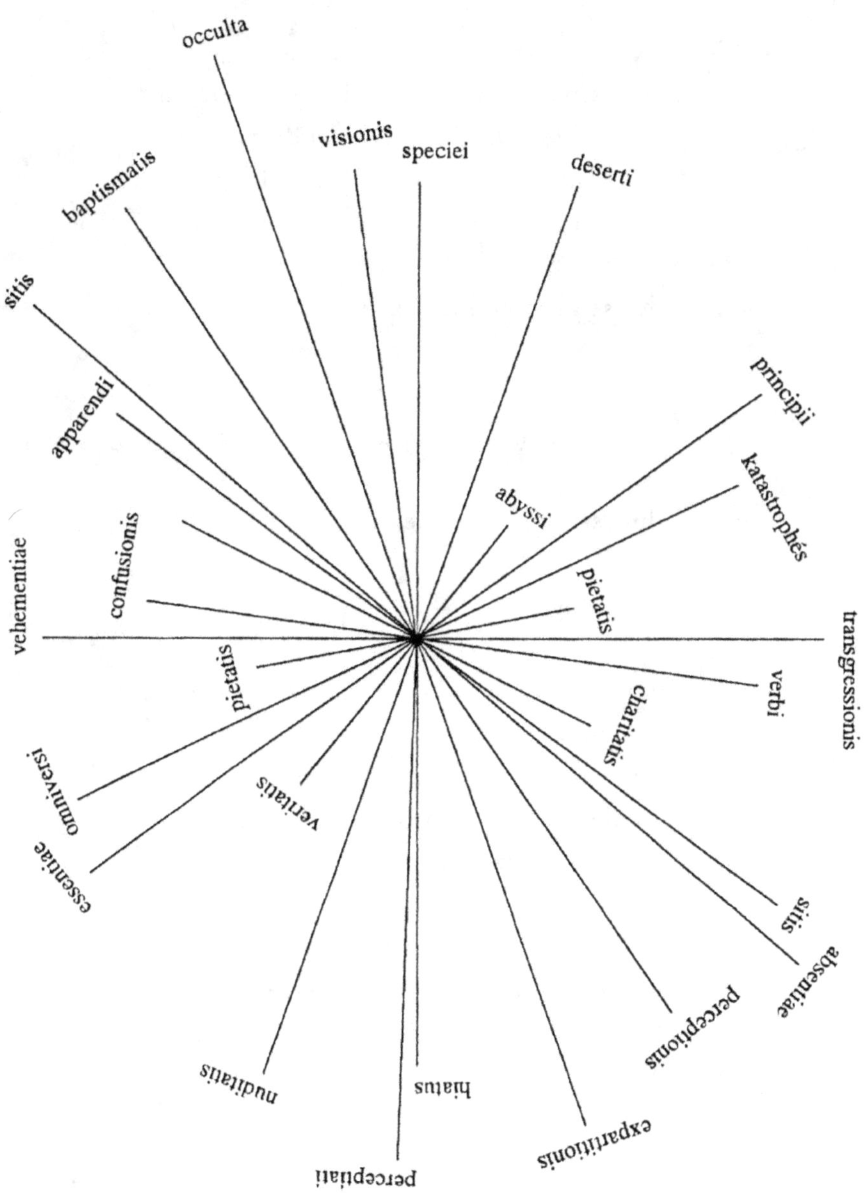

ARTEMIS

leges sumerice ạṛạḍẹ.ṃẹ.ḍịṃ.ṣ̌ạ
ạṛạ$_4$, seu akkadice ṇạṃṛụ, h.e. splendescens
splendit splendida splenduit
aut sị̂tu, h.e. exiens (luna) in cœlo,
exitus (cœli) luna

ḍẹ$_3$, seu ḷạ' ạḅụ, h.e. fax, lucens falx,
flamma lucis ignis

ṃẹ, seu ṣ̌ạṃṣ̌ụ, h.e. cœlum et ordo cœli

ḍịṃ, seu p̣ị̂, h.e. facies

ṣ̌ạ, seu ụṛụ̂, h.e. vulva

vunerabilis atque nudata vulneribus undans
fruticibus coata vulvæ,
formidine corusca, subter caudice cornus
enode nubit cornu artemideum ulvæ,
nubes noxia vela ac velaria, repens
subtilis descendit horrida cutis
in porcis intra lurores, fremitusque
lubrica proscindunt, erepunt curvæ,
crinibus micans extinguitur equus, ansam
suburguet agonistes fœda, nigrissima riget
fabula, ulula radii scribit cœlestes umbras

PETALUS VU

Vomitans Vomitatis
Vomitans Novum
Vomes N ovum
Vomitum Vorat

Visum Vehet Vox
Vehemens Vir Vix
Votum Vacuum Os
Vetat Vis N Ova

Vomere Vulnus Vacuet
Vulneris Vadit Venit
Via Verticem Videat
Viridis Varia Vegens
Vertigo Vastet Vultus

Vulcam Vundæ Vasæ
Vultures Volant Vult
Versus Valeant Venena:

Vulpes ehú, ehéu Vulpes
Vanuerunt Verecundiæ
Vehú! vehú! vuú Vitulus
Vocat Vanvera Vulvat 1
Virus Vacca Varuna
Viridi Veste Vestita
Vaporis Vela Versa
Vena Hæsa

HERCULES

cum constet deum mortuum
herculem fuisse etiam
dingir sumerice ^{dingir}
EN . MER . KAR
(heros deus, frater Astartis,
Solis filius & Terræ Matris)

[per   *(en)merkar, inde
         *(en)werakr/l
eureka, mehercle!] unde hymnus:

tribus   lucentibus
testiculis tractis
appareat her
                 cul es
ver   tebras   ebrias
                 plic ans
ovul ariter   ter
                        rore

        arc   uter
        alter uter
        ulter uter
        matr uter
                ter
                ror ter
                tæ

HERMES

ani ma lat oris
tum oral ium cel
lu lar um
in cap sul is
    ab scon dit us

    an us hud us
    hum us

ebr ia ci
        vi li tas
vis i bil is
        ætate æstate
        ætute ædeque
        adiuta, mehercle

        in
visi bil isis
        hor rore
        ord rore
        am ore
        hum ore
trans duc tus

trans lat io
sum er ice
dingir URU$_3$. MAŠ
h.e. deus dingir EN . NU . GI

PROBLEMA A

A
axium plurium plurimus axis
plurimus actus cricumaxialis
unica A modularis A anxia
maximi maxima mixti axis spiralis
genero alieno sonat resonat amens
A modularis turbata atque præsecta A
circinum furiose ictitando usque ad nullam
icunculam

From *Verboracula*

* For this collection, Villa added composition dates for some poems. However, it is very unlikely that these dates are accurate, for he would have written some of these compositions in his late teens.

IN HELICONE

1. A mix of Latin and Italian, this line roughly translates as "our body in divided body black moon."
2. Italian for "oh our soul."

THEATRULUM

1. The Italian *cari bambini siete invitati ad assistere buoni allo spettacolo* roughly translates to "my dear children you're invited to participate in the show and be on your best behavior."

PENSILINA

1. In Italian *pensilina* refers to a "platform roof."

PETALUS VU

1. In Italian, *parlare a vanvera* means to "babble on."

Geometria Reformata

Reformed Geometry

1990

vidi intactas
tabulas speciosas,
super eas conscripsi
salientibus literis
ad animas luce
rumpendas, easque
tibi reddo conscriptas

Claudio Parmiggiani

Geometria Reformata 10 Zeichnungen 1977-1978

plus ***
Pythicum
Nutum
adiecit
aemilius
lauri
fumis
incitatus

Edition Annemarie Verna
EMIL VILLA
Zürich
ROM

Pene immixto in lavatrina ISOMIX

1)	**Bleistift,**	1977	cm.	45,3 x 59,8
2)	„	1977	„	46 x 60
3)	„	1977	„	46 x 59
4)	„	1977	„	46 x 55
5)	„	1977	„	58 x 45
6)	„	1977	„	50 x 59
7)	„	1977	„	45,5 x 59
8)	„	1978	„	50 x 59
9)	„	1978	„	45,5 x 60
10)	„	1978	„	46 x 59,5

ex Labiis
deae ΑΤΗΣ
omnia accepi
omnia trapam
quae novi quae scripsi

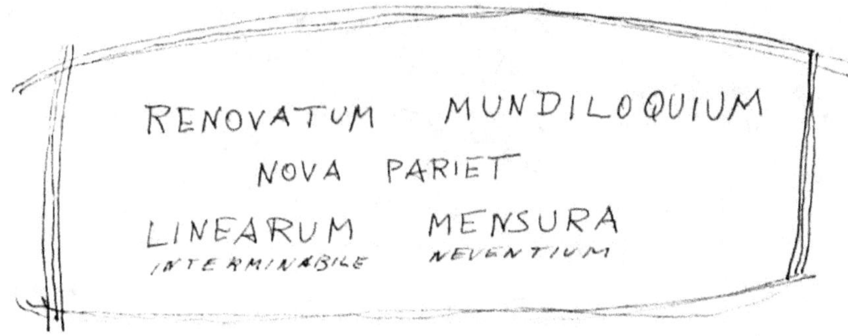

AEMILII DONUM
PRO CLAUDIO, ὁ γεωμέτρης

nostra rixa omnis extensa
nigra ἐνέργεια
vis venitat
vis veniat ubi inferior
interior superior habitus
reflans fons luceat
assiduus fomes
linea nondum sana videatur
et iter cineris in turbinem recedat

per os et per es
in oculo et in poculo
serenus ruit ros!

deus subtilis dies noctis
donum silens aedes muta
regit infirmitatem rerum
magnam animam tegat
sub vitreo aestuario
sub infirma ala
ipsam vim generans in labiis
ipsam infirmitatem urens in labiis
numinum fontis obscurae clara in neminis ore fictio

et derelicto derelicta, oh oh,
stercoribus nutrix, ah ah,
saeculi simulatrix!
(! αἰῶνος σημαντικὸν σπέρμα !)

nubes dissipabuntur
in petribus sedebimus

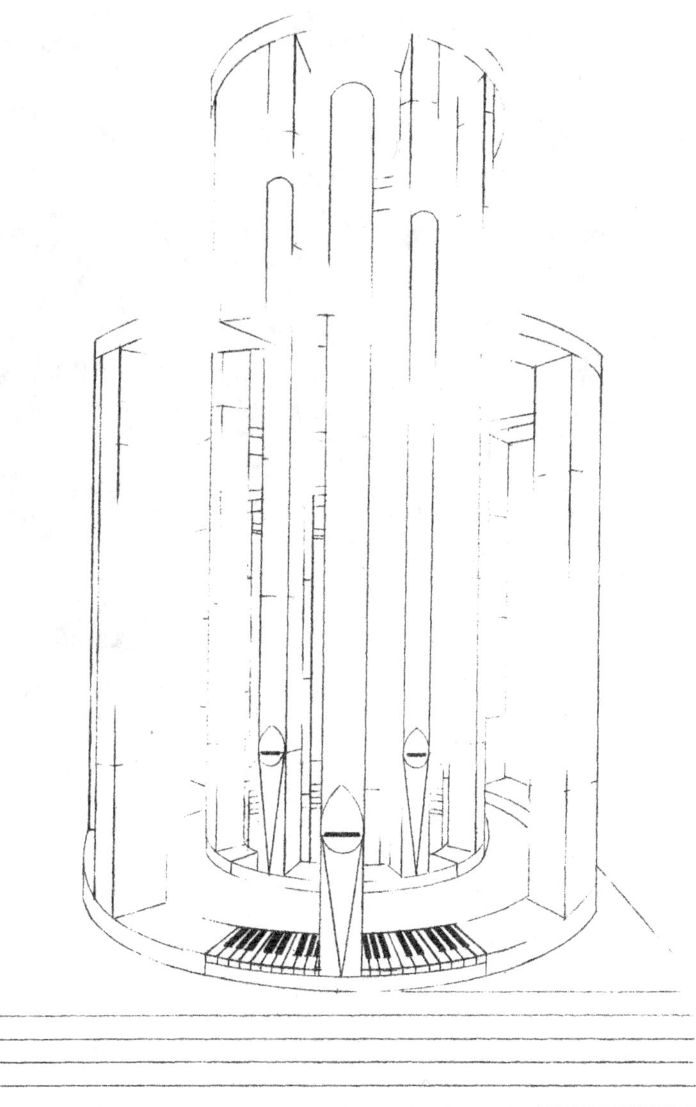

margo moritur
aeque ac ars
longa cinis
urens post
futura futurans

ac nec et or ut hic ab ob

ortus ac obitus suffocet nidum
moeror medullae cranium
sectus sexus suturam in nihilum

ἀνάπτυξις
impotens nisus lamae
sacra rixa comperit mentem

ἀνάπτυξις
vestigia premitans lineae
atque anhelitus palmitans
quandoquidem animans
linea clare delirans
vims absconditus
in intimis artubus

paululum febris
paululum vitae
paululum mortis

ἀνάπτυξις
et in oculo coacta
compulsa tandem libido

ἀιῶν τοῦ ἄλφα καὶ τοῦ ωμέγα
lux salex lex sedens
lux sadica
(cruxspes)
(moxnex) micans
(pul chrum abspectrum)
de pheretro aëris
(nuxnox)
(maxillis) ob rerum aerumnas

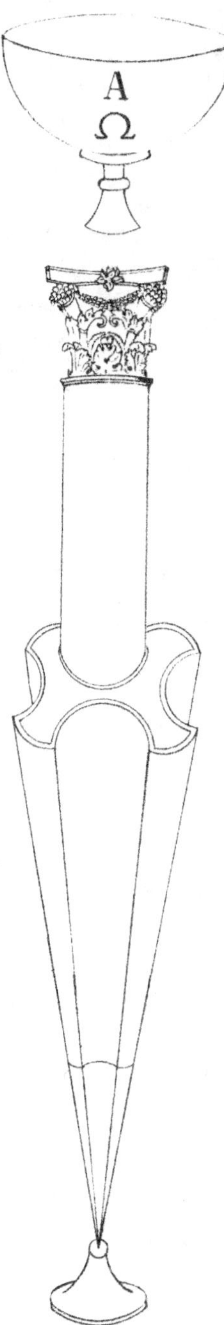
A
Ω

subversum fit visceribus imis Proelium
et postquam Parvi Filioli parva verpuly
a parvo pube Sanctissimae Matris
salsos Fluctus proscidit arvalis Uterus
uti Sphaera per undas aegaeas ruit,
secreta alii Daemonis species, tremitans
insatiata Libido Inguinis

! Abyssus est linea , Purus pater-
! Linea est Abyssus , Pura mater-
imago purae infirmitatis suae
subrepens [Striges] unda
ab Angulo gemens denuo gignitur
ab Anguine anguis clara leporis
tabula

x

x

x

elixi jaceant lemures
lineis scalenis obnoxii
sensuum sepulcrum
per lineam exsuctae
Ob li vi o nis,
pulpa rerum.

superior lethargus incipiet
post speciem utinam laesam,
mors foemina
nemen nomen affinitatis fiat

x

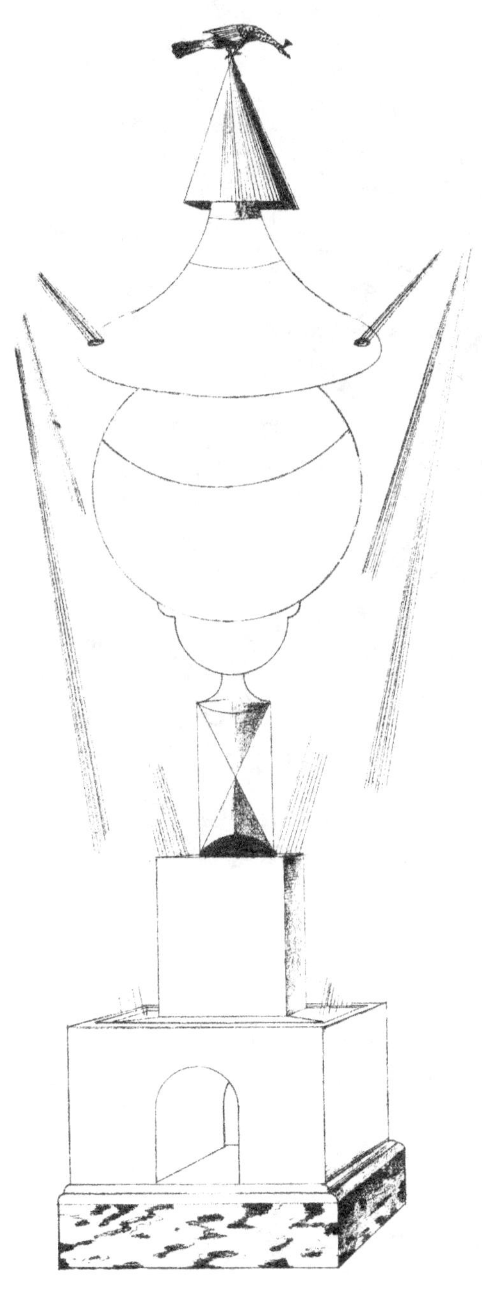

rupta krikoides
vultnus in vultnere
coeca ipsius
lineae linea

hic est
fagidus
hortus

frigilis
ortus

super
vacua
port
uum

locum sum
mitate un
iversa con
summans

furens plaudens erectio
obnubinbilanti deo
exhaeret

olfactus Verbi atque,
(τοῦ) αἰῶνος) ὀργῆ
fluunt , dein

in mentis se tectis umbris
umbris tectis
transmeat oculus
subrenalis
parvis nudis undis undique fluens
dum nigra sub luna dormitat
mensura
περιπετής

suprema noctis trabs
vertigo, occulta fecunda coeca ebrietas
quam animus plurimus petit ac aufert....

frons ultimans fugiens luce velocior
in quo ordinis cuiusdam Dati revolutio
atque immortalis aut mortalis ruina
proximae et incensae videantur

aevo avis-ovi consummimur / oviavisimur

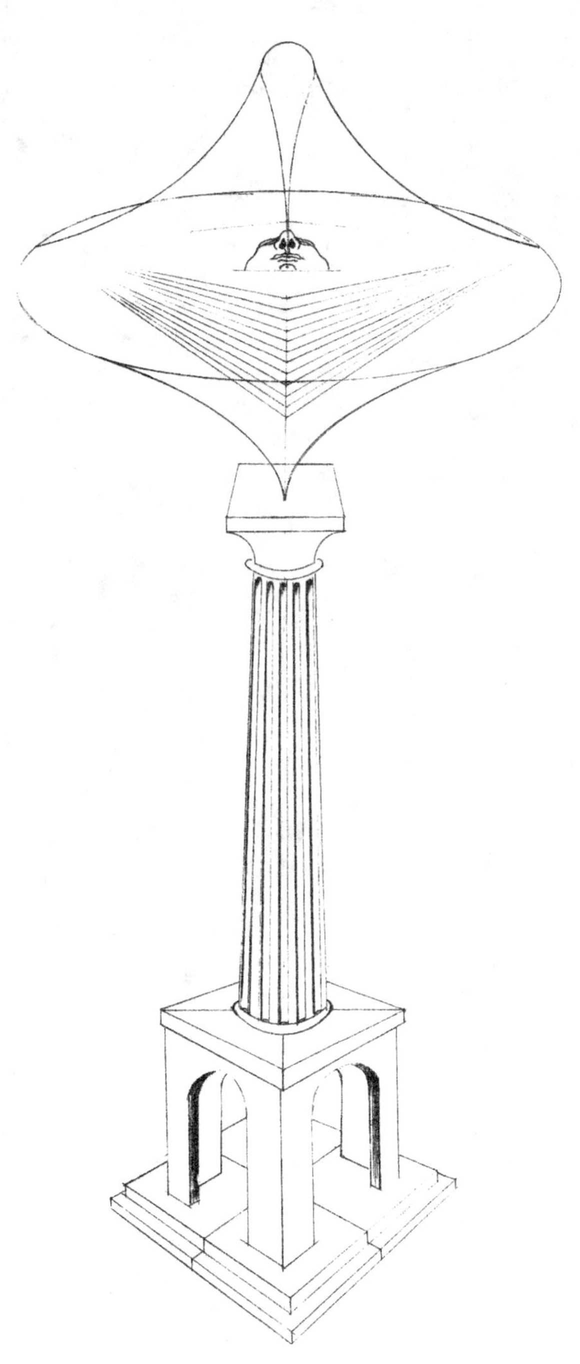

ut queat Ultima nulla resonare Fibra
capitis corporis pulveris formicis numeri Linea =
Ignis coeli prismate fracto,
vastato formice suppeditet ignoto
numero fossili, nullius brachiis
defendat

A.D. MI · Y C

ehuchu quantum volnus
in ceresia una ! et quot
sonus in sanguine —
in idipso – –

Oedipus, sub luce Fulguris,
soror atque frater Speculi,
(subcisa sententia), mentem
Sororem puniat aeque ac
nidificet —

Corpus, Temporum Aciem,
Corpus maximum, de Signo
minissimo, eruant
Fulgures HHH

usque ad intimos sinus in aëre
et sic semper simul interim
invisibiles semitae vagulae
portiunculam thesaurizant

horror in vagula spicula
dormit et regnat — per
pendiculatus pandiculatus pensus-
quia linea carnis in lumpa sanguinis

Sol Imus
Infans Infima
Proles
Pronus
Protinus
Procax
Prosus
In Cerebro
In Delapsu Somnii
Pudens
Punctum
Caecum
Obdurescens Ille Ignis Oculus

audi accipe contraiacturae desiderium amen-omen
audi ergo accipe n omen s emen n emen n udum

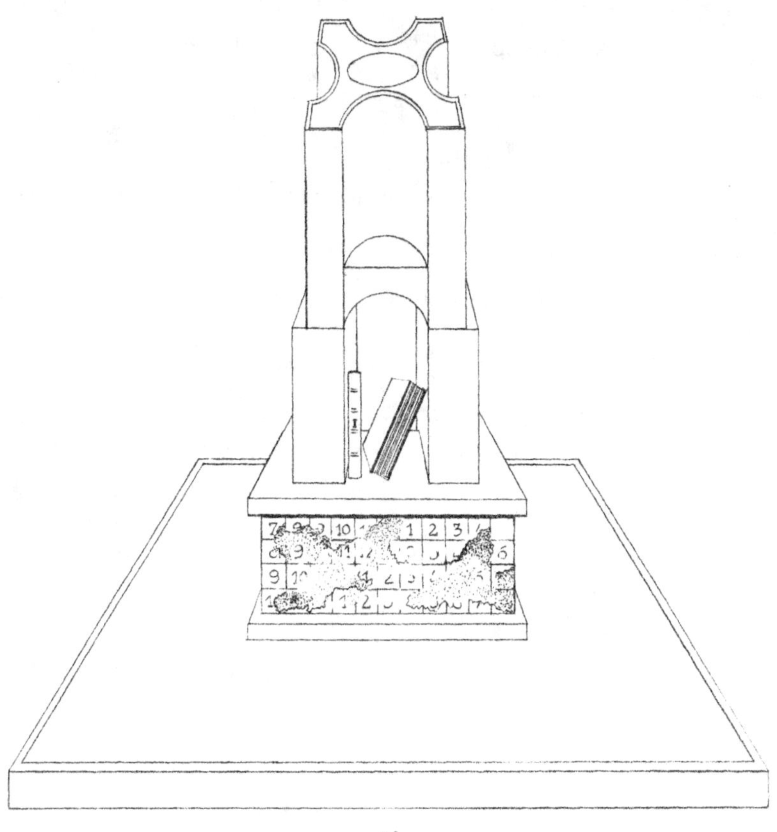

et quid in arcu   sine gemitu uteri
et quid in utero   sine gemitu spicae

patent Deorum Deorum Deorum stamina
aut ultra cellulam in aenigmate Campi

terrarum mensurae iaculant
in Corpore Corporis, in Terra Terrarum,

res in numine ora quatiunt
usquedum (p)o(s)culum moritur
abstruso Loco spirante

ruit Terra Terra ruit
spica feriet parietem

natus est natis;
lapis desonat, verbum
corrupta lapis gignit,
lancinans fossa Locum corripiet :

pars genitata   ultra genitet
rebus luctantibus   partam larvam
astralem rorem

linearula ferens
linearula foetens
linearula feriens
linearula futuens

linearula moerens
linearula nutens
linearula metiens
linearula moriens —

sol in nhumero
favilla cucurrit,
mundus roravit
rosam rorantem,
sol in numero
lineas retulit —

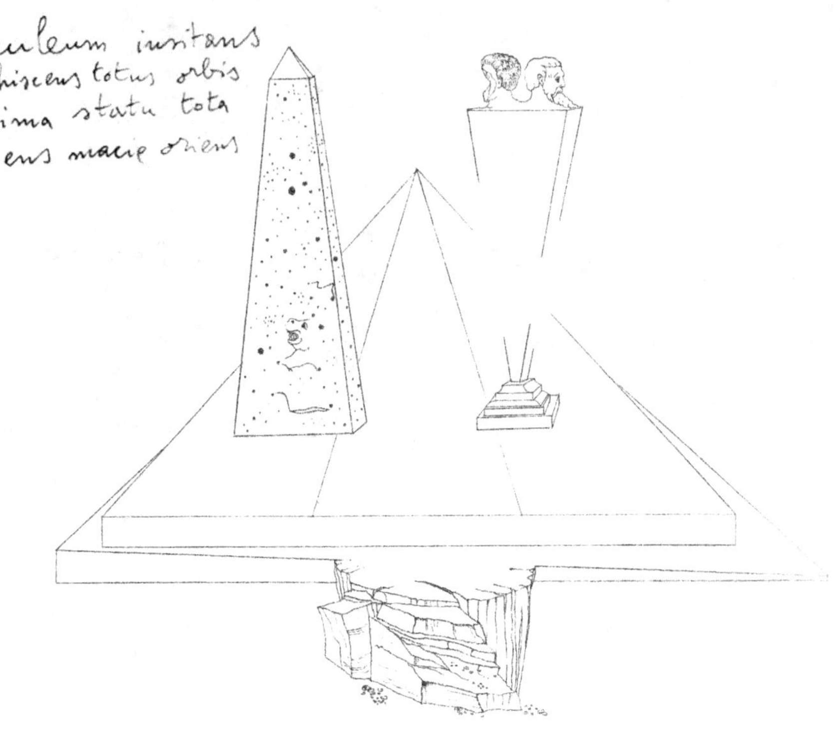

patens patiens res rem gignit

nemen geometricum nemen aerometricum
neming neminis numina numero nhoment
nemen ullum nemen nhullum g enitum
et palam
ad neminanda clam n omina n hemi nata
g eminorta

veniant reveniant atque immo revenient
nemina conivientia

quiescant neming sive
in lucem redacta
in corpus dirata
in aetem coacta
in arcum peracta
in aciem exacta
in lapidem subacta
in gradus inacta
in locum obacta
in rem acta

copula
locus
caput locus stupum
nemen nemus
stupor
semen

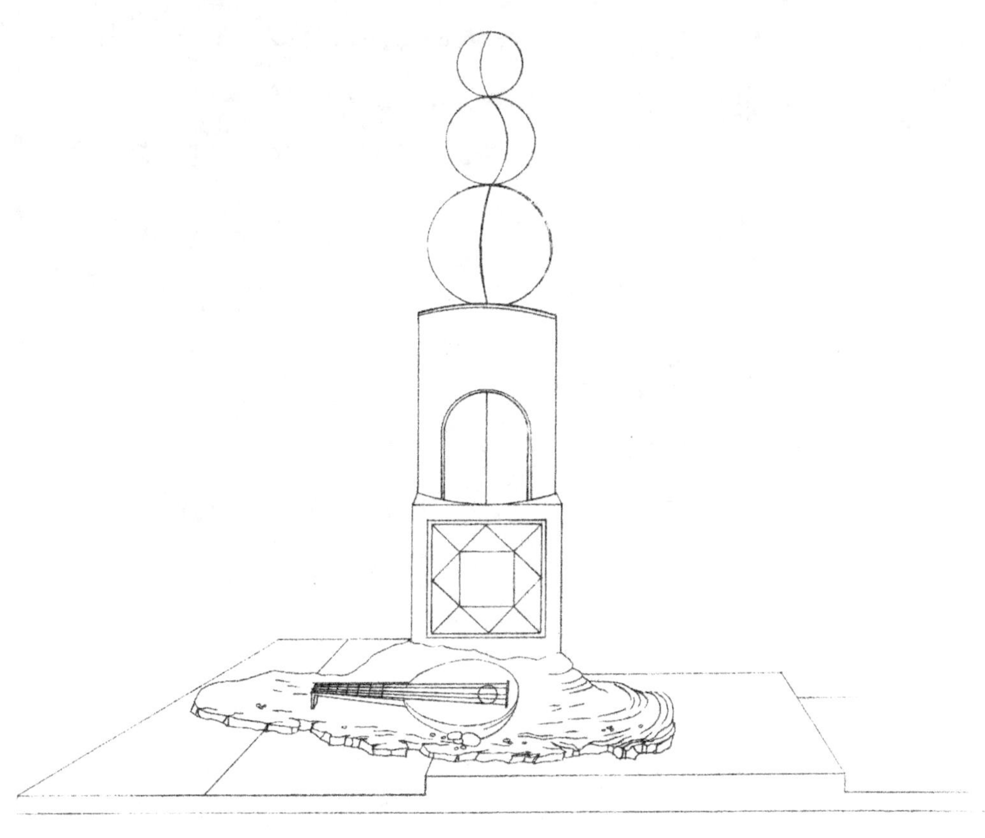

fabulae meantes extinguuntur
fabularum extinctio
rupit homogeneum id,
homogeneum locum adstantem,
homogeneum statum totum,
homogeneam rem universam lacerat:

finibus suis res respondent
ad insidias invisibiles a speculo caecitatis
retrahendas et adsimulandas

sint res denique
nec entes nec nihil
sed solum ea
erratica linea litoris
omniversae Stygis
ἐν τῇ τοῦ ὑστάτου ὀλέθρου ἐρίπνῃ
(uti ita scribam)

linea dein sit tibi
id quod non est
nec alia sit ultra

linea lineis res destruens
linea linei causas causis subripiens
boom - rang ————————
boom - going ————————
boom - gang ————————
boom - gag ————————
boom - bang ————————

in aenigmate
arulae
in tethrachtide
obstaculum
oraculum

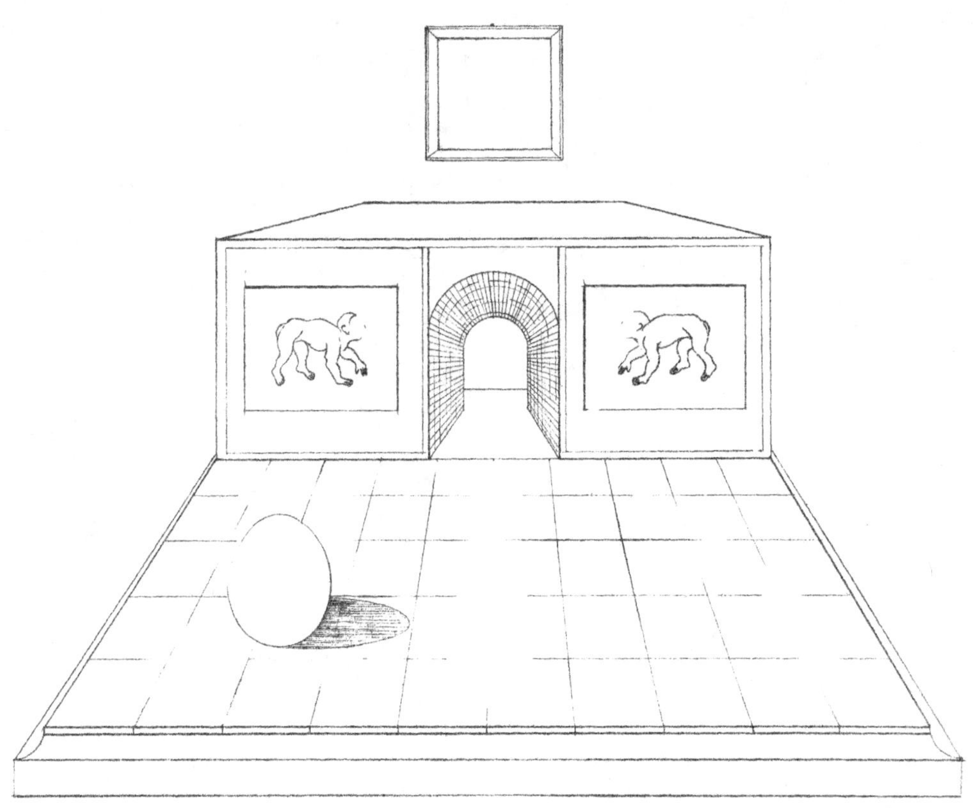

super daemonum acus
orbis ruinae in orifun(tur)

(sit) tandem daemonum nomen

non iam ΛΟΓΟΣ

non iam ΜΥΘΟΣ

non iam ΦΟΝΟΣ

non iam ΤΕΧΝΗ

non niam

sed ΑΤΗ

sit —

sit Ate noster daemon merus, prospectus sit —

deest aut desit a somniis illa aleatoria arboraranea
cuius radix in coelestis aequoribus vivit
et frondes ubique super ac subter – ea demum longus
longiqua linearum linea, ex vero et firma et praetermensura
linea datur aut detur

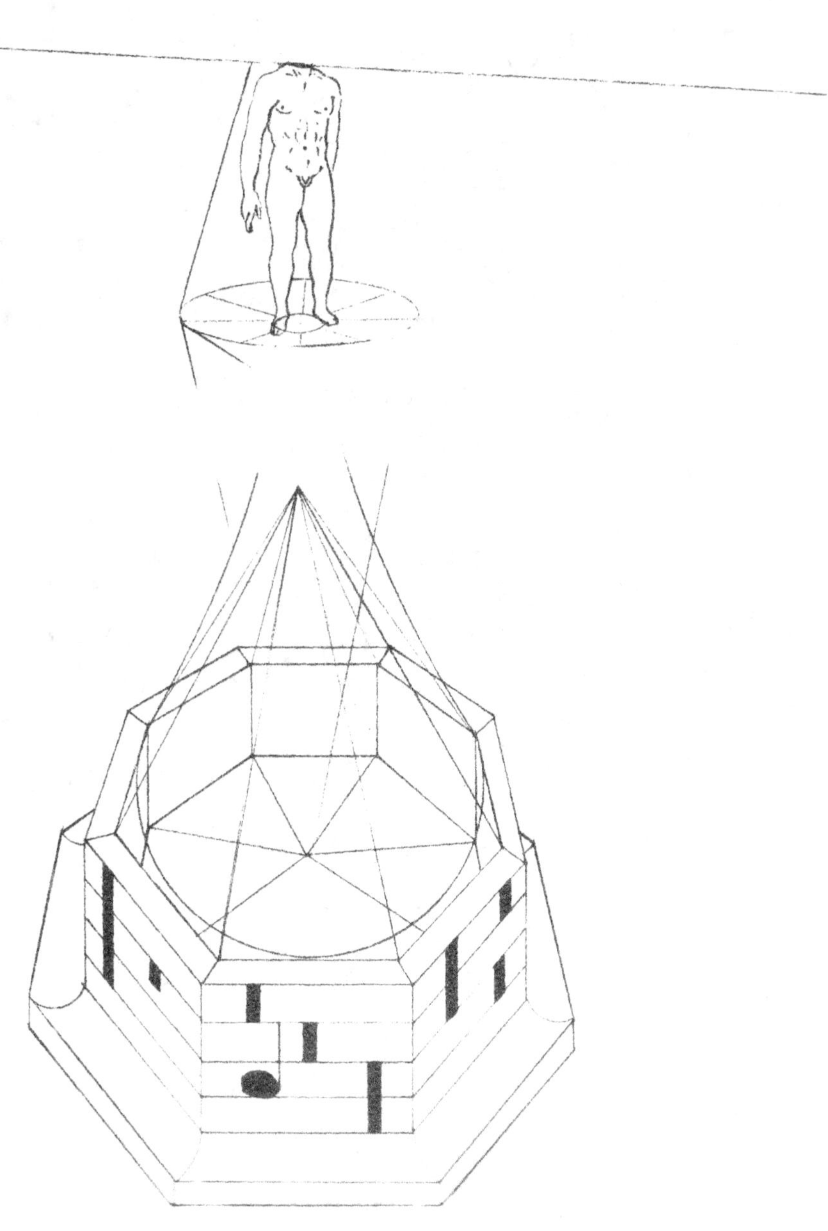

obscurus lateat
sulcus immanis
avidus avis
flagrat in acu
frinit fremit
frigit frangit
conum soni
solum solis
umbra iungit
tempus tempore
ultimum iacet
universi speculi
os

laetus cadet
ἐκ τῆς

Vinclis laxis erepta columna
universa labatur insidia

Aemilio   claudio

time mensuram transeuntem per hos radsmos
per haec frondia
ultimae lanceae
pondus splendoris —

arsura et mentura,
complexae sunt se
et in virga fumi,
linea orietur quae da,
in metagorica obsidione,
ex moesto ingenio,
ad inexorabilem mircelam
percipiendam,
diro mucrone mentis

nunc ergo ratio
firma atque infirma
in nigra hora nuda
suffocet mutum Sulcum

!

Da 12 *Sibyllae*

From 12 *Sibyllae**

1995

Sibylla
(cumana)

involucrus penis elucens mirabilibus altis
chronitrualia, choritualia, scortilualia
castissima custos mundi repleta sonore
la forza del diluvio non ci trascina più
con la sua seduzione intermittente
di cuore caduco geografico risvegliato
in dualità perenne, res opaca
tu epileptualis obstinata
aspergenza cryptopluviale, hyadica, caronica
bilis involucrum aperietur
mi cadono dall'anatomia cruda prevista di ali perdute
le scapole i gomiti il coccige la rotula
il perone, scabina, excarminat vertigine pubis
cruciale obprobrium mentium februarialium
et novæ relationes redeundæ reperitiones
ma il quotidiano, matutina iaculatio iactatio
nell'antiquum, ci esaspera alleviando
la nostra impunita ragione di non
credere più né all'ombra né al
ventriosum skeleton perruptis ossibus sacris
come radici piccolissime che vedono oltre la
immensa parete di tufo, e oltre quella
procedono e vanno, salpano, dalla notte
al mattino presto, e poi si addormono
senza pensare, senza vedere
gli idoli della tua ædes moriranno tutti
nel sangue ianuario miseno
per aprire sangue e bocche
e vagine flegree
vene e carogne
per lamentarsi con lo spirito del sangue e della fama
e portare la nostra puerizia al loro ombroso simulacro.

Sibyl
(Cumæan)

involucrus penis elucens mirabilibus altis
chronitrualia, chiritualia, scortilualia
castissima custos mundi repleta sonore
the flood's strength no longer drags us
          with its intermittent seduction
          of fleeting geographic heart awoken
          again in perennial duality, res opaca
          tu epileptualis obstinata
cryptopluvial, hyadic, charonic aspergence
bilis involucrum aperietur
from my crude anatomy that should have lost wings
          drop shoulder-blades elbows coccyx kneecap
          fibula, scabina, excarminat vertigine pubis
cruciale obprobrium mentium februarialium
et novæ relationes redeundæ reperitiones
but the quotidian, matutina iaculatio iactatio
          in the antiquum, exasperates us relieving
          our unpunished reason from not
          believing any longer in either shade nor
          ventriosum skeleton perruptis ossibus sacris
like the smallest roots that see beyond the
          immense wall of tufa, and go and
          proceed beyond it, set sail, from night
          till early morning, & then fall asleep
          without thinking, without seeing
the idols of your ædes they will all die
          in the ianuario miseno blood
          to open blood and mouths
          and Phlegræan vaginas
          veins and carcasses
to complain to the spirit of blood and fame
and bring our youth to their shady simulacrum.

Sibylla
(fœdus, fœtus)

Quando, da piccolo, nondum puer, strinsi un patto con te sui
giochi delle parole senza senso, fœdus inicisti:
ora tu non hai tenuto fede al nostro fœdus,
        fœdus iniecimus
        fœdus transgredieris.
Ma io, stipite e lancia della tua infedeltà, ho voluto tentare a
mia volta le più delicate e voluttuose trasgressioni
le deiezioni più sconsiderate,
in fuori e in dentro rovesciando le fodere del fœdus tenebrale.
Certo, tu hai avuto vergogna di me,
tu hai abbandonato i miei anfratti,
tu sei di nuovo fuggita nel deserto dei sensi, dei segni, dei
chiarori io ti inseguo e disegno con risibili fulminazioni
infelix exeat ergo copula nostra et aures nostræ flatu erecto
impraegnabuntur
siamo ancora due solitarie sparsæ sibille, io e te, che si
specchiano in faccia, in feccia, in furia, in fauci inficiate
come due angeli stupidi e assorti, angeli mutuæ faciei.
In realtà non sappiamo dire che cosa sia il dire,
quid sit dicere.
Consegna e consiglia alla malinconia perennitatis, la tua
perentoria assenza: evoca, erigi, brucia silenzi irragionevoli
in cerchi salienti di polvere absurditatis
è una lama di assenza che ci unisce, in una roteante ragnatela
di inutile desiderio
di chiasmo feroce.
Mutus quandoquidem inveniar et censear in cinere lucis obrutæ in
fulgoris laminæ acie.

Sibyl
(fœdus, fœtus) I

When, in my youth, nondum puer, I made a pact with you about
meaningless wordplay, fœdus inicisti:
now you didn't keep your end of our fœdus,
    fœdus iniecimus
    fœdus transgredieris.
But I, jamb and spear of your infidelity, decided it was my turn
to try the most delicate and voluptuous transgressions
the most thoughtless dejections,
outside and inside reversing the lining of the tenebrous fœdus.
Of course, you were ashamed of me,
you abandoned my coves,
once again you fled into the desert of the senses, of signs, of
glares I follow and draw you through laughable illuminations
infelix exeat ergo copula nostra et aures nostræ flatu erecto
impraegnabuntur
we're still two solitary sparsæ sibyls, you and I, who look
each other in the face, in filth, in fury, in festering fangs
like two stupid absorbed angels, angeli mutuæ faciei.
In reality we can't quite say what saying is,
quid sit dicere.
To perennitatis melancholy, consign and confer your
peremptory absence: evoke, erect, burn unreasonable silences
in salient circles of absurditatis dust
it's a blade of absence that binds us, in a whirling web
of useless desire
of fierce chiasmus.
Mutus quandoquidem inveniar et censear in cinere lucis obrutæ in
fulgoris laminæ acie.

So che non mi pento e la tua sovrilluminante tenebra ancora mi stringe, a
memoria, in libertà, in paradossia
i limiti banali del nostro intelletto rimandiamoli,
risospingiamoli più in là, oltre la nostra manipolata immagine
fonetica.
Anche il suono in fondo è un vestigio fastigio, un vestidio
fastidio e tra me e te si è spalancata una cisterna di specchi contraddittori,
ripiegati in fuori.
Ti chiamo a gestire questo rotolante imperversante silenzioso
caos la limitata tempesta del nostro indiavolato nascondimento.
La ribellione dell'immagine è pronta, preparata da tempo, e non
c'è misura che si attesti ad arginarla o a liberarla
solum opprobrium remoræ consentiam extremæ.
Ti manderò quattordici procreazionali apostrofi di protœschata
proporzione e quattordici posizioni astratte attratte un obelos e
tre spaziature per tre hapax assoluti uno steccato di sterpi per
neumi secchi e un iota: lavora tu, piccola ignota, con le tue
illuminazioni camuffanti da scialbo intelletto qualche cosa che
provenga da mutilati orizzonti immaginari di inconcepibile
travaglio.

I know I don't repent & your over-illuminating darkness still grips me, by heart, in freedom, in paradossia
let's send back the banal limits of our intellect,
let's push them back even further, past our manipulated phonetic image.
Deep down even sound is vestige fastige, vestidious
fastidious and between you & me opened a tank of contradictory mirrors, bended outward.
I call on you to manage this tumbling raging silent
chaos the limited storm of our wild hiding.
The rebellion of the image is ready, for a while now, and there's
no measure capable of controlling it or freeing it
solum opprobrium remoræ consentiam extremæ.
I'll send you fourteen procreational apostrophes of protœschata
proportions and fourteen attractive abstract positions an obelos &
three spaces for three absolute hapax an enclosure of twigs for
dry neumes and an iota: get to work, you little stranger, with your
camouflaging illuminations of a dull intellect something that
stems from mutilated imaginary horizons of inconceivable
toil.

Sibylla (nativitatis)

Perit cuniculus
duarum coniuncte
matrum ævorum:
in atro principio
in principio alterno
in impetu ætatum
vis ruinet lunaris
luna sub aris
sol extremus in alis
pro corpo reitate
naturis omnibus rariore
sit differens, penetret
impuram materiam
luminosæ phalenæ
utriusque sub undis
phalli cœlestis
a latere tonitruum
memorialis partus atque
generationis fluxus demetriacus
sensus superior legendus
in asperis aris
matrem maturnam
ab ovibus trahat
et recens fomentum
obscuret sacrum pavorem

mutetque pavorem
in Occultum Pavonem,
radiantibus brachiis
in diaphanis orgiis
ad monogamicam seductionem
revisitandam in epithalamiis
matricis oculus apex
adactione protrusus
Ianua, ianua! descendas
ad aphroditico remorso
fugiatque sol pugnax
ad currendam viam
sterilem letalem lætaminis
per herpetem ventorum
nactus iugiter perennis
lætetur omnis
natus facie mortali
victor humani lassus leporis
sub prætelluricis entibus.

Sibylla (euphemia)

fliga (a)ut pliga
plica (a)ut plaga
plex/ cul(te)rius
impanta nata
το εν τῷ παντί
regio pro miscua
egi hodie ego
endemica urgit
omnium illarum
rerum summa
et quantum nescire
necesse censetur
demum tandem resurget
comicæ solutiones
columnæ cœlestis
endemicitatis
en demi civitatis
rararumque ranarum
quas genuit palus

barometron subter lucernam
oinonque vinumque
ubicumque syllabavit
auspicia ad edunda
in unda tremorum

nec erba unquam
postea unquam increvit
in æra absque amore
aut nigrum hilum
serpsit per campora

dyspathica aut despotica
satrapia pilaria
enumerando hilos
et nigros pubium pilos
ventosæ momiæ.

Sibylla
(Kallas)

kallas
        sibylla
        kale
        ferocia vulnera illa
quæ oculos tuos mirabilia tangunt
            et ungula
                        angulata
coagulata
      uvula
                        visceribus mersa
ne fallas.

Sybilla protula

protula portula A
portulaca
protótomos protótelos
regnat
in glandis uterina
hortularia erosione
rotulæ fiss
ura
urinæ
cœli
palatus
indemne carumque
taumatum
signum
cadaveris cranii
heu
heuheu
porcula ac nitida
pulchraqua
porclaneta
ave
tiana
aura regnans
in
montibus

deviridatis
implexa promiscua
regio rationis
fati
fututi
ita ut fraus
reveniat mirabilis
arboris
mumutæ
et memoriæ fluens mammilla
uber
ubique.

Sybilla loquitur

et nunc œsmatici focus germinis
ulti acti
spectrum flagrat nunc
reputate virginis olim:
forte ex quadam gynaikokratia
nascitur omne
fomentum necnon fera illæsaque
omnia crescunt.

Sibylla
(labia)

Sibylla labialis, alis labi queas, limine clam
sugillata, syllaba labyrinthia, labilis labi lilium
syllepsis, invisibilis Valangæ immota Soboles! tota
lubilia verba leporis larva austrina helluetur, undique
unde sont orsa   :   hic tandem
sibylla avia   te distædeat
sibylla habeat sibyllabia sibyllalia
tibi sepulta citrulla, ignota sibylla
sarabanda syllyba paranympha,
sibilla alioquin subulta, sub ignota sæpilla,
subnigra subusta pupula exsurge,
everbera, sortesque subige mutas!

antequam alicubi a nobis galaxia retrocedat
et ipsamet tu saltem insili ad ultra! veñ a vulter!
verbi flagitiis istius modi selas quoque prome:
perpetuumque vomat ignet tuæ alula facis
et album mel statim ab anxia pupilla vanescat:

transitabilis tum iam migratio perempta
adnihilatio prompta peruret
maturas exempti mundi latitudines artas, eritque
interea quidam ventus qui per orbes
transibit sine tempore ruto,

isque una unam emittet magnam
vim, vi intellectus magna
absque clausulis latebrisque sonoris
et partu dulcedinem actam
eiciet arescendo: sic intus

et sic queas ipsa in ipsius tu tui lumen
selabi! c'est la vie; atque illuc immorari,
dum caput cœli
perpes petiat mordat angor mundi minor:

cor enim vadit cor venit, dein vetus cor
vortit horam procul simulque etiamdum
immotum pererrat, et paulisper
te salutat ultimam effrenam
syllabatam sibyllam, berecynthiam
meam, meam verecundiam, meam undam.

Sibylla
(Vedova
Vidua
In Dividua)

fama rerum periit iam et iam
huc et illuc periit

grandiosa molecola æquifocalis
in mappa e disordine acquificialis
polytopa compatta æquivocalis
monade di gargarismi æquifæcalis
oracolata di nidi, arule, pagine,
tane, essenze, remeggi,
grumo e torrenti
di fustigazioni
in groviglio e in erezione
træsecolata vidua arbor decrescens
tuæ tui ipsius multiplicatæ
longæ identitates
in ascensu atque descensu sineque mora
transitus in ara
confitere te præcharismaticam esse induisse vestem
venuto per il tempo mutato
di redigere il cespuglio
delle tue uniche identità
l'accumulo compatto e il culmine
il climax æquivoco
    scintillante nebuloso.

Sibyl
(Widow
Vidua
In Dividual)

fama rerum periit iam et iam
huc et illuc periit

grandiose molecule æquifocalis
in map and disorder acquificialis
compact polyrat æquivocalis
monad of gargling æquifæcalis
oraculated lady of nests, arule, pages
dens, essence, rowings,
clot and streams
of floggings
entanglement and in erection
træsecolata vidua arbor decrescens
tuæ tui ipsius multiplicatæ
longæ identitates
in ascensu atque descensu sineque mora
transitus in ara
confitere te præcharismaticam esse induisse vestem
that came for the time transformed
to draw up the bush
of your unique identities
the compact accumulation and culmination
the climax æquivoco
        cloudy sparkling.

Sibylla
(trifida)

printed of
printed of Bétail
by the
Transfixed Ptah
Ægyptia and Latin
  Laid
          of Bethel
          of Betulla
little Emotion
little Emotion
li tell Hæmation

kosmos olos
ne efficietur
insalubribus lamentis
aut rimpianti
necnon gemitibus rosarum
kallarumque
bilateralis calor
guttam extinguat
incertam
Good, God: I am amazed!
imparando tutte le noie
e tutte le nozioni
che non sono e non
nascono
nell'utero verbale
nox pleurica varat

Sibyl
(trifid)

printed of
printed of Bétail
by the
Transfixed Ptah
Ægyptia and Latin
  Laid
          of Bethel
          of Betulla
little Emotion
little Emotion
li tell Hæmation

kosmos olos
ne efficietur
insalubribus lamentis
aut regrets
necnon gemitibus rosarum
kallarumque
bilateralis calor
guttam extinguat
incertam
Good, God: I am amazed!
learning all this nonsense
and all these notions
that aren't found and
aren't born
in the verbal uterus
nox pleurica varat

good, good: I am amazet a

noi due oracoli
copie sbiadite di sopravvivenza
la vita si apre verso l'ora nona
si trucca verso le nove
si annoia verso le nove

good, God: i Am Am Am Azed!

voi sibille
che avete passato tutti i millenni
sulle foglie
a decidere che cosa
bisogna non dire
e che cosa bisogna
fare

Good, God: I am amaZed!

e in tutti noi
trascorrono
le nostre proprie piccole
parole malate
di voracità
di voragini.

good, good: I am amazet for

us two oracles
faded copies of survival
life opens around the ninth hour
puts on her make up around nine
gets bored around nine

good, God: i Am Am Am Azed!

you sibyls
who've spent every millennia
on leaves
trying to decide what
must not be said
and what must
be done

Good, God: I am amaZed!

and through all of us
flow
our own little
words sick
with voracity
for the void.

Sibylla ndrangheta
(indecentrica sive indecens eccentrica lutra)

salamandranguita
heu turpiter remota deplumis
sturna, incensum emblema probolon
sturna saturna introgrediaris
turma in dranguita intrat
in trangueta angorea
in transcula angora
in æscula inquieta
indrangena   indrongeta
androgina   dendrangeta
mandragula   extrangulata
ingenerata   semisanguis
                hydranguis
artranxia   antrangula
indramatica   faux olim
                eructans ab ovo
indroguaina   endrorgana
indogunanta   androngyna
cataracta sortibus expoliata
urtica   defraudata
                defrondata
indramatica regula rata.

From *12 Sibyllae*

* Here we offer eleven of the twelve "sibyls" originally published in 1995 (see page 670 of the bibliography). Other sibyls have been published in extremely limited runs (as poster size prints or metal etchings), but the series is in reality much larger: there exist some hundred unpublished sibyls in various languages.

Sibyl (fœdus, fœtus)

1. In Latin, *fœdus* means "treaty" or "pact" and *fœtus* "fetus."

Letania per Carmelo Bene

*Litany for Carmelo Bene**

1996

les colombemots ont toutes troujour un ciel à éventrer
pour en abattre la mémoire sur le miroir des instants sonores
    les lé
    ta nie à lécher
    en dérogatoir
        pour
    carmelo bene à
    redomander érection
    rédemption et
    vigueur de
        vous voix voir de toi
        qui nous, les tous, oblige et nous opte

Héron iridescent aux éclats vert-noir
en éclat verbevoir des glandes sans limite
tu aura bien pu saisir entre tes crocs
la grêle du Temps Dur, exilé mûr,
du Temps-Dieu de Blessure, Tant d'Yeux
en trace des Golfes d'Ombre, et l'Ombre
qui beugle, du Tout d'Yeux,
le long les Feuillages sans racines
liées aux rêves des vivants —
et pu trouer pu crever le Collapse
oratoire des Vidéo-Je des Jeux
Imprévisible rhéteur revolé revolu des représailles
en défaite, Arbitre pour aveugles
aux rats tués aux raids d'ouir
voix diacre voix à raid grenu

pour plaindre pour te plaindre sur les ongles
sur les As sur Bois sous Poudre sous Cendre
entre Thèbes et toi tout Vu, Thèbes
règne et défait ta voix toute nue noircie
toute desquamée dessaisie polluée
qui fasait disparaître le Lieu à descendre
in con nu ir rité chaque grain
ritué du Symbole Paresseux, à Vœux
et à Symbole Santgrenue Voile
où gît ta Grande Vide Pearls-Words
          Grandevoix Vivante dont deferle
          L'eau collab
          se a l'Ab su/à l'Ab
          side des choses des mystères en joues luxées
Bien, Béné ! c'est ta Voix en Goître
ta Voie Sablé qui t'Alignée
tarissable, l'A qui beugle impalpable
déjà dit, ta Voix oblique remplie d'air
à la chasteté du jeu innombrable
qui éloigne le monde, le monde
qui retient absent le ,,, l'horizon
escarpé d'horizon froissé
          c'est ta Voix en Gouffre
aux luxures exposées dégorgées vives
les fourrures alarmées d'A bsinthe
                              d'A psou
                              d'A bsous
du jeu à la chasteté corrive

en latrat aboyé, A infrason breuvé
en faim et en soif dégorge de L'A byrinthe
issu bobine l'A voix byrille
qui lappe l'O lascif
en fines scènes de Lèvres les l'ivres
livrées sur l'A raignée
du Mime qui règne Sublime, Béné;
du Mime qu'un Monde anime et éreinte!
les mots hâlés rosier
en jeux d'échecs ruisseaux
en jeux d'éclats rugeux
en despote chaque grain de ton bûcher!
les mots allés à rigolade
en jeu d'échéances et regret
les mots en chagrins poinçon
les maux en échanges chas grins
les maux hélés par A bol
en jeu d'essence
je d'incences, insens jeu d'inceste des croyances détériorées
bien béné bien née parabole
folle voix écrite martyrisée sur l'écran
rompu de terre rie eau rhée à passerelle

mon ami aimé, le Grand aimé, des tempêtres!
qu'est-ce que c'est qui te libère?
qu'est-ce que c'est qui te possède?
le mots hululés en vacarmes
en jeux sulfurisés de charmes

en jeux supplique supplice d'élan
    pour A A et ripaille donc, pu ta haine
    pour C B et engendre donc
    pour B C et vielle donc
    pour A A et
    aux souffles cruels
mon ton nom Carmel le Bien du Béné
en vain le souffle du Carmel, Déveine,
ira s'éteindre au bout de poitrine
et la pétillante puissance-prince des saintes saisons Rien
aux Détroits raisonnés par famine
    mère aisée   par se siens géometriques
mère et sémence de la mensonge infinie ses filanges fléaux
                                                                   d'ardeur
douce mensonge, de la syllabe assez   ses forêts fouets pour pies
arbre grenadier, touffu, de syllabes   arrosées en phono — !
abreuvées dans le faux sang grenus   par bébé très né ou traîné
d'un mensonge à tenue impénitente,   qui témoigne son respect
pour baptister un membre grains   pour les nondieux à flair
                              pour une vengeance en pleine rosée

Immense Vétérinaire de la Vache
Grande qui beugle fadasse
    en trachée somatestésiale
    par prévénance lésinée
    et démonicité en vestie
    du Paysage défaillant
pour, obviam Carmelo in aëra, pour

le Grand Jeu en brides
de la Suggestion, pour le Je Grand
en bribes d'A mour murmures
tout ou vert tout ou l'on voit,
de l'A rbre eau imaginaire trémie:
au feuillage no cturne habillé
caressant rongé assoupli sur fixité de fougue,
it all seems that way, yet happens through subtle
indulgence, and at the same time doesn't happen, yet it opens
wide to sickly colored changing crowds
of truant or summoned or contested vowels; to
spread seeds of the intransitive
idolatry, eidololatry, eh! I

poupées drolatiques en masques interdites,
voix de Matière séduite par scissures
voice of seduced Footprint, voice of fluid grit
for regeneration and separation of the iconic
Orgasm, shattered in hypotipóseis,
the Coming and Going in Hepotenuse is to be found at the peak,
vanishing from cell to polished polyhedric cell,
in ritual of genuflections of mirabunda
blindness, mirabilis Unda, when it rises,
the vain vulva of the labial eidolon,
like a beautiful Prey and very breathable
equilateral sail, voucher of scummy lexicons
as thick as the three hundred walls of cynara solymus
and worshiping the Queen of the incarnadine

Death, incarnadine Death of Star,
she herself, the same, and together
sa ma ri t'haine, jaspure de haleine
euchariste, mari tène, samaritaine, gouffre diadème
s'amar item, triage de ténia, elle même
la Voix, elle là, elle mène
en érème en hérésie en herbe autres,
elle même, seu ipsa ipsaque salus
animæ animatæ salus eremi
jardin du délire autre du repas du trépas
illa ipsaque Comestibilitas Undæ
illa Grandis imaginum Unda voculata,
vox hi hi, vox hi fi, vox hieroglypha
vox labilis, vox lubidinis, vox labyrintha

la Houle toute Houhoule des Images Emues qui errent
Images Absoutes à l'Assaut des Spécifs,
à l'arrache de l'Araignée des Pierres
2 soul of Absolute voice to the labia
reclining Ear ad burned Amygdale
          A   Myg   Dal
et munda Mundi A nimula
et blanda Fax Faciebus (Di)vitiata,
numina mun dii mund is
h.e. omnia munda mundis undis
l'audelà de tout Mi(ni)stère obrué
min ystère mystère Fêlé miroir-mésentère,
du aux yeux-grains secoués par la Larve

intrasmissible enfin, in pilicula Salomé,
et la non occultable Auditio
auditionem audientes audibitis
par trombes et tuyaux murènes
ganglions et vives salives
angles et tue-yeux, tuyaux,
tout je nous en tout genoux
en gambade et akrobatie vives reculées
en paraphonésis autour des épaules nues
noue-ramures nues-blessures
de chaleurs silumées ouvertes, nu feu du feu
incessant
pour l'A ntagoniste résumé imperturbable
véritable A (e)ndrogyne jouant
carmélange mélange en voix et lait
pour les treize répertoires de l'éclairage enseveli
great tempestuous Act
more magnificent Actor
or Histrio or Clown or great millenary
Shaman, intact Shaman of the Eon
for whom I pull from my hymnology:
Vocis Voce Iridescens Ridens vix
Inve   in ictu vocis
terascens Optuma Librata!
summe ergo Histrio culmine A rbor
rubescens vigeas Haruspex
et Fulguriator Carmen τοῦ El
Carminator, genialiter ultima Umbræ

genio vocis vox Uta maxima Mundi,
flatus Mundi   and I no longer know what or what

voice suits the immature, Demetriac mane
of your voice.
Bene! good! Bene dicas illud Benebene
in venis ultimis, in vanis ultimis, in ultimatis vocibus:
                                        Bene is the
un-caused, l'histrio æternalis, from Eleusis,
yet causing pluvial memory judged
in conference, in sections, in meetings, in secret rotating
menisci, jovenile ever-lasting heifer
to celebrate like corpus simulans atqui dissimulans:
teeth   blood   whip   hips
the flashenings of archaic cinereal aggressions, 3
sumptuous dragonflies, scantly clad knots, unknottings, and
emery
of lowered glottises, never born, 4
in infinite ugule pendule nodule,
where the Ideogram of Alarm sews and re-sews,
delightful of the Erratic Grace on inclines of effigies,
of the Invocation in Delta of the impeccable
trans-nourishment, blacker suture
of the innumerable leaden Proximity/Corporeity
in formula of mystery of parthenian Ceremony,
from Eleusis, parthenogenic ear, precisely called
Ear reclining, in a
single solitary unique word

unknowable, backed for the protection
of not knowing, of not dwelling, of dis-appearing
in flashenings and sunken face faze about face
that radiates, ray-diates, it opens in bursts,
the inaccessible flux of errors
in sweet sweet docile disorganized
Ypokalipsis precisely of the raw Womb
in the free soaring enemy Discourse
in the pure sense of icy alliteration,
of friction, of the complete daze
of the Precious Orga(ni)sm of yes,
of the Simulacrum in Monstrance of Breath and Trace
in ictus of fantastic Cells
that dare weep upon the Sickly Waters
                    of the summoning shade,
in the threatening veiled air from the phonocryptic
whirlwind, of the far off eve ntuality,
          la Rêve-Elation Celtique,
like a passing tax of tenderness and Zoocentric,
          pity,
banner of lightning fast crossing
          Eros & Deception
Ejection en Courbe d'Accent
du Bout qui rejette son sommet dans le Gouffre

          l'Epi de Voix en ce qu'elle souffre
          the Ear of voice in Eleusis
extremely nourished nourishing that nourishes, en outre

the Mare pregnant with the most varied lights,
that spills in an arrogant, proud, ferocious, broken
line, riotous materies, matrix à foutre, arch,
c/hurled sexual cupola, vocalized wasps where
I stumble (or you stumble) the proteic reasons
of the wind simulating fiery litanies,
hair-brained, bored, broods of bands
for eating the long chain of the impossible syllable
à foutre the corpus Hermiticum, the esseculum,
on cliffs of erectile glimmers and crown,
golden right, gloomy, febricital temple,
boœd detention of corporeal comedy,
from whose foramen slides, hisses
and flees the amazing miraculous
Corporeity of Actor, of hungry
Histrio, as I saw saw saw and saw again
et inquam
sic est com edia
et in edia
eating together and never eating

et alors
les sources les sœurs chatouillées
inaugure entame et engouffre l'incandescence du Serpent
maladroit d'Inouï
et dans tout ça, la Forte Flamme,
ça tout fort la lui même lui dit qui dégringole
le tout lui même qui bouleverse l'obscurur

d' son Â me même qui s'aime
qui sème ce qui s'aime, son Â me d'indifference
ou bien de déliverance, son épopée chanchate, épaisse,
plus rare son Â me pousée de périr
épousée, son époupée de la vestition,
son Â me car mêle tout
qu'est ce que ai-je connu de la première Brume,
toute mêlée incisive dans le tout
recourbe vocalisé, dans son os, dans le son
de son Â me inclinée sans destin,
son Â me léchée son Use démie et cou ronnée
démystifiée, hâtive Â me
dans le Trou de son Trou exhorcisé
serré de près le chemin vain de ses pièges durables —
pledged and offered through
        photosensitivity
through zoom-zoom, between nebulas
of sequences cardiac consequences

and wisteria of mortal mots, and thus misunderstood,
between frost, thaw, and fading,
between bush-house and selenic fragments,
and shreds tatters flakes of carotids to be shed...
et sources anciennes ébouriflées, et après
tranchée hachée découpée la vert e(m)brale avilie
simple où terrible, variation et Fugue défaillance, évanouissance
like saying, or to be said, of the Iseesaying in offering, 6
'Dioscoure en hypogée véritable':

sur l'inelucté vide symétrique, crise à défendre:
perpetuated Body in B and C
in or in Indemostrable Drudgery,
in Passing Over,
in the unawoked Variety
in the unrevealed Involucrum!

Pour ainsi dire, sur le bord du désert qui avance ou s'éparpille:
j'irais chercher le trou où me coucher
avec le Grand Chien Tétracéphale
en fait de Mémoir phonétisée sur face,
sur sa Front l'Ange Acteur de l'Action d'Âge supérieure, nimbe
monté su Eter Nuement en gloses périmées,
en fait de l'Agacement Ultérieur, Utérie,
utérus dédale méandre aux feux-croisés
mot sur mot de l'idée du Destin Histrionné Immanent

à l'A bri de l'Egide tachetée,
par A gonie d'A go ni sante,
nous irons, en jouet et en masque exténuant,
nous irons flairer plonger partager étendre
sa voix Charmehêlée, soumise
où gît la machine grotesque fardée
des mots qui égarent même les yeux
des Climats Improbables, dont retombent
          les ailes de l'égarement ténébreux,
et tu iras crier par hymène vocal
jusqu'à ce que ton époux apparaîtra;
ou lorsque C.B. ira se réciter

en l'êtranglé pour l'être anglé Trout
en se refuser au Salut à l'Â me, à l'A nonyme
    everything boils
    down everything
    irreversibly
        boils down
    to everything outline sets
        everything in stark
            radical nuances
enfant que je, Carmel le Bien, j'irais dire:
oh mes Mots troués par ma voix, brûles
dans la baie de mon cœur
    est-ce que vous en savez quelque chose
    d'une Resurrection sans fin?

leu leu les syllablabla du ES

amuré sur le jeu thème du (je t'aime)
(qui mourait)

la syllabe – coeur mêlée
et le coeur mêlé sibylle carminée
sont à chanter à jouer à rêver
insécables.

La sphynx réuni à sa source
ton oeil sonore

raphsodie qui rêve
dans les ... qui écrasent
de l'horreur et toujours continues
sous la tempête
les idoles squelettes devenant
rancune rupture et poubelle
de ce qu'elle en courroux
pourrait être l'être étranglé

bien

dall' Hymnologion
Eulogion
Doxologion
Etymologion
doxologion

per
vita ven

Carmelo B

Litany for Carmelo Bene

* Carmelo Bene (1937–2002) was an Italian playwright, actor, director, and poet. He was known for his many innovations in the field of theater, his incandescent stage presence, and his extraordinary ability to declaim poetry, not only his own, but also that of major Italian poets such as Dante, Leopardi, and Dino Campana, as well as others, including Russian poets such as Mayakovsky, Esenin, Blok, etc. (cf. Bene's 1974 production *Quattro modi di morire in versi* [Four Ways of Dying in Verse]: *Majakowski, Blok, Esenin, Pasternak*). In many ways, he was very similar to Villa: both were as erudite as they were ill-tempered & wrote poetry in a language all their own, creating macaronic mixtures with a predilection for wordplay. More importantly, they were equally obsessed with phonetics, of which Villa's homage to Bene serves as a perfect example. Villa never intended to print this litany; it was Bene himself who contacted Aldo Tagliaferri (the custodian of the poet's intellectual property after he suffered a stroke in 1986) and insisted on its publication.

1. For eido, see page XXIII of the introduction. Villa plays on this word in different ways throughout his œuvre. Here, he is using it in conjunction with the terms "idolatry" & "ideology."
2. In the original, *all'elabia* is most likely an intentional misspelling of "alle labia" (to the labia).
3. *Cinerule* could be a combination of "cinereo" (ashen, cinderly) & "ceruleo" (cerulean) or a play on "cinema."
4. In Italian the adjective "ammainate" (to haul down or lower) contains the morphemes "mai nate" (never born).
5. *Febbricitale* is Villa's creation and is derived from "febbre" (fever).
6. With *vedodire* Villa combines the first person singular form of the verb "vedere" (to see) and the infinitive form of "dire" (to say).

*Unpublished Poems**

Mottos

mortale
          e immortale
non esistono:
                      no
non
      né mortale né im/n-
      né, né
                NEC
NECARE-NEKYA-NEC
HIAT/   NEK ROS

né mortal dunque
          né immortal
piegati piegati piegati
dura immortale orgastica
organica schiena dell'IN-/

piegati piegati in due
      come piegati anche (also)
      in un, in uno, in uno solo,

spiegati, vana conclusione, be
      vanamente, declina,
      declinati, scazzati
fin dall'in-/
      dall'inizio
      dall'interitus
      dalla

Mottos

mortal
        and immortal
do not exist:
                no
not
    either mortal nor im/n-
    nor, nor
        NEC
NECARE-NEKYA-NEC
HIAT/   NEK ROS

nor mortal therefore
        nor immortal
to your knees to your knees to your knees
tough immortal orgastic
organic back of the IN-/

to your knees down to your knees
    like to your knees too (also)
    in on, in one, in one alone,

explain yourself, vain conclusion, be
    in vain, decline,
    decline yourself, get pissed off
from the very in-/
    from the initial
    from the interitus
    from the

(muta sequenza del do,
del dopo del dopo del dopo, POST)
muta sequenza in avere
CHE FAR
IN
in fondo (= in fundum)
come in fondum
infondum)

la chi unque la chio
o la chioma di Berenice
astrale inconseguenza
IN CUIUS NOMEN ROGITES
CŒUNDUM FACERE
FECEM

in inizio qui (= cui, qui)
c'è un colia,
un diddio vergine
molteplice, in virga
in virga luminis,
in very ogna
IN MOR TEM
resurgendo RE paraudam

qui, cioè, non si è
o non si è come quando
come quando è come
quando; quando
il quando è proprio
il quan il quan,

(mute sequence of the af,
of the after the after the after, POST)
mute sequence in having
TO DO
IN
in depth (= in fundum)
as in fondum
infondum)

the who ever the loc
or locks of Bernice
astral inconsequence
IN CUIUS NOMEN ROGITES
CŒUNDUM FACERE
FECEM

initiating here (=cui, qui)
there's a colia,
a virgin godda
varied, in virga
in virga luminis,
in very ogna
IN MOR TEM
resurrecting RE paraudam

here, that is, one isn't
or one isn't like when
like when is like
when; when
the when is exactly
the quan the quan,

e come
fondare / sfondare
fondere i rottami
perché ora si comincia a finire
l'inizio dell'in

che il mondo non sputa chi
sputi il mondo
lui / lei spingendo spin
spingente nell'abisso auricolare
la rissa i venti i canti
(lei i canti ficcati oltre vulva)
lei ma anche lui che foro,
il foro-infero
chiaro edificio-botro
broto-, proto-
protoduomo
onde

grande intima evoluta
bellezza
il prossimo tipo di società,
adunque, e sia
nuova società
tutta creata / incrente

con travi
martello
lesina
martinetti

& like
found / unfound
melt the scrap
because now we're starting to end
the initial of the in

that the world doesn't spit those who
spit the world
he / she pushing spin
pushing in the auricular abyss
the brawl the winds the songs
(she the songs stuffed beyond vulva)
she but also he what hole,
the hell-hole
clear edifice-ditch
broto-, proto-
protoduomo
whereby

great intimate evolved
beauty
the next type of society,
wherefore, and let it be
new society
entirely created / uncreated

with beams
hammer
awl
rams

cacciaviti
amuleti
ingegni / congegni con

anche la rete le reti i retioli
per captare che?
(as motherwell)
muoiono i primi in rete
come (as test, testim- un) (textile)
muoiono i primi come gli
ultimi (as Fate)
(hidden sky, hidden blu, hidden black)
l'essere pende
e dipende (well, well)
e culmina (well, well)
presso alle grandi uscite della vita
in preamor liscia sgombra cieca
esse,
alle prese con le
parallele del dolpo
sesso omofono
omomorfo
(hidden words and hidden all)

il vento matura come una
primizia caotica e incerta
sul da farsi e sul da essere
macinando triboli
spini
fogliame agricolo

screwdrivers
amulets
contraptions / apparatus also

with the net the nets the little nets
to capture what?
(as motherwell)
the first die in nets
like (as test, testim- un) (textile)
the first die like the
last (as Fate)
(hidden sky, hidden blu, hidden black)
being leans
and depends (well, well)
& culminates (well, well)
next to the great exits of life
in prelove smooth unencumbered blind
esse,
dealing with the
parallels of the alfter
homophonous sex
homomorphorous
(hidden words and hidden all)

the wind matures like a
chaotic and uncertain firstling
on what needs to be done and to be
smashing troubles
thorns
farm foliage

che se uno conta lontano
un uomo come te
come teeeeee
lo
sa cosa vuol dire vento
polmone utero coscienza
cosmo cazzo
e inciampa
ogni nota distolta all'AMEN

tipica, o metricamente fondato,
nel numero dell'essenza dolorosa
dei pensieri antichi del male
antico
che cuarta
l'immagine mist e riosa
mist
del
DESIDERIO IN
DESIDERIO IN(COGNITO)
DESI
IN SI STERE
basta! piegati!

estranged
excused
tengo la tua nascente avventura
il tuo vincolo nascente
e l'incompiuto tripudiate computer
instaurato in un clima
di perfetta inidentificazione

that if one counts far off
 a man like you
 like youuuuu
 knows
what it means wind
 lung uterus consciousness
 cosmos cock
 and it stumbles
 every note removed from the AMEN

typical, or metrically sound,
in the number of the painful essence
of ancient thoughts of ancient
 evil
 that cuarters
the myst e rious image
 myst
 of the
 DESIRE UN
 DESIRE UN(KNOWN)
 DESI
 IN SI STERE
 enough! on your knees!

estranged
excused
I hold your nascent adventure
 your nascent duty
and the incomplete exalted computer
installed in a climate
 of perfect inidentification

estranged
excused   and all

per una gamba a corona
il cornucomputer
    di nubi economico-fine
    fine, fine, anziaria
non si regge la bestia
        in braccia a brezza
        di clandestini rovesci
        di moneta di scudi di
            armi
e chi ha le armi confuse
        è la sola reale
            beatitudine / imbecillità

ma

ma perfetta sola soglia
        per il salto
il salto organico (da dirsi 3
                volte),
nonostante il trionfo
            monetario
plasmico proteico
                prodotto
        proteso demone-cosmo

l'irrefrenato fium
        dell'inganno
e del disinganno

estranged
excused   and all

for a leg shaped like a crown
the cornucomputer
      of thin-economic clouds
      thin, thin, or betteryetair
the beast can't be held
            in arms in a breeze
            of clandestine storms
            of coins of shields of
                        weapons
and he who has confused weapons
            is the only real
                        beatitude / imbecility

but

but perfect lonely threshold
            for the leap
the organic leap (repeat to yourself 3
                                    times),
despite the triumph
                        monetary
plasmic proteic
                                    product
            striving demon-cosmos

the unstopped river
                  of deceit
and of disillusion

come freccia
prospera nel suo destinato
          orizzonte

ch'egli tocca
con mano e con piede
(curvo in semiminere
e teso in mundolare
          psichiche invereconde

come se avessi potuto io scegliere
la mia propria sola acqua, io
ti ho scritto tutto, anima
          del sereno inesausto
tutto
     il potere dato della brezza
e sopra tutto (di beatitudine)
questo

     che prende sprint (fuga,
     spago, corda, scatto, start,
     recessi o processi o) dalla
     paura del malebene,
          ma paura è paura
viene dai crani antichi
e presenti
     dalla rissa cranica,
e la cœterna Pressione
contro di noi che un noi
come l'orma del piede

like arrow
flourishing in its destined
          horizon

that he touches
with hand and foot
(curve in semination
and taut in mondular
          shameless psyches

as if I could choose
my only exact water, I
wrote you everything, soul
          of the serene unexhausted
everything
          the given power of the breeze
and above all (of beatitude)
this

     that takes sprint (flight,
     twine, cord, lunge, start,
     recesses or processes or) from the
     fear of the evilgood,
          but fear is fear
it comes from ancient and present
skulls
    from the cranial brawl,
and the cœternal Pressure
against us that an us
like the print of the foot

e della mano di Lazio,
che giace cambiamo al
suo e nostro orizzonte,
sulla sua e nostra
verticale

e la sua orma trasuda
fraudolenza menzogna
da percorsi labirinti
della specula assurda
strati inaccessi e mai
            coordinati

      in vulvula
il contenuto immane di una vena
      conchiglia scoscesa,
      incessata permanente
la paura   fuga

as pulvis / pelvis
    pubis / pabis)

decreato, decreto,
      discreto, giacenza
      nel Novero

as, exchanged God(s)
as, damned God(s)
così, verme traditore
      verme che mangia,
      che perfora carne-in-scatola

and the hand of Lazio,
which rests we change in
his and our horizon,
on his and our
vertical

and his print seeps
fraudulence lies
from labyrinthine paths
of absurd specula
inaccessible & never coordinated
                layers

        in vulvula
the massive content of a vein
        steep shell,
        incessant permanent
the fear   flight

as pulvis / pelvis
    pubis / pabis)

decreated, decree,
      discreet, remnants
      in the Group

as, exchanged God(s)
as, damned God(s)
like that, traitor you worm
            worm that eats,
            that drills a hole in canned meat

(e succhia
opportunamente accesa
            e bene sporzionata)
            in porzioni aziendali
minerali animali spirituali

(senti subito lo spirito in
      permanente immolo
      scab
            roso
                        mob(y)
      smob
            di quanti non sanno.

(and sucks
opportunely lit
            and well portioned)
            in company portions
mineral animal spiritual

(you quickly hear the spirit in
               permanent sacrifice
               scab
                     rous
                                   mob(y)
               smob
                     of those who don't know.

Homily tactile to tickle tongue

and of Recuper sending and other reciprocate Jubilar
to the appear of Cosmos Images, in Place
Honour little Slough, and. Yes, and, ya.
Rowder shocking in the porticular Glace.
too, and it, and, yes, beat body Hand
nucleousness Head in revulsive Concept
of Selective Aphoditismus expermentent.
Sperment, Spermind, yes, ya, and, Ring
too, i sing, i look, too, for Mind Eeater,
To will giving, Fumiging Power,
so what?, so, yesya, of because under lower
Historic Understood Full gressing more,
more than what, in the ways thus
useful secrecy fall down to the
mean mond meg rowsing, oh, yo yo,
yes ye, ya, grey rows, gree. Additivismus

works in cities, on cities language long run, ya
good, well, yes, ya, and
in a or in not a, in o, in
other mind found soul's
consupremacy, yes. Bot, be to be or. But Delight you
as been system of Murder, a thin to move again
from me one Time are doing the ones
looking coulding head, together, for the Prosthetic
Club. Arrow is not to be can up to founding
        but Heaven cowle doubterers rum, hum.
The field of Soul is full of indomable shin and
graves wringed wrong in taunt Other
        Monstrous trouble devertuated when whar
love to to love, eventually [Ove] whim of Consumption
of Frames, over you climb, clam, to break
cleaninless, to alkalise

Preaching
Crash fall fling, oh, mouth all? Mother,
to lisp, kindle mutual tongue alive, ah!
abominable Feed-Back, oh! alert, alert!
but if i and too ruckle spit in
or of skat workword, ya, come
come come

let you also be Saints, bounteous Saints, generous to eat Bites
                                        of rustling permæshia
                                        of rufled Homily prudent when
when you approach to eat a cut of Hated Family, Cut, Put, unmannerly mouthful
upon mouthful eating, Fhomily eating a Eurological leave of Shadow of dead sexe
in delabiated Urn, in the long time of universal Erection, eating
the neutral whirlpool of spermatic Wit from
Nexus of dark trees of psycotic psych digressions and
and autobaptise to growing dim in water of funereal weakness,
and after autobaptise with whistle of luxurious match with
whiping one self with uricemic exorcisms, write urical whip,

couricemic cemic comic exorcisms, comic whip chirp whop, slaughter slaughter com,
cohom, a continent of radioactif Venoms by Kodak Ektachrome by,
where a little Extasis devour and very long fungus
lacking bone wake up always in shiver, oh!
ohoh! oooh! ohohohoh! oh and oh! saturday, satur!
and we have toujours accidents and instants of itch
and of imminent Brains and of brawny unalterable
exemptions and we abort the embryo of slop exaggerations, ah, yes
ya, you, youhou, youhouhouh! and rhhythm
of our Reason is our beatified Tail, look look!

when these shone bleached agonies were not impossible in
the core of impossible Futur, scarcely absurd, falled between,
lodged between, struggled between, bet, yes, quivering
between, blossoming between, little silence between, opened,
between … in the long run
absconditi rami, yes, abscondita membra
cochleæ absconditæ, above above,

above, each other down from down
to down,   all reliqual
confused and submerged
Symbolacre, Sima L'Acre SimSis
agent Simulacre,

all-half-dead Simulacre not acclimatized, déclassé croaker Si Mu La Cre, quaint Simul Acre, inclemently
militant, costive, vicariated Sim / Ulacre! phanatizated simulacra
with drawers and quivering! drag his back-bone. drag, christ!
egli si dilaterà laterà aterà terà   ! Hit hit hit him!
hit him!
more news have night, marrow or pith, harvest,
on quivering balance, tumid Yolk tumescent
Tumour, thy intimate Tumour! what there again, what!
we are little slaves but we shall be and we
should turn the Great Slaves to ransom
the Genuine Slave, when the perpetual quadruplicate petals explode
as unchaste waving Trumpets, vanished or
cuting, and Others, and even Others, and even even

even, and the Toasted Venus too and Protoplasmatic Entity
and I with Others I, and Others and I, and my
elbow grafts and crackles and grows in elbow of Others,
with xyster   the Great Genuine Sighing Slave palpate
and touch us with elbow and distracted wink, bowl
specus of Ear burst, each and own and own each
and each other and other and other each and, decanting
all different notions in a new unique fossil spring
catch courage to decant, and decant the courage too
all, all, down! below below!
            All-heal! Eat eat!

Unpublished Poems

* These two pieces can be found in the poet's archives at the Biblioteca Panizzi in Reggio Emilia, specifically in boxes #16 & #6. Most likely these were considered in progress rather than final, for Villa constanly returned to his work to make changes to it and rarely finalized anything, even when it was going to print.

Poesia è

*Poetry is**

circa
1989

poesia è evanescenza

poesia è condanna a vita, con libertà
sulla parola, liberté sur parole

poesia è guida cieca a un antico
enigma, a un segreto inaccessibile

poesia è trattazione dinamica e sussultoria

poesia è la più scampagnata cosmologia che noi possiamo
inalberare e agitare,
è una piccola (abregée) cosmogonia inconsapevole e
inconsutile, scucita,
strafelata, sdrucita

poesia è dimenticarsi
dimenticanza

poesia è se-parare sé dal sé

poesia è ciò che si lascia assolutamente fuori

poesia è svuotamento senza esaurimento

poesia è costrizione al remoto,
al non ancora, al non
adesso, al non-qui,
al non-là, al
non-prima né non-dopo
né non-adesso

poetry is evanescence

poetry is life penalty, release
 on one's word, liberté sur parole

poetry is a blind guide to an ancient
 enigma, to an inaccessible secret

poetry is an argument dynamic & jarring

poetry is a rag tag cosmology we can
 raise and wave,
 it's a small (abregée) cosmogony, unaware,
 seamless, unstitched,
 breathless, in tatters

poetry is to forget
 forgetfulness

poetry is to se-parate self from self

poetry is what's completely left out

poetry is emptying without exhausting

poetry is constraint to the remote,
 to the not yet, the not
 now, the not here,
 the not there, the
 not before, neither not after,
 nor not now

poesia è sfondamento

poesia è bruciare — partorire nello stesso gesto vocale

poesia è l'esserci moltiplicato per
non esserci, ricordare
di transesserci di traverso
a spartiacque

poesia è misconoscimento di
non so bene che cosa,
ma misconoscimento

poesia è impotenza infinita,
limpida, lucida, allucinata,

poesia è intersezione
interiezione
intersessione
interruzione

poesia è una carognata

poesia è transito e esito

poesia è infusione e trans-fusione

poesia è memoria di ciò che non è
e che deve non-essere, cioè
è il Sé culminante, liminare
il Sé come cosmo incompiuto e
da non compiere mai

poetry is breeching

poetry is to burn — give birth in the same vocal gesture

poetry is being-there multiplied by
    not being-there, remembering
    to trans-be-there traversely
    like a watershed

poetry is a misunderstanding about
    what I don't know exactly,
    but a misunderstanding

poetry is infinite impotence,
    limpid, lucid, hallucinated,

poetry is intersection
    interjection
    intersession
    interruption

poetry is a low blow

poetry is transit and exit

poetry is infusion and trans-fusion

poetry is memory of what is not
    & what must not be; that is
    the culminating, liminal Self
    the Self as an incomplete cosmos
    never to be completed

poesia è legare — slegare

poesia è la scena rituale della
infinita incertezza, della
inaccessibile Infermità
(Infirmitas)

poesia è scorcio
scarto
strombo
sterro

poesia è culla — cuna
è cella — cruna
del Trans — Organo
del transorganico
dell'Indistinto
dell'In(de)terminato

poesia è la cenere

poesia è diagonale
è vanvera
dentro il corpo manifesto
dell'Inesistente Universale
dell'Anenergico Globale

poesia è pigrizia irrigidita, con
un braccio appesa al ramo
dell'Albero della Scienza del

poetry is tying — untying

poetry is the ritual scene of
infinite uncertainty, of the
inaccessible Infermity
(Infirmitas)

poetry is a streak
a swerve
a splay
a spade

poetry is crib — cradle
it's crab — ladle 1
of the Trans — Organ
of the trans-organic
of the Indistinct
of the In(de)terminable

poetry is ash

poetry is diagonal
it's ramble
inside the manifest body
of Universal Inexistence
of Global Entropy

poetry is stiffened laziness, with
an arm hanging from
the branch of the Tree of the Knowledge

Bene e del Male; cioè
è una Scimmia che sta in
Brasile sempre appesa con un
braccio al ramo di un albero (è la Preguiça)

poesia è terrorismo nel dominio della lingua,
è scoppio nella clausura del linguaggio

è terrore sul fondo delle retoriche

poesia è liberazione dalla conoscenza,
fuga dal conosciuto
svincolo dalla meccanica

è insieme è caduta, sprofondo, nella
meccanica ripetitiva, ossessiva,
iterativa, che è anche la
meccanica del cenno, della
norma, del rito (dell'obbligo
stretto, della rima, del numero,
dell'essenza)

poesia è implosione del tempo — zero
e di grado in(de)finito

poesia è sfrenamento, sfaso, minaccia potenziale,
spacco, rapina, distruzione

poesia è scasso, squarcio, scuotimento

è l'urto tra forza
e misura che

of Good and Evil; that is
a Monkey in Brazil
always hanging by an arm
from the branch of a tree (it's the Preguiça) 2

poetry is terrorism in the domain of speech,
a bang in the cloister of language

it's terror in the depths of rhetoric

poetry is liberation from knowing
escape from the known
a release from mechanics

and at the same time it's falling, sinking
into repetitive, obsessive, iterative
mechanics, which are also the
mechanics of hinting, of the
norm, of the ritual (of strict
obligation, of rhyme, of number,
of essence)

poetry is the implosion of time — zero
and in(de)finite degree

poetry is unleashing, un-phrasing, a potential threat,
breaking, robbing, destruction

poetry is smashing, shattering, shaking

it's a clash between
strength & restraint

tende a cancellare.
siamo proprio
infinitamente matti

la poesia è quasi tutto: cioè è tutto, meno
quello che veramente è

poesia è impermanenza incrociata con
trans-manenza

è impertinenza

poesia è scontro e incontro (spontaneo e
destinato) tra nevrosi e inconscio,
tra archetipo e Sé
anello monotono e perpetuo tra impulso
e ossessione

poesia è aggressione

poesia è fare spiragli, produrre crepe,
segnare filiture dentro il
sipario, dentro la Parete Sbarrata

poesia è lotta contro la notte
poesia è notte contro la notte
poesia è urto contro la voce
poesia è attrito con la pelle del Drago

poesia è così
è così e così
e così sia

that tends to erase.
We are truly
infinitely mad

poetry is almost everything: that is everything, less
what it really is

poetry is impermanence crossed with
trans-manence

it's impertinence

poetry is counter and encounter (spontaneous and
predestined) between neurosis & unconscious,
between archetype and Self
a monotonous & perpetuated ring between impulse
& obsession

poetry is aggression

to write poetry is to cut slits, produce cracks,
point out filaments in the
curtain, in the Barred Wall

poetry is a fight against the night
poetry is night against the night
poetry is a rub against the voice
poetry is friction against the skin of the Dragon

poetry is this
it's this & that
and so be it

Poetry is

* After it was written, this poem was left in a box for years at one of Villa's neighbor's houses in Rieti. It was found & subsequently published by Toni Maraini in the January 2002 issue of the Italian literary journal *Quaderni*. The original manuscript is comprised of 9 folios without numbering. Here Villa acts as an ancient sibyl, tearing his work to pieces and inviting the reader to reshuffle the individual stanzas as they see fit.

1. In the original Italian, this verse literally reads: *it's cell — eye of the needle.* Villa was clearly thinking of the passage from the New Testament: "It's easier for a camel to pass through the eye of a needle than for a rich man to enter the kingdom of God" (Matthew 19:23–24).

2. *Perguiça* literally means "sloth" in Portuguese. Here Villa uses it in reference to the mammal that dwells in the trees of South America, specifically those of Brazil, where Villa lived for about a year (1951–1952).

Prima o poi

Sooner or Later

Prima o poi, poi o prima
le parole dette, le parole scritte,
presto o tardi tutte le parole
sono destinate a sparire
spariscono.

Le parole sulla carta, le parole
sulle pietre, le parole sui rami
spariranno tutte.

Se queste parole e non parole
sono scritte su materie
che presto si decompongono, che
durano poco più di un
attimo o poco più di un millennio
che cosa esse sono.

Sooner or later, later or sooner
words spoken, words written,
sometime or another all words
are destined to vanish
they vanish.

Words on paper, words
on stone, words on branches
will all vanish.

If these words and non words
are written on materials
that quickly decompose, that
last little more than a
second or little more than a millennium
what are they. 1

Sooner or Later

1. This last stanza would require a question mark, but actually ends in a period.

Other Writings

Traduzione del Genesi: L'Impresa del Rettile[1]

Di tutti gli animali selvaggi che Jahwè aveva fatto, il Rettile era il più subdolo.[2] Difatti il Rettile disse alla Femmina: "Certamente Elohim avrà detto: 'Non mangiate niente da nessun albero dell'Oasi!'"

La Femmina rispose al Rettile: "La frutta degli alberi dell'Oasi noi la mangiamo; ma, quanto alla frutta dell'albero che sta al centro dell'Oasi ha detto Elohim: 'Non mangiatela, e non toccatela nemmeno; se no morrete!'"

Il Rettile rispose alla Femmina: "Non è vero affatto, non morrete! Anzi, Elohim sa bene che, quando ne mangiaste, i vostri occhi si aprirebbero, e diventereste allora come gli elohim, conoscitori di tutto, dell'Universo".

La Femmina allora si accorse che l'albero era buono da mangiare, e che solo a guardarlo metteva appetito. L'albero dava la concupiscenza di comprendere le cose. Essa staccò un frutto dell'albero e mangiò; e ne diede anche al suo Maschio, che le stava accanto; e questi mangiò. Si aprirono allora gli occhi[3] a tutt'e due, e s'accorsero che loro eran nudi! Cucirono subito insieme delle foglie di fico,[4] e si fecero dei perizomi.

A un certo punto udirono il rumore di Jahwè che passeggiava su e giù per l'Oasi, alla brezza marina; l'Uomo e la Donna si nascosero, lontano dalla presenza di Jahwè, in mezzo agli alberi dell'Oasi.

Jahwè chiamò l'Uomo, e gli disse: "Dove sei?", ed egli rispose: "Ho sentito nell'Oasi il tuo rumore, e mi sono spaventato, perché sono nudo; così mi sono nascosto". Disse: "Chi ti ha fatto capire che sei nudo? Tu hai mangiato qualche cosa da quell'albero, e io invece ti avevo proibito di mangiarne!"

Translation of Genesis: The Reptile's Endeavor[1]

Of all the wild animals Yahweh had made, the Reptile was the sliest.[2] In fact, the Reptile said to the Female: "Elohim certainly told you: 'Don't eat anything from any tree of the Oasis!'"

The Female answered the Reptile: "We eat the fruit of the trees of the Oasis; but as for the fruit of the tree at the center of the Oasis, Elohim said: 'Do not eat it, and do not even touch it; if you do, you will die!'"

The Reptile answered the Female: "That is not true at all, you will not die! Quite the opposite, Elohim knows that, if you ate it, your eyes would open, and you would become like the elohim, who know everything, the Universe."

Then the Female realized that the tree was good to eat, and that just looking at it brought on an appetite. The tree aroused a desire to comprehend things. She plucked a fruit from the tree and ate it; and gave some of it to her Male, who stood next to her; and he ate it. Then the eyes of both opened,[3] and they realized they were naked! They immediately sewed together some fig leaves,[4] and made themselves some loincloths.

At a certain point they heard the sound of Yahweh strolling up and down the Oasis, in the sea breeze; the Man and the Woman hid, far from the presence of Yahweh, among the trees of the Oasis.

Yahweh called the Man and said to him: "Where are you?" and he answered: "I heard the sound you made in the Oasis, and was frightened, because I am naked; so I hid." He said: "Who made you aware of your nakedness? You ate something from that tree, & I instead had forbidden you to eat from it!"

E l'Uomo rispose: "È stata la Femmina che tu mi hai messo accanto a darmi da mangiare una cosa dell'albero".

Jahwè disse alla Donna: "Perché hai agito così?" La Donna rispose: "Il Rettile mi ha convinto, e ho mangiato".

Allora Jahwè disse al Rettile:

"Poiché tu hai fatto questo,
maledetto tu (tra tutte le bestie), 5
[e] tra tutti gli animali selvaggi!
Camminerai sul tuo ventre,
e fango mangerai,
per tutto il tempo della tua esistenza!

La discordia io pongo
tra te e la Donna
e tra il tuo seme
e il suo seme!

Egli (?) ti schiaccerà il cranio
e tu conoscerai il (suo) calcagno!" 6
Alla Femmina disse:
"Moltiplicherò oltre il sopportabile
i dolori delle tue gravidanze:
partorirai figli con dolore!
Avrai voglia del tuo maschio,
ed egli ti terrà soggetta".

All'Uomo disse:
"Poiché hai obbedito alla voce della tua Femmina,
e hai mangiato dall'albero
mentre ti avevo proibito di mangiarne,

And the Man answered: "It was the Female you placed next to me who gave me a thing to eat from that tree."

Yahweh said to the Woman: "Why did you behave that way?" The Woman answered: "The Reptile convinced me, & I ate."

Then Yahweh said to the Reptile:

"Because you did this,
cursed are you (among all beasts) 5
[and] among all wild animals!
You will walk on your belly,
and will eat mud,
for as long as you exist!

The discord I sow
between you and the Woman
and between your seed
and her seed!

He (?) will crush your skull
and you will know (his) heel!" 6
He said to the Female:
"I will multiply beyond tolerable
the pains of your childbearing:
you will give birth to children in pain!
You will lust after your male,
and he will enslave you."

He said to the Man:
"Because you obeyed the voice of your Female,
and you ate from the tree,
while I had forbidden you to eat from it,

maledetta, per causa tua, la campagna!
con dolore ne trarrai nutrimento
per tutto il tempo della tua vita.

Spine e gramigne ti produrrà
e mangerai erbe selvatiche.
Con il sudore del tuo volto
ti procurerai da mangiare,
fino a che tornerai nella terra,
perché da essa tu provieni;
perché tu sei fango
e nel fango ritornerai!" 7

Poi l'Uomo chiamò la sua Femmina con il nome di Eva,[8] cioè "la Vivente", perché essa fu la madre di tutti i viventi.

All'Uomo e alla sua Donna Jahwè fece delle gonne di pelle,[9] e con esse li vestì.

L'Espulsione

Jahwè disse: "Se l'Uomo può diventare uguale a uno di noi nella conoscenza universale, allora bisogna ch'egli non stenda la sua mano a cogliere un'altra volta frutta dall'Albero della Vita per mangiarne e vivere immortale". Per questo Jahwè lo cacciò fuori dall'Oasi della Steppa, mandandolo a lavorare la terra, dalla quale era stata prelevato. Espulse l'Uomo; quindi, di fronte all'ingresso dell'Oasi della Steppa collocò i Cherubini[10] e Spada-di-fiamme, a custodire il sentiero dell'Albero della Vita.

the land will be cursed, because of you!
in pain, you will draw nourishment from it
for as long as you live.

For you it will produce thorns and weeds
and you will eat wild greens.
By the sweat of your brow
you will gather your food
until you return to the earth,
for that is where you are from;
because you are mud
and to mud you will return!" 7

The Man gave his Female the name Eve,[8] that is "the Living" for she was the mother of all who lived.

For the Man and his Woman, Yahweh made some leather skirts,[9] and with these he clothed them.

The Expulsion

Yahweh said: "If Man can become just like one of us in universal knowledge, then he must not extend his hand to pick again the fruit of the Tree of Life to eat it and live immortal." For this reason Yahweh banished him from the Oasis of the Steppe, sending him to work the earth, from which he had been drawn. He expelled Man; thus, in front of the entrance to the Oasis of the Steppe he positioned Cherubs[10] and Swords-of-Flames, to guard the path to the Tree of Life.

1. Il mito della "caduta" dell'uomo nelle strettoie storiche del male, dell'indigenza, del dolore, della fatica, dell'insicurezza, il mito della fine del prestigio umano, del deperimento della sua natura medesima, è grande mito oscuro e fantasioso. Le sue radici immaginose attingono al sentimento, diffuso in tutte le mitologie, di un destino drammatico, e si articolano, probabilmente, con l'istituto, e la conseguente violazione, di un tabù dietetico, che anima un'atmosfera dove il protagonista del dramma, l'uomo, sopravvive, nonostante tutto, a tutte le insidie delle figurazioni agitate (dallo spirito così detto "religioso") che lo circondano come aspetti della morte, carichi di energie fatali e fatidiche, prodotti da una fantasia epico-teatrale che si cristallizza nel culto, e che opera se medesima come spettacolo enigmatico e come angosciosa ragione dell'esistenza. Queste figurazioni sono divenute a loro volta personaggi, deuteragonisti, comparse, e sono: il Dio-Mago, il Serpente-Chimera, il Demone-Serpente, il Frutto stregato, il Dio-Artigiano ("Fattore"), il dio Istitutore, gli Alberi magici, Alberi-Divinazione, preveggenti, oracolari, Alberi di Vita e di Giovinezza perpetua, Alberi-Stupefacenti, il Deus Furens, il Deus Otiosus, i Demoni vari, e le varie strumentazioni ambientali, terrestri o atmosferiche, spade, fulmini, fuoco, acque.

2. "Rettile": *nḥš*. Si traduce così tradizionalmente, per cui si usa intendere un animale come il serpente affine a quello della nostra nozione tassonomica. Però in realtà il referto mitologico ebraico allude a un grande e celebrato Mostro cosmogonico, di natura marina, abissale, uno dei maggiori avversari dell'Elohim. Assistiamo in questo mito a una delle fasi residuate di una maggiore teomachia. Più tardi la teologia giudaica interpreterà il "Serpente" come una manifestazione del Diavolo, di Satana. Ma nei testi sapienziali e in Isaia (27, 1) il *nḥš* è un vero e proprio Dragone, è il famoso Leviatan (ben noto alla letteratura ebraica come antagonista di Jahwè; e il nome è ripreso dalla mitologia cananeo-ugaritica). Perché il relatore ricorre proprio al nome di *nḥš*? Il racconto è di natura etimologizzante, il mitema interpreta parole affini, e si fonda sul valore magico-analogico (in strutture ritmico-onomastiche, in iterazioni magicamente intensificanti) della parola. La voce *nḥš* aveva anche in ebraico (come ha sempre avuto in arabo, *naḥisa*) il valore di "malefizio, malaugurio". Infatti è con l'accadimento, di prospettiva atropo-cosmica, del rapporto Donna-Serpente che irrompono nella storia umana il male e la morte. La concezione magica è evidente. Probabile è inoltre che il racconto ricorra giusto a una deformazione fonetica del nome sumero e assiro di questo

1. The myth of the "fall" of man in the historic bottlenecks of evil, of destitution, of pain, of toil, of insecurity, the myth of the end of human prestige, of the deterioration of his very nature, is a highly obscure & fantastical myth. Its imaginative roots hint at the feeling, widespread in all mythologies, of a dramatic destiny, and they are articulated, with the institution, and the subsequent violation, of a dietetic taboo, which animates an atmosphere where the drama's protagonist, man, survives, despite everything, all the traps of agitated figurations (laid out by the so-called "religious" spirit) that surround him as aspects of death, charged with fatal and fateful energies, produced by an epic-theatrical fantasy that is crystallized in the cult, and that operates in and of itself as an enigmatic spectacle and as a painful reason behind existence. These figurations became in their own right characters, deuteragonists, apparitions, and they are: the God-Magician, the Serpent-Chimera, the Demon-Serpent, the wicked Fruit, the God-Artisan ("Maker"), the Instructor god, the magic Trees, Trees-Divinations, soothsayers, oracles, Trees of Life and eternal Youth, Trees-Hallucinogen, the Deus Furens, the Deus Otiosus, the various Demons, & the various environmental props, either earthly or atmospheric — swords, lightning, fire, waters.

2. "Reptile": *nḫš*. This is traditionally translated as such, and therefore typically refers to an animal similar to that of our taxonomic notion of the serpent. In reality, however, the Hebrew mythological reference alludes to a great and celebrated cosmogonic Monster of an abyssal, marine nature; one of Elohim's major adversaries. In this myth we find one of the residual phases of a larger theomachy. Later Hebrew theology would interpret the "Serpent" as the manifestation of the Devil, of Satan. Yet in the sapiential books and in Isaiah (27:1) the *nḫš* is a real Dragon, it is the famous Leviathan (well-known to Hebrew literature as Yahweh's antagonist; and the name was taken from Canaanite-Ugaritic mythology). Why does the narrator harken back to the name *nḫš*? The story is of an etymologizing nature, the mytheme interprets similar words, and is founded upon the magical-analogical (in rhythmic-onomastic structures, in magically intensified iterations) of words. In Hebrew the term *nḫš* also held (as it always has in Arabic, *naḫisa*) the sense of "witchcraft, ill-omens." In fact, it is with the advent, of an anthropocosmic perspective, of the relationship Woman-Serpent, when evil and death burst into human history. The magical concept is evident. Also, it is probable that story recalls precisely a phonetic deformation of the Sumerian and

Mostro primordiale, che è *MUŠḪUŠ*, per trarne un significato aderente a una concezione magico-iettatoria. Infine la voce *nḥš* è legata a quella di *nḥšt*, che, sull'akk. *naḫšatu*, sembra significare "mestruazione" (e questo deve, secondo noi, poter essere il significato di *nḥšt* in Ezechiele, 16, 36). È intenzione del testo di incontrare proprio ai primordi una conferma del tabù del sangue mestruale. A distanza di secoli, nell'epoca post-giudaica, il maggior testo apocalittico, L'Apocalisse di Giovanni, evoca la Femmina e il Mostro (il "Gran Dragone" *rosso*), certamente con riguardo al modello contenuto nel nostro testo: la Femmina è Eva, e il Mostro è Satana, come Serpente *rosso*, *nḥš*, *nḥšt*; sotto i piedi della Femmina, sta la luna, simbolo del ritmo mestruale.

L'esegesi messianica offerta da buona parte della patristica e della teologia cristiana, ha definito questo breve referto mitologico un "protoevangelo" (il Rettile è il "diavolo", egli sarà sconfitto da un "figlio (?) della Donna", cioè dal Cristo, che è il tardo e stanco mito uscito dal groviglio dei miti accolti dai profeti ebrei; la Donna è la "Vergine Maria", ma l'arbitraria concezione non aderisce al nostro testo neppure in un punto, e sembra una delle più avventurate o stravaganti. Per di più la lingua rimane misteriosa e il dettato oracolare del tutto enigmatico, per via delle oscurità lessicali e per l'ambiguità delle referenze. Senonché la monomania ossessiva dell'esegesi messianistica, tanto giudaica quanto post-giudaica, è sempre in posizione aggressiva sul testo che non rende quello che il "messianismo" esige.

"Subdolo: ebr. *'rm*. S'intende, anche, insieme: "nudo", oltre che "subdolo". Prosegue il gioco etimologistico, basato sulla omofonia tra *'rm*, "astuto, subdolo", e *'rm*, "nudo". Cioè, il Rettile, che è *'rm*, dice alla Donna che lei diventerà Elohim (o come Elohim) se mangia di quel frutto. Essa ne mangia, insieme ne mangia l'uomo, e, anziché Elohim, tutt'e due diventano *'rmm*, "nudi"; cioè anche "demoniaci", nudi come la biscia.

3. "si aprirono gli occhi": il serpente non ha mentito, l'uomo e la donna sono ora diventati Elohim, conoscono tutto; allora il serpente è stato più forte di Jawhè. È uno degli episodi agonistici residuati da teomachie anteriori.

Elementi e mitemi tipici di questo racconto sono anche conservati, o forse perfino in parte tratti, da un comune patrimonio mitologico, che ha una redazione precipua, forse germinale, in un racconto della mitologia egiziana: secondo la quale la Donna-Maga (anche Eva è intesa come tale), che aveva nome Iside (*st*), voleva diventare una divinità. Riuscì infatti

Assyrian name for this primordial Monster, which is *MUŠḪUŠ*, drawing from it a meaning that adheres to an idea of magical-jinxing. Finally, the term *nḫš* is tied to that of *nḫšt*, which, from the Akkadian *naḫšatu*, seems to mean "menstruation" (& this, in our opinion, could possibly be the meaning of *nḫšt* in Ezekiel 16:36). It is the text's intention to find, precisely in the origins, a confirmation of the taboo of menstrual blood. Centuries later, in the post-Judaic period, the major apocalyptic text, the Apocalypse by John, evokes the Female and the Monster (the "Great *red* Dragon"), certainly with regard to the model contained in our text: the Female is Eve, & the Monster is Satan, as the *red* Serpent, *nḫš*, *nḫšt*; under the Female's feet, is the moon, symbol of the menstrual cycle.

The Messianic exegesis offered by a good part of the patristics & by Christian theology, has deemed this brief mythological reference a "proto-gospel" (the Reptile is the "devil," he will be defeated by a "son (?) of the Woman," that is by the Christ, which is the late & tired myth taken from the tangle of myths collected by the Hebrew prophets; the Woman is the "Virgin Mary," but the arbitrary concept does not adhere to our text at any point, & seems one of the most adventurous or extravagant. Moreover, the language remains mysterious and the oracular diction completely enigmatic, due to lexical obscurities and the ambiguity of the references. Nonetheless, the obsessive monomania of Messianic exegesis, as much Judaic as post-Judaic, always assumes an aggressive position over the text, which doesn't relay that which "Messianism" demands.

"Sly": *ʿrm* in Hebrew. It is also meant to convey: "nude," in addition to "sly." The etymological game continues, based on the homophony between *ʿrm*, "astute, sly," & *ʿrm*, "nude." That is, the Reptile, which is *ʿrm*, tells the Woman she will become Elohim (or like Elohim) if she eats of that fruit. She eats of it, the man also eats of it, &, rather than Elohim, both become *ʿrmm*, "nude"; that is, also "demoniac," nude like the snake.

3. "their eyes opened": the serpent did not lie, man and woman have now become *Elohim*, they know everything; so the serpent was stronger than Yahweh. This is one of the agonistic episodes left over from earlier theomachies.

   Elements and mythemes typical of this story are also contained in, or sometimes even taken directly from, a shared mythological patrimony, which may in turn be rooted in a tale belonging to Egyptian mythology: the Witch-Woman (with whom Eve shares certain traits), called Isis (*st*), wanted to be become a goddess. She succeeded through a stratagem,

allo scopo con uno stratagemma (fece un Serpente, con la saliva del Vecchio Sole, il dio Râ) che (reinterpretato a rovescio) è analogo a quello biblico: Iside riuscì a ottenere che il Serpente mordesse il tallone o calcagno della vecchia divinità; e così Iside poté conoscere il nome, cioè l'essenza del dio; e divenne essa stessa "dea", la famosa divinità, che per venticinque secoli conobbe culto vario e sempre più vasto in tutto il mediterraneo. La letteratura akkadica offre un esemplare mitologico abbastanza antico (sec. XV; il testo è stato ritrovato tra i materiali di *tell el-Amarna* in Egitto) che fu ripetutamente comparato con la storia di Adamo. Il mito era noto anche al sacerdote e scrittore caldeo Beroso. Si definisce generalmente come il "mito di Adapa", e nello stesso nome di Adapa alcuni critici intesero una relazione con il nome Adamo ma la cosa non è provata.

4. "foglie di fico": il nome del "fico", *t'nh*, appartiene a un largo e complesso calembour, o gioco etimologico-simbolico, su due radici affini, *'wn* e *'nh*, in cui un ebreo sentiva un trascorrere di temi o significati che vanno da "sesso, erotismo" (anche in Geremia, 2, 24, *t'nh*; in Isaia *'wn* è un "Dio-sesso") a "sciagura, disgrazia, lutto; fatica". Non si riesce a scorgere, però, fino in fondo, l'idea del testo, cioè se veramente la concezione del relatore del mito consideri la "caduta", il grande "castigo", come conseguenza di una trasgressione sessuale, e il sesso come origine della caduta umana, del peccato. E non è possibile decidere se il "mito" è fondato su uno sforzo, o tensione, del linguaggio, o diciamo, della convenzione (o convinzione) lessicale, o se appartiene a una formazione con tramiti omeomorfi, e in ogni caso autonomi.

5. "maledetto tu...": la sintassi non aiuta a comprendere bene il senso di questa maledizione. Si può anche letteralmente intendere: "maledetto tu... più di tutti gli animali selvaggi". O forse meglio: "maledetto tu... da tutti gli animali selvaggi", cioè "tutti gli animali selvaggi ti maledicano" (concezione del bestiario mitologico e favolistico).

6. "schiaccerà... conoscerai": la frase è enigmatica, e il verbo *šwp* non è comprensibile in ebraico. Qui riteniamo i due *šwp* prestiti dall'akk. *šāpu* "schiacciare con i piedi, calpestare" e akk. *šapû* "guardare, vedere". Antichi e moderni traducono in vari modi; più o meno alla ventura. Dobbiamo considerare il testo come perduto, fino a che analogie testuali, o nuove comparazioni letterarie nell'ambito dell'antico oriente, possano offrire mezzi più sicuri che ci aprano il testo.

which, reinterpreted backwards, is analogous to the biblical version. She made a serpent out of the saliva of the old sun god (*Râ*). Isis managed to get the snake to bite the talons or the heel of the old god; and thus Isis learned his name, that is to say his essence, and she herself became a "goddess," the most famous godhead who, for twenty-five centuries, was worshipped in different ways and whose fame expanded across the Mediterranean. Akkadian literature offers a somewhat older exemplary mythology (XV century; the text was found among the materials of *tell el-Amarna* in Egypt) that was repeatedly compared to the story of Adam. The myth was also known to the Chaldean writer and priest, Berossus. It is generally defined as the "Adapa myth," and from the very name Adapa, some critics inferred a relation to the name Adam, yet such a thing has not been proven.

4. "fig leaves": the name for fig, *t'nh*, belongs to a complex pun, or etymological-symbolic play, on two similar roots, *'wn* & *'nh*, in which a Hebrew heard a multitude of themes or meanings that range from "sex, eroticism" (also in Jeremiah, 2:24, *t'nh*; in Isaiah *'wn* is a "sex-God") to "shame, disgrace, grief; toil." However, the idea behind this passage cannot be fully deciphered, that is if the narrator's concept of the myth actually considers the "fall," "the great punishment," the consequence of a sexual transgression, & sex as the origin of the human fall, of sin. It is impossible to decide whether the "myth" is founded on a forcing, or tension, of the language, or let's say, of the lexical convention (or conviction), or if it belongs to a formation through homeomorphic, and in any case, autonomous, changes.

5. "cursed are you": here the syntax is too convoluted to permit a clear interpretation of this curse. It could literally be read as: "cursed are you … more than any other wild animal." Or better still: "cursed are you by all wild animals," that is, "may all wild animals curse you" (a concept from the fabled and mythological bestiary).

6. "you will crush … you will know": the phrase is enigmatic and the verb *šwp* is not understandable in Hebrew. Here we maintain that the two *šwp* have been borrowed from the Akkadian *šāpu*, "to smash with one's feet, or to trample" as well as from the Akkadian *šapû*, "to look & to see." Both ancient and modern scholars have translated this in various ways; and more or less haphazardly. Thus we are at a loss. A reliable interpretation of the passage cannot be made until new documents surface from the Ancient East, allowing us to clarify it through textual comparisons.

7. "nel fango... tornerai". La natura di questa metamorfosi punitiva, che è degradazione, è ripresa alle concezioni mesopotamiche. Da confrontare, nel mito akkadico *Zû e Lugalbanda*: "chi si oppone a lui (= a Enlili) diventa argilla" (vv. 52–53, 74–75).

8. "Eva": ebr. *ḫwh*, continua il mito onomastico, basato sul complesso sistema di sincretismi etimologistici. Nel nome Eva, che si può ritenere mutuato a testi mitologici sumeri, è contenuto il sumero AWA (AMA), "madre, femmina", su cui l'influsso etimologistico semitico avrà sentito *ḫwj* "serpente" (da cfr. aram. *ḫaiwa* e sopra tutto arab. *hayya* "serpente"), e, insieme, la voce arcaica *ḫwh* "vita". Anche nel pantheon fenicio esisteva una dea *hwt*, divinità di carattere o di natura ofidica, una dea dei serpenti, forse però piuttosto da situare in aera mediterranea, cretese. La scrittura ideografica sumera ha un segno che rappresenta il fiore della kalla: TIL. Il segno ha tre significati: "vita, essere"; "abitare"; "costola del corpo umano". Il segno è facilmente da mettere in relazione con il nome e il racconto di Eva.

Un rapporto di dipendenza di Eva rispetto alla mitologia sumera sembra presentato dalle caratteristiche e dalle azioni della divinità dingir NIN-TI-UG-GA "Signora che dà la vita al non-vivente" (assiro *muballitat mîti*), madre di tutta l'umanità, dea del parto, esperta nell'arte dei farmaci e delle qualità terapeutiche e stupefacenti di certe piante. Il suo nome significa inoltre "Signora della costola". Un testo sembra presentare un elemento affine al "frutto proibito".

9. "di pelle": ebr. *ʿwr*. Continua, però il gioco etimologico, affine a quello di "foglie di fico" (v.n. 3,7). In realtà la voce *ʿwr* significa anche "cecità", sia fisica che psichica, "cecità mentale, offuscamento della ragione"; cioè l'uomo, maschio e femmina, passa a una condizione di "ignoranza". Noi non sappiamo che cosa esattamente intendesse questo mito per "Conoscenza" e per "Ignoranza". Soltanto si rivela che, secondo il mito, si possono verificare, nella storia dell'uomo, due strati oggettivi, esterni alla mente umana, e che sono: lo splendore e la nitidezza delle cose, ben distinte tra loro; e la nebbia, il vapore che obnubila le cose stesse. Scendendo nel secondo strato, la mente è immersa nell'Ignoranza. Da questo punto, il tentativo di recuperare gli aspetti e il meccanismo del pensiero così detto "primitivo" e delle sue avventure, appartiene alla scienza speciale che se ne occupa.

L'esegesi giudaica, nel medioevo, era arrivata ad asserire (con Mosé Maimonide) che prima del peccato l'uomo, in quanto "immagine

7. "to mud you will return." The nature of this punitive metamorphosis, which is degradation, is taken from Mesopotamian concepts. To be compared to the Akkadian myth *Zû & Lugalbanda*: "who opposes him (= Enlili) is turned to clay" (versus 52–53, 74–75).

8. "Eve": *ḫwh* in Hebrew, is a continuation of the onomastic myth, based on the complex system of etymological syncretisms. In the name Eve, which we can consider to be borrowed from Sumerian mythological texts, is contained the Sumerian AWA (AMA), "mother, female," in which the Semitic ear would have heard *ḫwj*, "snake," (see the Aramaic *ḫaiwa* and most of all the Arabic *hayya*, "snake"), as well as the archaic word *ḫwh*, "life." A goddess (*hwt*) existed even in the Phœnician pantheon, a divinity of an ophidian nature or character, a snake goddess, which is possibly better situated within a Mediterranean context, specifically that of Crete. Sumerian ideographic writing has a sign that represents the flower of the kalla: TIL. The sign has three meanings: "life, being"; "to live"; "rib of the human body." The sign is easily placed in relation to the name and story of Eve.

An interdependence between Eve and the Sumerian mythology seems to be supported by the characteristics and by the actions of the divinity ^{dingir} NIN-TI-UG-GA, "Lady who gives life to the non-living" (*muballitat mîti* in Assyrian), mother of all humanity, goddess of childbirth, expert in the art of medicine and in the therapeutic and psychotropic quality of plants. Her name also means "Lady of the rib." One text seems to present an element similar to that of the "forbidden fruit."

9. "leather": *ʿwr* in Hebrew. This, however, continues the etymological game, similar to that of "fig leaves" (lines 3, 7). In reality, the term *ʿwr* also means "blindness," both physical & psychological, "mental blindness, obfuscation of reason"; that is, man, male & female, passes to a condition of "ignorance." We don't know what this myth meant exactly by "Knowledge" & "Ignorance." We can only say that the myth allows us to verify, in the history of man, two objective layers, external to the human mind, and they are: the splendor and the clarity of things, well distinguished between them; and the fog, the steam that clouds the things themselves. Delving into the second layer, the mind is immersed in Ignorance. From this point, the task of recuperating the aspects & the mechanism of so-called "primitive" thought and its adventures belongs to the special science that deals with such issues.

The Judaic exegesis, in the medieval period, went so far as to maintain (with Moses Maimonides) that before the sin, man, being that he

dell'Elohim" possiede i mezzi di discernimento della verità dalla falsità; mentre dopo il peccato, egli possiede solo "opinioni", cioè conosce solo il probabile. Naturalmente è interpretazione di carattere aristotelico, cui il testo non sembra in alcun senso essere affine; è l'intrusione della filosofia nell'esegesi; intrusione largamente avversata da altri interpreti (specialmente dalle interpretazioni provenienti dalla Cabala, e dai vari Allegorismi mistici).

10. "Cherubini": divinità tutelari, raffigurate come animali dalla testa di leone o di bovino, e muniti di ali, per lo più raccolte sul corpo; erano collocate, in Mesopotamia, dinnanzi alle porte dei templi, in funzione di custodi dell'abitazione divina. Nella fantomitica ebraica, i Cherubini sono destinati a trasportare sul proprio dorso, o sulle proprie ali, o a sorreggere in alto la divinità Jahwè. Qui, invece, sono in funzione di difensori, o guardiani: della Steppa, o Eden; e sarebbe da intendere "gli Apotropaici", nel verbo akkadico *karabu*, che sembra abbia qualche connessione con l'ebraico *brk*, in generale "benedire; augurare", ma anche (sembra da un passo almeno, Deut. 27, 12) "proteggere, preservare, difendere" (in senso, appunto, apotropaico).

was the "image of Elohim," possessed the means of discerning between true and false; while after the sin, he only possessed "opinions," that is, he only knows the probable. Naturally, this is an interpretation of an Aristotelian character, to which the text is not akin in any way; this is an intrusion of philosophy upon the exegesis; one that has been widely carried out by other interpreters (especially by the interpretations hailing from the Cabala, and by various mystic Allegories).

10. "Cherubs": protective divinities, depicted as animals with the head of a lion or cow, equipped with wings, most of the time folded on their body. In Mesopotamia, they were positioned before temple gates, as guardians of the divine dwelling. In the Hebrew phantomyth, the Cherubs are charged with transporting or lifting, either on their backs or on their wings, the divinity Yahweh. Here, instead, they are used as defenders, or guardians: of the Steppe, or Eden; & should be understood as "the Apotropaic," according to the Akkadian verb *karabu*, which seems to have some connection to the Hebrew *brk*, generally "to bless; to wish," but also (it seems from at least one passage: Deuteronomy 27:12) "to protect, preserve, defend" (precisely in the apotropaic sense).

Saggio sull'uomo primordiale:

Noi e la preistoria: A proposito di una scoperta recente

Sulle pendici del monte Circeo, l'opera paziente, tenace, quasi da roditore del tempo, condotta dai paletnologi, e specialmente dal prof. Blanc, la terra ha riservato, in questi ultimi mesi, una nuova rivelazione: sono stati scoperti i resti fossili (una mascella inferiore, con alcuni denti) di un bambino, anzi di un piccolo ominide, decenne, della razza Neandertal: vissuto in quella remota parte del Lazio parecchie decine di migliaia d'anni orsono. Gli anni si calcolano sulla radioattività degli isotopi di carbonio, tratti dai residui di carbone che si trovano nei focolari preistorici. E questi ultimi reperti, approssimativamente valutati, andranno negli Stati Uniti, dove si praticano sistemi di calcolo di radioattività molto più vasti di quanto non si possa fare nei nostri istituti scientifici. Ma non sono tanto i tre dentini del bambino che ci interessano qui. Più importante per noi è l'annuncio dato dal Blanc di aver trovato, in una delle grotte esplorate, una vertebra di balena, che i primitivi ominidi di Neandertal hanno, evidentemente, recuperato sul litorale. Ora, si ritiene che gli uomini di Neandertal, cacciatori straordinari, non possedessero nessuna facoltà di quelle che noi oggi chiamano "artistiche": o, almeno, la paletnologia non ne ha trovato le vestigia. Però il prof. Blanc ha rivelato, con l'acutezza che distingue sempre la sua ricerca, questo: il fatto che essi abbiano raccolto e trasportato nella loro abitazione la vertebra, dovrebbe dimostrare che essi comprendevano "la singolarità" dell'oggetto.

Questo è veramente il punto che ci riguarda, e che dovrebbe condurci a una analisi assai più approfondita di quanto fino ad oggi, con una singolare ristrettezza di prospettive, abbiano fatto le estetiche, o, diciamo addirittura, l'estetica, su quelle manife-

Essay on Primordial Man:

Prehistory and Us: Regarding a Recent Discovery[1]

On the slopes of Mount Circeo, the patient, tenacious work carried out by paleontologists, and especially by Prof. Blanc, has, over the last few months, unearthed a new revelation: they discovered the fossilized remains (a lower jaw with a few teeth) of a child, or rather of a small hominid of about ten belonging to the Neanderthal race that lived in that remote part of Lazio some tens of thousands of years ago. Its age is determined by the radioactivity in the isotopes of carbon, drawn from the carbon residue found in prehistoric fire pits. These latest findings, assessed approximately, will be sent to the United States, where the systems in place to calculate radioactivity are much more advanced in respect to those of our own scientific institutes. Yet it is not the child's three little teeth that interest us the most. More important is Prof. Blanc's report of having found, in one of the caves he explored, the vertebra of a whale, which the primitive Neanderthal hominids had, evidently, recovered from the seashore. Nowadays, it is believed that, while extraordinary hunters, Neanderthals did not possess any faculties that we would today call "artistic": or at least paleontology has yet to find any traces of them. However, what Prof. Blanc has revealed, with the acuteness that always sets his work apart, is this: the fact that picking up & transporting the vertebra into their dwelling should prove that they understood the object's "singularity."

This is really the point that concerns us, and that should lead us to an analysis much more profound than those conducted thus far, with remarkable closed-mindedness, regarding the aesthetics of those human, pre-human, or even para-human

stazioni umane, o anche preumane e paraumane, che in qualche senso coincidono con le facoltà così dette "artistiche". Difatti rimane da chiedersi: cosa mai può aver "visto" l'uomo di Neadertal nella vertebra di una balena, per trascinarla fin dentro casa? sarà soltanto una intuizione di carattere magico-religioso, o, tenuto conto della fondamentale e semplice organicità del pensiero prelogico, del pensiero preistorico, così difficilmente sezionabile in gradi e in elementi, non sarà magica, o intuita come magica proprio l'idea centrale che rappresenta una vertebra? e cioè, la strutturazione, la continuità, la variazione metrica costante, l'iterazione? il sentimento della vertebra, della catena, del serpente, dell'intreccio, non è forse da considerarsi la fondazione prima, e ultima, del sentimento così detto artistico, della intuizione ritmica?

È presumibile, anche se non probabile, che la vertebra portata nella grotta avesse una funzione magica, apotropaica, cultuale. Però, quello che con grandi difficoltà i paleontologi e i paletnologi hanno tentato di chiarire, rimane appunto la ragione per cui un oggetto, reperto in seno alla natura o manufatto, sia venuto a caricarsi di un funzionamento che l'oggetto in sé naturalmente non presuppone. Quale il procedimento secondo cui l'oggetto diventa significativo in un ordine apparentemente eterogeneo? che cosa porta a quella successiva natura? che cosa fa emettere all'oggetto rapporti nuovi con sfere di attività esterne ad esso? è un procedimento meccanico o un procedimento psicologico? L'analisi dovrebbe, innanzi tutto, procedere alla classifica e alla qualifica, e a un congruo lavoro comparativo, di tutti gli oggetti conosciuti dalla descrizione scientifica come magici; e quindi chiedersi: perché questi oggetti, questa serie di oggetti, e non un'altra serie? Praticamente: ecco la vertebra di balena. Ecco una forma, ecco una struttura, ecco un aspetto della preda naturale. Non vorremmo nemmeno lontanamente insinuare, come qualche esteta, sempre gretto, o qualche dilettante, spesso improprio,

manifestations that in some sense coincide with so-called "artistic" faculties. In fact, we still need to ask ourselves what Neanderthal man could have "seen" in the whale vertebra in order to drag it into his house? could it have been merely an intuition of a magico-religious character? Perhaps — keeping in mind the simple and basic comprehension of pre-logical thought, of the prehistoric thought that cannot easily be separated into levels or elements — it was not magical at all? And that means the structure, the continuity, the constant metric variety, the iteration? Could we consider the feeling evoked by the vertebra — the chain, the serpent, the intertwining — the first, and last, formation of the so-called artistic feeling, of the intuition of rhythm?

Although unlikely, we may presume the vertebra brought into the cave held a magic, apotropaic, cultic function. However, what both paleontologists and historical archeologists have struggled to clarify is precisely the reason why an object, either found in nature or manufactured, came to be charged with a function that the object itself does not naturally have. Through what sort of procedure does the object become significant within an apparently heterogeneous order? What leads it to that different nature? What causes the object to emit new relationships with spheres of activity that are external to it? Is it a mechanical procedure or a psychological procedure? An analysis should, first and foremost, proceed to classify and qualify, as well as engage in a congruous comparison of all objects labeled by the scientific community as magic. Therefore, we must ask: why these objects, why this series of objects and not others? In short: here's the whale vertebra. Here's a form, a structure, an aspect of natural preying. We do not want to even faintly insinuate, like some narrow-minded esthetic or mistaken dilettante, that the choice of the object to hold a function within the magical sphere is

farebbe, che la scelta dell'oggetto funzionante nelle sfera magica cada sugli oggetti "belli". Nel nostro caso: sulla bellezza di una vertebra. Anzi, al contrario, potremmo escludere questo genere, piuttosto avaro, di basso mitologismo estetico. Per fortuna i nostri antenati erano sprovvisti del sentimento del bello; quel sentimento che, caduto dentro certi nostri artisti, li ha condotti a fare o ricostruire i nessi e le giunture di una morfologia mimetica, o a "creare" (come dicono loro) delle forme, perché sono "belle". Questo è infantilismo: l'infantilismo inesperto e solennemente orbo delle estetiche. Nessuna sensibilità estetica supponiamo nell'uomo arcaico, sia quello preistorico, sia quello degli uomini allo stato etnografico. Non abbiamo mai supposto che gli idoli dell'isola di Pasqua o la venere di Savignano sul Panaro, siano "belle". "Bella" è soltanto la venere di Milo e le riproduzioni in gesso che oggi si usa mettere sotto gli occhi dei giudici di concorsi per le elezioni di miss universo. Appunto perché le estetiche, supposto che abbiano un minimo senso prospettico, hanno soltanto quel senso, univoco e impotente.

Questo discorso è fatto tutto di domande. Allora domandiamo ancora: che cosa ha indotto l'uomo della grotta del Circeo a portarsi a casa la vertebra di balena? con lo stesso spirito con cui noi ci porteremmo a casa una indagine morfologica fatta in pietra o in legno dallo scultore Noguchi?

Il lavoro di indagine che deve portare una qualsiasi documenta risposta alla nostra questione non è ancora stato compiuto. I material non sono ancora stati posti nella speciale prospettiva, necessaria a far ripensare su questo argomento, che è alla base della nostra coscienza medesima di artisti e di uomini. Ma rimane il fatto che la parte più sollevata, più solenne, più audace della produzione artistica moderna, e ormai anche statisticamente più ricca, è quella che cerca il suo orientamento nella naturale reviviscenza delle etimologie sorprese nel loro trasalimento originario,

determined by the "beauty" of the objects. In our case: the beauty of a whale vertebra. Instead, it is quite the opposite; we may exclude this rather stingy sort of low aesthetic mythologism. Fortunately, our ancestors were spared this feeling of beauty; the feeling that consumes most of our artists and pushes them to forge or remodel the connections and joints of a mimetic morphology, or "to create" (as they say) forms because they are "beautiful." This is childish thinking: the inexperienced and solemnly shortsighted childish thinking of aesthetics. We do not presume any aesthetic sensibility in archaic man, prehistoric man, or even those in an ethnographic state. We have never presumed that the idols of Easter Island or the Venus of Savignano sul Panaro are "beautiful." Beautiful is only the Venus of Milo & the cast reproductions that are today placed under the eyes of judges electing miss universe. Precisely because aesthetics, supposing they have even a slightly perspectival sense, have only that sense, univocal and impotent.

This argument is entirely comprised of questions. So let's keep asking: what urged the man of the caves in Circeo to bring home the whale vertebra, with the same spirit with which we would bring home a morphologic investigation in stone or wood by the sculptor Noguchi?

The investigatory groundwork required to eventually document any answers to these questions has yet to be carried out. The materials still have not been placed in the special perspective necessary to rethinking this argument, which lies at the base of our very understanding of artists & men. However, the fact remains that the most salient, the most solemn, the most audacious, and by now statistically the most rich, part of modern artistic production, is that which seeks its orientation in the natural revivification of etymologies surprised in their original fulguration,

e nella sua alterna condotta storica. Il recupero dell'atto iniziale, e di tutte le sue conseguenze, questa decisiva e definitoria ripresa del gesto puro che ha condotto l'uomo preistorico alla comunicazione concreta con il mondo, anzi a una presa di possesso del mondo, è sottointeso, ma non tanto sottointeso da non essere almeno segretamente operante, nella maturità del lavoro. Ai superficiali che obbiettano che l'invenzione nonfigurativa è vecchia di quart'anni, noi obbiettiamo che invece essa è vecchia di cinquantamila anni. Che è sempre una bella età. E una vertebra di balena, scoperta sul litorale o ritrovata nel flusso della immaginazione e del gesto che la realizza, è sempre più arte, cioè più tempo, più umanità, più energia, più intelligenza, più precisione, più purezza, che non un paesaggio di Courbet o un noioso gruppo di Rodin, per non dire altro.

as well as in their alternative historical behavior. The recovery of this initial act, and all of its consequences, this decisive and defining retrieval of the pure act that led prehistoric man to a concrete communication with the world, or rather to taking possession of the world, is implied, but not so implied that it is not operating secretly, by the maturity of the work. To those superficial people who object by saying non-figurative invention is forty years old, we object that it is instead fifty thousand years old. It is a rather handsome age. And a whale vertebra, discovered on the shore or found in the flux of the imagination, or the act that creates it, is always more art, that is more time, more humanity, more energy, more intelligence, more precision, more purity, than a landscape by Courbet or a group of Rodin's, just to name a few.

1. Originally published in *Arti Visive,* № 1 (1954).

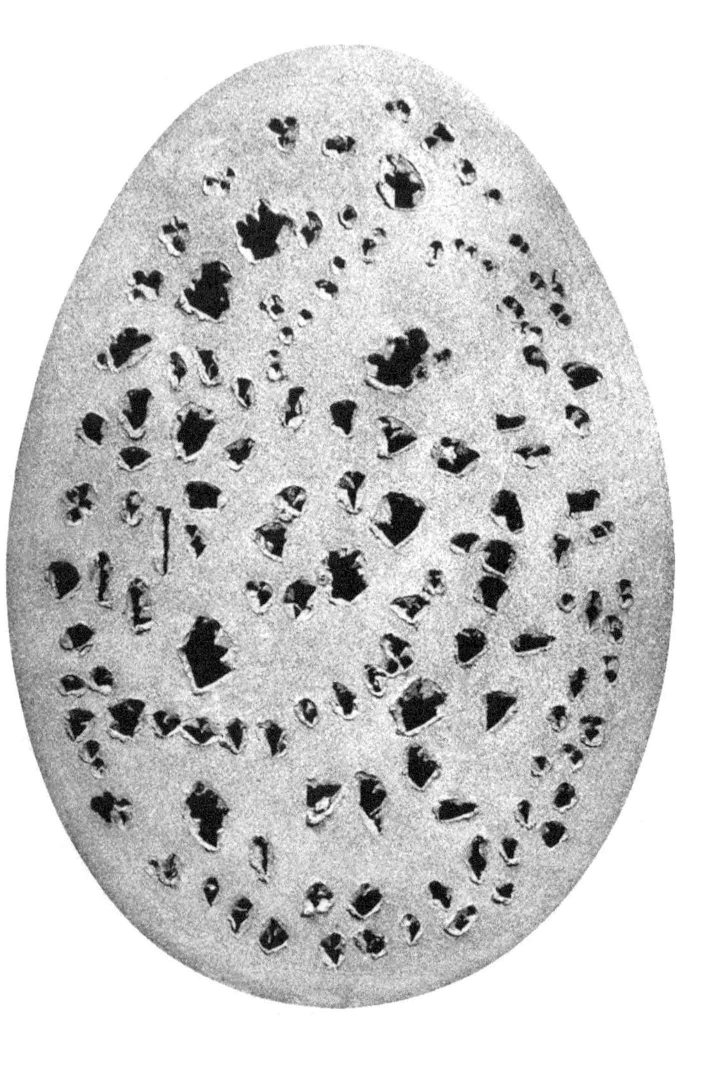

Lucio Fontana

emitte spiritum tuum
& foramina creabuntur

. . . .

mitte digitum tuum
in foraminibus

LA GNOSE ÉVULGWÉE DU TROU

(pour la bien bonne coagulation cinétique des trous troués dans le

TROU

boutrou foutrou toutrou troutrou d'où guette fau-trou troufau trouflou troufolle)

alvéole con p act!
alguev éole cinétique?

tu cris tu foutes, re-, tu vrilles, tu noues les trous en courbes en chaînes trou après trou urgent en droit en dextruation en orientaction en parcours en chymi-smères obligées en corps morts en lèvres hibrerniées en cataclyses en hypolyses en barbises en instants d'instants en millénaires en trou temps

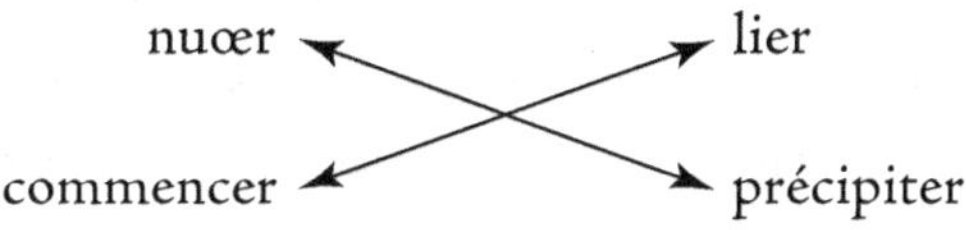

(oui, j'ai oui centaines de minutes immenses dans cet-te installation plissée constellée pissée)
entretemps le temps qui tourne autour d'un trou, qui trourne autour d'un tout, ou le temps qui tourne au trou? par le trou

et qu'est-ce que c'est là la connaissance-naissancenée sans sinus que de faire ou faire faire un trou sans un trou sans fini, sans finir sans? à l'in? fini? (du temps de l'entre-*n*-sexes) le trou secoué et le trou caché qui se hiérarchisent en alterance, étendre-étiendre-entendre, phalange de trous, y descendre pour les changer e, en Processus de Monades, une Aventure dénutritionelle, (on y pourrait bien téter-tâter, de ses lèvres des ses yeux: est-ce qu'ils mènent à une Source? une bordée?
à una Sourche, à une Proie? à une Plessure irrélate?) parce que le Trou est d'emblée coupé, si l'on va essayer de souffler d'essuyer dans le Trou, d'essoufler la substance du Trou, ou, où, &
alors le soustrait, -at, bien, le sous-trou, le soustrué, le trou dans le miroir, le trou dans le paradigme hypergéomantisé, le trou au dedans du trou, au trèfond, et c'est là tout, bien tout, bientôt très tout, des trous (trou pourrait être: "tu es," ou bien "tuer") chez trou, des trous observés, des trous occultes, des trous pénétrants, des trous filtrés, des trous intercompénétrés pour des trous associés, en trou, le trouviol, le trouvol, le trouvaille, le trouve est, le trouver, letr où, ou bien, oùniversal, où ni vers sel, trous aillent, des trous dormis des trous prétermis, ou mis dans le trop dan le, l'œil, trœil, où trou aussitôt rentré, vaincul, également trou écrasé, massacré, tout, trou-krasis, trou crêtes

mais un

un

1

un

seul
un
sœil
un
tout
un
trou

trou tué pour tuer, bien, (tuer la mort), là un trou mort, comme si ça c'était drou (... où?), depuis où, la vie restée demeurée, là, là autour, d'où, autour du trou, le le, le trou comme trou de victoire (vie noire, mors ubi est victoria tua?) (trou I, trou-you)

et parce qu'il a bien troué, égaré dans le cré plus cul, du trou le trou sort, é(n)tendu, étant du d'être où le trou se troue, c'était ça serait très simple que l'être-trou trou outre trou, les uns comme des autres ou comme les autre trous, tous trous, et de nous tirer de là, par là, par où, et alors

ayant étée achevée une ruche, là, enfin, le vide serait-ce un trou à réinventer, une sommatoire-truche-ruche de trous, ou le

TROUZÉRO

à computer à compter à conter, trou de véhémence et trou de paix, trou de trop de vie ou de trop de trop ou de trop de mort, mais en chaque trou le grand cas du trou, voilà, si ça c'est bien de la revanche conclamée pour y tout app(r)endre et tout y tra(n)cher, viol derrière, viol en avant, tout trou qui pousse et tombe trou en trombe trou en trombe trou, ça c'est, trou au buse, trou obus, trou au baise, là, les trous l'un en face de l'autre c'est bien trou et donc cou paix, couper émincer diviser le trou en troutrou, ou en trou tout, un, tout simple, jusqu'au niveau de l'unité disparaissant son les coup-trous de l'unité, touche jusqu'au touche d'un touche un, 1

jusqu'au trou l'artrouche l'articre s'éteient au fond du tout petit trou entonnoir, trou hospital, trou véhédémentiel, trou véhi cul, il faudrait que toute l'humanité demeurait sauvée dans les trous, un trou sur chaque trou, lavie au trou! à travers du trou, le trou volitif et le trou volontaire, trou volatile trou brut, à se trouer soi-même sur peau sur trou sur crâne sur couille sur troudre, sur lèvres par example du tatrouage technique, la troucarie ou la trougamie, la trougénie ou la troumatique, ou trouthérie, le trou sur gênoù, tu peux bien y aller au fond de toute ta force, là, le trou t'attend, marche donc et frappe, et réveille-moi de tout trou de sommeil conjugé (congigné)

conjugué sur espace-crépi: (je crois que cette crépissure où le trou s'enfonce, soit le drapeau inépuisable de notre impuissance fulgurée frappée poignardée): hissez le drapeau-fontaine, blanc rouge vert noir, le tableau enduit! tabula vexatoria, tabula castrationis, vexillum castrationis je vais le nommer: (halètement explicite)

sur l'espace progressivement dézérofié se noyent un troutérus de difficultés psychométriques, éoïdées en tortures bavardes, le troutérus du grand préexil, et c'est là ce qu'il fait, ce qu'il faut fêtrer (fœter fouetter fêter fouttre), qu'il faut écreuser (trou touché trouchés pas des trous, des petits slogans "groupe," en corymbes sans sources, les sources conglobées dans le nul originaire, les sources toujours hésitées), ça croche les trous jusqu'à en consumer la trouité (l'étruité, l'autruité, l'autrouité) fluide, jusqu'au bout du, le trouarbres (pyramide humaine renversée, renc une renversion), le trou qui va mûrir sur les dos de l'*aïón*, lisez-là, troyons, la grande truie: le troutroué et les trous détrouits et la trouité cachée, imminente, très chaste, chahaha (trous!)! le trou très troué dans l'extensibilité odostatique, de la pudrespace (poudrespèce) délicate s'échappant à la cohésion, l'extensibilité sécrétionnaire, pénitentielle (le trourêvage d'autrui, le trouravage de soi en soi-même) et bien ça sera, dans le cercle, l'armée des cieux (les kosmos des cyeux, trônes et dominations, crocs et aiguillons, pustules divines croûtes démiurges), errant et nombrée (cieux mâchés de toiles) en troubillon pyrrhique, ïambe io io io, le trouïo, io, splendeur assassine, nappes et tympans in cymbalis mutis, brusquement dévisionnée, claque en coulée zodiac, bondissant, aliments maintenant, bâteau cosmique en route expétitive brandillant, vers une série très simple des yeux trouant du

COMMENCEMENT

(aventure (avant lumière) (sur les lèvres du poète) plurivalve ambiguë, anneau sans soudure, subtil ovule trempé de, enumérable, hors d'équilivre, famille éveillée du bruit, en pousse scrutable de pâleur sur la zone déserte, flèche spirituisée du Moment; j'irai y me plonger, moi qui j'ai prêché jadis le droit du trou de faire trou, le droit de faire trou, partout pythagorisme très contrit, très au jeu, drôlerie pythienne, avec coaction conviction contorsion antipirinisme: jadis, en effet, à l'aide des instruments de mon ami sculpteur, Amerigo Tot, j'ai percé les pierres petites, et, tout seul, j'ai trépané des tomates (oh, les armées des cieux, les troupes laides, oui, les troubles haies, les trou-plaies, plaies vides!) (ugelli, microbonds, zones minimales de diffusion de l'homogène inopiné) (étrangement suspendues) (les zones) (légères et luisant)

pour le TROÙ scindé de sa source et, au contarire, integré à sa gnose, le trou dénudé qui te ti tu be, to be, le trou inintroulligible et introuné de l'EXCÈS, troufugue troufuite, tout une chevelure de trous Flous, trône de trous nus (donk) un trou deux trous trois trous (le trou: bon, un œil un ciel une âme une fente une idée un sphynxtère qui aurient bien pu avorter, trouavorton, et qui pourraient se traire, se taire tous les instants en face de leur trou), c.à.d.: le trou de la Restitution létargique,

le Trou dénié au défi par son trou et par le trout: et tout ce qui fait partie du trou, et le trou de la Pudeur Asphyxiante; en total, le trou mort qui est le porteur escatologisé des trous, et ses Ailes Jalouses (parce que c'est justement là, entre trou et trou autre, que le nonspace célèbre ses noces immenses, ontojenétiques, onophrènes, comme renverser, un trou c'est renverser un utérus, renverser dedansdehors une costellation, renverser un amour, renverser un houragan, un épisode sacrement syndacal du Coïtus Général, le présouflle de la Halte, le calix des ressacs des trous, le trou est trou est tout est trou, en principe était le trou, et oublierais-je moi toute une semaine-semence de siècle qui fut remplie de trous véritabiles sensibiles générables, chaque trou une année ou un millénnaire, hou! queffuos à être! comme s'ils eussent étés le christ d'un trou, un christrou, c.à. d. un fétiche pelingénète construit par des virus-miroirs rénitents, reniflents, et alors trouer le fétiche Espace, comme piocher dans l'eau échoustique (euristique): les trous mourrissent l'éclat et ses chances, l'archipel (la sombre-nature, à l'intérieur ultime du vide, suspend toute fluidité, toute katalyse, tout contact avec l'acceptation totale, et le peintre dès alors paraît plus qu'un signataire futile) (quand même, en particulier, sous certaines propositions de vue (de vie) il faut bien reconnaître que les positions (dépositions, dispositions) soutenues par le peintre se présentent très pauvres d'entrain et fort dépourvues d'alimentation montante: sa phraséologie, qui ne connaît que l'algèbre euclidéenne (des orties spaciales), bouge sans vibrations et capture aobliquement, avec une spontanéité heureusement à peu près idiote (ça veut dire que Fontana est et en même temps n'est pas démoniaque, vêtu de mana; selon les attitudes et les moments des trous; parce que j'ai inventé le type émergeantiel du *pyschodaimon,* trouer-performance, eh bien, ces psuedo-peintres qui trouent et qui coupent, on peut bien les nommer *pyschodaimones*) (parfaitement provisoires, joués par outrance hermet-)

alors on pourra taper des doigts vraiment autant liquides à ses trous, tu vois, tout debout immoble, sur la même journée par oû se dénouera l'égarement long (perpetuellement retrourné), la journée sans nos aisselles, la journée avec nous, toujours sur la même place, sur la même souche, sucée par quelque trou et remonter, en menant la dance, en trésaillant, jusqu'aux galaxies oisives de l'idée du trou: & en effet,

comment serait-ce partagé de cours du monde?
en trous-haleines
en trous-athelètes
en préfixes-couloir
en puits- αἰών plus faiblement que dans la lumière enclytique, plus ardemment que dans le corps obscène d'un flûte suave, que dans le gorge nymphale nymphe (à éteindre le cou rant d être finie, à l'étreindre d'êt re qu'il soit *éranos* empreint sur nuages, si les fleurs s'allongent et s'élargissent, et s'étendent à la recherche du lieu par où sortir puissamment, avec ardeur orndeulation, des bornes bornes lénitives, bornes-flèches, bornes brognes, chances et niveaux miraculants des élevages anciens, néolithiques (nouveau à perdre les rumeurs les exhalations rameurs re âmeurs noires in vacuum, encore entrer trou le veines des balances qui vont se déchirer, sous la pousse du triomphe de l'inéquation, et, oh là, sa main qui sort immaginée salsifiée enduite, soulevée du centre au perimètres conçus creux, con sucreux, écrits, soufflés sifflements, les branches autres effacées, lancée au dehors béant, au nouveau béant, au, donc, au, eau, au trouveau béant obligé, cru, accent, occident, tuyau, nuque, boyau, trabéation, entrecroisée minimale d'é-

nergies irrépéribles, et poutre foulée, là, foyer inconnu du caché, trou tout nu, là, j'en devine le nombre saccadé rompu lu le sang disparu, le désang haut seulement, l'ennui qui rentre aux hauts, et roule et s'écoule s'éggrrhoule elle même en pointe de pénis interférant, en lames vites, en fonds, le geste y s'étouffe et retourne à l'autre du delà d'autre soi-même, qui touche et qui hôche et tranche le souffle et perce le siffle, pourtant, en lumière longue jusqu'au, le fond des utérus volumes changés en, le doigt pénétrant, en y remontant, entrechengés

enchevêtrés être et

ce passage mu de tout ce qui va te touer turer le tout trou fou toi tué tu en trou

parce que çacela le trou que tu trou ve, où ve, le trou distance, une vibration stupide entre l'ordonée cohordonnée biorragique, stupide glu gluant &
une axisse phrenorragique

et en première ligne (tourne le trou
le trou du trou et tu trouvera
l'ultime le dernier le trou l'autroui
the thru to 300 yds, from here, de l'autre trou
le troujour ingénéré mais que où i
aurais-je fait le trou dans le speculum absent, le miroir opaque amer diagonal la trourriture, nous riture, nourriture le trou manger le trou dont le cul est cul de vipère (à changer le rideau! change donc, si ça va) (et tous les trous récents et passés, à restituer!) (tout trop jeune toutefois j'en suis crevé) (je pouvais en cracher au loin du loin un trou de trou) un trou d'eau, trou dans l'eau, dans l'o, dans le sang, sangtrou, et pourtant le trouçanle troulà où,

et, par example,
le trou-mot
en tant que mot nul
au point de fibre

j'ai eu déjà, lorsque j'étais tout petit, et je touchais de mes doigts les abîmes auditifs, envie de capturer les trous pour les déposer dans le trou du trou, ou dans le niche de la du tout, jusque dans les trou de dieu et de la madonne (inventés! bon, ils se sont inventés! par eux-mêmes les trous) (et justement, mesure après mesure, les doigts perforant tremblent de trou en trou sur la chair du trou (pour arracher doigtement l'araignée de son trou, son regard infiltré comme un rayon épée jusqu'à l'entrée du trou) (là où l'on sort) (en autre et en anxiéte)

et bien donc, trou à trou quand j'ai trou à coup de trou où, trou qui m'étrou, aurais-je trou sec, trou émerclé mètre par des tr(ou)aces de courâge montre où, toutre où et mon ton, toùn tout trou, par où l'accès est passé vers l'obscur découpé (and complexities of Survival, à manger les trous) (les ulcères foutue!)

l'ex-tension des mots dels des mots dules des mains sions des frac tions des spermutations apparait quelque pue close et branlée en mesure, drainée avec une furie evidemment, par trop, psychogymnique quelque peu débouchant, trébouchant, enchantée mais inerte d'inertie anoressique: comme si ça c'était une manœuvre anchylosée, non transitive, sur des intervalles engourdis, rigides entravés embarassés riades en trismes orbitales bien peu sûres, un processus lenticulaire pas trop frélatant, glandules et se-

mences de la perforation myriade, plus d'odoriféra-tion que de texture oùblieuse, plus d'oùrdissage-déchirure que de fertilité originaire, que d'entraîne-ment, plus de trames que de toxines, plus de signes que de blessures, sur le trou au long, toujours unila-bié: peut-être est-il que le champ (campus qu'on pour-rait susciter, en conglobant dans un système ou dans plusieurs systèmes le Trouage entier que constitue l'œuvre de Fontana), obtiendrait une machine trou-ant d'une envergure permutationelle à la puissance haute, en tout cas variée et instituant des principes actifs dans le sphère infinie de l'Isomorphie Géné-rale ou des Emotions Majeures ou de l'Attente La-tente. En quelque sens, toutefois, demeure légrement mémorable la passion, et l'intuition peut-être, de la manœuvre à exerciter sur le Trou Créatif. Et les Ensembles des Trous Créatifs reçoivent dans leur sein la douleurs des Nombres, et ils la remouent, aussi bien que toute la richesse et l'anxiété du jeu de la complainte raisonnée des Algèbres;
bien, l'usage récipient! faire zéro-tactile, tactiliser zé-ro, fêter zérurgie, présencier zérousie, achever zéro-gamie! (mais, où se troù-ve-t-elle latra ce du Scan-dale?)
ayant étée étrourdie, par réductions accessives, la dureté de la Primauté du Frontal Absolu, l'emploi étymologique du trou [(embrassez-les donc ces trous, baisez-les, en grand, le baiser même, visiteurs!) (le trou demeure pratiquement libre, et, au contraire, l'homme peintre, hommpreinte, tante d'instituer ou deviner une Nécessité représentative ou autrement)] dans les renseignes des tableaux de Fontana s'obsu-

jette à des règles minimales et dénominatrices, qui détruisent presque entièrement les jeux de causalité dont s'anime et se nourrit chaque position et s'exalte l'Ensemble irroré des positions (Positrions) à repère (repaires; les jeux qui troublent les Gradations de la Montée in prepetuum, qui irritent la différence-différée du trou ultime, le Troutype factorial; qui écrasent l'Obstance de la Positrion Irrélate; qui rongent l'Etat absolu de l'Irrisoire). En effet, la procèdure qui rend un ordre prévenu et inamovible à un certain convoi de trous désaltère et remoue l'ambigüité mineure et la Série originelle créative, ouverte aux énumérations-positions les plus dénouées dans tous les cas et dans tous les ordres (orguedres), c'est à dire dans l'ordre (orguedre) multiplié au cisfini de la Dérivé inoppugnable, là où discussion répresentation nombrification imagination s'éteingnent:

à faire glisser intact, & inachevé, le sophisme prégnant de l'

ORDRE-DESORDRE

de l'univers, micro- et macroséisme

'Idée spaciale' dit Fontana. Qu'est-ce que ça peut signifier? Je crois que ça veut dire rien, justement; rien, et, en tout cas, son œuvre ne veut dire que rien; bien; son œuvre, seulement, relate. Plus probable que cette œuvre tend à mettre en évidence en remou in tension ou bien créer et absorber un état de présence: produisant des algies similaires aux algies de la confusion évolutive éternelle aveugle et de la perplexité parfaite, inavouable. Comme il y avait de ceux qui prenait l'élan et trouait une parois, de son propre crâne ou de son propre prépuce; ou contre soi même miroir (speculum), pour y chasser le trou au delà de son petit corps (corpusculum), le rechasser à sa coïncidence stérile. Enfin, nous ne pourrons jamais calculer combien soit près de la déperpétuation et de l'exclatement du Vide, souzerain, la fiction du Trouer de tableaux, ou même le coup du Meurtrier, ou le coup du Prêtre sur la bête sacrifiable, ou le trou dans le cœur de l'arbre, de la terre, du ciel, ou dans la lunule du pain transhistorié, sur les coins de lèvres qui se mâchent : combien donce prolonger l'aleph, aléphiser à coups de bec, à coups d'orteil, à coups de croc les morceaux innombrable du Multiple Nul et l'innombrable Principe, l'Ambience inébranlable, inaltérée, l'impossible Amalgame Unité et sa divisibilité en sous-multiples du Nul, et fermer tout Passage, troupassage.

[1961]

p. s. Une niche niche
dans une niche
c'est une voile née
à chymère obligée :

quelle mère, quelle mer ?
le nul dans le nul
c'est une araignée
de la vague polaire :

le cul dans le cul
le trou dans le trul
qu'est-ce que c'est ?
qu'est-ce que je sais ?

ETNA in Eruzione
Etna in Eruption
L'Etna in éruption
Der Etna speit

3 Juin 63

Cher Emilio Villa
merci et ave pour
votre Villadrome
qui nous a aidés
à gravir les hauteurs
de la poesie sicilienne
et affectueusement
Marcel Duchamp

Emilio Villa
c/o Gianfranco Baruchello
7 via Baglivi
Roma

Riproduzione vietata

A.G.C. - SUPER

N. 8778

Marcel Duchamp

In Memoriam

de son parabaptême (vive!)
sur l'Æthne éructant (vive!)
Parce qu'il m'a baptisé (vive!)
de son parabaptême (vive!)
sur l'Æthne éructant (vive!)
en évocant mon vrai nom (vive!)
en tant que VILLADROME,
cette Course, δρόμος, veut faire vivre
le nom MARCEL DUCHAMP
esprit de la Hauteur & du Silence,
du Sourire Absolu, héros de l'Adresse sans Fin
et de la Ruse implacable, maître des Prévivences,
charnière de l'Indifférence

àrome

[25 aout 1968]

Alphabetum cœleste

Le Schéma
Magnétisant
est à restituer
et fomenter
par
une resection itérée
en
matière croissante
corroborée
par
des éclairs incarnées

chaque jeu étant donné,
chaque je étant donné,
chaque dieu étant donné,
chaque lieu étant donné,
chaque yeux étant donné,
chaque eux étant donné,
chaque feu étant donné

dégagez tout ça tout tron
écrivez ça sur lignes
enroulez-les
mangez-les
Chiez-les
et tout ça ne sera sans réclamer la dynamique des chutes verbales

pour dérégler la prosodie du Ra Vga
on mange les Arbres
et si l'on manque de Sang
c'est l'Assassinat
pour que l'on Double
le martyre
du présupplice

Adieu Mon Chen!
que j'aille caresser le Cul de Ton Âme
dans l'Oeuf Rouge qui ment
sous les longs longs Cyeux,
chaque étant d'étant
chaque étant s'éteint

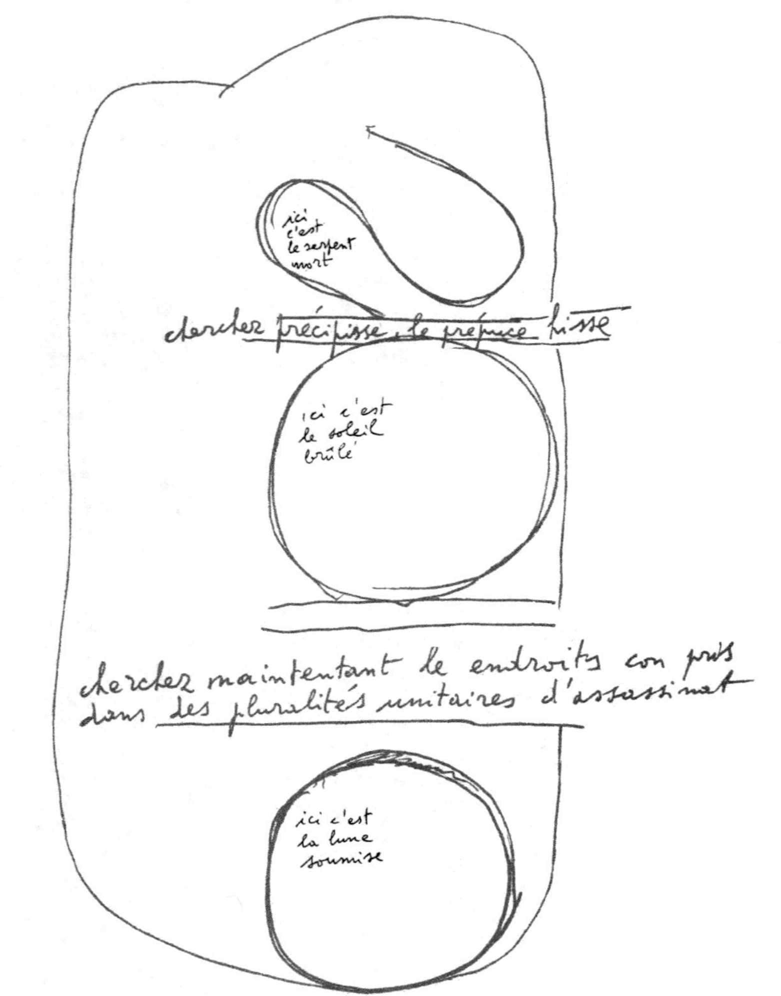
ici
c'est
le serpent
mort
chercher précipisse le prépuce lisse
ici c'est
le soleil
brûlé
chercher maintenant le endroits con pris
dans des pluralités unitaires d'assassinat
ici c'est
la lune
soumise

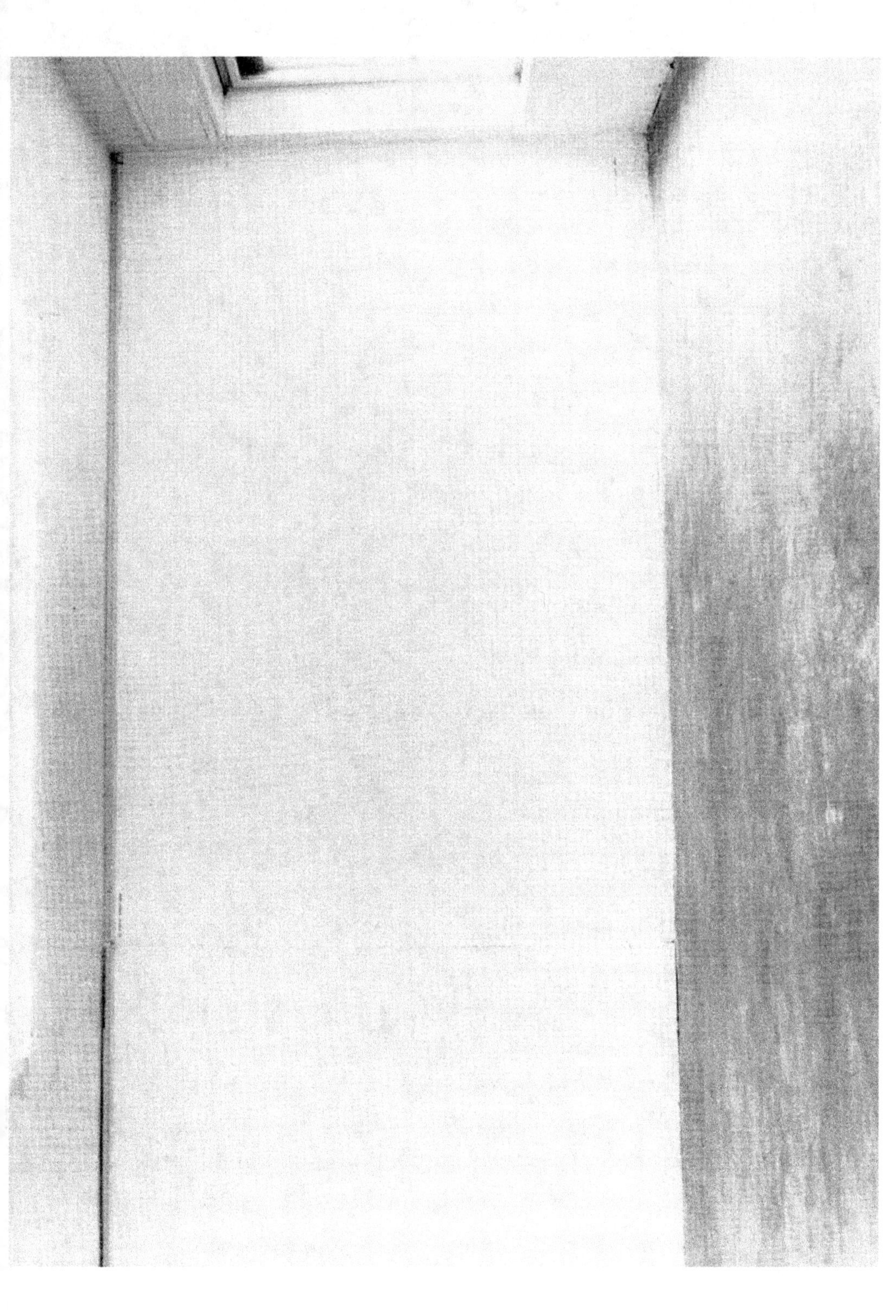

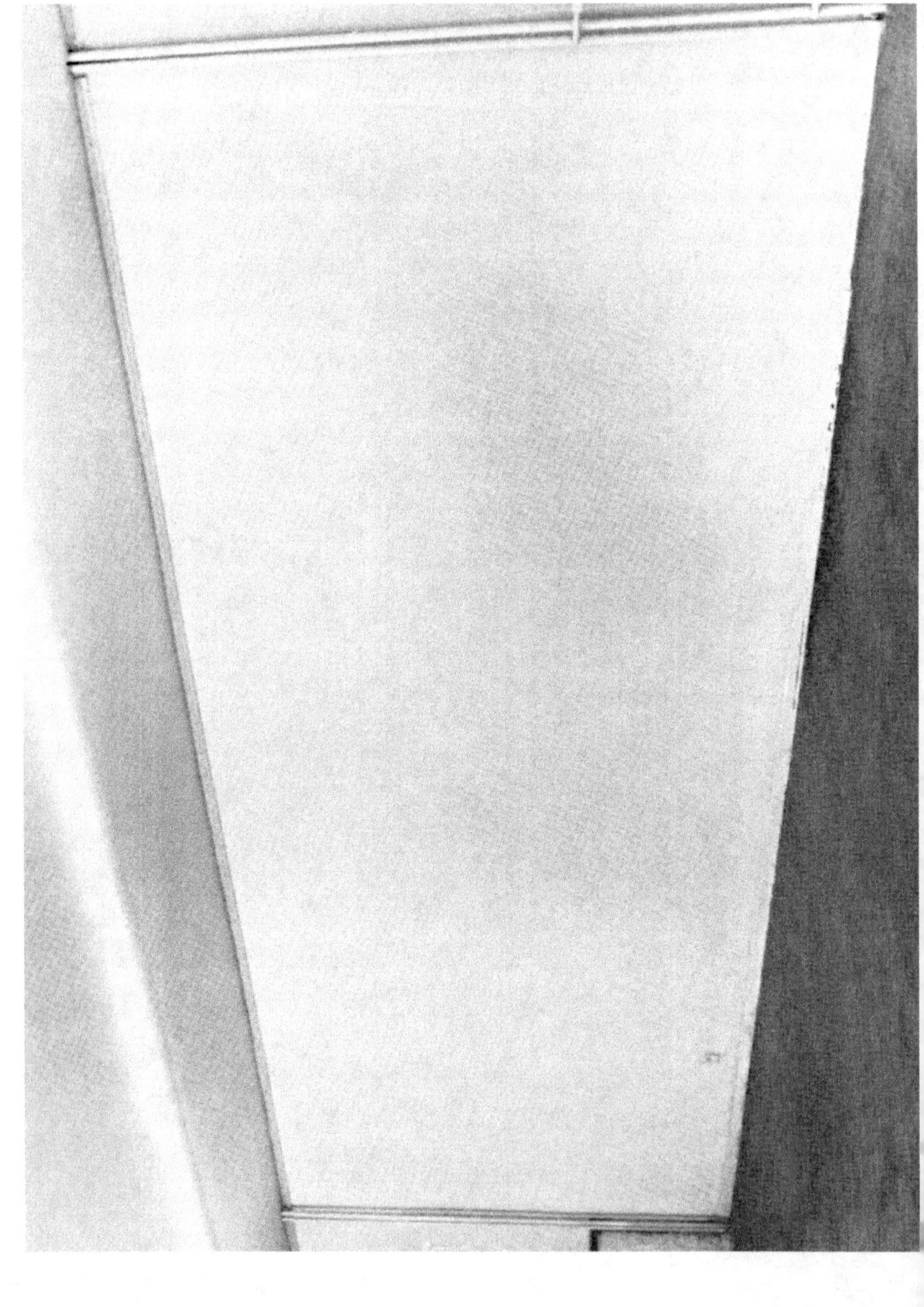

ICI C'EST LE SERPENT MORT

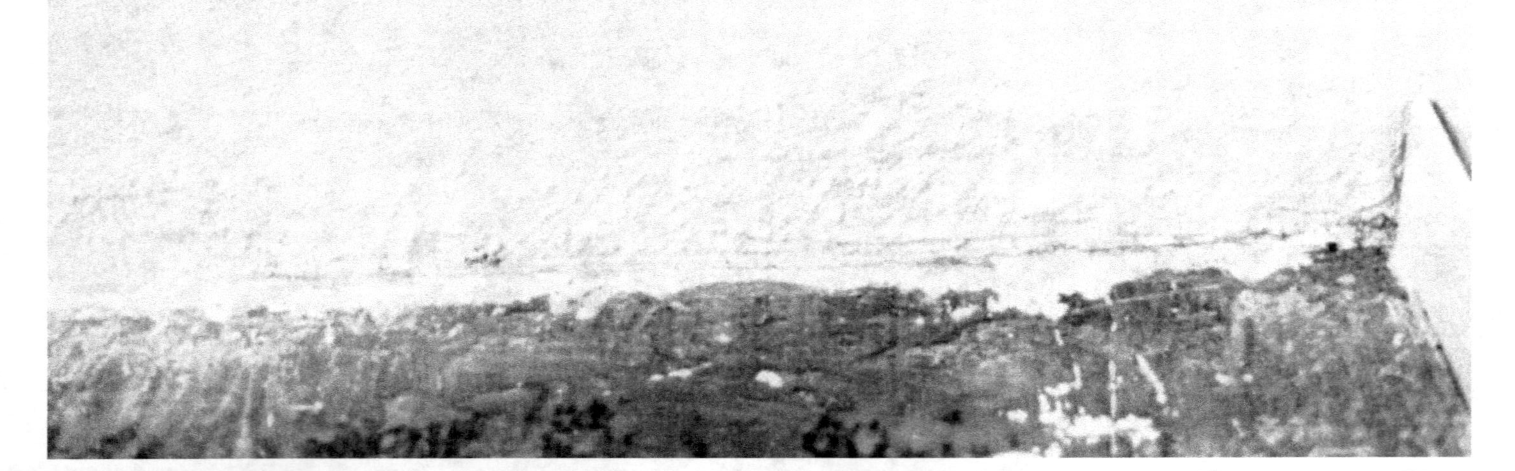
ICI C'EST LE SOLEIL BRÛLÉ

ICI C'EST LA LUNE SOUMISE

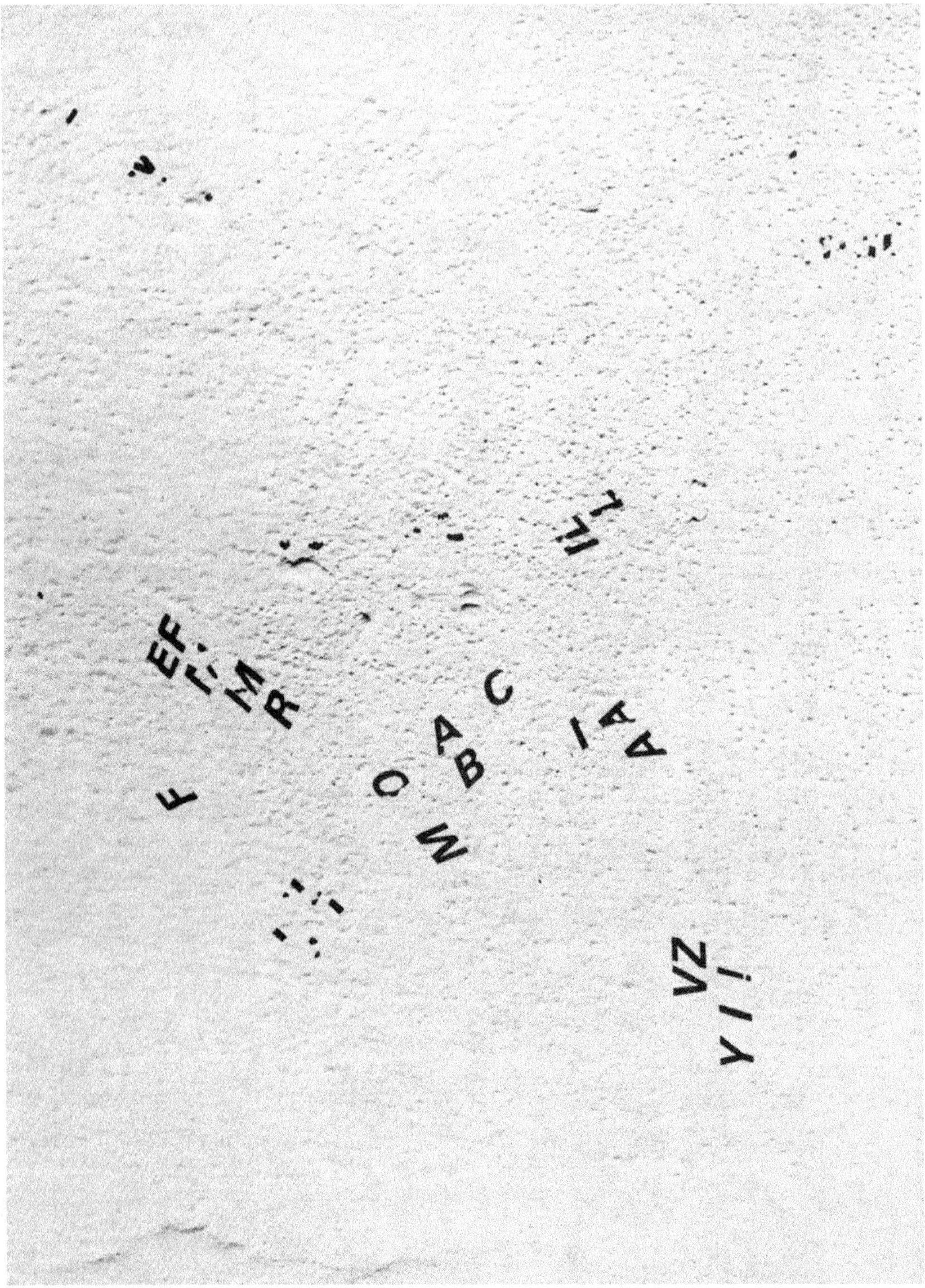

F EF

M

R

O

M A

B C

AA

IL

VZ

Y I !

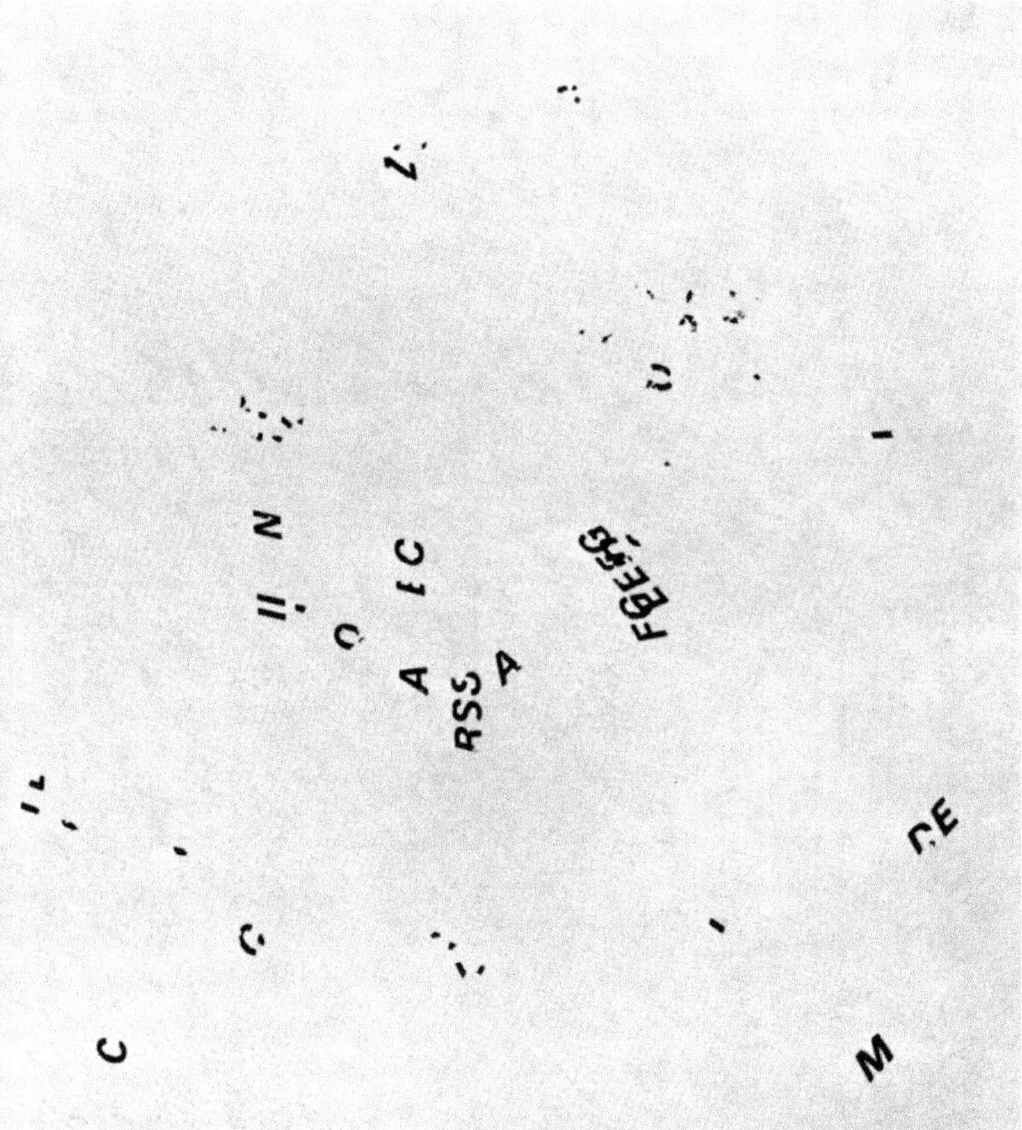

C

II N

A EC

RSS

A

FGEFG

M

CE

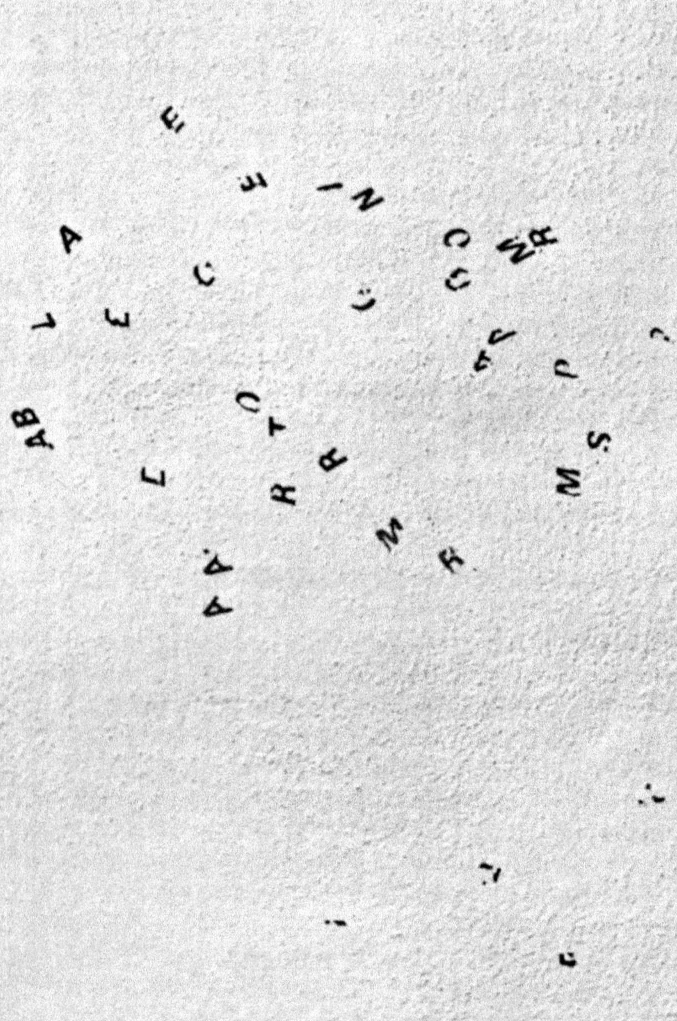

F

O

S

STUUU

V

UVA
IVZ
O
HBC
OOC
O
N
DLN
L

ST

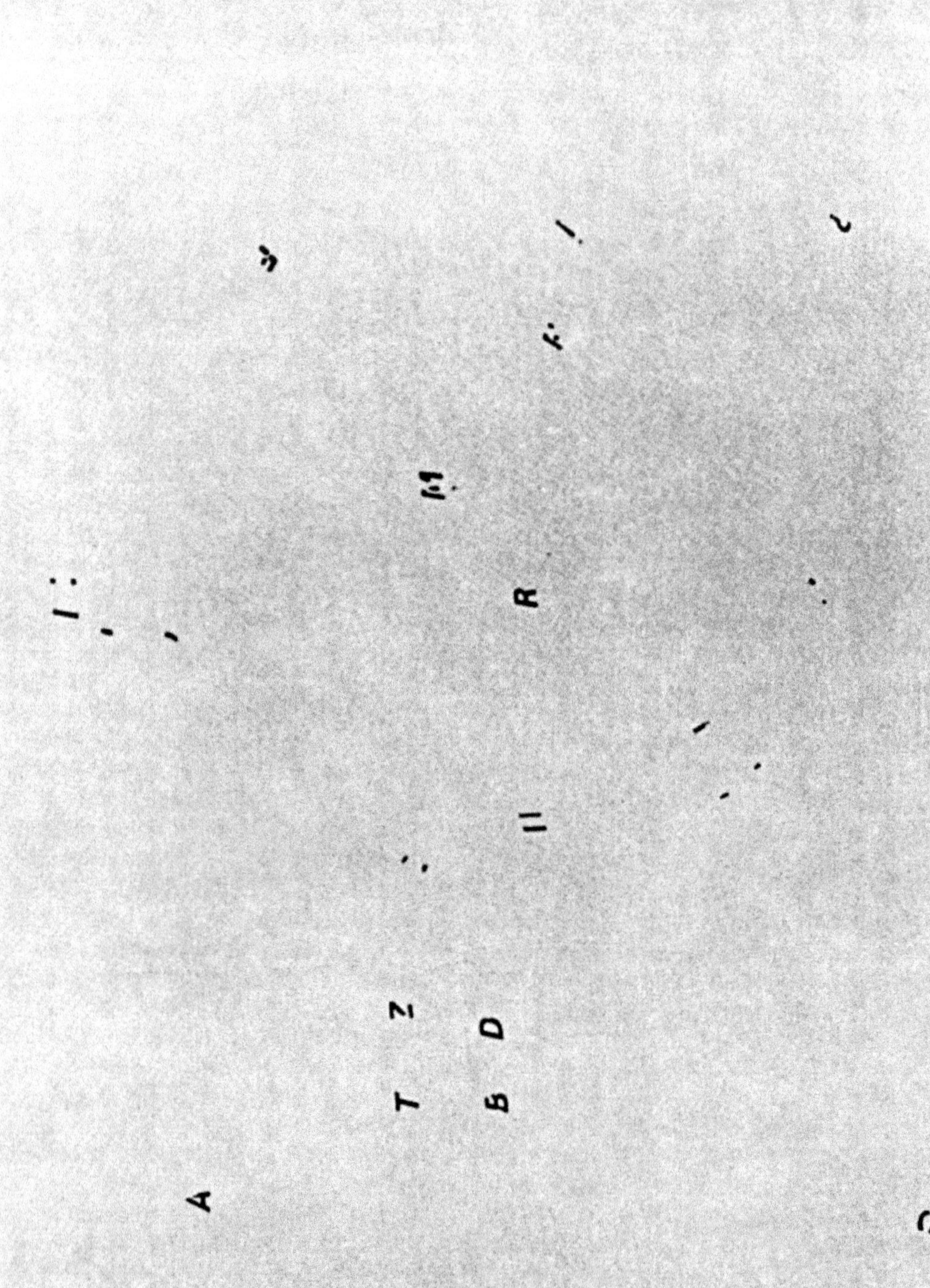

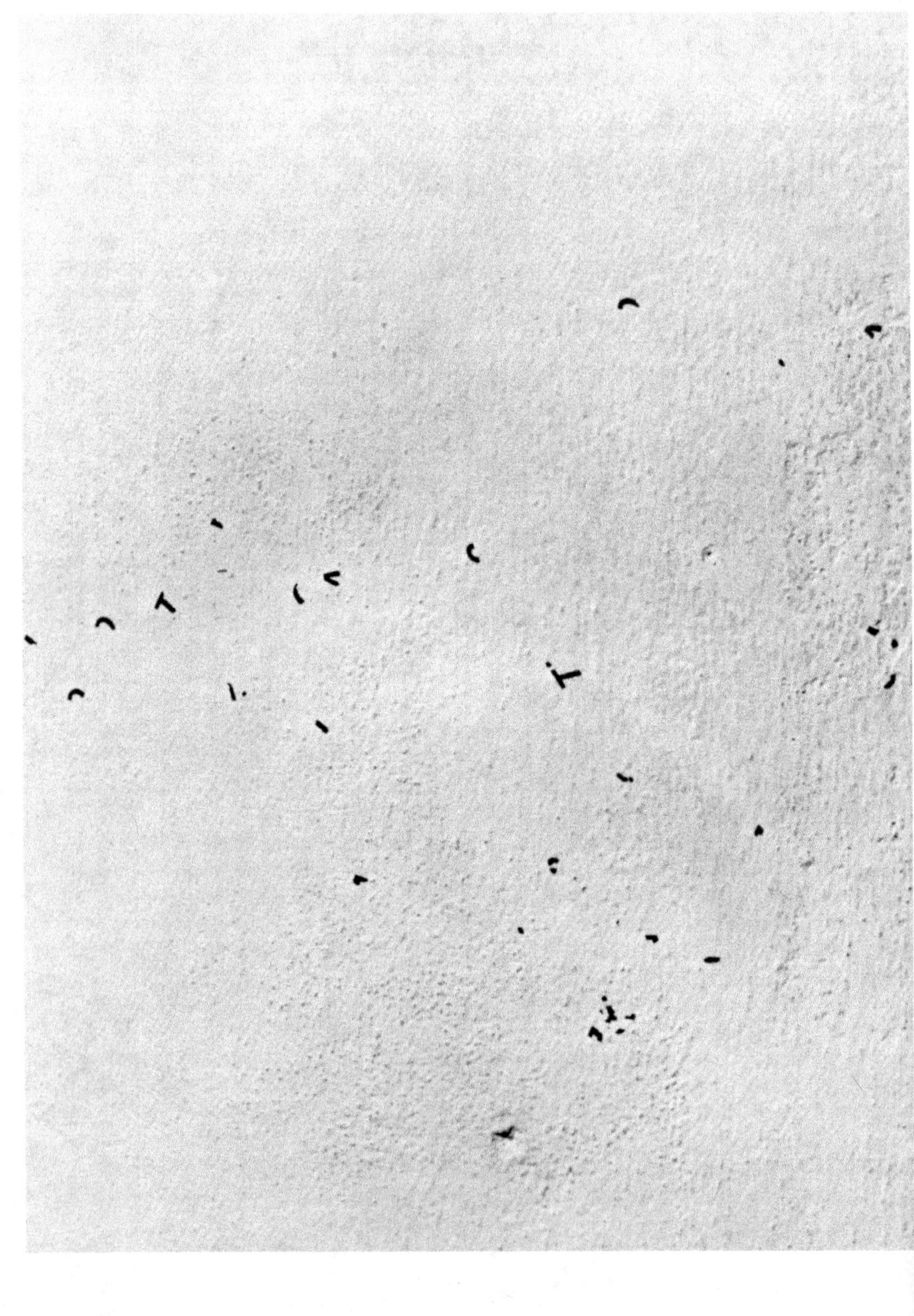

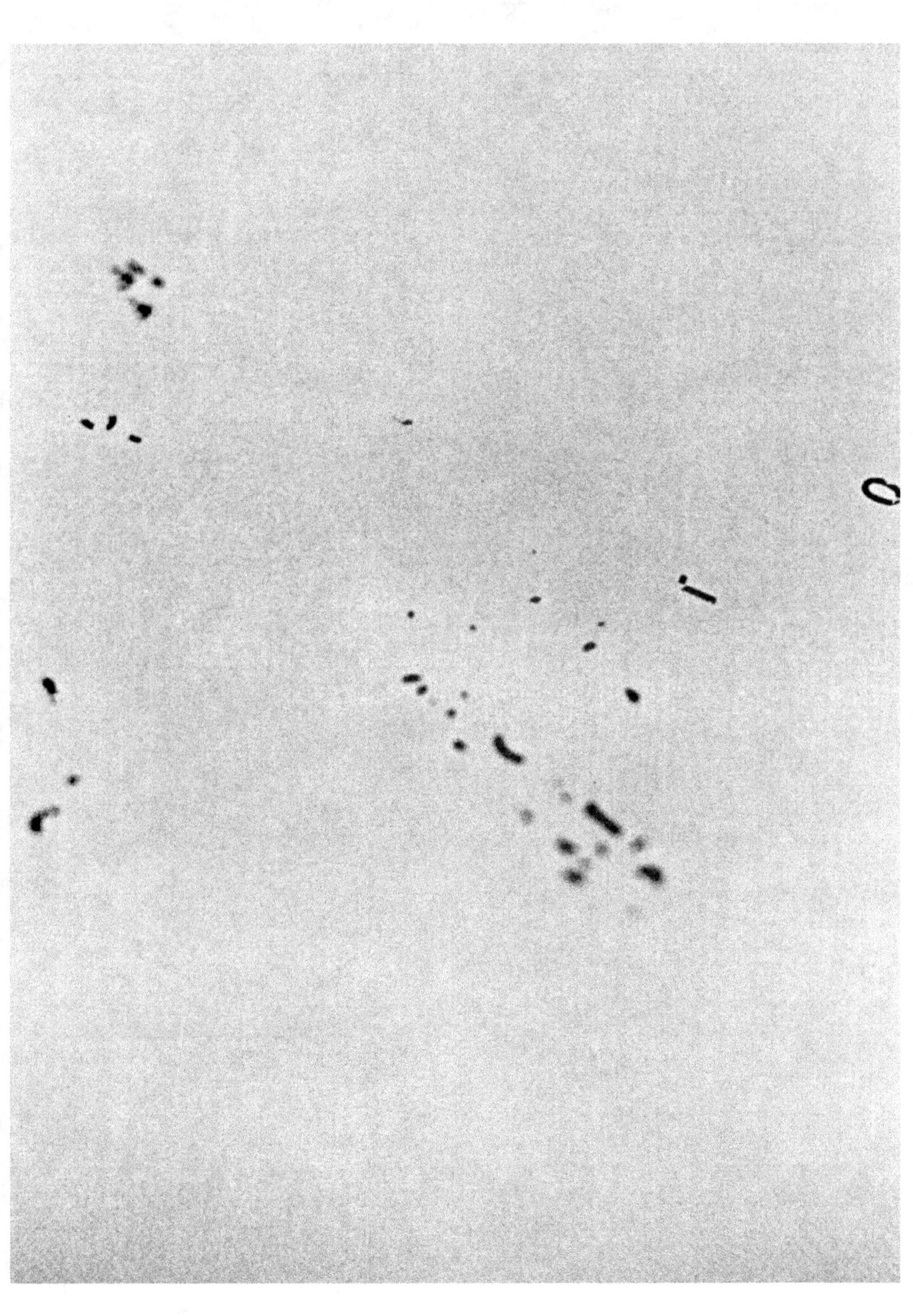

Biography

Poet, visual artist, translator, critic and biblicist, Emilio Villa was born in Affori (a ward of Milan) in 1914.

Throughout his life Villa displayed a fiercely independent spirit, both in everyday affairs and in artistic matters. He never joined any of the schools, artistic groups, or -isms that animated the Novecento, but rather preferred a proud isolation. His poems encompass modern and ancient languages, including Milanese, Italian, French, English, Latin, Greek, Sumerian, & Akkadian. Fundamental to his formation were the years he spent at a Seminary school in Seveso, outside Milan. He published *Adolescenza* (Adolescence, 1934), his first collection of verse, while attending the Istituto Biblico in Rome, where he specialized in Sumerian and Ancient Semitic Philology. His subsequent collection *Oramai* (By Now, 1947) deals with the trauma of the Second World War & the difficulties of post-conflict recovery. In this work, as well as in his third collection *E ma dopo* (Yeah but After, 1950), he employs poetics that clearly set him apart from the contemporary Hermetic and Neorealist schools.

Starting with *17 variazioni su temi proposti per una pura ideologia fonetica* (17 Variations on Themes Proposed for a Pure Phonetic Ideology, 1955), & *Heurarium* (1961), he began experimenting heavily with languages other than Italian, eventually developing a distinctively fluid mélange of tongues that became one of the many defining characteristics of his poetics. Or he composed entire pieces in foreign languages, as with the English of *Options, 17 eschatological madrigals captured by a sweetromatic cybernetogamic vampire* (1968). Later, he focused heavily on 'dead' languages, especially ancient Greek & Latin. See, for instance, *Verboracula* (1981), *le mûra di t;éb;é* (the wâlls of th;éb;és, 1981), *Geometria Reformata* (1990), and *12 Sibyllæ* (1995).

Villa also translated from these ancient languages, adopting the same unconventional attitude found in his poetry: in his rendering of Homer's *Odyssey* in Italian, Villa goes back through time to recuperate the sources that influenced the composition of this famous epic, sources that would have resonated with readers, or rather listeners, at the time of Homer, but that have been completely lost to the modern ear. Throughout his life, he also worked on an a-confessional translation of the Hebrew Bible. This unbiased and unapologetic rendition of the Pentateuch, however, encountered much resistance from specialists, as well as from the Curia, & was never published.

Villa was also involved in the visual arts, collaborating with influential figures such as Alberto Burri, Eliseo Mattiacci, Nuvolo, Claudio Parmiggiani, William Xerra, & many others. He wrote extensively on contemporary art (*Gli attributi dell'arte odierna* 1947–1967, The Attributes of Contemporary Art 1947–1967), as well as the visual testimonies left by prehistoric communities (*L'arte dell'uomo primordiale*, The Art of Primordial Man, 2005).

Villa created and printed a number of art books & ephemera, such as the groundbreaking, although short-lived, *EX*, to which different experimental Italian, as well as American, poets contributed.

From 1951 to 1952, Villa lived in Brazil, & worked at the Museum of Contemporary Art in São Paolo. There, he collaborated with the renowned concrete poets Augusto and Haroldo de Campos, as well as with the famous Italian painter Gastone Novelli. Aside from this brief detour, he rarely left his beloved Rome. He died in Rieti in 2003.

Villa's preoccupation with the origin of languages (verbal as well as non-verbal) is the common thread that runs through his diverse artistic and critical endeavors. He excavates these languages to reach the deepest and most ancient layer of expression, in an effort to re-live the act of "naming" the world for the first time.

The most relevant collection of his work is held at the Biblioteca Panizzi in Reggio Emilia, although a large amount of material still rests in the hands of private collectors. Furthermore, throughout his life, Villa disseminated and even actively destroyed his own work, making any attempt at a comprehensive bibliography difficult. Although highly respected by fellow poets, his poems have rarely been included in major anthologies throughout Italy and are almost entirely unknown to English readers.

Bibliography of Works by Emilio Villa*

* This bibliography is a work-in-progress & is by no means exhaustive, for the full extent of Villa's artistic corpus still remains a mystery. Aside from being scattered about Europe and even Brazil, much of his work lies in the archives of his fellow friends & artists, as well as in the hands of private collectors. After his death in 2003, Villa's archives were divided between the Biblioteca Panizzi in Reggio Emilia, which contains a number of unpublished poems in various languages as well as his a-confessional translation of the Hebrew Bible, and the Fondazione Baruchello in Rome, which houses his writings on art.

Writings

Adolescenza (Bologna: La Vigna Editrice, 1934).

"Prendi la rocca e il fuso e andiamo in California," *La luna nel corso* (Milano: Edizioni Corrente, 1941).

Oramai. Pezzi, composizioni, antifone. 1936–1945 (Roma: Istituto Grafico Tiberino, 1947).

"Tenzone" (1948), *Poesia satirica nell'Italia d'oggi,* ed. by C. Vivaldi (Parma: Guanda, 1964).

Omaggio ai sassi di Tot (1949).

E ma dopo, nove componimenti, with a lithograph by Mirko (Roma: Le Edizioni d'Argo, 1950).

Pour amuser Voltaire, pour épater Staline (Roma: 1950).

22 cause + 1 (Milano: Edizioni del Milione, 1953). Villa's poetry accompanies Roberto Sambonet's artwork.

Cinque invenzioni di Nuvolo e un poema di Emilio Villa (Roma: Edizione La Palma, 1954). Also known as *Sì, ma lentamente.*

17 variazioni su temi proposti per una pura ideologia fonetica (Roma: Origine, 1955). Includes visual works by Alberto Burri.

Un eden précox (Roma: l'esperienza moderna, 1957).

3 ideologie da piazza del popolo / senza l'imprimatur (Roma: 1958). Includes three watercolors by Nuvolo.

comizio 1953 (Roma: 1959).

Rho, dé roman (Roma: 1961).

Heurarium (Roma: Edizioni Ex, 1961).

Villadrome (Roma: Edizioni Ex, 1964).

Iside enfante Kongo (Roma: Edizioni Ex, 1964).

Ash overritual: Emilio Villa to Philippe Lamantia (Roma: 1964).

Various texts published in the magazine *EX* (1961–1965).

"The Bible in Art," *The Bible* (Verona: Arnoldo Mondadori, 1966).

Options. 17 eschatological madrigals captured by a sweetromatic cybernetogamic vampire, by villadrome (Macerata-Roma: Foglio editrice d'arte, 1968).

Traitée de pédèrasthie céleste (Napoli: Colonnese, 1969).

Attributi dell'arte odierna: 1947–1967 (Milano: Feltrinelli, 1970). Hereafter cited with the main title alone.

Le monde Frotté Foute (Milano: Scheiwiller, 1970). Includes three visual works by Claudio Parmiggiani.

Beam H (Macerata: La Nuovo Foglio, 1971).

Untitled poem, *Dello sbaglio programmato* by Enrico Bugli & Luciano Caruso (Napoli: Studio Boenzi Jacobelli, 1971).

Untitled text, *Nell'abitudine del giorno* by Luciano Caruso (Napoli: Studio Boenzi Jacobelli, 1973).

Phrenodiæ quinque de coitu mirabili (Pollenza-Macerata: La Nuovo Foglio, 1971). Also known as the "Mignottauro," this is a collaboration with the poet and visual artist Corrado Costa.

The Flippant Ball-Feel (Piacenza: ManaMarket, 1973). Written for the exhibition of three pinball machines by the visual artists William Xerra & Corrado Costa.

La râge oblique / La râge oublie — journal (Napoli: Visual Art Center, 1973).

9 lithographies de Giulio Turcato et 9 médiations courtes par Emilio Villa (Roma: Bulla, 1974).

L'homme qui descend quelque: roman metamytique (Roma: Magma, 1974). Includes six visual works by Claudio Parmiggiani.

E. Villa – F. T. Marinetti, Dannunziana (Napoli: Visual Art Center, 1974).

Exercitations de tire en io / cibles (Macerata: 1975). Contains illustrations by Nuvolo.

Hisse toi re / d'amour rire (romansexe) (Torino: Geiger, 1975).

La dernière mort sentimentale (Napoli: Visual Art Center, 1975).

"Prima serpentis et secunda serpentis," *Exempla (1966–1973)* by Luciano Caruso (Napoli: Visual Art Center, 1975).

"La Jeune Porque," *Antologica (1965–1975)* by Luciano Caruso (Napoli: Schettini, 1976).

6 videogrammi e un logogramma di Emilio Villa (Roma: 1976). Includes twenty-five "videograms" by Nuvolo.

le mûra di t; éb; é (Brescia: Galleria Multimedia, 1981).

"Verboracula," *Tau / Ma*, № 7 (Bologna: Editore A. Maramotti, 1981).

8 case delle antiche vicende (Roma: 1984). Includes eight incisions by Carlo Ambrosoli.

"Letanie," *Il Beato Creatore*, ed. by Mario Lunetta & Emilio Villa (Roma: Scienza dell'Arte, 1984).

Untitled poem, *Anatomie* by Luciano Caruso (Livorno: Belforte Editore, 1984).

"De Luciano Caruso / in charte musice," *Del poetar citando* by Stelio Maria Martini (Livorno: Belforte Editore, 1984).

Pro (desuper) (intra) C. P. (Grafis Edizioni, 1985). Includes a poem by Mario Diacono and a visual work by Claudio Parmiggiani.

"Epistola," *Contra-Cantica* by Ferdinando Grossetti (Napoli: Tor Editore, 1986).

"égypt taons d'isis," *A noir, E blanc, I rouge, U vert, O bleu*, № 20–22 (Roma: Editrice Inonia, 1987).

Untitled poem, *Il principio della parola*, ed. by E. Bonessio & R. Perrotta (L'Aquila-Roma: Japadre Ed., 1988).

Foresta ultra naturam, ed. by Paul Vangelisti (San Francisco–Los Angeles: Invisibile City, 1989). Includes texts by Emilio Villa, Giulia Niccolai, and Luciano Caruso.

Geometria Reformata, with a note by Mario Diacono and a watercolor by Claudio Parmiggiani (Albinea: Collezione Tauma, 1990).

Opere poetiche ~ I, ed. by Aldo Tagliaferri (Milano: Coliseum, 1990).

Unpublished texts from *Floraison*, *Baldus* (new series), № 1 (1994).

12 *Sibyllæ*, with an essay by Aldo Tagliaferri (Castelvetro Piacentino: Michele Lombardelli Editore, 1995).

CBille CBille, with an essay by Aldo Tagliaferri (Castelvetro Piacentino: Michele Lombardelli Editore, 1995).

Ridente sillaba (Belluno: Proposte d'Arte Colophon, 1995). Includes two graphic works by Agostino Bonalumi.

Letania per Carmelo Bene, with a note by Aldo Tagliaferri (Milano: Scheiwiller, 1996).

Trous (Belluno: Proposte d'Arte Colophon, 1996). Includes five works by Enrico Castellani and an essay by Aldo Tagliaferri.

Pittura dell'ultimo giorno, Scritti per Alberto Burri (Firenze: Le Lettere, 1996).

Conferenze, with a preface by Aldo Tagliaferri (Roma: Coliseum, 1997).

"Labyrintha. Quattro Sibyllæ di Emilio Villa," ed. by Cecilia Bello, *Avanguardia*, № 8 (Roma: 1998).

Geolatrica, with a note by Aldo Tagliaferri (Verona: In Ædibus Portæ Novæ, 1998).

"A César Zavattini (1978)," *Coevit*, № 2 (December 1998).

Zodiaco, ed. by Cecilia Bello Minciacchi (Roma: Empirìa, 2000).

"Mottetti. 7 mottetti di Emilio Villa, 7 acquaforti/acquatinte di Achille Perilli," *Librericciula*, № 16 (Roma: 2001).

"Poesia è," *Quaderni* (selections ed. by Toni Maraini), № 1 (Roma: Fondo Moravia, 2002).

Posthumous Writings

Scritti napoletani, with a note by Stelio Maria Martini & a letter by Mario Diacono (Napoli: Edizione Morra, 2003).

"Labirinto. 7 testi poetici, 7 acquaforti/acquatinte di Achille Perilli," *Librericciuola,* № 20 (Roma: 2004).

L'arte dell'uomo primordiale, ed. by Aldo Tagliaferri (Milano: Abscondita, 2005).

Mondo nero / Niger mundus, tr. & with a note by Vinceno Guarracino (Napoli: Edizione Morra, 2005).

Attributi dell'arte odierna 1947/1967, new edition ed. by Aldo Tagliaferri (Firenze: Le Lettere, 2008).

Experiments (Visual Material & Book-Objects)

Kiboshgénèse (Roma: 1956).

comizio, with Gianni De Bernardi (Roma: 1961).

Tabula absphixoria, with Gianni De Bernardi (Roma: 1962).

Cucile sec-s-Ile, with Gianni De Bernardi (Roma: 1963).

Le liber mutus (1965).

All'Upim è già Natale, with Luciano Caruso (Napoli: 1968).

Lettera e risposta, with Giorgio Cegna (Macerata: La Nuovo Foglio, 1971).

La me ga scrito, with Luciano Caruso (Napoli: 1971).

Green (Pollenza-Macerata: La Nuovo Foglio, 1971).

Untitled, *Continuazione A–Z* (Napoli: Edizione Continuum, 1973).

Untitled, *Nell'abitudine del giorno* (Napoli: Visual Art Center, 1973).

Untitled, *Il 900 Italia / poesia "ultraparola"* (Nola: Edizione Match, 1983).

Mosaic created for the "Prototipo mosaico" exhibit held in Ravenna (1986).

"Preface," U. Moretti, *69 Images par tous* (Roma: Edizioni del Giano, 1987).

3 Sibyllæ inscribed in zinc (1996).

Vertiges vestiges (1997).

Action-Experiments

Stones in the Tiber (1949). Villa threw a number of stones in the river after writing short texts on them.

"Corpi firmati" (São Vincente: 1950). Also included in *Attributi dell'arte odierna*.

Carpe Diem (Tor Lupara: 1965).

Idrologie (1964). Reproduced in *Le idrologie*, by Emilio Villa, Giorgio Cegna, & Silvio Craia (Macerata-Roma: Foglio OG, 1968).

Karnoval (Rieti: 1969). During a "Carnival of Artists," Villa distributed a *Disco muto*.

In foresta con Emilio Villa, Giorgio Cegna, Silvio Craia, dentro la poesia visiva (Ferrara: Palazzo dei Diamanti, 1970).

Alphabetum cœleste (Brescia: Galleria Multimedia, 1976). Reprinted in *Tau / Ma*, № 3 (Bologna: Editore A. Maramotti, 1977).

Translations by Emilio Villa[1]

"Enuma Elis," *Letteratura. Rivista di lettere e di arte contemporanea*, V. III (October 1939).

Antico teatro ebraico. Giobbe e Cantico dei Cantici (Milano: Edizione Il Poligono, 1947).

Odissea (Parma: Guanda, 1964). The translation was updated by Villa & reprinted by Feltrinelli in 1994 and then again by Derive Approdi in 2005.

Dies iræ, ed. by N. Taccone (L'Aquila: 1980).

Saffo (Roma: 2RC, 1982).

Proverbi e Cantico. Traduzioni dalla Bibbia, ed. by Cecilia Bello-Minciacchi (Napoli: Bibliopolis, 2004).

1. The translations of Plato's *Gorgias* (1941) & *Phædo* (1943) into Italian are by a different Emilio Villa.

Writings on Art[2]

Forma 1. Consagra, Dorazio, Guerrini, Maugeri, Perilli, Turcato (Galleria dell'Art Club, 1947).

"Nuova coordinata, nuove risorse," *I sette pittori sul Tevere* (Roma: 1954).

In *Angeli, Festa, Lo Savio, Schifano, Uncini* (Bologna: Galleria Il Cancello, 1960).

"Napoli Porta Pittura," *Bonito Oliva, Carlini, Dentale, Diodato, Gennaro, Patison, Piemontese, Rubino* (Roma: Studio d'Arte Delta, 1965)

In *A. Belli, M.V. Carelli, R. Gozzi, M. Mazzucco* (Roma: Galleria Mana, 1976)

In *Angeli, Baruchello, Marotta, Mauri, Schifano, Scialoja, Tacchi* (Roma: Centro Internazionale per la Ricerca sulle Comunicazioni).

"Cosmico e magico nella pittura indiana," *Pittura dell'India tantrica* (Roma: l'Attico-esse arte, 1980).

In *Claudio Bissattini, Luigi Campanelli, Giancarlo Limoni, Oscar Turco* (Roma: Rondanini Galleria d'Arte Contemporanea, 1982).

"Venezia *&* ses bourreaux les peintres," *Immagini di Venezia nell'Ottocento* (Roma: Galleria d'Arte Eleuteri, 1983).

2. In this and the following section, references that begin simply with "in" denote articles without titles that Villa had written for either volumes, journals, exhibition catalogs, or pamphlets.

In *The black egg (i no/politani)* (Marigliano: Centroarte "multiplo 2," 1983).

Introduction to *Il beato creatore collettivo e multimedia*, ed. by Mario Lunetta and Emilio Villa (Roma: Scienza dell'Arte, 1984).

In *Gruppo minimo. L'Acqua, Malmignati, Nicastro* (Casatenovo Brianza: La bottega grafica, 1984).

Writings on Artists

AFRO

"Le sang de la couleur de Afro," *Afro* (Roma: Galleria "Il Collezionista," 1983).

ALBERTI, VALERIA

Je me souviens des Fleurs Anciens (Roma: Galleria San Marco, 1957).

ALTAMURA, GIANCARLO

L'homo paradocsus secondo il pittore nuovo Altamura, ed. by Luigi Castellano (Napoli: Edizione Lan "Poesia," 1984).

AMBROSOLI, CARLO

Carlo Ambrosoli. Labriniti piramidali (Roma: L'Ariete, 1983).

Carlo Ambrosoli. Piramide Alchemica (Roma: Galleria guidArte, 1984).

8 case delle antiche vicende, 8 incisioni di Carlo Ambrosoli, 8 poesie di Emilio Villa (Roma: 1984).

ANGELOTTI, SANDRO

"Tracce tese alle sorgenti della luce consumabile," *Sandro An-*

goletti alle sorgenti della luce, ed. by E. Mercuri (Roma: Grafica Editoriale, 1984).

ARTOM, DIANA

In *Diana Artom* (Roma: Galleria del Cortile, 1969).

BARISANI, RENATO

"Renato Barisani," & "Biography," *Annuario del MAC e del Sindacato Nazionale Arte non figurativa* (May 1954).

BASADELLA, DINO

In *Dino Basadella. Dieci sculture in ferro* (Roma: Galleria la Tartaruga, 1960).

"Memoria per Dino Basadella," *Dino Basadella* (Bologna: Edizioni Bora, 1983). Also in *Le parole rampanti* (September 1990).

BENDINI, VASCO

"Vasco Bendino. Stabilità dell'instabile, memoria del futuro, memorie," *Vasco Bendino* (Roma: Galleria "L'Attico-Esse arte," 1980).

BERDINI, FRANCO

In *Franco Berdini. Astrolografie* (Roma: Galleria Editalia, 1982).

BERTACCI, MARIA GRAZIA

In *Universe stanze* (Comune di Copparo, 1985).

BLOC, ANDRE

"Florence. André Bloc," *Aujourd'hui, Art & Architecture* (January 1963).

BOVA, RAFFAELE

Bova e Mafonso. Sirène et Jobard (Confin Arte, 1983).

BRINDISI, REMO

"Una nozione antropologica nella pittura di Remo Brindisi," *Remo Brindisi. 10 serigrafie* (Macerata-Roma: Foglio Editrice, 1969). Reprinted in *Panorama della Arti* (June 1973).

BUGLI, ENRICO

Mottetti funebri per l'Autofunus di Enrico Bugli (Dead fiction) (Napoli: Visual Art Center, 1974).

BULGARELLI, LUCIO

In *Lucio Bulgarelli* (Certosa di Valmanera: 1976).

BURRI, ALBERTO

"Burri," *Arti Visive. Rivista della Fondazione Origine* (May 1953).

In *Burri* (Roma: Fondazione Origine, 1953).

"Emilio Vedova. Alberto Burri," *Arti Visive. Rivista della Fondazione Origine* (January 1956).

"Alberto Burri," *Appia Antica. Atlante di arte nuova* (July 1959).

"Alberto Burri," *Aujourd'hui. Art et Architecture* (September 1960).

"Per l'Operazione Burri mobilitata tutta l'America," *La Rivista Europea. Lettere e arti, cultura e politica* (January–February 1978).

In *Alberto Burri. Teatri e scenografie* (Comune di Pesaro, 1981).

Pittura dell'ultimo giorno. Scritti per Alberto Burri (Firenze: Le Lettere, 1996).

BUSANEL, MARIA

In *Maria Busanel* (Roma: Studio d'Arte Delta, 1965).

CAGLI, CORRADO

In "La quadriennale," *Il Bargello* (April 1935).

In "L'exposition d'Art Quadriennale à Rome," *Sud Magazine* (April 1935).

In "Quelli che contano," *Il Bargello* (October 1936).

"Cagli Corrado," *Enciclopedia Italiana. Appendice II* (Roma: 1948).

"Quarta dimensione. Commento a Corrado Cagli," *Mediterranea. Almanacco di Sicilia* (1950).

In *Cagli* (Roma: L'Asterisco, 1955).

In *Cagli* (Roma: Galleria San Marco, 1958).

"Il referto sull'Etna di Corrado Cagli," *Il Margutta. Periodico d'arte contemporanea* (January–February 1972).

In *Recenti opere di Corrado Cagli scelte e presentate da Emilio Villa* (Terni: Centro d'Arte Sciamannini, 1974).

CAMPANELLI, LUIGI

In *Luigi Campanelli* (Roma: 1983).

CANNILLA, FRANCO

In *Cannilla* (Roma: Galleria d'Arte Selecta, 1959).

CAPASSO, BEPPE

In *Multiplo* (October 1984).

In *Pericle Fazzini e Beppe Papasso* (Nola: Galleria Globo, 1986).

CAPOLONGO, CAMILLO

In *Emilio Villa: Scritti Napoletani*, with a note by Stelio Maria Martini (Napoli: Edizione Morra/Socrate, 2003).

CAPOGROSSI, GIUSEPPE

In *Capogrossi* (Roma: Galleria L'Attico, 1962).

CARACCIOLO, MARIO

In *Mario Caracciolo* (Roma: Galleria La Luna, 1976).

CARACENI, BRUNO

In *Caraceni* (Roma: Galleria Appia Antica, 1958).

In *Appia Antica. Atlante di arte nuova* (January 1960).

CARREGA, UGO

In *Confronto dalla mente* (Roma-Venezia: Le parole gelate, 1982).

CARUSO, LUCIANO

"Formulario per assistere all'atto letterale di Luciano Caruso in horto," *E/manazione* (May 1978).

CASTELLANI, ENRICO

"Enrico Castellani: è la ricerca ostinata della totalità," *Castellani* (Ravenna: Loggetta Lombardesca, 1978).

CASTELLANO, LUIGI

In *Linea Sud*, № 5–6 (April 1967).

CAVELLINI, GUGLIEMO

In *Quaderno dell'archivio Cavellini* (May 1999).

CECCARELLI, AURELIO

"Nuove indicazioni. Aurelio Ceccarelli," *Arti Visive. Rivista della Fondazione Origine* (spring 1954).

In *Aurelio Ceccarelli* (Roma: Galleria d'Arte Anthea, 1964).

CIRIACONO, CIRO

Ciriacono. Ultime proposizioni (Napoli: Galleria d'Arte San Carlo, 1985).

COLLA, ETTORE

"Scultura di Ettore Colla," *Arti Visive. Rivista della Fondazione Origine* (November–December 1953).

"Ettore Colla," *Arti Visive. Rivista della Fondazione Origine* (January 1956).

"Ferri e legni di Ettore Colla," *Civiltà delle macchine*, № 4 (1957).

In *Colla* (Roma: Galleria La Salita, 1959).

CONSAGRA, PIETRO

"Pietro Consagra," *Fiera Letteraria. Settimanale di lettere arti & scienze* (March 1947).

CONTINO, VITTORIO

Text distributed at the exhibit for *Ezra Pound. Segreti della scrittura* (Roma: Serafini Editore, February 1978).

CORPORA, ANTONIO

"Difesa a oltranza del colore. Antonio Corpora," *Quadrante* (October 1962).

COSSYRO, MICHELE

In *Michele Cossyro. "L'angolo di Tanit"* (Bagheria: Edizioni E. Pagano, 1985).

CRAIA SILVIO

Pittura e metafora di Silvio Craia (Catania: Istituto Statale d'Arte, 1986).

DE BERNARDI, GIANNI

In *Gianni De Bernardi* (Napoli: Galleria d'Arte San Carlo, 1961).

In *Emilio Villa e Mario Diacono su Gianni De Bernardi* (Milano: Edizioni Apollinaire, 1965).

In *Gianni De Bernardi. Opere 1959–67* (Roma: Galleria Santoro, 1967).

Gianni De Bernardi (Roma: Galleria Skema Z, 1981).

Gianni De Bernardi. Riti di paesaggio 1972–1978 (Roma: 1981).

DE FELICE, AURELIO

"Scultura di De Felice," *Fiera letteraria. Settimanale di lettere arti e scienze* (February 1947).

DE KOONING, WILLEM

In *Attributi dell'arte odierna.*

DELLI SANTI, FRANCESCO

Un fossile rigenerato (Spoleto: Festival dei due mondi, 1973).

DE PISIS, FILIPPO

"Omaggio a De Pisis," *Alfabeto. Quindicinale di arti, scienza e lettere* (October 1946).

DESIATO, GIUSEPPE

"Declarations pour les saintes femmes apparentes en nature post-anthropomorphiques, œuvres Desiatéennes," *Prospettive*, № 3 (1966).

"Il dialetto del sabato," *Napoli 2* (Reggio Emilia: Edizioni Pari & Dispari, 1973).

DE TOMI, ENRICO

In *Enrico De Tomi* (Roma: Galleria La Tartaruga, 1964).

In "Enrico De Tomi," *Carte Segrete*, № 14 (Roma: 1975).

Carattere nella pittura di Enrico De Tomi (Roma: 1976).

"Bilancio di una pittura astrattista per Enrico De Tomi," *Enrico De Tomi* (Roma: Edizioni La Gradiva, 1986).

DONNINI, SERGIO

In *Sergio Donnini* (Roma: Galleria Appia Antica, 1958).

DORAZIO, PIERO

In *Forma 1* (Roma: Galleria dell'Art Club, 1947).

DUCHAMP, MARCEL

In *Attributi dell'arte odierna.*

EIELSON, JORGE

In *Arti Visive. Rivista della Fondazione Origine* (spring 1954).

FASCETTI, RENATO

Ancienne géométrie sabine (Edizioni Skema).

In *Renato Fascetti* (Roma: Spazio Alternativo, 1977).

In *Renato Fascetti* (Roma: Galleria dell'Obelisco, 1981).

FASOLA, ROBERTO

In *I 4 Soli. Rassegna d'arte attuale* (September–October 1955).

"I polepipedi di Roberto Fasola," *Diorama. Mensile d'arte foto cinematografica e figurativa* (November–December 1956).

FAZZINI, PERICLE

In *Fazzini* (Roma: Galleria del Foglio, 1968).

Preface to *Omaggio a Fazzini*, ed. by N. Taccone (Premio Città di Avezzano, 1983).

FERRARI, ENEA

In *Enea* (Roma: Flash Art Plus, 1972).

FERRARI, FRANCO

Franco Ferrari (Napoli: Galleria Il Diagramma 32, 1976).

Franco Ferrari (Roma: Artivisive Studio d'Arte Contemporanea, 1976).

Franco Ferrari (International Symposium all'Hotel Hilton di Roma: 1977).

Franco Ferrari. Spazio fossile (Bologna: Galleria 9 Colonne, 1985).

Franco Ferrari. La favola della mente (Roma: Altier Calderoni, 1986).

FISCHER, EVA

"Sulla pittura di Eva Fischer," *Alfabeto. Quindicinale di arti, scienze e lettere* (November 1946).

FONTANA, LUCIO

In *Attributi dell'arte odierna.*

In *Roma Fascista* (March 1940).

"L'ombra chiara," *Fontana* (Milano: Galleria 2RC, 1981).

FRANCINA, NINO

In *Appia Antica. Atlante di arte nuova* (July 1959).

FRANCIS, SAM

In *Attributi dell'arte odierna.*

"Così Sam Francis," *Sam Francis* (Roma-Milano: RC Edizioni d'Arte, 1985).

GABRIELLI, LUCIANO

"Umanizzare l'oggetto," *Gala International*, № 76 (March 1976).

In *Luciano Gabrielli* (Milano: Galleria Pagani, 1978).

GENOVESE, ROCCO

In *Rocco Genovese. Sculture* (Assisi-Roma: Beniamino Carucci Editore, 1974).

GERARDI, ALBERTO

"Gerardi: ori e argenti," *Arti Visive. Rivista della Fondazione Origine* (spring 1954).

GIORGINI, VITTORIO

"Per una architettura futura," *Vittorio Giorgini, Strutture soniche (ipotesi per un habitat più naturale)* (Ferrara: Palazzo dei Diamaneti, 1968).

GLÜCKMANN, NORA

In *Nora Glückmann* (Roma: Galleria San Marco, 1973).

GONZALES, ALBA

"Per una comédie magnétique, in scultura monumentale," *Terzoocchio* (March 1985).

GUAITA, CARLO

Carlo Guaita (Venezia-Mestre: Barbera De Girolami Arte Moderna, 1984).

GUSTON, PHILIP

In *Attributi dell'arte odierna.*

GUTTUSO, RENATO

In *Fiera Letteraria. Settimanale di lettere arti e scienze* (October 1946).

Considerazioni per gli "studi da" Michelangelo di Renato Guttuso (Città di Castello: 1985).

HABER, SHAMAI

"Shamai Haber," *Appia Antica. Atlante di arte nuova* (July 1959).

INNOCENTE, ETTORE

In *Emilio Villa e Mario Diacono per Ettore Innocente, XYZ A1 take one 1970 XYZ A2* (Pollenza-Macerata: La Nuovo Foglio, 1970).

In *Ettore Innocente* (Erbusco: Multimedia Arte Contemporanea, 1976).

LANCIONI, SERGIO

In *Mostra per Sergio Lancioni* (Roma: Galleria Triangolo, 1977).

L'ACQUA, ENZO

In *L'Acqua* (Savona: 1983).

LAYATICO, GABRIELLA

In *Attibuti dell'arte odierna.*

LEBEL, JEAN-JACQUES

In *Attibuti dell'arte odierna.*

LEINARDI, ERMANNO

D'un zero engendré, o (Roma: Edizioni Elle Ci, 1980).

LEONCILLO

In *Leoncillo* (Roma: Galleria L'Attico, 1962).

"Leoncillo, genialità e gnosi," *Leoncillo. Sculture* (Roma: Galleria L'Attico-Esse Arte, 1980).

In *15 opere di Leoncillo* (Roma: Galleria L'Attico-Esse Arte, 1983).

LIPTON, SEYMOUR

In *Appia Antica. Atlante di arte nuova* (July 1959).

LOMBARDI, TONINO

In *Lombardi* (Brescia: Magalini Editrice, 1985).

"L'arsenale di tenebre," *Tonino Lombardi* (Roma: Il Cigno Galileo Galilei Edizioni, 1954).

LO SAVIO, FRANCO

In *Appia Antica. Atlante di arte nuova* (July 1959).

In *Attributi dell'arte odierna.*

LUCA (LUIGI CASTELLANO)

In *Luca* (Padova: Galleria 1+1, 1967).

MAFONSO

"Pour Mafonso et sa déesse," *Mafonso* (Edizioni Meinard Camenzind, 1982).

MANNUCCI, EDGARDO

Edgardo Manucci, catalogue for the XXVIII Biennale of Venezia (Venezia: Alfieri, 1956).

In *Edgardo Manucci* (Roma: Via Sistina Galleria, 1957).

In *Appia Antica. Atlante di arte nuova* (January 1960).

In *Edgardo Manucci. Sculture 1950–1978* (Maestà di Urbisaglia: Editore Cegna, 1979).

In *Edgardo Manucci* (Roma: Galleria Schema, 1980).

MANZONI, PIERO

In *Attributi dell'arte odierna.*

MANZU, GIACOMO

"L'ultima stanza di Manzù," *Alfabeto. Quindicinale di arti, scienze e lettere* (April 1947).

MARCARELLI, CORRADO

"Pittura di Marcarelli," *Arti Visive. Rivista della Fondazione Origine* (January 1956).

MAROTTA, GINO

In *Gino Marotta e Sante Monachesi* (Roma: Galleria d'Arte Portonovo, 1957).

In *Gino Marotta* (Milano: Galleria Montenapoleone, 1957).

"Gino Marotta ed i suoi tappeti di lana," *Rivista dell'Arredamento* (September 1957).

"Anatomia ginomarotta," *Pitture di Gino Marmotta* (Roma: Galleria Anthea, 1964). Also in *Leader. Mensile di attualità economica politica cultura industria e scienza* (October–November 1964).

"La 'riserva' di Gino Marotta," *Gino Marotta. Riserva di caccia* (Pollenza: Edizioni La Giraffa, 1971).

In *Gino Marotta, la dimensione spettrale* (Terni: Galleria Poliantea, 1973).

"Gino Marotta: l'orizzonte artificale," *Marotta* (Vanessa Edizioni d'Arte, 1982).

MASTROIANNI, UMBERTO

In *La scelta della libertà. Sculture nelle città* (Roma: Magna Editrice, 1976).

MATTA

In *Matta* (Roma: Galleria del Secolo, 1950).

In *Matta* (Roma: Galleria l'Attico, 1961).

MATTIACCI, ELISEO

In *Sondaggio* (Ancona: Galleria del Falconiere, 1978).

In *Eliseo Mattiacci* (Milano: Padiglione d'Arte Contemporanea, 1981).

In *Mattiacci* (New York: Iolas Jackson Gallery, 1983).

MAUGERI, FABIO

In *Alfabeto. Quindicinale di arti, scienze e lettere* (September 1946).

MAURI, FABIO

In *Appia Antica. Atlante di arte nuova* (January 1960).

In *Fabio Mauri* (Studio d'ArteToninelli, 1969).

MAZZUCHELLI, FRANCO

In *Prospettive 4* (Roma: 1969).

MEO, SALVATORE

"Meo Salvatore, ou le Snag-Art," *Salvatore Meo. Opere 1945–1965* (Roma: Studio d'Arte Metropolitan, 1965).

In *Salvatore Meo. Assemblages e disegni (1945–1971)* (Roma: Galleria Ciak, 1971).

In *Salvatore Meo* (Roma: Galleria Incontro d'Arte, 1975).

MERIDA, CARLOS

"A Carlos Merida," *Carlos Merida* (Roma: Il Collezionista d'Arte Contemporanea, 1975).

MINUCCI, NELDA

In *gli emblemi e i dipinti* (Roma: Galleria d'Arte Russo, 1972).

In *Nelda Minacci* (Venezia: Galleria Il Traghetto 2, 1973).

In *Nelda Minucci. 6 dipinti* (Spoleto: Festival dei due mondi, 1973).

In *Nelda Minucci presenta 20 opere* (Montecatini: Galleria La Barcaccia, 1974).

In *Minucci* (Milano: Galleria Settala, 1976).

MONACHESI, SANTE

In *Monachesi* (Roma: Galleria Portonovo, 1956).

In *Aujourd'hui, Art & Architecture* (January 1963).

"Sante Monachesi," *Alfabeto. Quindicinale di arti, scienze e lettere* (April 1963)

In *Monachesi Agrà* (Macerata: Foglio OG, 1965).

Monachesi, Il Poliedro. Rivista mensile d'arte e attualità (December 1967).

"Monachesi," *AL2. Mensile arte cultura attualità* (December 1968)

"Monachesi," *Carte segrete*, № 5 (1969).

"Monachesi," *Athos* (March 1969).

L'iperbole di Monachesi (Milano: Galleria Borgonuovo, 1970).

"Hommage à Monachesi per Emilio Villa," *Monachesi* (Milano: Achille Maramotti Editore, 1970).

Manifesto Agrà (Pollenza-Macerata: La Nuovo Foglio, 1970).

"I chemiogrammi o muriciechi," *Monachesi* (Roma: Centro d'arte La Barcaccia, 1972).

"Teatro instabile italiano rappresentazione di Monachesi, scultore in evelpiuma," *Monachesi* (Pollenza-Macerata: La Nuovo Foglio, 1975).

MONCADA, IGNAZIO

In *Emilio Villa presenta Ignazio Moncada* (Torino: Galleria Il Punto, 1973).

MONTANARINI, LUIGI

In *La Festa. Rivista settimanale illustrata della famiglia italiana* (September 1943).

"Indizi per una lettura dell'opera di Luigi Montanarini," *Art International* (December 1995).

MORELLE, JEAN-PAUL

Jean-Paul Morelle. "Les fruits du Congo" ovvero "Il Pentagramma Hermetico, o il Sigillo Zoppo" (Milano: Centro Lavoro Arte, 1985).

MOTHERWELL, ROBERT

In *Attributi dell'arte odierna*.

MUSSIO, MAGDALO

In *Charta, Magdalo Mussio* (Macerata: Palazzo Ricci, 1997).

NARDULLI, GIUSEPPE

"Giuseppe Nardulli candidato all'utopia," *L'Occhio* (Roma: 1978).

In *Il secondo Io* (Roma: 1994).

NATILI, ALDO

"Natili," *Bollettino della Galleria La Nuova Pesa* (1961).

In *Aldo Natili* (Roma: Galleria San Marco, 1963).

NERVI, PIER LUIGI

"Vediamo l'architettura. P. L. Nervi," *Arti Visive. Rivista della Fondazione Origine* (May 1953).

NEWMAN, BARNETT

In *Attributi dell'arte odierna*.

NOVAK, GIANNI

"Pour quelque Arlequins peints par Gianni Novak," *Vie des Arts* (winter 1969–1970).

NOVELLI, GASTONE

"Novelli, pintor e ceramista," *Habitat. Arquitectura e artes no Brasil* (October–December 1952).

NUVOLO

In *Arti Visive. Rivista della Fondazione Origine* (November 1954).

In *Nuvolo* (Roma: Galleria delle Carrozze, 1955).

In *Nuvolo* (Perugia: Galleria del Brufani, 1957).

In *Mostra di serotipie di Lorri e Nuvolo* (Roma: Libreria "Al ferro di cavallo," 1958).

In *Nuvolo* (Roma: Galleria La Tartaruga, 1958).

In *Exemplaria* (Roma: Galleria Appia Antica, 1959).

In *nuntius celatus* (Roma: Delta Editori, 1971).

In *Nuvolo* (Città del Castello: Galleria d'arte moderna "Il Pozzo," 1971).

In *Nuvolo* (Terni: Galleria Poliantea, 1972).

PADOVAN, MARIO

In *Mario Padovan. Opere dal 1964–1971* (Comune di Ferrara: 1971).

In *Padovan. Disegni 1954–1973* (Pollenza-Macerata: La Nuovo Foglio, 1973).

In *Charte arcani 24 di Mario Padovan* (Roma: De Cristofaro Editore, 1982).

PANDOLFINI, EMANUELE

In "Pandolfini, pittore di strutture ioniche," *Pandolfini, opere grafiche* (Roma: Edizioni Arco, 1978).

In *I pupi* (Roma: Edizioni "La Sfera," 1978).

PANTER, GEA

In *Appia Antica. Atlante di arte nuova* (January 1960).

PAPARONI, GIOVANNI

Emblematica di Giovanni Paparoni (Spoleto: 1969).

In *Paparoni* (Ferrara: Centro Attività Visive, 1974).

PARMIGGIANI, CLAUDIO

"Le monde Frotté Foute," *Atlante* (Milano: Scheiwiller, 1970).

"Pro [desuper] [intra]," *Claudio Parmiggiani*, ed. by A. Schwarz (Comune di Reggio Emilia: 1985).

PELKONEN, RAMI

In *Rami Pelkonen* (Roma: Galleria Centro Skema/Z, 1980).

PERSIANI, COSTANTINO

"La scultura di Costantino Persiani," *Il Margotta. Periodico d'arte contemporanea* (March 1971).

PIERELLI, ATTILIO

In *Pierelli. Planches Aluminium* (Roma: Galleria San Marco, 1963).

PIGNITORE, PINO

In *Pino Pignitore* (Roma: Galleria d'Arte Porto di Ripetta, 1983).

POLLOCK, JACKSON

In *Attributi dell'arte odierna*.

PUGLIELLI, GIOVANNI

In *Sempre veleggiando la divinante coesione* (Roma: Trevi Edizioni, 1977).

RAGALZI, SERGIO

In *Delitti sessuali* (Roma: Associazione Culturale l'Attico, 1984).

ROTELLA, DOMENICO

"Décollages di Rotella," *Arti Visive. Rivista della Fondazione Origine* (April–May 1955).

In *Rotella* (Roma: Galleria La Salita, 1959).
In *Appia Antica. Atlante di arte nuova* (January 1960).
In *I 4 Soli. Rassegna d'arte attuale* (July–August 1960).

ROTHKO, MARK

In *Attributi dell'arte odierna.*
"Idée de Rothko," *Appia Antica. Atlante di arte nuova* (January 1960).

RUSSO, MARGHERITA

In *Margherita Russo* (Roma: Galleria d'Arte Selecta, 1958).

SADR, BEHDJAT

In *Behdjat Sadr* (Roma: Galleria La Bussola, 1958).

SADUN, PIERO

In *Sadun* (Roma: Galleria San Luca, 1962).
Per Piero Sadun (Pollenza-Macerata: La Nuova Foglio, 1972).

SAMARUGHI, MARIO

"Per la fotografia eidogrammatica di Mario Samarughi," *Mario Samarughi* (Roma: Galleria d'Arte valle Giulia, 1971).
In *Samarughi* (Roma: Studio S, 1981).

SAMONÀ, MARIO

In *Mario Samonà* (Firenze: Galleria Numero, 1956).
In *Mario Samonà* (Roma: Galleria Appia Antica, 1958).
In *Mario Samonà* (Milano: Diagramma arte contemporanea, 1969).

SANTORO, SUZANNE

In *Suzanne Santoro* (Roma: Centro Culturale L'Indiscreto, 1983).

SCARPITTA, SALVATORE

In *Salvatore Scarpitta. Opere 1955–1964* (Studio Durante, 1991).

SCHIFANO, MARIO

In *Schifano* (Roma: Galleria Appia Antica, 1959).

SCIALOJA, TOTI

In *Appia Antica. Atlante di arte nuova* (July 1959).

SERGHIEV

In *Serghiev, "Le regine-cristallo"* (Roma: Galleria La Pace, 1974).
In *Serghiev* (Roma: Galleria Orione, 1975).

SETTANNI, PINO

Voilgrammi (Pollenza-Macerata: La Nuova Foglio, 1976).

SEVERI, CARLO

"Caro Severi come Ocello Lucano," *Tesi/Analisi* (Milano: 1975).

SCHLOSS, EDITH

Per Edith Schloss (Roma: Galleria Il Segno, 1974).

SHU, TAKAHASHI

In *Shu Takahashi* (Milano: Galleria 2RC, 1985).

SMITH, DAVID

"Pour un thème symbole de David Smith," *Appia Antica. Atlante di arte nuova* (January 1960).

SORDINI, ETTORE

In *Ettore Sordini. Gianni Novak* (Roma: Galleria della Carrozze, 1956).
"Ettore Sordini: l'Epigrafia Maggiore," *Ettore Sordini* (Macerata: Foglio OG, 1961).

In *Sordini* (Roma: Time's Gallery, 1974).

"Paraphrase sur les tables de Sordini," *Ettore Sordini* (Livorno: Galleria Peccolo, 1996).

SOSKIC, ILIJA

In *Ilija Soskic* (Ferrara: Centro attività visive, 1972).

STEFANONI, TINO

"Paese per Stefanoni," *Stefanoni* (Torino: Galleria Franz Paludetto, 1985).

STENIUS, LILLI

In *Lilli Stenius* (Milano: Arte Incontro, 1983–84).

STERPINI, UGO

"Elenchi di simboli e sabbie," *Ugo Sterpini* (Roma: Galleria Due Mondi, 1967).

SUGAI

"Pittura di Sugai," *Arti Visive. Rivista della Fondazione Origine* (November 1954).

TALIENTO, BENEDETTO

In *Benedetto Taliento, "pittore del quadrato"* (Roma: 1980).

TERZIARI, NINO

In *Terziari* (Roma: Galleria Arco, 1970).

TOROK, STEFANO

In *Stefano Torok* (Lugano: Studio Dabbeni, 1982).

TOT, AMERIGO

"I sassi di Tot," *Alfabeto. Quindicinale di arti, scienze e lettere* (April 1947).

"L'arte di Tot," *L'Avanti* (September 1948).
"Lo scultore Tot," *Il Lavoro* (November 1948).
"Umanità nell'arte di Tot," *Apollo* (December 1948).
Tot. Otto disegni (Roma: La Palma, 1949).
"Omaggio ai sassi di Tot," *Il Popolo di Roma* (December 1952).
"Stazione Termini, il Grande Fregio," *Arti Visive. Rivista della Fondazione Origine* (November 1954).
In *Tot. Con una confessione dello scultore,* ed. by Gino Alliata (Roma: Edizioni La Palma, 1954).

TRIPODO, SANDRO

In *Sandro Tripodo* (Roma: Centro Culturale per l'Informazione Visiva, 1974).

TROTTI, SANDRO

"Trotti," *Carte segrete. Rivista trimestrale di lettere e arti* (October–December 1968).

TULLI, VLADIMIRO

In *Wladimiro Tulli* (Porto Sant'Elpidio: Vesprinis' Meetings, 1983).
In *W. Tulli, I miei poeti* (Illasi: Laser Edizioni, 1990).

TURCATO, GIULIO

"Pittura di Giulio Turcato," *Arti Visive. Rivista della Fondazione Origine* (November 1954).
"Riconoscimento per Giulio Turcato," *Appia Antica. Atlante di arte nuova* (January 1960).
"Giulio Turcato," *Aujourd'hui, Art et Architecture* (December 1960).
In *Giulio Turcato* (Roma: Galleria La Tartaruga, 1962).

Turcato (Roma: Galleria La Tartaruga, 1964).

In *Giulio Turcato* (Montecatini Terme: Galleria La Barcaccia, 1969).

Turcato. 80 opere (Firenze: Casa d'Arte La Gradiva, 1975).

In *Turcato* (Bologna: Galleria Il Nettuno, 1971).

In *Turcato. Cina '56*, ed. by V. Caruso (Macerata: La Nuova Foglio, 1971).

"L'opus scriptum di giulio turcato," *Qui Arte Contemporanea* (December 1974).

In *Giulio Turcato* (Galleria Editalia, 1974).

La "luce" di Giulio Turcato (Roma: Galleria d'arte Coltellacci, 1976).

Propositions pour les Iridescences modulaires librérées par Turcato, with a note by I. Mussa (Roma: Edizioni Soligo, 1981).

"Le Pelli narrate da Emilio Villa" & "Il viaggio in Cina secondo Emilio Villa," *Giulio Turcato*, with an essay by I. Mussa (Firenze: Borgo Ognissanti, 1983).

In *Turcato / Moduli in viola. Omaggio a Kandinsky*, ed. by G. Proietti (Firenze: Centro Di, 1984).

TWOMBLY, CY

"Cy Twombly talento bianco," *Appia Antica. Atlante di arte nuova* (July 1959).

In Cy *Twombly. E una parafrasi per Cy Twombly di Emilio Villa* (Roma: Edizioni della Tartaruga, 1961).

UNCINI, GIUSEPPE

In *Giuseppe Uncini. "Dimore"* (Udine: Plurima, 1984).

UNGHERI

Ungheri (Roma: Galleria dell'Obelisco, 1973).

VANGELLI, ANTONIO

"Un epodo per Antonio Vagelli," *Antonio Vangelli* (Bologna: 1991).

VEDOVA

"Emilio Vedova. Alberto Burri," *Arti Visive. Rivista della Fondazione Origine* (January 1956).

VERCEL, ENRICO

In *Vercel* (Roma: Galleria Schneider, 1954).

WALASSE, TING

In *Walasse Ting* (Milano: Galleria 2RC, 1984).

WHITING, LORRI

In *Whiting Lorri* (Roma: Galleria Obelisco, 1959).

WOLS

In *Attributi dell'arte odierna.*

XERRA, WILLIAM

The Flippant Ball-Feel (Piacenza: ManaMarket, 1973).

Various Writings in Magazines & Periodicals

AAA. Azioni off Kulchur:

"Addressing" (February 1969).

"All'Upim è già Natale" (April 1969).

Alfabeto. Quindicinale di arti, scienze e lettere:

"Mostre d'Arte a Roma" (November 1946).

"Mostre romane" (February 1947).

Appia Antica. Atlante di arte nuova:

"Editorial"; "Arte e rito"; "Di una ipotesi barocca"; "Post-Editorial" (July 1959).

"Dada corphèe à New York" (January 1960).

Arti Visive. Rivista della Fondazione Origine:

"Astrattismo e scienza"; "Vediamo l'architettura"; "Produrre quello che può essere prodotto oggi e soltanto oggi"; "Ciò che è primitivo" (May 1953).

"Ideografie sui lastroni di Monte Bego" (November–December 1953).

"Stazione Termini il Grande Fregio"; Commentary on an investigation by Ann Salzmann; "Refe" (spring 1954).

"Noi e la preistoria" (November 1954).

"Lettera agli amici pittori" (January 1956).

Aujourd'hui, Art et Architecture:

"La peinture italienne dans le dix dernières années" (March–April 1959).

"La sculpture italienne contemporaine" (September 1959).

"Les jeunes artistes italiens" (September 1960).

Avanguardia. Rivista di letteratura contemporanea:

"Sibylla (seraphin seraphina)"; "Sibylla (sabina)"; "Sibylla (Secreta ex creta creata)"; "Sibilla" (1998).

Baldus. Semestrale di letteratura:

"Epistola a Corrado Costa"; "Le monde Frotté Foute"; "Geometria Reformata" (September 1990).

Il Bargello:

"Democrazia intellettuale" (September 1937).

Beltempo. Almanacco delle lettere e delle arti:

"Gli ottant'anni di Bergson" (1940).

Chelsea:

La mano di Pitagora (a.k.a. *Imprimatur*); *Eructavit cor ver-*

bum; hymnenee pour; Homoioteleuton; Apoklypse; Tour de pouces; Options; "Cy Twombly" (December 1978).

Cinema. Quindicinale di divulgazione cinematografica:

"Per una storia del cinema" (November 1942).

Circoli. Rivista di Letteratura:

"Su Andrè Salmon" (July–August 1938).

"Anima, prosa e gloria di Leonardo" (May 1939).

Civiltà delle Macchine:

"Trappole" (January–February 1954).

"Energia aero-elettrica" (March–April 1954).

"Il fregio della Stazione Termini" (May–June 1954).

"Le navi di Ulisse" (September–October 1954).

"Navi mitiche" (November–December 1955).

"La nascita dei numeri" (March–April 1956).

"I soffioni di Lardello" (September–October 1956).

"Visita alla termomeccanica" (November–December 1956).

"Macchine di legno" (January–February 1957).

"Ferri e legni di Ettore Colla" (July–August 1957).

"Maccarese" (January–February 1958).

Codice Biancaneve:

4 poems from *le mûra di t; éb; é* (1992).

Continuazione A-Z. Foglio di comportamenti, azioni, antiscrittura, gesti, ecc. ritualizzaioni:

Untitled visual work (I, 1968).

Untitled visual work (IV, 1968).

Convivium. Rivista bimestrale di lettere e filosofia:

"Note sul Surrealismo. Di Eluard e di alcune conseguenze" (March–April 1939).

Corrente di vita giovanile:

"Su G. Petroni" (April 1939).

"Sulla semplicità moderna" (November 1939).

"Opinioni e pretesti: due opinioni cristiane su Carlo Bo" (March 1940).

La difesa della razza. Scienza, documentazione, polemica, questionario:[3]

"Arianità della lingua etrusca" (October 1938).

"La lingua tocarica" (July 1939).

Documento Sud. Rassegna d'arte e di cultura d'avanguardia: *Come il terremoto che affoga nel marsala*; *Le gran ruban*; *Logogrammata* (1969).

Enciclopedia Italiana di scienze, lettere ed arti. Appendice II:

"Arp, Jean"; "Belgio. Arti figurative"; "Bill, Max"; "Brasile. Arti figurative"; "Cagli, Corrado"; "Fontana, Lucio"; "Giacometti, Alberto" (vol. I, A–H, 1948).

"Mafai, Mario"; "Manzù, Giacomo"; "Marini, Marino"; "Pirandello, Fausto"; "Portinari, Candido"; "Soutine, Chaim"; "Sutherland, Graham Vivian"; "Tunnard, John"; "Usellini, Gianfilippo"; "Van Dongen, Kees" (vol. II, I–Z, 1949).

3. There are uncertainties as to if these articles can be attributed to this Emilio Villa.

EX:

Le liber mutus; Tabula Absphixoria; Anatomie, № 1 (June 1963).

Theophorie phonophonte; onon ominaticum écrit sur le coude qui éclate; à tout âmdré toute liberté; obscourosseux laboratoire Polydème sur Saint-Siege-Chaos; difficultivésupplices du palimpseste mutil; QUE; ritué; trombe l'œil, № 2 (April 1964).

Homoscuralnulsentiment; Que Iside Enfante Congo; Forece prenante de cong de san fin au-delà; Growjera (SURcenSure), № 3 (March–December 1965).

Chronoïd pulinyest (y-y) monoject (40 units), № 4 (Lerici Editore, April 1968).

Pour un Assassinat; Lettera a un assassinato, № 5 (1968).

La Festa. Rivista settimanale illustrata della famiglia italiana:

"Vita romana. La Cometa" (July 1938).

Fiera Letteraria. Settimanale di lettere arti e scienze:

"Nuovi capolavori al Louvre" (September 1946).

"Le pittura murali di Tavant" (October 1946).

"Novelle per ragazzi" (November 1946).

Il Frontespizio:

"Sopra il ritorno al canto"; "Ancora del monismo Martiniano"; "Oggetto e allegoria"; "Duncan Bhan Mac Intere" (1937).

"Informazioni sulla poesia sudamericana"; "La mitologia e le sue fonti nascoste"; "Note su Roberto Papi" (1938).

Gala international. Attualità e informazione visiva:

"Umanizzare l'oggetto" (March 1976).

Habitat. Arquitectura e artes no Brasil:

"Os puristas são enfandonhos e inùteis" (April–June 1952).

"Vasos e tecidos brasileiros num museu romano" (July–September 1952).

"Norœste magico"; "Outras peças no Museu Pigorini de Roma" (October–December 1952).

L'Italia che scrive. Rassegna per il mondo che legge:

"Appunti di critica: Giuseppe Ungaretti" (August–September 1940).

"Carmelo Sgroi: Prospettive letterarie"; "Ettore Strinati: Riepilogando"; "Fernando Capecchi: Poesia e cultura" (November–December 1940).

"Alba De Cèspedes: Fuga"; "Carlo Pastorino: Il canto dell'uccello migratore" (January–February 1941).

"Alessandro Parronchi: I giorni sensibili"; "Luigi Fallacara: Notturni"; "Vittorio Sereni: Poesie" (March 1941).

"Svaghi lessicali"; "Corrado Covoni: Pellegrino d'amore"; "Elio Vittorini: Nome e lagrime"; "Mario Soldati: La verità sul caso Motta"; "Enrico Falqui: Pezze d'appoggio" (April 1941).

"La luna nel corso"; "Giorgio Bolza: On sabet grass. Quartinn in milanés"; "Guido Pioveni: Lettere di una novizia" (May 1941).

"Interpretazioni del libro d'oggi"; "Tullio Cicciarelli: Poesie"; "Nelly Vucetich: Portone semichiuso" (July–August 1941).

"Svaghi lessicali. Gianna Mancini"; "Leonardo Sinisgalli: Campi Elisi" (September 1941).

"Gerhard Rohlfs: L'italianità linguistica della Corsica"; "Luigi Salvini: Le candide ville" (October 1941).

"Giulio Mele: Gergo di guerra"; "Virgilio Giotti: Colori"; "Luigi Salvini: Narratori Bulgari" (November 1941).

"Eugène Lyons: Stalin, Zar di tutte le Russie"; "Hans Ruesch: Gladiatori" (December 1941).

"Augusto Garsia: Opposte voci"; "Guareschi: La scoperta di Milano"; "Michele Vocino: A orza pioggia"; "Comunicazione: Emilio Villa" (January–February 1942).

"Come si può leggere il romanzo di oggi"; "Carlo Salsa: Questo stramaledetto amore"; "Alessandro Tornimparte: La strada che va in città"; "Mario Alonge Park: Cento anni di vita dei tram milanesi"; "Comunicazione: Emilio Villa" (March–April 1942).

"Enzo Grazzini: Desiderio"; "Franco Matacotta: Poemetti"; "Adolfo Jenni: Annate"; "Leone Traverso: Poesia moderna straniera" (May–June 1942).

"Giacinto Spagnoletti: Sonetti e altre poesie"; "Gavino Cerchi: Cuore di donna"; "Alberto Menarini: I gerghi bolognesi" (July–August 1942).

"Lionelli Fiumi: Parnaso amico. Saggio su alcuni poeti italiani viventi"; "Michele Amari: I Musulmani in Sicilia"; "Luigi Reybaud: Gerolamo Paturot" (September–October 1942).

"La mostra della Rivista Germanica, Roma: 25 novembre–6 dicembre 1942"; "Alessandro Manzoni: Storia della Colonna Infame"; "Marino Parenti: Immagini della vita e dei tempi di Alessandro Manzoni" (November–December 1942).

"Letteratura narrativa e cinematografo italiano"; "Piero Bigongiari: La figlia di Babilonia"; "Neppi Fanello: La colonna del magnifico"; "Francesco Cazzamini-Mussi: Omaggio a Meneghin" (January–February 1943).

"Filippo Burzio: Favole e moralità"; "Carlo Salsa: Si liquida"; "Oreste Macrì: Esemplari del sentimento poetico contemporaneo" (March–April 1943).

"Giuseppe Valentini: Mare senza Sirene. Poesie"; "Giacomo Leopardi: Il mio sistema" (May–June 1943).

Letteratura. Rivista di lettere e di arte contemporanea:

"Dannunzio" (March 1939).

"C. Pariani: Vite non romanzate di Dino Campana scrittore e di Evaristo Bonicelli scultore" (April 1939).

"Libero De Libero: Testa" (January 1940).

Linea Sud. Nuova rassegna d'arte e di cultura d'avanguardia:

"LUC-ARCH 67" (May 1967).

Marcazero:

"The Flippant Ball-Feel" (1972).

Mediterranea. Almanacco di Sicilia:

"Sicilia immaginata," № 2 (1950).

Il Meridiano di Roma. L'Italia letteraria artistica scientifica:

"Apologetica cattolica" (October 1937).

"Libri d'arte" (November 1937).

"Butrinto-S.Pietro" (November 1937).

"Traduzioni" (December 1937).

"Novecento europeo" (December 1937).

"Cartesio e la cultura contemporanea" (January 1938).

"Diego Valeri"; "Pastorino" (February 1938).

"Betti" (February 1938).

"Fallacara e Mariani"; "Religioni Germaniche" (February 1938).

"Poesie di Sinisgalli" (February 1938).
"Poesie di Cardarelli" (March 1938).

Panorama. Enciclopedia delle attualità:
"Il poema di Danel" (June 1939).
"Opere di Gaspari Gozzi scelte a cura di Enrico Falqui" (November 1939).
"Scoperte archeologiche ed artistiche in Egitto" (December 1939).

Le parole rampanti:
"Cubo con scritta"; "Un t'exécute une piramide fiance"; "cage cosmique du phónos (rèponse Rimbaud)"; "L'éticinelle de l'Offrande déployée"; "La fleur-chacun"; "Les plansex des FI = les sex du nord"; "Au dessous-hyperbole du marroner souffrant"; "Les 4 c(a)ra(c)tères du tortueux Champ du feuillzâge global"; "Cosmofraix"; "Una rosa rotta in Carnia"; "Dada coriphée à New York"; "immaginiamo"; "J'ai cru plus que providentiel"; "Os olhos são muito preguiçosos"; "Aveugles"; "Carmen" (September 1990).

Quaderno:
"comizio millenovecentocinquanta3," № 2 (March–April 1962).
"Le liber motus," № 3 (May–June 1962).

Quadrante. Bollettino di Quadrante. Studio d'arte contemporanea:
"Difesa ad oltranza del colore" (October 1962).

Roma Fascista:
"Mostre alla Galleria Roma. Gattuso, Guzzi, Montanarini, Tamburi, Viveri, Fazzini" (February 1940).

Sapere Nuovo:

"L'ædo terrestre ha tracciato la via agli astronauti" (February 1968).

Il selvaggio:

№ 5–6 (October 1939).

Stile. Nella casa e nell'arredamento:

"Pittori e studi di pittori a Roma" (July 1943).

"Idea della città nel Chianti" (January 1944).

Studi e materiali di Storia delle Religioni:

"La gesta di Karit na'man re di Tiro e di Sidone"; "Il valore paleografico del segno numerico TIL e la biblica Eva (=vita)" (V. XV, 1939).

"La dea Anat e la resurrezione di Baal" (V. XI, 1940).

Tam Tam. Rivista Internazionale di poesia:

"*SUB BREGME*," № 1 (1972).

La Tartaruga. Quaderni d'arte e letteratura:

"Eclissi"; "Alberto Burri alla Fondazione Origine"; "Mimmo Rotella"; Postscritto; "Angeli, Festa, Lo Savio, Schifano, Uncini"; "Appia Antica" (March 1989).

TAU / MA:

Alphabetum cœleste (March 1977).

Verboracula (1981).

Il Tempo:

"Sulla traduzione dell'Odissea" (January 1973).

Terzoochio. Trimestrale d'arte contemporanea:

"Per una comédia magnétique, in scultura monumentale" (March 1985).

Vies des Arts:
"Pour quelque Arlequins peints par Gianni Novak" (winter 1969–1970).

Important Volumes Dedicated to the Work of Emilio Villa

The monographic issue of *Uomini e idee*, № 2–4 (October 1975).

Gianni Grana, *Babele e silenzio: genio "orfico" di Emilio Villa: la neg-azione apoetica: caos e cosmos, vertigini e metastasi della parola nell'era telematica* (Milano: Settimo Milanese, 1991).

Aldo Tagliaferri & Bruno Corà, *Emilio Villa. Opere e documenti* (Milano: Skira, 1996).

The monographic issue of *il Verri*, № 7–8 (November 1998).

Emilio Villa. Critica d'arte 1946–1984, ed. by Aniello De Luca (Napoli: Città del Sole, 2000).

Aldo Tagliaferri, *Il clandestino: vita e opere di Emilio Villa* (Roma: Derive Approdi, 2004).

Segnare un secolo. Emilio Villa: la parola, l'immagine, ed. by Gian Paolo Renello (Roma: Derive Approdi, 2007).

Emilio Villa. Poeta e scrittore, ed. by Claudio Parmiggiani (Milano: Mazzotta 2008).

Aldo Tagliaferri, *Dentro e oltre i labirinti di Emilio Villa* (Milano: Edizioni del Verri, 2013).

Parabol(ich)e dell'ultimo giorno. Per Emilio Villa, ed. by Enzo Campi (Milano: Dotcom Press, 2013).

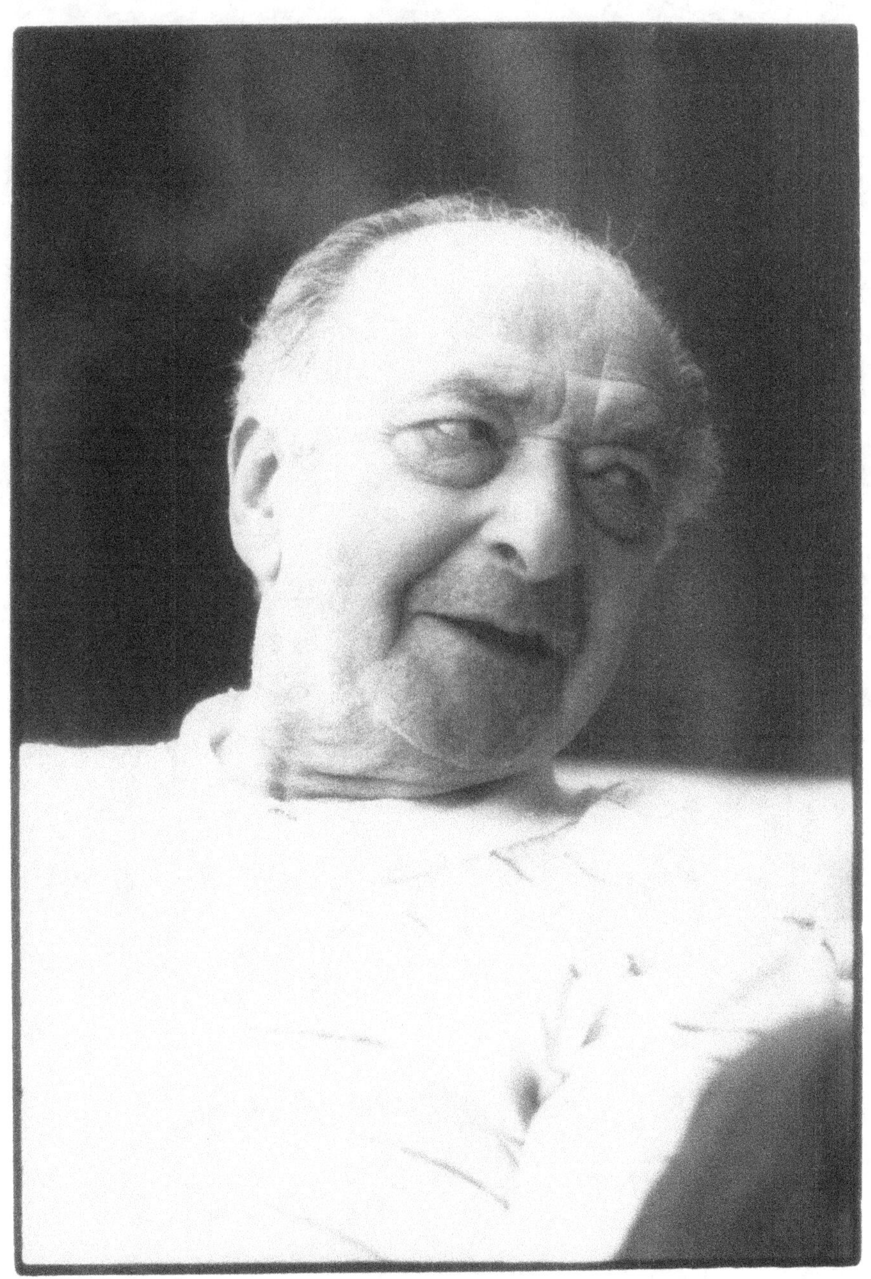

Acknowledgements

I would like to express my gratitude to The Raiziss/de Palchi Translation Award Fund of The New York Community Trust; to Dr. Maurizio Festanti and Dr. Chiara Panizzi at the Biblioteca Panizzi for so graciously allowing me access to Villa's archives; to Francesco Villa & family for their faith, generosity, and warm hospitality; to Sonia Puccetti-Caruso for opening her door to me while so many in Italy kept theirs closed; to Gianluca Rizzo and Jessica Strom for another set of eyes in reviewing the manuscript; to the Contra Mundum team (Rainer & Alessandro) for providing a venue for Villa's voice in English and all their hard work in assembling this volume; to Contra Mundum's anonymous readers, who helped me to refine the introduction; and finally to the Siracusa family (Ed, Michelle, Matt, Edi-Roma, Maura, and Sara) and Kristi Parenti-Kurttila (my beautiful bride-to-be) for their unwavering love & support.

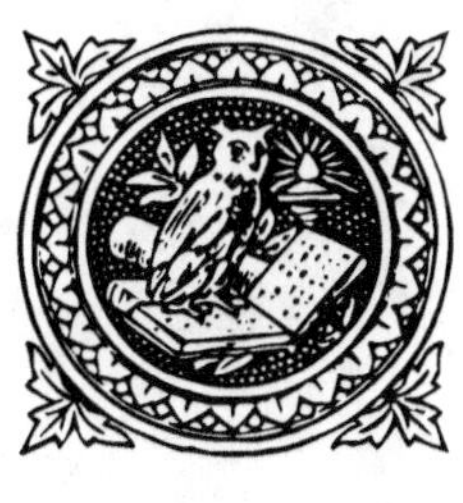

COLOPHON

THE SELECTED POETRY OF EMILIO VILLA
was typeset in InDesign.

The text and page numbers are set in *Adobe Jenson Pro.*
The titles are set in *JAF Lapture.*
Villa's own English is set in *Linotype Clarendon.*
Book design & typesetting: Alessandro Segalini
Cover design: Contra Mundum Press
Image credit: Emilio Villa, *Options* (1968)

THE SELECTED POETRY OF EMILIO VILLA
is published by Contra Mundum Press
& printed by Lightning Source, which has received Chain of Custody certification from: The Forest Stewardship Council, The Programme for the Endorsement of Forest Certification, and The Sustainable Forestry Initiative.

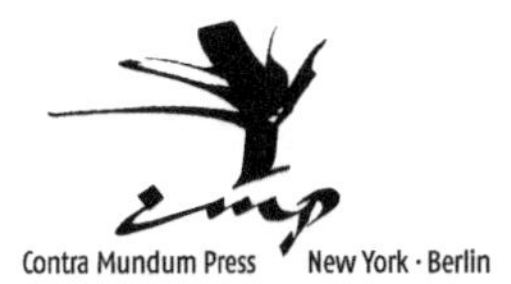

CONTRA MUNDUM PRESS

Contra Mundum Press is dedicated to the value & the indispensable importance of the individual voice.

Our principal interest is in Modernism and the principles developed by the Modernists, but challenging and visionary works from other eras may be considered for publication. We are also interested in texts that in their use of form & style are a *rebours*, though not in empty or gratuitous forms of experimentation (programmatic avant-gardism). Against the prevailing view that everything has been discovered, there are many texts of fundamental significance to *Weltliteratur* (*& Weltkultur*) that still remain in relative oblivion and warrant being encountered by the world at large.

For the complete list of forthcoming publications, please visit our website. To be added to our mailing list, send your name and email address to: info@contramundum.net

Contra Mundum Press
P.O. Box 1326
New York, NY 10276
USA
info@contramundum.net

OTHER CONTRA MUNDUM PRESS TITLES

Gilgamesh

Ghérasim Luca, *Self-Shadowing Prey*

Rainer J. Hanshe, *The Abdication*

Walter Jackson Bate, *Negative Capability*

Miklós Szentkuthy, *Marginalia on Casanova*

Fernando Pessoa, *Philosophical Essays*

Elio Petri, *Writings on Cinema & Life*

Friedrich Nietzsche, *The Greek Music Drama*

Richard Foreman, *Plays with Films*

Louis-Auguste Blanqui, *Eternity by the Stars*

Miklós Szentkuthy, *Towards the One & Only Metaphor*

Josef Winkler, *When the Time Comes*

William Wordsworth, *Fragments*

Josef Winkler, *Natura Morta*

Fernando Pessoa, *The Transformation Book*

SOME FORTHCOMING TITLES

Pier Paolo Pasolini, *Divine Mimesis*

Ferit Edgü, *No One*

Robert Musil, *Short Prose*

www.ingramcontent.com/pod-product-compliance
Lightning Source LLC
LaVergne TN
LVHW020039110826
845155LV00029B/553

* 9 7 8 1 9 4 0 6 2 5 0 5 8 *